Science Fiction, Fantasy, and Politics

RADICAL CULTURAL STUDIES

Series editors: Fay Brauer, Maggie Humm, Tim Lawrence, Stephen Maddison, Ashwani Sharma and Debra Benita Shaw (Centre for Cultural Studies Research, University of East London, UK)

The Radical Cultural Studies series publishes monographs and edited collections to provide new and radical analyses of the culturopolitics, sociopolitics, aesthetics and ethics of contemporary cultures. The series is designed to stimulate debates across and within disciplines, foster new approaches to Cultural Studies and assess the radical potential of key ideas and theories.

Titles in the Series

Sewing, Fighting and Writing: Radical Practices in Work, Politics and Culture, Maria Tamboukou

Radical Space: Exploring Politics and Practice, edited by Debra Benita Shaw and Maggie Humm

EU, Europe Unfinished. Europe and the Balkans in a Time of Crisis, edited by Zlatan Krajina and Nebojša Blanuša

Science Fiction, Fantasy, and Politics: Transmedia World-Building Beyond Capitalism, Dan Hassler-Forest

Austerity as Public Mood: Social Anxieties and Social Struggles, Kirsten Forkert (forthcoming)

Metamodernism: Historicity, Affect, Depth, edited by Robin van den Akker, Alison Gibbons and Timotheus Vermeulen (forthcoming)

Pornography, Materiality and Cultural Politics, Stephen Maddison (forthcoming)

Science Fiction, Fantasy, and Politics

*Transmedia World-Building
Beyond Capitalism*

Dan Hassler-Forest

ROWMAN &
LITTLEFIELD
INTERNATIONAL

London • New York

Published by Rowman & Littlefield International Ltd.
Unit A, Whitacre Mews, 26-34 Stannary Street, London SE11 4AB
www.rowmaninternational.com

Rowman & Littlefield International Ltd. is an affiliate of Rowman & Littlefield
4501 Forbes Boulevard, Suite 200, Lanham, Maryland 20706, USA
With additional offices in Boulder, New York, Toronto (Canada), and Plymouth (UK)
www.rowman.com

British Library Cataloguing in Publication Data
A catalogue record for this book is available from the British Library.

ISBN: HB 978-1-78348-492-8
       PB 978-1-78348-493-5

Library of Congress Cataloging-in-Publication Data
Names: Hassler-Forest, Dan, author.
Title: Science fiction, fantasy, and politics : transmedia world-building
  beyond capitalism / Dan Hassler-Forest.
Description: Lanham, Maryland : Rowman & Littlefield, [2016] | Series:
  Radical cultural studies | Includes bibliographical references and index.
Identifiers: LCCN 2016014471 (print) | LCCN 2016029533 (ebook) |
  ISBN 9781783484928 (cloth : alk. paper) | ISBN 9781783484935
  (pbk. : alk. paper) | ISBN 9781783484942 (electronic)
Subjects: LCSH: Science fiction—History and criticism. | Science fiction
  Films—History and criticism. | Fantasy fiction—History and criticism. |
  Imaginary places in literature. | Capitalism and mass media. | Culture and
  globalization. | Politics and literature.
Classification: LCC PN3433.8 .H376 2016 (print) | LCC PN3433.8 (ebook) |
  DDC 809.3/8762—dc23
LC record available at https://lccn.loc.gov/2016014471

∞™ The paper used in this publication meets the minimum requirements of American
National Standard for Information Sciences—Permanence of Paper for Printed Library
Materials, ANSI/NISO Z39.48-1992.

Printed in the United States of America

Dedicated with love and gratitude to my mother,
Laura Hassler, and to the memory of
my grandfather, Alfred Hassler.

Contents

Acknowledgments   ix

Chapter 1: Imaginary Empires: Transmedia World-Building
and Global Capitalism   1

Chapter 2: World-Building and Convergence Culture:
From Imperialism to Empire   23
    Tolkien's Middle-earth   27
    Star Trek   47

Chapter 3: Fantastical Capitalism and Postideological World-Building   67
    Game of Thrones   75
    Battlestar Galactica   92

Chapter 4: Revolutionary Storyworlds and Postdemocratic Capitalism   109
    Spartacus   118
    The Hunger Games   135

Chapter 5: Beyond Capitalism: Posthuman Storyworlds   151
    The Walking Dead   160
    Janelle Monáe's "Metropolis Saga"   174

Chapter 6: "Post"script   197

Bibliography   201

Index   225

Acknowledgments

This book began with an invitation from Amsterdam University Press to write a short introductory volume on transmedia storytelling. The topic had evolved, on the one hand, from my earlier book *Capitalist Superheroes* and, on the other, from a lecture series on transmedia and convergence culture that I had given for the John Adams Institute in Amsterdam. Both AUP and the JAI have never been anything but supportive and encouraging, and I would especially like to thank Ebissé Rouw, Jeroen Sondervan, and Jan-Peter Wissink at Amsterdam University Press; Russell Shorto, Maarten van Essen, Yara Deuss, and Tracy Metz at the John Adams Institute; and all the enthusiastic participants in the lecture series I gave in the spring of 2014.

As the book began to take shape, I must first thank my two online nemeses, Mark Bould and Gerry Canavan, both of whom offered invaluable advice and feedback in the early stages of development. Other crucial input at this point came from the incorrigible David Nieborg, whose recommendation of the book *Games of Empire* gave me an excellent model to copy shamelessly, and from fellow radical and comrade-in-arms Jan Teurlings, whose politely phrased feedback on a quite terrible early proposal draft pointed me toward ways of improving it.

A crucial event as my book proposal slowly took more definite shape was the wonderful conference "SF/F Now," organized at Warwick University by Rhys Williams with Mark Bould. At the conference, I finally got to meet in person long-admired scholars such as Carl Freedman, Sherryl Vint, and Mark Fisher, and I was given the opportunity to present an early version of my work on Janelle Monáe, which was published soon thereafter in a special issue of the journal *Paradoxa*. Rhys, Carl, Sherryl, Gerry, both Marks, and many others gave generous and extremely helpful feedback, both during and after the conference, and the delightful Stephen Shapiro was another presence there whose supportive and stimulating input has helped me enormously.

I also wish to express my deep and undying gratitude to the students who took action against the financialization and neoliberalization of academic life through a series of occupations at the University of Amsterdam. These student protests, undertaken by De Nieuwe Universiteit, Humanities Rally, and the University of Color, sparked a long-overdue debate about the nature of higher education that resonated throughout the academic community and far beyond. I feel pride beyond words to have been a small part of their movement, and my work on this book draws courage and inspiration from their anticapitalist chant "We are unstoppable / Another world is possible!" I also wish to thank the many former colleagues and friends who advised and supported the student protest as part of ReThink UvA. There are too many to mention, but my particular thanks and solidarity go out to Claire Weeda, Robin Celikates, Markus Stauff, Guy Geltner, Amade M'Charek, Pieter Pekelharing, Enzo Rossi, Julie McBrien, Umut Kibrit, Sicco de Knecht, Linda Duits, Natalie Scholtz, Joost de Bloois, Josef Früchtl, Sanli Faez, Mieke Aerts, Marco de Waard, Patricia Pisters, Geert Lovink, Ewald Engelen, and Gijs van Donselaar.

At Rowman & Littlefield International, I must thank commissioning editor Martina O'Sullivan, whose patience was sorely tested by my egregious failure to meet even the most generous deadline. Sinéad Murphy was similarly forced to put up with my bad behavior, and I thank both for their flexibility, their optimism, and their confidence-building faith in this project. Thanks also to Steve Coulson and Jackson Bird for graciously suffering through my inept interviewing style on Skype, to Colin Harvey for generously passing on a copy of his own recent book on transmedia world-building, and to Matt Hills for putting up with me while I kept prioritizing this book over our editorial work on the book series I'd gotten him involved in.

Above all, I wish to thank Debra Benita Shaw, the book series editor with whom I worked closely as I struggled to get the manuscript written. Debra was enormously supportive from the very start, and her incisive, articulate, and incredibly generous comments on every chapter draft kept the project's momentum going and helped identify and correct some of the worst weaknesses in my thinking and my writing. Collaborating with Debra on this project has been a rare privilege, and it is no exaggeration to say that this book truly wouldn't have been the same without her enthusiasm and most helpful support.

Other friends and colleagues I wish to single out for special thanks are Erik Steinskog for introducing me to Afrofuturism and the music of Janelle Monáe; my lifelong friend Bram de Beijer for having once made me a reluctant but undeniable Trekkie; Christoph Lindner for his always-helpful advice; my former student Meghan Schalkwijk for her invaluable research on Tolkien and political activism; and my brother Thom for getting me hooked on *Battlestar Galactica*. Thanks as well for being supportive, helpful, and/or awesome in ways they may not even realize, to Aaron Bady, Julian Brimmers, Jacob Brogan, Will Brooker, Bill Chambers, Walter Chaw, Istvan Csicsery-Ronay, Shane Denson, José van

Dijck, Pawel Frelik, Jeremy Gilbert, René Glas, Evan Gledhill, Rudolph Glitz, Joyce Goggin, Ted Gournelos, Dan Hartley, Frank Kelleter, Eloe Kingma, Jeroen de Kloet, Jaap Kooijman, Ishay Landa, Martin Lund, Tara MacDonald, Richard McCulloch, Jason Mittell, Pascal Nicklas, Roberta Pearson, Billy Proctor, Jason Read, Maarten Reesink, Suzanne Scott, Matthew Smith, John Storey, Chuck Tryon, William Uricchio, Ryan Vu, Johnny Walker, and my amazing students.

Finally, my love and eternal thanks to my family: my dad, who taught me to love fantastic storyworlds; my mom, who taught me to question everything; my sisters and brothers, with whom a real understanding of solidarity begins; Noah and Joshua, who are always in my heart; Sara and Sam, for whom we need to build a world worth living in; Mariecke, for not giving up on me; and my cat, Boris, for being the best of all cats.

Imaginary Empires

Transmedia World-Building and Global Capitalism

"Everything is awesome." Anyone who has seen *The LEGO Movie*[1] won't be able to hear those words without humming that mind-numbingly stupid but irresistibly catchy tune. The catchphrase is a perfect expression of the film's ambivalently satirical take on the LEGO brand, the movie itself, and the cultural logic of global capitalism. Both critical and celebratory, participatory and exploitative, independent minded and highly commercial, *The LEGO Movie* is the perfect cultural product for our times, blithely incorporating a vibrant anticapitalist sentiment into a framework that greases the wheels of global capitalism. So blatant is the film's overtly satirical take on consumerism, conformity, and commodity culture that film reviewers have described it as "practically communist,"[2] while commentators on Fox News attacked the film for indoctrinating children with anticapitalist values.[3]

As bizarre as it may seem to use the term *anticapitalist* for an animated film whose most obvious function is to advertise a popular toy brand, *The LEGO Movie* is an illuminating example of the many contradictions that inform twenty-first-century fantastic fiction and its relationship to capitalism. The ideological nerve it has struck is most visible in the film's early scenes, which depict an urban population that lives in a state of what can only be described as a classically Marxist false consciousness.[4] The narrative revolves around Emmet, a desperately ordinary construction worker who has been successfully integrated

---

1. *The LEGO Movie*, directed by Phil Lord and Christopher Miller (2014; Burbank, CA: Warner Home Video, 2014), Blu-ray.

2. Bilge Ebiri, "*The LEGO Movie* Is Practically Communist," *Vulture*, February 7, 2014, accessed December 27, 2015, http://www.vulture.com/2014/02/lego-movies-antidote-to-kids-movie-clichs.html.

3. Ben Skipper, "Fox News Takes Aim at *The LEGO Movie* for Being 'Anti-Capitalist,'" *International Business Times*, February 10, 2014, accessed January 29, 2015, http://www.ibtimes .co.uk/fox-news-takes-aim-lego-movie-being-anticapitalist-video-1435808.

4. See Ron Eyerman, "False Consciousness and Ideology in Marxist Theory," *Acta Sociologica* 24, no. 1/2 (1981): 43–56.

into an elaborate system of ideological mind control. Over the course of the film, Emmet is identified as the Chosen One, and his resulting adventures allow him to escape his desperately tedious life in the service of a vaguely North Korean variation on Starbucks capitalism.

In a more playful way than similarly organized dystopias in films such as *The Matrix*[5] and *V for Vendetta*,[6] the initial worldview presented in *The LEGO Movie* seems perfectly aligned with Guy Debord's famous critique of the "Society of the Spectacle"[7]: the power of capital has become so overwhelming that it encapsulates all of lived experience. The system's subjects are fully conditioned to take for granted the most monotonous daily routines, while mass media effectively brainwash entire populations. In the film, we are therefore introduced to Emmet as capitalist society's perfectly indoctrinated subject: consuming endlessly repetitive catchphrase-heavy TV comedies, happily purchasing $37 cups of coffee, and spending his working days singing along to insipid but catchy pop songs with lyrics that reassure him over and over again that everything is indeed awesome.

The fact that Emmet soon thereafter comes to lead a team of adventurous rebels is more or less irrelevant, especially because the increasingly incoherent narrative all but falls apart under the strain of its own metatextual irony. Far more interesting is how the film's imaginary world establishes itself not as ideologically neutral but as an environment where anticapitalist sentiment exists side by side with the most blatant promotion of a wide range of commodities and branded entertainment franchises. In this ambiguous context, "Everything Is Awesome" becomes a hilariously unsubtle articulation of neoliberalism's notorious mantra "there is no alternative," signaling that the world we live in is not just the best but also the *only* possible world. Just as Emmet learns that he can build whatever he can imagine as long as he builds it out of LEGOs, we, too, can do whatever we want, as long as we don't question the fundamental logic of capitalism.

But, at the same time, *The LEGO Movie* makes it impossible to take any of this seriously: its anticapitalist jabs, its casual sexism, its self-reflexive hyper-commercialism, and the finale's sentimental paternalism are all overshadowed by the film's tone of overwhelming irony. The obviousness of the film's many contradictions and the fun we have with its self-satisfied awesomeness make it an especially vivid illustration of the cultural, ideological, and narrative logic of participatory culture and media convergence. With a cast of characters that includes Batman, Wonder Woman, Gandalf, Albus Dumbledore, Lando Calrissian, and Shaquille O'Neal, the jokes and narrative twists rely heavily on viewers'

---

5. *The Matrix*, directed by Lana and Lilly Wachowski (1999; Burbank, CA: Warner Home Video, 2010), Blu-ray.

6. *V for Vendetta*, directed by James McTeigue (2005; Burbank, CA: Warner Home Video, 2008), Blu-ray.

7. Guy Debord, *The Society of the Spectacle* (New York: Zone Books, 1994 [1967]).

intimate familiarity with popular franchises and their many transmedia iterations. In this sense, the film's release is a culmination of the decades-long interaction between a wide range of popular narrative franchises and the LEGO brand. By its very design, LEGO is a toy that involves a highly participatory sensibility, with a productive tension (ultimately central to the film's plot) between straightforward assembly, as one follows the instructions to put together an X-Wing or a Quidditch arena, and creative production, as components from different sets are easily combined with others to create entirely new hybrids.

The contradiction between these two coexisting perspectives is remarkably similar to the relationship between canonical storyworlds in fantastic fiction and the creative fan cultures that have nourished and sustained them. Fandom is hardly ever limited to a single franchise or storyworld, typically spreading out across genres and media, as evidenced by the organization of fan conventions: *Star Trek* fans, for instance, will most commonly not only know and enjoy other sf narratives across numerous media but also be familiar with other related genres like fantasy and horror. What most forms of sf and fantasy fandom have in common is an interest in world-building as a limitless and continuously expanding narrative environment.

Matt Hills has described this kind of infinitely expansive storyworld as a *hyperdiegesis*: "a vast and detailed narrative space, only a fraction of which is ever directly seen or encountered,"[8] offering the dual attractions of ontological security[9] and endlessly deferred narrative.[10] The ongoing expansion of these storyworlds is primarily the result of fan culture's own creative and transformative activity, especially since fantastic storyworlds offer "creators and fan-bases coherent ways of suturing together gaps or contradictions in narrative when they occur."[11] But what fans also add creatively is a continuous hybridization of these storyworlds: just as children can have Dora the Explorer team up with Spider-Man to defeat an evil Papa Smurf, fan culture thrives on the imaginative work of crossovers, mashups, and creative appropriation. The many forms of mashup culture that have emerged over the past two decades attest to this continuous hybridization of fan texts and collaborative creative production.

This tension between internally coherent storyworlds and the fandom's radically heterogeneous creative work is central to any understanding of what I define in this book as transmedia world-building. While most other studies have chosen one perspective, focusing either on the construction of complex, coherent storyworlds or on fan cultures' creative appropriation of popular culture, I see this internal contradiction as an expression of the two faces of global capitalism:

8. Matt Hills, *Fan Cultures* (London: Routledge, 2000), 137.

9. Hills, *Fan Cultures*, 138.

10. Hills, *Fan Cultures*, 142.

11. Colin Harvey, *Fantastic Transmedia: Narrative, Play and Memory Across Science Fiction and Fantasy Storyworlds* (Basingstoke: Palgrave Macmillan, 2015), 38.

On one face, Empire spreads globally its network of hierarchies and divisions that maintain order through new mechanisms of control and constant conflict. Globalization, however, is also the creation of new circuits of cooperation and collaboration that stretch across nations and continents and allow an unlimited number of encounters. This second face of globalization is not a matter of everyone in the world becoming the same; rather it provides the possibility that, while remaining different, we discover the commonality that enables us to communicate and act together.[12]

The discovery of this commonality is central to the imaginative and collaborative work of transmedia world-building. Even as popular storyworlds are constantly being appropriated by capitalism's incontrovertible logic of accumulation, and as audiences' creative work is transformed into immaterial labor at the service of media corporations, there remains a valuable radical potential that is clearly worth salvaging. By emphasizing the radical spirit of collectivity that underlies so many fantastic storyworlds, I will attempt to make sense of the central contradictions of transmedia world-building by relating them back to Hardt and Negri's influential work on global capitalism. But before I explain in more detail this theoretical connection between fantastic storyworlds and politics, I will first unpack a few central terms, beginning with *transmedia world-building*.

MEDIA CONVERGENCE AND TRANSMEDIA WORLD-BUILDING

The most commonly used definition of the term *transmedia storytelling* was introduced by Henry Jenkins, who described it as a single narrative that is spread out across multiple media, "with each new text making a distinctive and valuable contribution to the whole."[13] Later debates about the term have expanded its range somewhat from Jenkins's original definition, adding in further important factors such as branding, adaptation, extension, seriality, and radical intertextuality.[14] Some have even rejected the term due to its implicit focus on narrative coherence, preferring instead a more traditional industrial term like *media franchising*.[15] Without entering into a semantic discussion of the exact limitations of the term and to what degree any given transmedia narrative is fully consistent across any given number of textual formations, I use the term in combination

---

12. Michael Hardt and Antonio Negri, *Multitude: War and Democracy in the Age of Empire* (London: Penguin, 2005), xiii.

13. Henry Jenkins, *Convergence Culture: Where Old and New Media Collide* (New York: New York University Press, 2006), 97–98.

14. See the articles "Transmedia 101" and "Transmedia 202" on Jenkins's blog (http://henryjenkins .org) for elaborate discussions of competing definitions.

15. Derek Johnson, *Media Franchising: Creative License and Collaboration in the Culture Industries* (New York: New York University Press, 2013), 31.

with world-building to indicate commercial franchises that develop complex fantastic storyworlds across a variety of media. Transmedia world-building thereby articulates a fundamental element of convergence culture: boundaries between media have blurred to the point at which it makes little sense to foreground fundamental distinctions between contemporary media. Instead, the term helpfully foregrounds the fact that our immersion in imaginary storyworlds takes place not within but *across* media.[16]

My use of the term *transmedia world-building* is therefore primarily meant to emphasize a few key points about the cultural logic of fantastic storyworlds in the context of media convergence:

1. Transmedia world-building takes place *across* media.

2. Transmedia world-building involves *audience participation*.

3. Transmedia world-building is a process that *defers narrative closure*.

As a complex set of layered and interlinked cultural, social, and industrial practices, transmedia world-building in sf and fantasy first emerged across a range of distinct subcultures that found forms of meaning through the appropriation and collaborative development of imaginary worlds.

But although the term *transmedia* is associated by many with digital culture, it is important to remember that it has a much longer history. Fantastic storyworlds first gained prominence, "persistently available and collectively envisaged," in European and American popular culture of the late nineteenth century,[17] as highly detailed and immersive narrative environments were developed by authors such as Arthur Conan Doyle, H. P. Lovecraft, and Edgar Rice Burroughs. Some of the most enterprising authors of fantastic fiction responded to readers' appetites for immersive storyworlds by embracing multiple media for their world-building: L. Frank Baum's popular world of Oz is a well-known early example of transmedia world-building, carefully integrating text and illustrations to create a seamless whole, and spreading out across other platforms until it encompassed nearly all existing media of its time.[18]

But while transmedia world-building has a long and rich history, it has also clearly gained a much higher relevance and visibility in the twenty-first century. Over the past two decades, a complex and diverse set of mutually reinforcing cultural, technological, economic, and political changes resulted in what we now

---

16. In a similar way, Mark Deuze has argued that our lives no longer take place *with* media but *in* media. See Mark Deuze, *Media Life* (London: Polity Press, 2012), 6–9.

17. Michael Saler, *As If: Modern Enchantment and the Literary Prehistory of Virtual Reality* (Oxford: Oxford University Press, 2012), 6.

18. Mark J. P. Wolf, *Building Imaginary Worlds: The Theory and History of Subcreation* (London: Routledge, 2012), 117.

refer to as convergence culture. The simultaneous processes of globalization and digitization have helped transform transmedia world-building from a cultural activity that existed on the margins of mainstream culture to one of the cornerstones of popular entertainment. What had for decades been a culturally marginalized and ghettoized culture of niche fan communities had undergone a transformation by the late 1990s: media industries no longer viewed fans as eccentric irritants but as loyal and highly valued consumers.[19] And with the rise of digital culture, those very fans were increasingly mobilized as essential "influencers" whose endorsement of a particular product was essential to generating the necessary "buzz" that would help attract a mass audience.

As the activities and interests of fan culture have by now become an essential part of a widely shared popular culture, the industrial organization of our media landscape has shifted as well. The growing power of media conglomerates with control over multiple platforms has altered the relationship between producer and consumer, raising new questions about the tension between global capitalism and the collaborative creative development of imaginary worlds. The benefit of the "mainstreaming" of genre fiction and fan culture is that a much larger audience now engages with fantastic storyworlds that can help question, challenge, and perhaps even change the world we live in. If it is indeed the case, as Fredric Jameson has famously suggested, that it has become easier for us to imagine the end of the world than the end of capitalism,[20] then we desperately need fictions that not only offer possible alternatives but also involve us as active participants in their construction.[21] This combination of audience participation and the creative development of imaginary storyworlds is what I describe as the political potential of transmedia world-building in sf and fantasy. If one is willing to embrace the notion that transmedia world-building involves not only the audience's creative transformations of commercial entertainment properties but also the active development of alternate imaginary worlds, its political potential becomes impossible to ignore.

THE POLITICS OF WORLD-BUILDING

Most of the existing scholarship on the imaginary worlds of cross-media storytelling franchises has described them thus far primarily in formalist and/or sociological terms: the exhaustive detail, the elaborate histories, the complex

---

19. Hills, *Fan Cultures*, 36.

20. Fredric Jameson, *Archaeologies of the Future: The Desire Called Utopia and Other Science Fictions* (London and New York: Verso, 2005), 199.

21. The additional benefit of a narrative environment that is experienced as not merely immersive but also participatory is that it foregrounds its own construction, thereby pointing the way toward the inherently political organization of our own world.

relationships between fans and producers, and the variety of media that make up convergence culture have encouraged many scholars working on such franchises to focus on their forms and the cultural practices that surround them rather than theorize their political implications. Mark J. P. Wolf's *Building Imaginary Worlds*, the first academic monograph to focus extensively on world-building as a set of cultural practices and textual conventions, discusses it primarily in precisely such terms. Wolf takes as his point of departure J. R. R. Tolkien's concept of "subcreation,"[22] which he views as an inseparable combination of process and product resulting in the development of a fictitious "Secondary World."[23] The "secondariness" of this imaginary environment is more a question of degree than absolute separation, depending on the ways in which familiar defaults are transformed into imaginary alternatives:

> Fictional worlds can be placed along a spectrum based on the amount of subcreation present, and what we might call the "secondariness" of a story's world then becomes a matter of degree, varying with the strength of the connection to the Primary World.[24]

Wolf's book subsequently offers an overwhelmingly detailed historical overview of many varieties of imaginary worlds with varying levels of subcreation, each of which is to some degree separated in one form or another from the ways in which the "Primary World" is commonly represented. For instance, Baum's world of Oz is an example of an imaginary environment where the presence of talking trees, flying monkeys, and magical slippers indicates a high level of "secondariness" that separates it from a primary reality that is also represented within the text. The imaginary world of the film *Blade Runner*,[25] by the same token, "is as much a constructed environment as Oz, yet it depicts a Primary World location, set in an alternate version of 2019 . . . in which replicants, artificial animals, flying cars, and gigantic buildings not only exist but are common."[26] Wolf's definition of world-building thus relies on a commonsense distinction between what constitutes a "realistic" representation of a diegetic world and a fictional environment that defamiliarizes conventional defaults by altering a number of these coordinates.

Besides this conscious deviation from realist narrative conventions, which is obviously a defining general characteristic of all fantastic fiction, a second crucial aspect Wolf identifies is that of scale. World-building franchises are typically developed not only across many different texts but also across multiple media.

22. J. R. R. Tolkien, "On Fairy-Stories," in *The Monsters and the Critics and Other Essays*, ed. Christopher Tolkien (London: HarperCollins, 1997 [1983]), 138–41.

23. Wolf, *Building Imaginary Worlds*, 24.

24. Wolf, *Building Imaginary Worlds*, 25.

25. *Blade Runner*, directed by Ridley Scott (1982; Burbank, CA: Warner Home Video, 2013), Blu-ray.

26. Wolf, *Building Imaginary Worlds*, 27.

For example, the world-building that followed the release of *Star Wars*[27] was as much the result of the production of toys, videogames, television programs, comic books, novelizations, and role-playing games as it was the mere process of serialization through the production of sequel films. This multidirectional proliferation of transmedia world-building has thus transformed literary theory's traditional focus on the single narrative as a linear and internally coherent text, and it also destabilizes discourses of individual authorship, especially once the audience starts contributing actively to the development of the imaginary world.

The resulting scale of any such imaginary world is defined firstly by its aforementioned hyperdiegetic qualities, or what Lisbeth Klastrup has described as "worldness"[28]: the storyworld in question provides an environment in which a potentially unlimited number of narratives can take place, but this storyworld will always by its very definition exceed in scale any single representation of it.[29] The resulting "multitext"[30] and its fundamental multiplicity therefore shifts the focus from the more traditional literary notion of narrative closure to the open-endedness of serialization and the active navigation of imaginary geographical spaces. The activities associated with world-building, at the levels of both pro- duction and consumption, are for this reason much more closely aligned with the serialized narratives of television series, comic books, and pulp literature, on the one hand, and videogames' common emphasis on spatial exploration, collabora- tive interaction, and kinetic immersion, on the other.

While world-building therefore clearly shifts our focus from the linear and teleological structure of narrative to the environment that surrounds and sus- tains it, this changes nothing about the ways in which we might interrogate and historicize the resulting multitexts as expressions of tensions and contradictions that are ultimately social, material, and political. Therefore, if we wish to gain a better understanding of the politics of world-building, we must start by asking questions similar to those that help us explain any other narrative text's "political unconscious."[31] Following Jameson, a useful starting point would therefore be "by asking of what real contradiction a given text is an imaginary or symbolic resolution."[32] A text is thereby not approached as a self-contained system of signs

---

27. *Star Wars Episode IV: A New Hope*, directed by George Lucas (1977; Century City, CA: Twentieth Century Fox Home Entertainment, 2005), DVD.

28. Lisbeth Klastrup, "The Worldness of EverQuest: Exploring a 21st Century Fiction," *Game Studies* 9, no. 1 (2009).

29. In terms of scale, it also bears mentioning that the term *world-building* is most commonly applied to fantastic fiction that stretches far beyond any single world: the term is derived from possible world theory, as fantastic storyworlds often encompass entire universes. See Lubomír Doležel, *Heterocosmica: Fiction and Possible Worlds* (Baltimore: Johns Hopkins University Press, 2000).

30. Clare Parody, "Franchising/Adaptation," *Adaptation* 4, no. 2 (2011): 210–18.

31. Fredric Jameson, *The Political Unconscious* (Ithaca: Cornell University Press, 1981).

32. William C. Dowling, *Jameson, Althusser, Marx: An Introduction to the Political Unconscious* (London: Routledge, 1984), 121.

that carries its own meanings inside it but as a reflection of a specific organiza-tion of historically grounded social relations. Any attempt to better understand the politics of a fictional storyworld must therefore begin, in Jameson's famous words, with "the recognition that there is nothing that is not social and his-torical—indeed, that everything is 'in the last instance' political."[33] Developing a political understanding of fantastic world-building therefore implies a certain expansion of the framework Marxist theory provides for cultural analysis and ideology critique. In this analysis, I take as my point of departure the historical-materialist proposition that the fantasy offered by these storyworlds expresses the tensions and contradictions that inform our material world.

When applied to world-building, this form of ideological analysis seemingly faces a challenge in the absence of a single structuring narrative, where the ex-pansive framework may most commonly present minor variations on a familiar theme but also often spirals outward in unexpected directions. The Frankfurt School tradition of media criticism is notorious for emphasizing the monolithic repetitiveness of this form, running counter to Cultural Studies' interest in the way communities and individuals find value and meaning in what may appear to outsiders as insignificant details. At the same time, storyworlds are continuously undergoing expansions in numerous directions: prequels, sequels, "side-quels" featuring alternate timelines, retcons, and reboots[34] add endlessly to the story-world's byzantine chronology, while the many maps of various scales provide interpretive guides to the storyworld's spatiotemporal organization. These maps almost by definition impose an emphatically modern and specifically capitalist worldview on these imaginary empires (a point I will return to in more detail in later chapters). For these reasons, any given storyworld's spatiotemporal organi-zation is at least as crucial to understanding its political and ideological implica-tions as the narratives that take place within it.

As a set of cultural and economic practices that emerged under late capital-ism, my main point of interest throughout this book is therefore how transmedia world-building offers immersive, complex, and endlessly expansive spatio-temporal environments that provide pleasurable negotiations of global capital-ism's contradictory logic. The immersive engagement provided by transmedia storyworlds offers many potential lines of flight that mobilize an anticapitalist imagination, and which may even open up a shimmering "communist horizon."[35] This operation is threefold: at the level of narrative, at the level of storyworld organization, and at the level of collaborative and creative participatory work on the audience's part. At each of these levels, the case studies in the following

33. Jameson, *The Political Unconscious*, 5.

34. William Proctor, "Beginning Again: The Reboot Phenomenon in Comic Books and Film," *Scan: Journal of Media Arts Culture* 9, no. 1 (2012), http://scan.net.au/scn/journal/vol9number1/William-Proctor.html.

35. Jodi Dean, *The Communist Horizon* (London and New York: Verso, 2012).

chapters illustrate the radical political potential offered by many of these popular imaginary empires, each of which ultimately negotiates central contradictions within capitalism.

But, at the same time, we must acknowledge the challenges posed by the continuous absorption of those practices by the system it has such power to critique. The radical potential of fantastic genres is constantly being contradicted and curtailed on those same three levels: first, at the story level, as the narratives' anticapitalist and democratic energies are counterbalanced by their ideological opposite. To return to my earlier example, *The LEGO Movie*'s satire of capitalist reification is counterbalanced by the restoration of a benevolent patriarchy at the film's end. Second, at the level of storyworld organization, the emphasis on mapping out space and time to make these worlds navigable and internally coherent also articulates the imperial logic of capitalism. In *The LEGO Movie*, this compulsion to map out stable and canonical "worlds" is among the film's main satirical targets. And third, at the level of participation, where the audience's contributions to these transmedia storyworlds are increasingly being appropriated as a form of immaterial and unpaid labor. Both aspects are again illustrated with perfectly appropriate ambivalence in *The LEGO Movie*, as fandom's creative work is presented first as an invaluable quality that ensures victory for the heroes, while the ending rearticulates its liberating force in a way that infantilizes its audience and reintegrates it into the main circuitry of benevolent patriarchal capitalism.

By adopting a dialectical perspective on the organization of commercial transmedia storyworlds, their narratives, and their fan cultures, we can learn more from their internal tensions and contradictions than from any dubious assumptions concerning textual or ideological coherence. Adopting such a dialectical perspective is even more important when discussing audiences' own creative efforts, which have become difficult to discern from global capitalism's forms of affective and immaterial labor. Carlo Vercellone has described the dominant logic of these productive forms as *cognitive capitalism*: a term that helps us understand the nature of a phase in capitalism in which "the relation of capital to labour is marked by the hegemony of knowledges, by a diffuse intellectuality, and by the driving role of the production of knowledges by means of knowledges connected to the increasingly immaterial and cognitive character of labour."[36]

To put it in simpler terms, the dominant logic of labor in the post-Fordist economies of cognitive capitalism is not one of production in the traditional sense. In the advanced capitalist nations, capitalism's focus has shifted from industrial production to immaterial labor, bringing with it a cultural and economic order that perfectly suits the participatory forms of transmedia world-building. This obviously affects our understanding of mass culture: just as the development of twentieth-century industrial capitalism was accompanied by commodities,

---

36. Carlo Vercellone, "From Formal Subsumption to General Intellect: Elements for a Marxist Reading of the Thesis of Cognitive Capitalism," *Historical Materialism* 15 (2007): 16.

fashions, and media whose massive production scales made their cultural effects relatively homogeneous, the far more flexible "just-in-time" or "on-demand" production systems of the neoliberal era have by now transformed the very nature of mass culture.[37]

It therefore no longer makes much sense to think of mass culture as being some monolithic entity, in the way that Adorno, for instance, once described it—that is, as a unified and machinic "culture industry,"[38] irrespective of the question of whether this was ever a very accurate description. Instead, the multiple economic and political reorganizations associated with global capitalism have thoroughly transformed the workings of popular culture. In this context, audiences involved in participatory cultures of transmedia world-building should also no longer be viewed primarily as textual poachers "operating from a position of marginality and social weakness,"[39] nor is it really helpful to categorize fans' practices as the resurrection of a romanticized preindustrial folk culture, "accelerated and expanded for the digital age."[40] Instead, I approach it in this book as a form of immaterial and affective labor that operates both in opposition to *and* in collaboration with new forms of corporate power. I place the recent growth of this phenomenon in the context of what Hardt and Negri have described as a new age of Empire, where political alternatives to capitalism have become increasingly difficult to imagine. But, at the same time, the only way forward is precisely by intensifying the very practices that give Empire its ubiquitous but deeply unstable power.

EMPIRE AND CONVERGENCE CULTURE

When the publication of Michael Hardt and Antonio Negri's *Empire*[41] in 2000 introduced a new term for the workings of global capitalism, it sparked a wave of interest and excitement. And it isn't hard to see why: their work expresses in easy-to-understand terms a forceful critique of what they see as the key central dynamic of globalization. Combining Marx's historical materialism with a theory of subjectivity derived from Spinoza, *Empire* gives a passionate and highly readable theoretical account of the challenges and opportunities they see as specific to our own historical era. In brief, they view twenty-first-century globalization as a new phase in the history of capitalism.

---

37. "The era of mass culture is over, and it is now clear that it was only ever typical of one specific form of industrial capitalism, adapted to the technological capacities and limitations of the early-twentieth century." Jeremy Gilbert, *Anticapitalism and Culture* (London: Bloomsbury, 2008), 116.

38. Theodor Adorno, *The Culture Industry* (London and New York: Routledge, 1991).

39. Henry Jenkins, *Textual Poachers: Television Fans and Participatory Culture* (London and New York: Routledge, 1992), 27.

40. Jenkins, *Convergence Culture*, 141.

41. Michael Hardt and Antonio Negri, *Empire* (Cambridge, MA: Harvard University Press, 2000).

Empire is Hardt and Negri's term to describe the new ways in which capital's power is organized in the postindustrial era. They use it as a provocation that has the enormous benefit of identifying in no uncertain terms the struggle any anticapitalist movement now faces. Central to their thinking is the notion that our age of global, postindustrial, financial, or cognitive capitalism brings with it new forms of power that are specific to the richest nations' dominant mode of immaterial production. The result is something they describe as a "properly capitalist order" defined by "a new notion of right, or rather, a new inscription of authority and a new design of the production of norms and legal instruments of coercion that guarantee contracts and resolve conflicts."[42] Unlike the dominant order that informed capitalism in its industrial phase, they see the age of Empire as fundamentally networked, decentered, and—using a term from key influences Deleuze and Guattari—*biopolitical.*[43]

Their theory, as influential as it has been controversial, offers its own kind of world-building: an articulate, impassioned, and ultimately optimistic way of imagining the relationship between capital and proletariat—or in their terms, Empire and the multitude. Like every such Grand Theory, the obvious disadvantage of Hardt and Negri's sweeping rhetorical gestures is that their terminology works better as a generalization than as a precise history of global capitalism.[44] But the authors' combination of theoretical sophistication and political radicalism has made their intervention one of the most widely read critical perspectives on anticapitalism in the twenty-first century, and one that has the massive advantage of crystallizing with elegant simplicity the opposing sides in the anticapitalist movement. Or, as Jeremy Gilbert put it so succinctly, "that which stands in the way of so many democratic demands, that which blocks so many lines of becoming today, deserves a name: and Empire is as good a name as any."[45]

Moreover, what makes their work particularly useful to the field of Cultural Studies is the way it foregrounds the massive forces of commodification and capitalist hegemony without simultaneously depriving the system's many "victims" of agency. Instead, Hardt and Negri's polemical dedication to creativity, solidarity, and joyful collaboration as productive forces resonates with Cultural Studies' investment in audiences' active engagement with culture. Their central concept of the multitude rids itself of the homogenizing implications of more traditional "masses" based on class, race, gender, or any other unifying characteristic. But, at the same time, their theorization of "multitudinous subjectivity" as a positive

---

42. Hardt and Negri, *Empire*, 9.

43. Hardt and Negri, *Empire*, 23–27.

44. For explanations of why Hardt and Negri's work is of limited usefulness to historiographers of capitalism, see Chris Harman, *Zombie Capitalism: Global Crisis and the Relevance of Marx* (London: Bookmarks Publications, 2009), 93; Leo Panitch and Sam Gindin, *The Making of Global Capitalism: The Political Economy of American Empire* (London and New York: Verso, 2013), 26; and David Harvey, *The New Imperialism* (Oxford: Oxford University Press, 2005), 169.

45. Gilbert, *Anticapitalism and Culture*, 166.

category is not automatically also an uncritical validation of some vaguely defined spontaneous and autonomous critical consciousness. For Hardt and Negri, the multitude does have an inherently revolutionary potential, but this has yet to be realized by collective political action. Their radical critique of global capitalism is therefore at the same time a call to action: the radically heterogeneous multitude of diverse subjects must ultimately break free from capital's biopolitical enslavement through the creative reappropriation of the very forms of immaterial labor that are currently regulated by the power of Empire.

This new age of Empire has followed that of imperialism, in which multiple powerful nation-states competed globally for access to resources and labor. While the nation-state as an entity existed under imperialism to facilitate the development of capitalism, its highly striated global territory would become an impediment to capital's requirement of boundless growth in the post–Cold War age of global capitalism. The late twentieth-century dissolution of the Soviet Union as a competing world power ushered in an imperial age in which capitalism no longer had any "outside" to contend with, and the many borders of the imperialist order were rapidly restructured under the flag of deterritorialization.

From the nineteenth century until close to the end of the twentieth, this imperialist system existed in combination with industrial capitalism. Because it created continuous limits for capital's access to labor and resources, national governments were the most important agents in the regulation of these processes. The substantial advances that were gained by women, labor unions, migrants, and ethnic minorities over the forces of capitalism were made possible by these limitations, their struggles in many cases resulting in more open and inclusive forms of democracy. Michel Foucault's work offers the most widely read theoretical description of imperialism's sovereign practices. Throughout his major works, he describes modern capitalism's obsession with the creation of boundaries that differentiate and discipline its subjects into behaviors that enhance the regulatory forms of productivity that sustained capitalist development.[46] Above all, Foucault's writing teaches us that subjectivity under imperialism is constructed through institutional norms that exercise power while simultaneously producing resistance.[47]

While Hardt and Negri extend Foucault's ideas, their postimperialist worldview is crucially different in the sense that the boundaries that defined industrial capitalism are being erased:

> Empire establishes no territorial center of power and does not rely on fixed boundaries or barriers. It is a *decentered* and *deterritorializing* apparatus of rule that progressively incorporates the entire global realm within its open, expanding frontiers.[48]

---

46. Michel Foucault, *Discipline and Punish: The Birth of the Prison* (New York: Vintage, 1995).

47. Michel Foucault, *The History of Sexuality: 1—The Will to Knowledge* (London: Penguin, 1981).

48. Hardt and Negri, *Empire*, xii.

This more fluid environment is the natural extension of the development described by Foucault in his most influential books: once there is no longer any outside beyond modernity's normative frameworks of the prison, the asylum, the factory, the school, and the army barracks, the institutions themselves begin to evaporate and biopower comes to define subject formation more than ever. In other words, individuals had already absorbed the systematic nature of institutionalized power that operates by "structuring the parameters and limits of thought and practice, sanctioning and prescribing normal and/or deviant behaviors."[49] Accompanying the transition from industrial to global capitalism, the modern age's regime of disciplinary power has moved beyond Foucault's panopticism into something more akin to Gilles Deleuze's "society of control."[50] Even more than the decentering effects of panoptic power and disciplinary institutions, this society of control is organized entirely through "flexible and fluctuating networks" that are biopolitical in nature: "In the passage from disciplinary society to the society of control, a new paradigm of power is realized which is defined by the technologies that recognize society as the realm of biopower."[51] In this "new milieu of maximum plurality and uncontainable singularization,"[52] we witness biopower at its most effective, but also at its most vulnerable.

Even if Empire has adapted remarkably well to the multitude's activities within a more participatory culture of media convergence, its hybrid networks still offer the opportunity to break free from capital's hold on the multitude and its creative energy. Henry Jenkins, Nicholas Negroponte, George Landow, Frank Rose, Lev Manovich, and many others have celebrated the advent of digital media as the return of a more participatory form of culture. While these authors' many examples of fan culture and appropriation are both credible and appealing, such approaches also gloss over the complex political economies that ultimately determine the form as well as the contents of digital media. One of Jenkins's main reasons for celebrating the cultural practices of convergence culture is precisely the fact that he regards it as a politically productive activity: the networked, low-threshold nature of web culture, for instance, is an ideal form of grassroots self-organization. But his perspective on political engagement too easily equates liberal activism with political agency, implying that the kind of participation facilitated by Web 2.0 automatically yields increased participation in the social-democratic system. To put it more plainly, Jenkins's work tries to offer solutions to capitalism's problems without seriously challenging capitalism itself.

In the context of cognitive capitalism, what Jenkins calls participatory fan culture is in fact difficult to distinguish from other forms of consumerism without imposing arbitrary-seeming boundaries and fairly dubious assumptions about

---

49. Hardt and Negri, *Empire*, 23.

50. Gilles Deleuze, "Postscript on the Societies of Control," *October* 59 (1992): 3–7.

51. Hardt and Negri, *Empire*, 24.

52. Hardt and Negri, *Empire*, 25.

the nature of political agency. Derek Johnson has argued in his book on media franchises that these kinds of participation would be more accurately described as "collaboration," a word that has far more ambiguous associations, especially in the context of political conflict.[53] Johnson goes against the political economy approach by making abundantly clear that corporate-owned transmedia storyworlds are the product of constant negotiation between multiple parties with competing, often contradictory interests. But his conclusions also demonstrate clearly that the relationship between producers and audiences is still a hugely asymmetrical one, and that the power of global conglomerates remains a massive obstacle for actual media democratization.

However, just as Hardt and Negri rightfully point out that the decentered and networked structure of Empire releases a democratic energy that is fundamentally uncontrollable, the same logic holds true for the imaginative work of transmedia world-building. The struggle to release our culture from the stranglehold of intellectual copyright and commercial franchising may be an asymmetrical battle, but it is certainly not a lost cause. Important advances have been made by the copyleft movement, by fan communities' organized pushback to nervous corporations' bullying, and by advocates of file sharing and online "piracy" that pose severe challenges to the existing order of commercial media production and capital accumulation. Authors, filmmakers, and musicians have explored alternative ways of financing their work through crowdfunding and direct distribution, sometimes with success. It therefore seems at the very least worth considering fantastic storyworlds both as texts with radical potential and as sociocultural practices that can play a role in anticapitalist imaginative *and* organizational work.

STRUCTURE AND CASE STUDIES

This book approaches the creative, cultural, and social work of transmedia world-building from a radical political perspective informed by Hardt and Negri's theoretical approach to global capitalism. Throughout the following four chapters, I argue that our age of post-Fordist cognitive capitalism and immaterial labor shapes and determines the complex and highly profitable imaginary empires that dominate our narrative culture. My central thesis is that in both form and content, popular fantastic storyworlds articulate the cultural and political logic of Empire, giving us helpful tools to better understand the contradictory nature of global capitalism. In terms of form, this means that the variety and complexity of medium-specific incarnations perfectly suit neoliberalism's dominant logic of flexible and immaterial labor, information economies, and cognitive capitalism. And in terms of content, these popular fantastic storyworlds offer immersive, participatory, and endlessly

53. Johnson, *Media Franchising*, 198.

expansive environments in which audiences can safely negotiate the tensions of capitalist culture. Fueled by a narrative dynamic that all too often foregrounds an anticapitalist spirit, this energy is at the same time counterbalanced by ideological values and media-industrial practices that reinforce Empire's framework of biopower and capital accumulation.

Convergence culture's collapsing of barriers between media corresponds to the ways in which the institutions that shape capitalist subjectivity also collapse and bleed into each other: in the words of Hardt and Negri, "today the enclosures that used to define the limited space of the institutions have broken down so that the logic that once functioned primarily within the institutional walls now spreads across the entire social terrain."[54] This breakdown of divisions also challenges many of our preconceptions about the importance of fantastic fiction. While twenty-first-century world-building often presents a fantasy of pastness that brings to mind Jameson's "nostalgia mode," it isn't any longer typically the kind of depthless play with empty signifiers that makes up postmodern pastiche.[55] Nor do we find as a dominant mode of engagement the kind of full immersion popularly dubbed "escapism" that is so often attributed to genre fiction in general, and to fantastic genres in particular.

Instead, transmedia world-building provides a form of engagement that involves a constant negotiation between sincere immersion and radical self-reflexivity: viewers of a series like *Game of Thrones* can watch a new episode breathlessly, fully captivated by its storyworld, and then go online to post the mashup video or humorous "meme" image they have created, while at the same time engaging in Facebook discussions about plot inconsistencies, casting issues, or the differences between the novels, the TV series, and the videogames. In other words, transmedia world-building depends on and demands from its audience a high degree of participatory activity, media literacy, and a playful sense of engagement with the storyworlds it creates. One of the most typical features of these popular franchises is their "drillable"[56] nature: highly accessible to casual audiences but deliberately layered to offer rewards to "fannish" groups willing to invest more time and energy.

Now that a first generation of millennials has come of age within the context of ubiquitous digital culture, we find that one of the effects of media convergence is that it has made us much more omnivorous in our relation to narrative culture. Digitization, the social and technological transformation that has brought all our media together within a single device, has also flattened the traditional hierarchies that existed between media, which always privileged the

---

54. Hardt and Negri, *Empire*, 196.

55. Fredric Jameson, *Postmodernism, or, The Cultural Logic of Late Capitalism* (Durham: Duke University Press, 1991), 17.

56. Jason Mittell, "*Lost* in a Great Story: Evaluation in Narrative Television (and Television Studies)," in *Reading* Lost, ed. Roberta Pearson (London: I. B. Tauris, 2009), 119–38.

old over the new. So even though it would be hard to argue that videogames are now perceived in the same way as the opera or the ballet, it has become commonplace to discuss the literary qualities of the latest HBO television series, even in previously maligned genres like horror or fantasy. At the same time, it has become far more socially acceptable to exhibit fannish behavior than it once was, as the widespread emergence of geek culture has resulted from the radical individualization that marks our social media environment in the current "postdemocratic" context.[57]

The triumph of geek culture and its "everything is awesome" mantra has in recent years created the seductive illusion that fans have graduated from consumerism to full participation in media production. But their actual degree of agency all too often resembles the quite limited movements available to a single player within a videogame: while experiencing the sensation of directing an avatar freely through an immersive and richly detailed environment, the player's control is in fact limited by the design of the game to encourage and reward certain forms of behavior, while discouraging and even actively precluding others. In this sense, our narrative media and the ways in which they have become more participatory simultaneously produce new biopolitical subjectivities that are regulated by the forms these media take and by their content.

The reterritorialization that is thus taking place is propelled by powerful media producers' frantic and increasingly canny efforts to direct the energy that has been unleashed in directions that will maintain the existing balance of power. Just as twenty-first-century geopolitics has been defined by the wide reach of global capitalism, the social, cultural, and technological changes that have transformed our media landscape are similarly being reappropriated by the very powers they had once seemed destined to displace. As the rhizomatic virtual networks of the Internet are absorbed and contained by corporations such as Facebook and Google, working in close partnerships with hardware suppliers such as Samsung and Apple, what was once perceived as subversive and transformative appropriation increasingly comes to function as the kind of collaboration that simply rearticulates the immaterial logic of global capitalism.

This book therefore combines a critical analysis of transmedia world-building with a more optimistic quest for these storyworlds' radical political potential. It focuses on the tension between the anticapitalist building blocks that are essential to these franchises' mass appeal and the multiple ways in which they are incorporated within global capitalism's mechanisms of commodity circulation and capital accumulation. From Middle-earth to *The Walking Dead*, a crucial part of the appeal of fantastic world-building lies in its representation of social, cultural, political, and economic systems that offer more fantastical imagined alternatives to our own. But, at the same time, their anticapitalist potential is undermined on

---

57. Jeremy Gilbert, *Common Ground: Democracy and Collectivity in an Age of Individualism* (London: Pluto Press, 2014), 19.

two levels: first, within the storyworld's multitext, where contradictory ideological systems coexist that can offset or at least diminish more radical political currents; and second, at the level of audience participation, as fans' creative work is appropriated as immaterial labor.

In each of the four following chapters, I discuss two primary case studies that give a political analysis of the forms, narratives, and ideological foundations of these fantastic storyworlds. I have taken as my main objects of analysis some of the most popular and commercially successful narrative franchises to discuss the radical potential that resides both in the ideological organization of their storyworlds and in the collaborative cultural practices that have developed around them. While lesser-known fantastic storyworlds often have a far more obvious radical direction, a key point of interest for me is how the common language of popular culture can be appropriated and politicized. Each chapter therefore looks, on the one hand, at how the political and ideological organization of these imaginary worlds contain anticapitalist elements that can contribute to the important cultural work of imagining viable political alternatives and, on the other, at how the user practices that are essential to the construction of these worlds can all too easily be reappropriated as forms of immaterial labor.

Chapter 2 engages with two key fantastic storyworlds that have largely developed the conceptual vocabulary and tools for transmedia world-building. I approach the "Secondary Worlds" of Tolkien's Middle-earth and *Star Trek*'s universe as transitions between the older imperialist paradigm and the global reign of Empire. Both provide imaginary empires that would largely define the genres of fantasy and sf in the late twentieth century, the former offering a representation of magical pastness with its nostalgia for a premodern, precapitalist world; the latter articulating a human future that on the surface at least seems postcapitalist and postimperialist. While each of these storyworlds' longer histories has been essential to the development of world-building as a cultural and industrial practice, they have also been exhaustively documented from every conceivable angle elsewhere. My chapter will therefore focus primarily on how recent transmedia iterations have connected them directly to the political logic of Empire. For Tolkien, Peter Jackson's two film trilogies and their multiple transmedia paratexts have adapted the original text in a way that perfectly suits the context of media convergence and participatory culture. And while the original *Star Trek* TV series seemed to anticipate the age of cognitive capitalism, I focus more strongly on *Star Trek: The Next Generation*, the series in which the franchise developed explosively in terms of world-building, and which accompanied the historical emergence of global capitalism in the early 1990s.

While *Star Trek* and the "Tolkien-verse" clearly negotiate the transition from imperialism to global capitalism, the two storyworlds that make up chapter 3's central case studies offer examples of global capitalism's "postideological" spirit, and the contradictions of constructing a coherent storyworld from a neoliberal framework that Mark Fisher has described as "capitalist realism."[58] Just as *Game of Thrones* can be read as global capitalism's response to Tolkienian high fantasy, the twenty-first-century *Battlestar Galactica* reboot delivers neoliberalism's postideological reaction to *Star Trek*'s humanist sf. Both of these influential and hugely popular transmedia storyworlds offer complex negotiations of a politics of cynicism through the combination of a realist aesthetic, on the one hand, and the ambiguous embrace of religion and mysticism, on the other. But besides the profitable gentrification of genre that this process has entailed, the worldview that they represent provides an uncannily accurate reflection of neoliberalism's postideological spirit.

Chapter 4 then shifts over to storyworlds that explicitly foreground class conflict and revolutionary political action. They show the transformative potential that is contained within the biopolitical organization of Empire, which in its deterritorialization has unchained energies that challenge the hierarchical power structure informing the imperialist project. I begin by discussing the Spartacus narrative as an allegorical mythology for representing a specifically modern "communist imaginary." The character's cultural legacy of anticapitalist energy also informs the twenty-first-century *Spartacus* franchise, a transmedia storyworld that draws upon a wide variety of sources from various genres and media, ranging from historical fiction to fantasy and exploitation cinema. It locates in the popular mythology of Spartacus a central motif of exploitation that it places within a fantastical version of the Roman Empire where power and ideology operate along the lines of Debord's Society of the Spectacle: the class struggle that is central to the storyworld is ingeniously intertwined with a self-reflexive representation of the media industries' own sensational output.

This anticapitalist energy is even more evident in *The Hunger Games*, a franchise that expresses class consciousness in a way that opens up a space for more radical alternatives, even if this is simultaneously counteracted by the logic of commodity culture. My argument here is that the positive revolutionary energy these highly commodified media tap into cannot be fully contained by the capitalist machinery that attempts to regulate and contain it. In the particular case of *The Hunger Games*, I argue that the franchise's overt anticapitalism has saturated the cultural vocabulary in spite of the fact that the storyworld's ideological organization is oblique and profoundly contradictory. While *Spartacus* is in every way more radical and subversive as a transmedial multitext, its "cult" status as a franchise associated with exploitation cinema has clearly reduced its potential as a shared language for political activism.

Chapter 5 introduces the framework of critical posthumanism as a way of constructing a subject position with the potential to think beyond capitalism. By moving beyond the oppressive hierarchies of liberal humanist binaries, radically posthuman storyworlds can produce narrative frameworks that destabilize the

---

58. Mark Fisher, *Capitalist Realism: Is There No Alternative?* (Hants: Zero Books, 2009).

ontological basis of capitalist realism. By presenting the human subject as a construct and technological hybrid, critical posthumanism can interrogate the politics that inform our affective relationship with transmedia world-building. As popular culture's primary posthuman tropes, the zombie and the cyborg embody some of the key concepts underlying this form of anticapitalist imaginary. This chapter therefore examines the ways in which such posthuman tropes can affect the political implications of popular fantastic world-building by looking at two case studies in which the prominence of posthuman bodies focuses the storyworlds' ideological organization on posthumanism's radical political implications.

In the hugely popular transmedia franchise *The Walking Dead*, the outbreak of a zombie pandemic brings about a postapocalyptic environment in which small groups of survivors attempt to rebuild society through the establishment of small, precarious communities. While their repeated failure seems to align this storyworld with the postideological politics of cynicism I discuss in chapter 3, the zombie genre's long history of social satire and subversive politics informs this franchise's unique attempt to sustain a zombie narrative that resists closure. The formal properties of this transmedia multitext therefore align themselves uniquely with the critical potential of posthumanism and "zombie theory," resulting in often fruitful and complex explorations of postcapitalist alternatives, on the one hand, and the obstinate legacy of capitalist realism, on the other.

Similarly, transmedia artist Janelle Monáe's series of concept albums depicts a future society of massive social and political oppression where resistance takes a looser, more playful form than that of linear narrative media. Repurposing and transforming the cultural legacy of Afrofuturism, Monáe's world-building project spans not only her pop albums and music videos but also a wide variety of participatory and collective projects that also include social justice and antiracist movements. Moreover, her stylistically eclectic work simultaneously embraces and transforms the logic of Empire, with her Wondaland Arts Collective both establishing an elaborate imaginary world that circulates in conventional commodity form and operating as a creative collective that puts her utopian vision into practice. Monáe's world-building project is therefore one of the most vivid examples of transmedia culture that uses the multitudinous energy unleashed by Empire and directs it in a deliberately subversive way.

By emphasizing commercial storyworlds that subvert and transform the ways in which transmedia world-building operates as an industrial practice, this book consciously foregrounds an aspect of multiplatform media franchises that is too often and too easily overlooked. One may be tempted to observe that the majority of successful transmedia storyworlds incorporate Empire's logic of cognitive capitalism, disciplining their participatory audiences in ways that reflect the overwhelming power of immaterial labor and neoliberal biopower. This book thereby embraces the necessity to move beyond mere critique and joins forces with the growing number of voices calling for a radical political perspective on contemporary culture. It combines critical theory and the Marxist tradition's radical perspective with the more utopian and celebratory approach often found within fan studies to explore productive ways of thinking about the contradictory nature of fantastic world-building. Just as Walter Benjamin saw both great liberating potential and grave danger in mass media like cinema, convergence culture similarly offers radical political opportunities that capital continuously seeks to control, regulate, and diminish. This book attempts to identify and acknowledge this radical potential without underestimating the powerful forces that contain it.

2

World-Building and Convergence Culture

From Imperialism to Empire

"Which is better: *The Lord of the Rings* or *Star Trek*?" On Saturday, April 20, 2013, the big question that may or may not have divided sf and fantasy fans for decades was going to be settled once and for all on the TV show *The Nerdist*.[1] In nine minutes, both of these storyworlds would be championed by a solitary fan in an epic debate on their relative strengths and weaknesses. Topics of comparison included Great Leadership, Ultimate Goals, Cool Weapons, and Great Villains, and the comedian-debaters made every attempt to express in words the awesomeness of their own favorite while making merciless but benevolent fun of their opponent's. Points were scored with the studio audience by ridiculing "creepy" Commander Riker's facial hair, harping on Gollum's skin condition, emphasizing *Star Trek*'s ethnic diversity, and comparing Gandalf's return to the resurrection of Jesus Christ.

This humorous exercise was clearly not designed to give any kind of real answer to the segment's main question. Instead, it provided the participants with an opportunity to show off their appropriately "nerdist" sensibilities in an affectionate send-up of fan culture. In the context of a weekly TV show adapted from a popular podcast, the comical discussion followed the familiar trajectory of devoted but self-aware fans geeking out over the genre fiction and pop-cultural items that are fan culture's stock-in-trade. On the program's website, host Chris Hardwick explains in remarkably similar terms how the program's creators "gush about the things we love constantly, and the fact that BBCA[merica] lets us do that as OUR JOBS puts me forever in their debt." Both the style and the content of this remark vividly illustrate the kind of affective energy that typifies fan culture. As John Fiske has expressed in his defense of fan culture, "fandom

---

1. "Fantasy Nerdist," *The Nerdist* (BBC America, April 20, 2013).

is a heightened form of popular culture," where the fan's "excessive" form of readership is just one degree removed from a "normal" audience's engagement.[2]

The segment also demonstrates the inclusive nature of fandom: the debate is presented on the surface as if it seeks to establish which of these two fan favorites is the greatest, but its actual function is all too obviously a celebration of both. This dialogic, affective, and collaborative attitude, which has typified fan culture for many years,[3] has in the twenty-first century become increasingly visible and influential as part of a wider, more mainstream popular culture. Countless twenty-first-century sitcoms[4] offer celebrations of geek sensibilities, giving fandom a heightened visibility and cultural legitimacy. The twentieth-century perception of the fan as the "vulnerable, irrational victim of mass persuasion"[5] is clearly no longer the dominant perception of this kind of sensibility. Instead, digital culture has fostered the image of the fan as Jenkins's textual poacher: an active, productive, and self-reflexive cultural magpie whose cultural preferences thrive in a media landscape dominated by immersive transmedia storyworlds.

As the playful *Nerdist* segment also illustrates, Tolkien's fantastic realm of Middle-earth and the long-running *Star Trek* franchise remain the two best-known and most beloved paradigms of transmedia world-building. Within fan culture, each functions as the classic example of a major strand of fantastic genre fiction: just as Tolkien's elves, wizards, orcs, and hobbits came to define high fantasy, *Star Trek*'s warp drives, transporter beams, and phasers signaled the cultural vocabulary of "hard sci-fi."[6] Both therefore also articulated and sustained a clear distinction between the fantasy and sf genres and their associated fandoms, which for many years functioned as a meaningful boundary between separate cultures, aesthetics, philosophies, and politics. But besides their historical importance to the development of transmedia world-building as a cultural and industrial practice, these two examples are particularly relevant as introductory case studies for this book because of their similarly ambivalent relationship to capitalism: as my analysis will show, each in its own way embeds a radical anticapitalism within forms and structures that support and even strengthen capitalism's most basic coordinates.

---

2. John Fiske, "The Cultural Economy of Fandom," in *The Adoring Audience: Fan Culture and Popular Media*, ed. Lisa A. Lewis (London and New York: Routledge, 1992), 46.

3. Henry Jenkins, *Fans, Bloggers, and Gamers: Exploring Participatory Culture* (New York: New York University Press, 2006), 150.

4. Prominent examples of Anglo-American comedy shows celebrating "geek culture" include *The Big Bang Theory* (CBS, 2007–present), *The Office* (NBC, 2005–2013), *Parks and Recreation* (NBC, 2009–2015), *Community* (NBC/Yahoo, 2009–2015), *How I Met Your Mother* (CBS, 2005–2014), *The IT Crowd* (Channel 4, 2006–2013), and *Peep Show* (Channel 4, 2003–2015).

5. Joli Jenson, "Fandom as Pathology," in *The Adoring Audience: Fan Culture and Popular Media*, ed. Lisa A. Lewis (London and New York: Routledge, 1992), 14.

6. As the third obvious paradigmatic franchise in fan culture, *Star Wars* perfectly occupies a middle ground between fantasy and sf, combining elements of both in its hybrid "science fantasy" form.

My focus in this chapter will therefore be on these two storyworlds' representation of (respectively) pre- and postcapitalist storyworlds, and on how their twenty-first-century circulation has contributed to a form of popular fantasy we might describe as "postgenre."[7] My discussion will focus on some of the main contradictions that illustrate the storyworlds' dialectical relation to the history of capitalism: first, by looking at the tension that exists on the textual level, as both Tolkien and *Star Trek* present storyworlds that are defined internally by the ideological tension between an anticapitalist spirit and a more reactionary conservatism; and second, on the level of reception and circulation, as fan culture is increasingly absorbed and reterritorialized as a valuable new form of immaterial labor, thereby further diminishing the storyworlds' political potential. But first, I must give a short explanation of the transformation from imperialism to Empire, and the ways in which the dawn of global capitalism has remapped our political, economic, and cultural reality.

IMPERIALISM AND THE TWENTIETH-CENTURY MEDIA LANDSCAPE

The mass media landscape of the early twentieth century was organized in ways that reflected the industrial organization of its era's mode of production: the media companies that produced mass entertainment for film, radio, comic books, and genre literature were each centrally organized, with a highly compartmentalized and classically Fordist organizational form. While many popular characters would appear across a wide variety of different media, this would not be in a centrally controlled or consistently organized way. Instead, copyright holders would license characters to other media companies, which would then reinvent elements of the story to suit their own specific needs and available formats. In this way, multiple incarnations of characters and their settings would proliferate across different media platforms, each of which would define these elements in its own terms. Comic book characters like Superman and Batman are obvious examples of this cross-media logic, which resulted not in structured transmedia world-building but in highly diverse and varied histories more accurately described as a kind of palimpsest.[8]

This dominant approach to the development of cross-media storyworlds and narrative figures directly reflects the institutional organization of Fordist capitalism at its peak, which followed the logic of imperialism. In the same way that imperialist practices were defined by a small number of competing European

---

7. Ramzi Fawaz, "'Where No X-Man Has Gone Before!' Mutant Superheroes and the Cultural Politics of Popular Fantasy in Postwar America," *American Literature* 83, no. 2 (2011): 356–57.

8. Will Brooker, *Hunting the Dark Knight: Twenty-First Century Batman* (London: I. B. Tauris, 2012), 56.

nation-states, each of which imposed clear borders around the territories it had usurped, commercial narrative media would compete with each other in ways that restricted transmedia world-building. Following this logic, film studios, book publishers, and broadcasting companies defined themselves in relation to their direct competitors within the same medium (e.g., Marvel versus DC Comics), while other narrative media were most commonly viewed as competitors rather than as potential collaborators.[9] This imperialist paradigm thus fostered an atmosphere in which the worlds of mass-produced communication platforms such as radio, television, cinema, and print were predominantly experienced as a clearly bounded "hierarchy of media."[10]

The post–World War II dissolution of European colonial powers made possible a radical remapping of global boundaries that ushered in the age of Empire, as nation-states were now redefined as three "worlds": the First World of the US and its capitalist allies; the Second World of the Soviet Union and other "socialist" states included in the Warsaw Pact; and the Third World of "developing nations," consisting mostly of former European colonies.[11] This transitional phase from imperialism to Empire saw the first major steps in the deterritorialization of nation-states that would ultimately result in what Philip Bobbitt has described as the constitutional order of the market state.[12] He describes the onset of globalization in terms remarkably similar to Hardt and Negri's: as one in which the sovereignty of individual nation-states is progressively weakened by the growing power of transnational corporations, especially once we enter the post–Cold War years in which capitalism is no longer forced to compete with an alternative system.

During this transitional period, the forces of modernization quickly reshaped the landscapes and local cultures of First- and Second-World nations on the "blank canvas" left in the wake of World War II's devastation. At the same time, a broad interest in narrative world-building began to emerge from within the genres of sf and fantasy: postwar sf authors such as Isaac Asimov developed serialized epics that mapped out elaborate fictional chronologies,[13] while organized sf fandom continued to develop as a grassroots phenomenon in North America and northern Europe. While these practices were initially limited to relatively marginal subcultures, world-building during this transitional period

---

9. There was, for example, a firm boundary between film and television, with very few actors or other creative personnel transitioning from one medium to the other.

10. Jay David Bolter and Richard Grusin, *Remediation: Understanding New Media* (Cambridge, MA: MIT Press, 2000), 100.

11. Michael Hardt and Antonio Negri, *Empire* (Cambridge, MA: Harvard University Press, 2000), xiii.

12. Philip Bobbitt, *Terror and Consent: The Wars for the Twenty-First Century* (New York: Alfred A. Knopf, 2008), 86.

13. Asimov's *Foundation* series is a paradigmatic example that would shape many later world-building narratives, including *Star Trek*.

did important cultural work in the development of new collaborative practices that would reflect and negotiate the emerging cultural logic of global capitalism. The first of these paradigmatic world-building projects was J. R. R. Tolkien's development of the imaginary world of Arda, and its genre-defining history and mythology of Middle-earth.

NOSTALGIA FOR AN IMPERIALIST WORLD: TOLKIEN'S MIDDLE-EARTH

Hobbits, wizards, orcs, elves, Gollum, Mordor, the One Ring: Tolkien's imaginary world established an abundance of characters, species, and locations that have by now become part of the shared vocabulary of global popular culture. This paradigmatic world-building project began as an Oxford philologist's stated intention to invent a new language while simultaneously creating a full-scale premodern mythology for what he perceived as an "enfeebled" Anglo-Saxon narrative culture.[14] Combining elements from multiple European traditions of folklore and fantastic literature, he constructed a storyworld that would provide the template for the high fantasy genre as it took shape from the early 1970s onward. Introduced in *The Hobbit*[15] and substantially expanded in *The Lord of the Rings*[16] (hereafter *LOTR*), Tolkien's immersive world-building would become the standard by which all subsequent fantastic storyworlds in the genre would be judged.

The books' "topofocal" approach to narrative, in which the mapping out of an imaginary geography is as important as the plot, emphasizes the strong connection between the characters and the environment they traverse.[17] This combination of the text's foregrounding of its massively detailed and extraordinarily textured storyworld, its explicit rejection of technology and modernization, and the trilogy's availability as an inexpensive paperback[18] helped make *LOTR* massively popular among the emerging American countercultural movement. In 1965, *LOTR* outsold all other book titles on American university campuses,[19] and

---

14. Brian Attebery, *Strategies of Fantasy* (Bloomington: Indiana University Press, 1992), 14–16.

15. J. R. R. Tolkien, *The Hobbit (or There and Back Again)* (Boston: Houghton Mifflin Books for Children, 1973).

16. J. R. R. Tolkien, *The Fellowship of the Ring: Being the First Part of the Lord of the Rings*, 2nd ed. (Boston: Houghton Mifflin Company, 1965); J. R. R. Tolkien, *The Two Towers: Being the Second Part of the Lord of the Rings*, 2nd ed. (Boston: Houghton Mifflin Company, 1965); J. R. R. Tolkien, *The Return of the King: Being the Third Part of the Lord of the Rings*, 2nd ed. (Boston: Houghton Mifflin Company, 1965).

17. Stefan Ekman, *Here Be Dragons: Exploring Fantasy Maps and Settings* (Middletown: Wesleyan University Press, 2013), 2.

18. Mark J. P. Wolf, *Building Imaginary Worlds: The Theory and History of Subcreation* (London and New York: Routledge, 2012), 130–34.

19. Michael Coren, *J. R. R. Tolkien: The Man Who Created* The Lord of the Rings (London: Boxtree, 2001), 98.

its surging popularity soon spread to similar-minded alternative communities across Europe. Before long, T-shirts, posters, buttons, and bumper stickers bearing slogans like "Gandalf for President" proliferated among the book's growing number of fans, many of whom perceived Tolkien's imaginary world as an idealized expression of their own environmentalist, communitarian, and anticapitalist views. At the same time, the text's metaphorical demonization of industrial labor and technological innovation connected to the American counterculture's rejection of the Western world's burgeoning materialism and consumerism.

Most of the existing scholarly writing on Tolkien's world-building falls rather neatly into two camps. On the one hand, authors within the growing field of "Tolkien studies" celebrate its richly intertextual incorporation of elements from North European mythology, linguistics, and philology. But in their attempts to discuss him as a literary figure without alienating his countless fans, Tolkien scholars tend to tread lightly when it comes to a more critical approach: all too often, Tolkien studies "focuses on comparisons with other writers, pursues linguistic investigations, or examines popular topics, sometimes from poorly-informed points of view."[20] Scholars writing in the Marxist tradition of literary theory, on the other hand, have roundly condemned Tolkien's work for its overwhelming conservatism, one-dimensional characters, inconsistent and often overblown prose, and reactionary politics.[21]

Both sides have made compelling points. Tolkien's writing does indeed offer a massively detailed and highly immersive storyworld that is experienced as meaningful by a great many readers, for a variety of contradictory reasons. At the same time, the organization of Middle-earth's history and geography expresses an overwhelmingly Eurocentric worldview that thrives on grossly offensive racist stereotypes, a phallocentric and largely masculine perspective on human agency, and a blanket condemnation of progressive forms of social and political change. Because of these factors (and several others besides), the Marxist perspective on Tolkien's writing, and by extension on the larger genre of late twentieth-century fantasy literature, has ranged from dismissive to overtly hostile.

Approaching Tolkien's storyworld from an emphatically dialectical perspective, my interest lies in the political and ideological contradictions that define the storyworld's structural organization and in the ways in which these tensions are negotiated, both inside the text and outside it. To put it more plainly, I am purposefully seeking out those Tolkienian elements that are worth salvaging from an anticapitalist perspective, while also identifying and critiquing the factors that impede or even contradict such a reading. This dialectical approach will allow

---

20. Norbert Schürer, "Tolkien Criticism Today," *Los Angeles Review of Books*, November 13, 2015, accessed January 12, 2016, https://lareviewofbooks.org/essay/tolkien-criticism-today.

21. Carl Freedman's polemical dismissal of Middle-earth as an "extremely light façade" that is "a mile wide but only an inch deep" typifies the general Marxist response to Tolkien. Carl Freedman, *Art and Idea in the Novels of China Miéville* (Canterbury: Gylphi Books, 2015), 19–20.

me to discuss its political potential and its obvious mass appeal without glossing over or understating the aforementioned problematic aspects of Tolkien's narrative universe, many of which have been exacerbated by the film adaptations of *LOTR*[22] and the lamentable prequel series loosely based on *The Hobbit*.[23] My attention will be focused on the relationship between Tolkien's structure of feeling[24] and the contradictory ways in which it negotiates specific ideological tensions inherent in twentieth- and twenty-first-century capitalism.

THE IDEOLOGICAL CONTRADICTIONS OF MIDDLE-EARTH

Capital's response to the global recession of the 1970s has been exhaustively described, by Hardt and Negri as well as many other theorists and historians of capitalism.[25] But only rarely do these authors include in their analysis the ways in which these changes received crucial support from the cultural realm. It is therefore worth examining in more detail how fantastic storyworlds that have resonated under these historical and material conditions articulate the tensions and contradictions that emerged under global capitalism. In this period, Tolkien's world-building was adopted as the basic template for fantasy literature, role-playing games, fan fiction, and Hollywood's late 1970s transition to nostalgically oriented popular fantasy as a key element of its "high concept" business model.[26] While it would take many more years before *LOTR* would itself become a mass media phenomenon, its influence on post-1960s fan culture and popular entertainment is nevertheless impossible to exaggerate. This makes the "Tolkien-verse" worth

22. *The Lord of the Rings: The Fellowship of the Rings*, directed by Peter Jackson (2001; London: Entertainment in Video, 2011), Blu-ray; *The Lord of the Rings: The Two Towers*, directed by Peter Jackson (2002; London: Entertainment in Video, 2011), Blu-ray; *The Lord of the Rings: The Return of the King*, directed by Peter Jackson (2003; London: Entertainment in Video, 2011), Blu-ray.

23. *The Hobbit: An Unexpected Journey*, directed by Peter Jackson (2012; Burbank, CA: Warner Home Video, 2013), Blu-ray; *The Hobbit: The Desolation of Smaug,* directed by Peter Jackson (2013; Burbank, CA: Warner Home Video, 2014), Blu-ray; *The Hobbit: The Battle of the Five Armies*, directed by Peter Jackson (2014; Burbank, CA: Warner Home Video, 2015), Blu-ray.

24. I take this term from Raymond Williams, as used and developed throughout his work, but defined most clearly as a nonreductive way of articulating "concepts of 'world-view' or 'ideology'" in a way that foregrounds "meanings and values as they are actively lived and felt." Raymond Williams, *Marxism and Literature* (Oxford: Oxford University Press, 1977), 132.

25. See, for instance, Gilles Deleuze and Félix Guattari, *A Thousand Plateaus* (New York: Continuum, 2004 [1987]); David Harvey, *A Brief History of Neoliberalism* (Oxford: Oxford University Press, 2006); Leo Panitch and Sam Gindin, *The Making of Global Capitalism* (London and New York: Verso, 2013); Manuel Castells, *The Rise of the Network Society*, 2nd ed. (Chichester: Wiley Blackwell, 2010); Chris Harman, *Zombie Capitalism* (London: Bookmarks, 2009); Thomas Piketty, *Capital in the Twenty-First Century* (Cambridge, MA: Harvard University Press, 2014).

26. Douglas Gomery, "Hollywood Corporate Business Practice and Periodizing Contemporary Film History," in *Contemporary Hollywood Cinema*, ed. Steve Neale and Murray Smith (New York: Routledge, 1998), 47–49.

discussing in more detail from the perspective of anticapitalism, not only because it supplied the basic mold for so many other fantastic storyworlds but also because it has resonated so strongly with activist and countercultural projects, many of whom saw in Tolkien's work the possibility of another kind of world, and who embraced his writing as a "voice for the dispossessed."[27]

If we then wish to salvage at least some elements of Tolkien's world-building for their anticapitalist potential, we might begin by focusing on how strongly the books' portrayal of rapid modernization resembles the most familiar critiques of capitalism's destruction of all previously existing communities and cultural forms. Tolkien's misgivings about modernization represent similar anxieties as those felt more recently by the European Left in the face of neoliberal globalization, as his work pines nostalgically for "the reconstruction of the unified social body and thus the recreation of the people."[28] His imaginative dramatization of the effects of capitalist modernization and industrialization even bring to mind those well-worn lines from *The Communist Manifesto* that equate the rise of capitalism with the rapid destruction of all previous forms and traditions, as "all fixed, fast-frozen relations, with their train of ancient and venerable prejudices and opinions, are swept away."[29] Hardt and Negri describe the sped-up process of globalization in remarkably similar terms:

> The contemporary processes of globalization have torn down many of the boundaries of the colonial world. Along with the common celebrations of the unbounded flows in our new global village, one can still sense also an anxiety about increased contact and a certain nostalgia for colonialist hygiene. . . . Nothing can bring back the hygienic shields of colonial boundaries. The age of globalization is the age of universal contagion.[30]

In articulating an anxiety that reflects twentieth-century capitalism's passage from these "hygienic" colonial boundaries to Empire's "radical deterritorialization,"[31] Tolkien's storyworld provides an imaginary framework from which this larger transformation of capitalism can be negotiated. The slow process of disenchantment in fantastic fiction, as "magic and wonder are crowded out by science and technology,"[32] is commonly referred to as "thinning." It forms a common ingredient in many varieties of fantastic fiction, as "fantasies set in

---

27. Jane Chance, *The Lord of the Rings: The Mythology of Power*, revised edition (Lexington: Kentucky University Press, 2001), 2.

28. Michael Hardt and Antonio Negri, *Multitude: War and Democracy in the Age of Empire* (London: Penguin, 2005), 191.

29. Karl Marx and Friedrich Engels, *The Communist Manifesto: A Modern Edition* (London and New York: Verso, 2012), 38.

30. Hardt and Negri, *Empire,* 136.

31. Hardt and Negri, *Empire*, 137.

32. Ekman, *Here Be Dragons*, 90.

history almost invariably deal with the loss of the old richness."[33] It is especially apparent in *LOTR*, where "the passing away of a higher and more intense Reality provides a constant *leitmotif*,"[34] and the storyworld's residual magic is displaced by an emergent modernity. Viewed from this context, the structure of feeling that permeates Tolkien's world-building is one that associates a utopian ideal of community with the clearly bounded and compartmentalized reign of imperialism, while the intensified deterritorialization of an increasingly global capitalism is presented as a form of sad but inevitable deterioration.

The most common misreading of Tolkien seems to be derived most strongly from his work's many imitators, as well as from the many film and videogame adaptations that have helped popularize the genre of high fantasy. This understandable but inaccurate critical perspective interprets his work's teleological imperative to be that of stasis and salvation,[35] as the premodern world of Middle-earth is ultimately kept safe from the corrupting influence of Sauron and his proletarian legions of orcs, on the one hand, and Saruman's destructive industrialization, on the other. While the storyworld's multiple antimodern currents do superficially support this kind of reading, the central historical development around which *LOTR*'s storyworld is organized is not about avoiding the transition into modernity but about ensuring that this inevitable thinning occurs in the least objectionable way. The structure of feeling that informs Tolkien's work most strongly is therefore defined by the dialectical tension between a thoroughly anticapitalist spirit and the reactionary desire to resist not only industrial modernization but also any social movement that challenges class power.

Of these two competing energies, the most universally recognized element in Tolkien's popular appeal—as evidenced by fans' widely shared expression of the storyworld's "spiritual essence"[36]—is its sense of nostalgia for an older world of myth, magic, and Elvish wisdom that has been tragically lost. Paradoxically, this fantastic world of invented languages and imaginary beings is experienced by many readers as more "real" than our own postmodern condition, in which the human subject struggles to find clear and tangible meaning, and where traditional forms of knowledge appear to have lost their sense of legitimacy.[37] Tolkien's easily ridiculed but also intensely beloved "pseudo-medievalism"[38] should therefore not be interpreted as an actual desire to return to some form of premodern

---

33. John Clute, "Thinning," in *The Encyclopedia of Fantasy*, ed. John Clute and John Grant (New York: St. Martin's Griffin, 1999), 942.

34. Clute, "Thinning," 942.

35. See, for instance, Fredric Jameson, *Archaeologies of the Future* (London and New York: Verso, 2005), 57–71.

36. Giselinde Kuipers and Jeroen de Kloet, "Spirituality and Fan Culture around the *Lord of the Rings* Film Trilogy," *Fabula* 48, no. 3–4 (2007): 317–18.

37. Jean-François Lyotard, *The Postmodern Condition: A Report on Knowledge* (Minneapolis: Minnesota University Press, 1984), 37–41.

38. Umberto Eco, *Faith in Fakes: Travels in Hyperreality* (London: Vintage, 1986), 62.

feudalism. Instead, it presents a selective and massively contradictory fantasy that allows readers to negotiate tensions inherent in late capitalism. As with Jameson's postmodern "nostalgia mode,"[39] the fantasy in the case of Middle-earth is even more literally the invention of a generalized sense of "pastness" that fetishizes highly selective and grossly superficial aspects of an earlier historical period. At the same time, the storyworld's imaginary past carefully removes or displaces any internal contradictions that might disrupt the pleasurable fantasy of its supposedly precapitalist environment.

The sense in which such pseudo-medieval storyworlds thus offer a kind of "utopia for the before" by imagining a life *before* capitalism[40] is contradictory in the first place because the organization of this world is so clearly based on a fundamentally capitalist paradigm. While the means and relations of production throughout Tolkien's Middle-earth are largely and quite deliberately obfuscated, the world the characters inhabit is organized entirely on the basis of the class hierarchies and geographical boundaries that typify the "striated" landscape of capitalism in its imperialist phase.[41] Like many other popular fantasy narratives, *LOTR* presents a world populated by many distinct and homogeneous local communities. These communities are strongly embedded in their geographical and ecological environment, and individual characters have specific and identifiable customs, languages, and cultural idiosyncrasies that identify them clearly as members of those communities.

Besides the larger distinctions between various imaginary humanlike races (hobbits, elves, dwarves, trolls, orcs, etc.), the cultural identity of each particular community is similarly determined by its direct physical environment. For example, the elves who reside in the peaceful and secluded hamlet of Rivendell are markedly different from the fiercer, more warlike elf tribes in the dangerous forests of Mirkwood. The lands of Middle-earth are therefore clearly defined by the many boundaries that exist between races, regions, and cultures. While fans often celebrate Tolkien's work for its alleged diversity, it is at the same time quite obviously an essentialist and therefore inherently racist kind of diversity, where ethnic and cultural identity tend to strengthen and reiterate each other.[42] For this reason, the structure of feeling that permeates this variety of fantastic world-building expresses a strong sense of nostalgia for the imperialist and colonialist paradigm.

---

39. Fredric Jameson, *Postmodernism, or, The Cultural Logic of Late Capitalism* (Durham: Duke University Press, 1991), 279–96.

40. Alexander R. Galloway, "*Warcraft* and Utopia," Ctheory.net, February 16, 2006, accessed January 26, 2015, http://www.ctheory.net/articles.aspx?id=507.

41. Deleuze and Guattari, *A Thousand Plateaus*, 540–43.

42. Tellingly, Tolkien's attempt to demonstrate his sensitivity to racism and anti-Semitism is the slowly developing friendship between the (Aryan) elf Legolas and the (Jewish) dwarf Gimli. But this highly selective, thoroughly individual, and obviously exceptional possibility of cross-cultural and interethnic relationships clearly does not extend to races coded in the text as non-white.

And while Tolkien's storyworld cannily avoids direct representations of capitalism's most recognizable signifiers, it is nevertheless defined both in its ideological content and in its spatial organization in ways that only make sense from the context of twentieth-century capitalism. It is therefore little wonder that this fantastic storyworld was interpreted as an allegorical indictment of modernity and embraced so enthusiastically by anticapitalist and antiauthoritarian movements in the 1960s and 1970s. For the students, activists, and revolutionaries who saw in Tolkien's storyworld a powerful alternative to capitalism, "the United States government took on the guise of a Dark Lord demanding universal domination."[43] A wide variety of radical activists and anticapitalists at this time united under the catchphrase "Frodo Lives!" which proliferated on T-shirts, banners, and pamphlets across antiwar and anticapitalist protests. Alternative youth culture thus clearly saw in young Frodo's steely resolve in the face of a seemingly unstoppable force a direct reflection of their own asymmetrical struggle against American capitalism's economic, military, and cultural imperialism.[44]

But the problem with Tolkien's anticapitalism is quite obviously the form it tends to take. The static and ostentatiously romanticized world it portrays is essentially that of European feudalism, but one that is—as Slavoj Žižek might state—deprived of its essence: in Middle-earth, the European agrarian mode of production is able to exist, but without the forms of class struggle and exploitation that defined it historically in the Middle Ages. Instead, this tension is displaced onto an external threat of some Great Evil that is explicitly associated with xenophobia, orientalism, racism, and (perhaps more than anything else) the fear of revolution. The contradictions of class conflict that make up the storyworld's political unconscious are most obvious in the dynamic between Frodo and Sam: their relationship is presented to us not on the basis of its master-slave dialectic but as a deeply personal, even profoundly intimate friendship that nevertheless always maintains its completely hierarchical character.

To borrow another famous Žižekian phrase, one is indeed tempted to describe this displacement of a structural internal tension as an example of "ideology at its purest": the Shire, as the crucially significant symbolic site of innocence and purity around which the larger quest in *LOTR* ultimately revolves, is structured by a set of social relations without any substantial internal contradictions, thus "presenting itself as an alternative reality only through a process of ruthless and radical *over-simplification*."[45] It presents an ideal of community dominated by unmediated face-to-face communication, strong social controls, and lives lived in harmony with a nurturing natural environment. Hobbit society in fact presents the

---

43. Chance, *The Lord of the Rings: The Mythology of Power*, 2.

44. "There is a seed of courage hidden (often deeply, it is true) in the heart of the fattest and most timid hobbit, waiting for some final and desperate danger to make it grow." Tolkien, *The Fellowship of the Ring*, 151.

45. Freedman, *Art and Idea in the Novels of China Miéville*, 20.

superficially attractive fantasy of a perfect balance between human industry and the ecological environment, predicated entirely on traditionally gendered terms: hobbit culture is an expression of patriarchal, masculine agency that is nurtured and sustained by the feminine fertility of the land.[46] Obviously, the residential hobbit-holes represent not only this "ideal" harmonious balance between culture and a fully domesticated nature but also (in a somewhat filthy metaphor) the penetrative force of capitalism's dominant masculinity, which has literally taken up residence in the most womblike domicile imaginable.

Michael Saler's excellent study of Tolkien's storyworld focuses precisely on this weird incongruity between irrational, premodern fantasy, on the one hand, and modernity's "instrumental rationality," on the other.[47] For him, Tolkien's storyworld offers a precarious form of fantasy that is "enchanted in a disenchanted way"[48]: it provides a premodern environment of seemingly irrational fancy, but one that is organized on the basis of "rigorously rational" coordinates, and which is subject to the thinning that accompanies capitalism's inevitable disenchantment.[49] His analysis articulates very clearly one of the most crucial contradictions in Tolkien's storyworld, as it plays upon a tension between modern and antimodern forms, aesthetics, and sensibilities. The benefit of this approach is first that it helps historicize Tolkien's work and legacy precisely by emphasizing the contradictory elements in the political organization of his storyworld, and second that it emphasizes how what is so often experienced as a "timeless" fantastical narrative is in fact fully enmeshed in tensions that are historical and material.

This perspective also points the way toward a further unpacking of this storyworld's political organization, and how its contradictions reflect those of twentieth-century capitalism. The geopolitical structure of Middle-earth clearly illustrates its historical contingence with industrial capitalism's framework of imperialism, which revolved around the ongoing competition between European nation-states, and the constant negotiation of globe-spanning border systems:

> Imperialism was really an extension of the sovereignty of the European nation-states beyond their own boundaries. Eventually nearly all the world's territories could be parceled out and the entire world map could be coded in European colors: red for British territory, blue for French, green for Portuguese, and so forth.[50]

---

46. It is worth mentioning that the Shire, as a fictional environment that falls firmly within the English pastoral tradition, reflects a very specific sense of Englishness that obviously (if paradoxically) resonated with the American counterculture's wider interest in Great Britain as a site of musical, cultural, and political innovation. See Patrick Curry, *Defending Middle-earth: Tolkien: Myth and Modernity* (Boston: Houghton Mifflin, 2004), 24–35.

47. Michael Saler, *As If: Modern Enchantment and the Literary Prehistory of Virtual Reality* (Oxford: Oxford University Press, 2012), 9.

48. Saler, *As If*, 13.

49. Saler, *As If*, 159.

50. Hardt and Negri, *Empire*, xii.

Tolkien developed the imaginary world of Arda in a historical period where capitalism's inherent instability took on previously unimaginable forms: from the mechanized mass slaughter of World War I (which Tolkien witnessed firsthand) to the economic crisis and emergent fascism of the 1930s, and from World War II's calculated genocide to the emergence of consumer society in the 1950s. In many ways, *The Hobbit* and—even more obviously—*LOTR* have strong anti-capitalist tendencies that were certainly recognized by many readers in the 1960s counterculture, and which give the text a radical potential that has been too often and too easily overlooked by Marxist critics.

But as more scholars have come to acknowledge fantasy as a popular genre with as much radical political potential as sf, even Tolkien is slowly being re-evaluated. In his article "Slaves of the Ring: Tolkien's Political Unconscious," Ishay Landa makes a strong case for Tolkien's thematic preoccupation with capitalism and the concept of private property, reading the Arkenstone in *The Hobbit* and the Ring in *LOTR* as central objects around which the characters' ambivalent relationship to capitalism is constructed. His admirably dialectical reading of the "Tolkien-verse" emphasizes the perfectly contradictory way in which Tolkien's storyworld resolves its anxieties about imperialist capitalism's increasingly inescapable power. Rightfully dismissing the "mythical" aspects of the metaphysical battle between opposing forces of good and evil as historically meaningless, Landa mounts a compelling argument that sees in the Ring a distillation of some of capitalism's most fundamental contradictions:

> Tolkien's great achievement is in the way he was able to compress into the Ring . . . the historical dilemma of capitalism. For, in the Ring, are congested all the immeasurable contradictions of the capitalist system: the enormous productivity with the annihilating destructiveness, the unlimited power of the few with the utter impotence of the many, the extravagant luxury and the epidemic poverty, the sanguine promise with its horrible betrayal. All are there in the greatest miniature.[51]

This historical-materialist perspective on Tolkien's mythical storyworld salvages an element of the text that not only is worth considering in more detail but also helps us better understand its enduring influence and popularity, which has grown explosively in the age of global capitalism. More than mere escapism to a seemingly precapitalist fantasy world, the narrative trajectories of *The Hobbit* and *LOTR* potently dramatize the notion that radical political change is possible and sometimes even desirable. But, at the same time, it clearly concludes that this can never be achieved without also abandoning one's most basic ideological values. Therefore, as the Ring comes to stand in for "that most uncontrollable of all historical modes of production,"[52] even its destruction cannot reverse its

---

51. Ishay Landa, "Slaves of the Ring: Tolkien's Political Unconscious," *Historical Materialism* 10, no. 4 (2002): 122.

52. Landa, "Slaves of the Ring," 122.

harmful effects on the world. The organization of Tolkienian storyworlds thus provides an environment in which the developing tension between industrial and postindustrial capitalism can be negotiated in ways that are nostalgic and pleasurable but also deeply contradictory.

These contradictions concern not only the enormous discontinuities in style, narrative pace, and character motivation both within and across his major works but also a striking tension between competing modes of temporality, especially in *LOTR*. The trilogy's narrative is set at the end of what Tolkien calls "the Third Age," one of four distinct eras in the development of his imaginary world of Arda.[53] While following Frodo and the other characters in their journey from the northwest of Middle-earth to the most southeasterly corner of the map, the reader encounters a landscape rich in history and mythology, its various peoples all struggling in their own way to negotiate a world that is rapidly making the transition from enchantment to modernity, as the magical Age of Elves gives way to the rational Age of Men.

While Tolkien famously rejected the idea that *LOTR* might be interpreted allegorically, the mournful nostalgia that dominates his writing clearly corresponds with the mid-twentieth-century waning of European imperialism and the rise of a US-dominated global capitalist order.[54] The endless song verses that interrupt the narrative, the ruins and architectural wonders of previous ages encountered across Middle-earth, and the (white, Eurocentric) assortment of peoples and customs communicate above all a sense of overwhelming loss, as the magical and mythical elements of the world are swept away by the rising tide of rationalism, industrialism, and the orcish threat of universal proletarianization. Though writing in an entirely different register and for a different audience than authors such as T. S. Eliot and Virginia Woolf, Tolkien's bewilderment over the traumatic shock of the modern age is in this sense fundamentally identical to that of more highly acclaimed modernist figures.[55]

In Tolkien, this advent of a homogeneous and rational age of modernity alters the organization of Middle-earth most notably in the loss of the many specific "polders" that previously checkered the map of this imaginary empire: areas that not only are geographically separate from their direct surroundings but also have their own unique temporal organization. Such polders "belie the static impression of many worlds, demonstrating how the present of the story . . . differs from

---

53. Tolkien's storyworld was not initially intended to be set in a different, "Secondary" World but in an imagined past of our own, "Primary" World, further strengthening the notion that there is a strong correspondence between Tolkien's story events and their relation to human history.

54. Panitch and Gindin, *The Making of Global Capitalism*, 67–72.

55. Note also the obvious similarities between T. S. Eliot's "The Waste Land" and Tolkien's vivid descriptions of Mordor and the heavily industrialized Isengard. See Theresa Freda Nicolay, ed., *Tolkien and the Modernists: Literary Responses to the Dark New Days of the 20th Century* (Jefferson: McFarland, 2014).

the past as conserved within their boundaries."[56] Time in the Elvish realm of Lothlórien, for instance, moves more slowly than it does directly outside its borders, as a period that is experienced as a mere few days for the Fellowship later seems to have taken much longer in measurable "objective" time. The crucial moment in which the Fellowship lingers in the more leisurely "premodern" time of Lothlórien brings into sharp relief one of the text's key contradictions: while early chapters in the book have a more picaresque structure,[57] the time spent with the elves increases the temporal urgency of the central quest. The point here is that *LOTR*'s enchanted and premodern storyworld has strong boundaries that separate clearly defined cultures, identities, and even temporalities from each other, all of which are crucially portrayed as entering into a more modern state of rapid disintegration and deterritorialization. At the same time, the book's formal structure increasingly foregrounds the necessity for linear progress toward a single main goal.

The central choice in terms of storyworld organization is therefore no longer between the magical world of elves, dwarves, and hobbits, on the one hand, and the rational world of men, on the other. The fate of Middle-earth will be decided by the choice between two different forms of imperial rule: the malevolent dictatorship of dark lord Sauron or the "natural" reign of Aragorn, the messianic human king descended from the ancient "Dunedain" of Westernesse.[58] While the eponymous Return of the King is clearly preferable to the threat of Sauron's dictatorship of the proletariat, either outcome would still bring about the demise of the author's beloved world of magic and enchantment. As China Miéville has pointed out in his nuanced critique of the book, it is precisely this "tragedy of the creeping tawdry quotidian" that gives *LOTR* its powerful sense of melancholia, making it to some extent at least "worth celebrating and reclaiming."[59] In a register that at times shows some provocative similarities to Marx and Engels at their most colorfully ambivalent, Tolkien also mourns the universal destruction of "all that is holy" by the forces of modernity.[60]

The problem with the politics of Tolkien's world-building is therefore not so much the absence of any sense of historicity, which clearly takes abundant and

---

56. Ekman, *Here Be Dragons*, 125–26.

57. Not only are the chapters in the first volume more leisurely paced, taking abundant time for the singing of songs and reciting of poems, but the hobbits' encounters with Old Man Willow, the Barrow-wights, and Tom Bombadil are only of tangential interest to the book's narrative trajectory. These sections foreground the world-building that in the later volumes will be more rigidly interwoven with *LOTR*'s teleological portal-quest.

58. As the wizard Gandalf describes Aragorn's lineage, these superior men are "the last remnant in the North of the great people, the Men of the West" (Tolkien, *The Fellowship of the Ring*, 233).

59. China Miéville, "There and Back Again: Five Reasons Tolkien Rocks," *Omnivoracious*, June 15, 2009, accessed January 26, 2015, http://www.omnivoracious.com/2009/06/there-and-back-again -five-reasons-tolkien-rocks.html.

60. Marx and Engels, *The Communist Manifesto*, 38.

fascinating forms at multiple levels, both within the text and in its explicitly modernist resonance. It is felt much more strongly in the restoration of a patriarchal monarchy where the author's political conservatism is perfectly complemented by his Roman Catholicism. As in the iconic dystopian city of Fritz Lang's tedious modernist allegory *Metropolis*,[61] the text's solution to class conflict lies in the acknowledgment of religion as a "middle way" between capitalist exploitation and proletarian revolution. Or, as so often occurs in popular narratives, the problem is made to appear to lie not with capitalism itself but with those powerful individuals who practice it excessively. Aragorn's rule offers the promise of a benign dictatorship in comparison to Sauron's unquenchable thirst for power, the inherent desirability of his monarchy articulated through his emphatic affinity with nature, on the one hand,[62] and his affiliation by marriage with the aristocratic elf maiden Arwen, on the other.[63] The coronation that ushers in Tolkien's "Fourth Age," in which the thinning process fully transforms Middle-earth, thereby symbolically represents the beginning of an era in which previously existing boundaries are dissolved and the deterritorialization of Middle-earth truly begins. The defeat of Sauron and Saruman has not halted the inevitable onset of modernization per se, but it has slowed down the accelerated deterritorialization associated with capitalism's most powerful globalizing tendencies and—even more crucially—the troubling specter of revolution.

From this point of view, the long series of endings that follows after the Ring's destruction brings the storyworld's most startling contradictions into vivid relief, as the Scouring of the Shire and Frodo's departure from the Grey Havens represent the sometimes desperate-seeming maneuvers of an author struggling to contain the political consequences of his work's anticapitalist implications. First, the hobbits' return to the Shire expresses the reactionary position that the form of monopoly capitalism resulting from Saruman's dictatorship somehow leads to some form of communism, as Lotho Baggins and other henchmen impose a form of rule based on the pretense of "fair distribution."[64] Quickly displacing the storyworld's powerful critique of capitalism onto a stereotypically dystopian representation of communism, "the real fault of imperialist capitalism is diagnosed as residing not so much in its own wrongdoing . . . but in the fact that it paves the way of a much more sinister, properly inhuman evil: the revolutionary forms of darkness."[65] This is where we see *LOTR*'s radical potential contradicted by a counterrevolutionary spirit that fears a popular uprising as much as the imposition

---

61. *Metropolis*, directed by Fritz Lang (1927; London: Eureka Video, 2010), Blu-ray.

62. Introduced as the humble ranger "Strider," Aragorn only reluctantly embraces his destined position as monarch.

63. Troublingly, the imagined path to a better future lies in eugenics: Tolkien explicitly cross-breeds Aragorn's "Man of the West" with the elf maiden Arwen to establish a superior bloodline.

64. Tolkien, *The Return of the King*, 292.

65. Landa, "Slaves of the Ring," 131.

of an evil dictatorship. Like someone who can't make up his mind which is worse—capitalism or communism—Tolkien ends up demonizing both with his elegy to a precapitalist world that never was.

The routing of Saruman and his henchmen from the Shire thus sets up yet another contradictory movement in mutually exclusive directions, as an insincere and grossly caricatured form of communism is prevented through the rejection of monopoly capitalism. In the extended epilogue that follows, it is up to Frodo, Bilbo's official heir and the obvious "rentier" figure of petit bourgeois property ownership,[66] to make the ultimate sacrifice and bequeath his possessions along with his place in the social hierarchy to his loyal servant Sam. The trilogy therefore ends on a symbolic moment of class mobility, with Frodo being elevated (along with Bilbo, Gandalf, and the elves) to a truly mythical form of immortality by departing for the unknowable new world of a "far green country" that lies across the sea in the distant West.[67] Having completed his quest in spite of the fact that he was unable to destroy the Ring's power, the narrative's endpoint is nevertheless a Pyrrhic victory, as social relations in Middle-earth have not been substantially transformed. The books' ending therefore by necessity finds itself in a sort of ideological and historical no-man's-land: the magical world of Middle-earth now belongs definitively to the past, while the unavoidable future of industrial modernity has at the same time been indefinitely deferred. No wonder, then, that this phase in the storyworld's history no longer holds any interest for the books' protagonists: Sam's final words "Well, I'm back" impart a fantastic storyworld's resigned acceptance of a new bourgeois norm of domesticity.[68]

Unsurprisingly, Tolkien's Fourth Age of intensified thinning has generally proved to be of fairly minor interest to fan communities devoted to Middle-earth's storyworld. Videogames, RPGs, film and cartoon adaptations, and fan fiction have focused above all on the much more exciting Third Age, in which the events in *The Hobbit* and *LOTR* take place, and—though to a somewhat lesser degree—on the First and Second Ages, which are sketchily described in publications such as *The Silmarillion*,[69] *Unfinished Tales*,[70] and several other fragmentary works published posthumously.[71]

In this way, we can recognize clearly in Tolkien's storyworld a contradictory negotiation of the spirit of capitalism: as a popular storyworld produced, distributed, and consumed in the context of a dwindling imperialism and the inevitable-seeming rise of a global capitalist Empire, Middle-earth offered an

---

66. Freedman, *Art and Idea in the Novels of China Miéville*, 20.

67. Tolkien, *The Return of the King*, 310.

68. Tolkien, *The Return of the King*, 311.

69. J. R. R. Tolkien, *The Silmarillion* (Boston: Houghton Mifflin Company, 1977).

70. J. R. R. Tolkien, *Unfinished Tales* (Boston: Houghton Mifflin Company, 1980).

71. While some fan fiction set in the Fourth Age does exist, its relative lack of interest testifies vividly to the storyworld's fundamentally nostalgic, backward-looking tendency.

imaginary space where the contradictory logic of twentieth-century capitalism was transformed into a desirable fantasy—while at the same time locating this fantasy in an irretrievable past. With its thematic energy oscillating nervously between an implicit anticapitalism and a determined social and political conservatism, the resulting dialectical tension has given the storyworld a momentum and affective power that has only increased as our own inability to think outside of capitalism has diminished. And while the 1960s counterculture and "Frodo Lives!" movement recognized a radical spirit in Tolkien's work that reflected their own anticapitalism, the storyworld's adaptation into a commercial transmedia franchise would transform these perceptions of the storyworld itself and of the role of fandom's participatory and interpretive communities.

RETERRITORIALIZING FANDOM:
FAN CULTURE AND IMMATERIAL LABOR

Organized sf and fantasy fandom emerged visibly in the American landscape in the wake of the countercultural movements of the 1960s. The first San Diego Comic-Con, now the most influential fan convention in the Western world, was founded in 1970 in the context of a developing grassroots fan culture. As fan conventions dedicated to comic books and fantastic genres grew and developed throughout the 1970s, fans self-identified as members of a subcultural group that existed outside of the mainstream. The pleasure of congregating at conventions like Comic-Con, WonderCon, FedCon, and many others is all too often described as a celebration of this shared outsider status: fans of imaginary storyworlds engage in cosplay by crafting staggeringly elaborate costumes to resemble their favorite characters and indulge publicly in other forms of "excessive" enthusiasm in ways that are remarkably different from the kind of aggressive tribalism associated with sports fandom. Instead, communities of genre fandom have traditionally been marked by their radically inclusive spirit: an enclave of nerds, geeks, and others who saw themselves as social outcasts excluded from hegemonic mainstream culture.

This makes such fantastic fandom a very specific type of community that goes against at least one basic understanding of the term. As political philosopher Iris Marion Young has argued, communities are typically constructed on the basis of the violent exclusion of otherness.[72] The kind of "natural" balance that is so clearly visible, for instance, in Tolkien's representation of the Shire is commonly perceived as authentic, organic, and pure. But the hobbits' "pure and authentic"

---

72. Iris Marion Young, "The Ideal of Community and the Politics of Difference," in *The Blackwell City Reader*, 2nd ed., edited by Gary Bridge and Sophie Watson (Chichester: Wiley-Blackwell, 2010), 231–32.

community[73] can obviously exist only through exclusionary processes of racism, homophobia, and sexism.[74] The model she proposes as a more productive alternative is what she calls a *politics of difference*: a set of social relations that fully embrace radical diversity, starting with the acknowledgment that the individual subject is itself multiple and uncontainable. Therefore, only by rejecting the Cartesian notion that the subject is singular, rational, and knowable can one arrive at a set of social relations based on solidarity, inclusiveness, and social justice.

Young's ideal strongly resembles Hardt and Negri's definition of the multitude as a fundamentally and irreducibly heterogeneous category that embodies this very politics of difference. The creative and self-organizing world of fan culture does indeed resonate with their description of the multitude's political mobilization: a sense of community that isn't based on a single common trait but on a solidarity that emerges partly through the shared sense of exclusion from a hegemonic mass culture, and partly from the creative energy of participatory culture and collective intelligence.[75] Several arguments along these lines have of course been made by Henry Jenkins many times over, and they have by now even come to dominate in many ways the growing academic field of fan studies.

But, at the same time, the hyperconsumerism and general lack of radical political activity in these groups has become more problematic as fan culture has been increasingly absorbed by the mainstream. The many grassroots forms of organized fandom that emerged in the 1970s as a provocative alternative to mass culture can now no longer be approached with the same naïveté.[76] Visiting a fan convention or watching a documentary such as *Comic-Con Episode IV: A Fan's Hope*,[77] one is struck by the overwhelming reproduction of an intense market logic, with fans desperately attempting to achieve the kind of fame and fortune

---

73. Tolkien's ambivalence toward hobbits is evident in the way he combines a pastoral fantasy of "unspoiled" rural Britain with his patronizing and often hostile sensibility toward the "simple life" he both romanticizes and ridicules. This precisely mirrors Raymond Williams's dialectical treatment of the relationship between the country and the city, in which "the distinction between built environments of cities and the humanly modified environments of rural and even remote regions appears arbitrary except as a particular manifestation of a rather long-standing ideological distinction between the country and the city." Raymond Williams, *The Country and the City* (Nottingham: Spokesman Books, 2011 [1973]), 119.

74. A minor controversy during the preproduction of *The Hobbit* illustrated this very precisely, as the "open" casting call specified "light skin tones." See Mary Elizabeth Williams, "'Hobbit' Controversy: When Is Casting Racism?" *Salon*, November 30, 2010, accessed January 13, 2016, http://www.salon.com/2010/11/30/racism_the_hobbit.

75. Henry Jenkins, "Interactive Audiences? The 'Collective Intelligence' of Media Fans," in *Fans, Bloggers, and Gamers*, 134–51.

76. Even Henry Jenkins, self-proclaimed "aca-fan" and godfather of fan studies, concedes as much in his recent work, as he retreats somewhat from his earlier hopes for politically transformative fandom. See Henry Jenkins, Mizuko Ito, and danah boyd, *Participatory Culture in a Networked Era: A Conversation on Youth, Learning, Commerce, and Politics* (Cambridge: Polity Books, 2015), 1–2.

77. *Comic-Con Episode IV: A Fan's Hope*, directed by Morgan Spurlock (2011; Antwerp: Remain in Light, 2013), Blu-ray.

associated with celebrity culture, competing fiercely in one of the many cosplay shows, or else embracing consumerism to the fullest by paying extortionate fees for celebrity photos and autographs, and by the never-ending quest to seek out the most valuable collectables and "limited collector's editions."

This transformation of the fan from marginalized outsider to collaborative hyperconsumer is illustrated vividly by the production and reception of Peter Jackson's first series of Tolkien adaptations. Before the *LOTR* film trilogy's production, fans had mainly been perceived by Hollywood film studios as irritants: niche groups of excessively invested consumers whose limited numbers rendered their voices insignificant in terms of desired audiences. The 1989 blockbuster *Batman*[78] is a clear example of this kind of perception, as director Tim Burton and film studio Warner Brothers explicitly tailored their film for the largest possible audience, while the character's most devoted fans were "fated to watch helplessly as 'their' treasured possession [was] given over to the whims of the majority."[79]

But less than a decade later, when Jackson's film trilogy went into production, the fan's status in the media industry was about to change. The clearest illustration of this transformation is the fan-driven website The One Ring.[80] The site was established in 1998 with the explicit goal of reporting on the films' production. Individual *LOTR* fans from New Zealand, known online by their Tolkienian aliases, sought to develop a network of spies that could report exclusive news related to Jackson's massive production. Webmaster "Tehanu" first attempted to infiltrate the closed set where the town of Hobbiton was being constructed and was unsurprisingly escorted off the site by security guards as soon as her presence was noticed. But shortly thereafter, she received an invitation to return to the set the next day, where she was given a guided tour by Peter Jackson himself.[81] "Tehanu" was told that she was free to take photographs and post them on her website, and, before long, The One Ring had become one of the key resources for publicity and breaking news surrounding the highly anticipated film trilogy.

The unusual alliance that was forged between the production company and the fan community The One Ring testifies to the shifting relationship between fan culture and media industries in the early twenty-first century. In this process, fans were addressed not only as the ideal consumers of a commercial fantastic franchise but also as valuable contributors to the process. The Tolkien enthusiasts who ran this website were quickly reframed by the production company not as hostile spies but as brand ambassadors, thus legitimizing both their affective investment in the text and the sociocultural practices they had developed. Jackson's

---

78. *Batman*, directed by Tim Burton (1989; Burbank, CA: Warner Home Video, 2011), Blu-ray.

79. Will Brooker, *Batman Unmasked: Analyzing a Cultural Icon* (New York: Continuum, 2000), 280.

80. See http://www.theonering.net.

81. Kirsten Pullen, "*The Lord of the Rings* Online Blockbuster Fandom: Pleasure and Commerce," in *The Lord of the Rings: Popular Culture in Context*, ed. Ernest Mathijs (London: Wallflower, 2006), 182.

collaborative approach thus explicitly established fans as both participants and crucial "influencers" and legitimizers: getting the most vocal Tolkien fans to support the film adaptations became the first important step toward bringing in a larger audience while positioning the *LOTR* films as "cult blockbusters" that cannily bridge the divide between "authentic" cult property and "artificial" mainstream.[82] As a result, a set of "fannish" practices that once constituted an alternative to a corporate-driven mass culture was all too easily absorbed by the system it had previously resisted. This process illustrates how sub- and counter-cultural activities that emerged and developed outside of the mainstream can be reterritorialized by the media industries as valuable forms of immaterial labor.

In the context of Empire, immaterial labor has become the hegemonic form of work, where it has been able to intertwine the production of subjectivity with the production of things.[83] Unlike the physical products that result from indus-trial processes, immaterial labor involves "the less-tangible symbolic and social dimensions of commodities."[84] In this sense, fandom's labor in creating valuable "buzz" around a transmedia franchise like *LOTR* typifies capital's new reliance on participatory audiences in the age of media convergence. Like the fans who became instrumental in promoting and legitimizing Jackson's film project from its early stages to the later prequel trilogy, these influencers have only increased in relevance as media industries have come to rely more and more on networked cultures and "spreadable media."[85]

But this form of collaboration is ultimately much less participatory than the fan cultures from which these practices were derived. The grossly asymmetrical relationship between media producers and fans results in a continuous negotiation of questions of ownership as media corporations seek to maintain control over what they consider their intellectual property.[86] When storyworlds like Tolkien's become highly profitable global entertainment brands, they no longer make up a form of cultural commons that can be appropriated, embellished, transformed, or subverted by anyone freely. Instead, they become lucrative corporate franchises made up of a wide range of commodities, most of which are dependent upon fans' affective and immaterial labor to achieve their desired commercial value: "What gives these commodities value beyond their initial sales price is what fans add to them—the new uses to which fans put old things and the emotional landscapes

---

82. Matt Hills, "Realising the Cult Blockbuster: *The Lord of the Rings* Fandom and Residual/Emergent Cult Status in 'the Mainstream,'" in *The Lord of the Rings: Popular Culture in Context*, ed. Ernest Mathijs (London: Wallflower, 2006), 169.

83. Hardt and Negri, *Empire*, 29.

84. Nick Dyer-Witheford and Greig de Peuter, *Games of Empire: Global Capitalism and Video Games* (Minneapolis: Minnesota University Press, 2009), 4.

85. Henry Jenkins, Sam Ford, and Joshua Green, *Spreadable Media: Creating Value and Meaning in a Networked Culture* (New York: New York University Press, 2013).

86. Derek Johnson, *Media Franchising: Creative License and Collaboration in the Culture Industries* (New York: New York University Press, 2013), 25.

that fans construct around them."[87] The irony is that as the successful incorporation of fandom's affective energy changes its direction from "transformative" to
"affirmational,"[88] the radical spirit that informs these storyworlds simultaneously
seems to diminish or even evaporate.

The emotional landscapes constructed around storyworlds like Tolkien's are
more than merely the result of fans' immaterial labor: these practices have also
been absorbed and rearticulated by corporate forces that constantly seek out new
ways to monetize the cultural logic and affective spirit of fan culture. A new generation of self-proclaimed "geek directors" such as Peter Jackson, Joss Whedon,
J. J. Abrams, Brad Bird, Guillermo del Toro, and James Gunn has rapidly become
a defining force in twenty-first-century Hollywood. Much of their appeal seems
to derive not only from their repeated self-identification as members of the fan
community but also from their successful incorporation of fan discourse both in
their films and in the voluminous materials that accompany them: trailers, interviews, posters, making-of documentaries, toys, and promotional features all function as what Gérard Genette has described as "paratexts."[89] It is worth quoting
Jonathan Gray at length on the importance of such paratexts as a way of framing
a text or franchise in relation to fandom:

> Paratexts are the greeters, gatekeepers, and cheerleaders for and of the media, filters
> through which we must pass on our to "the text itself," but some will only greet
> certain audiences. Many fan-made paratexts, in particular, address only those within
> the fandom. Other paratexts will scare away potential audiences, as the semblance of
> being a "fan text" is often enough to detract some. In such cases, though, the para-
> texts create the text for the fleeing would-be audience, suggesting a "geek factor" or
> an undesired depth that may turn them away. In other instances, paratexts will insist
> that a text is more mainstream, less niche or fannish.[90]

The home video release strategy following the first *LOTR* film offers a vivid illustration of this phenomenon and the way in which the categories "mainstream"
and "cult" are becoming more difficult to separate.

After the blockbuster success of *The Fellowship of the Ring*, New Line an-
nounced that there would be two separate DVD releases of the film for home
video consumers: first the theatrical version of the film, accompanied by a few
short "making-of" specials, and then, in the months preceding the next film's

---

87. Abigail De Kosnik, "Fandom as Free Labor," in *Digital Labor: The Internet as Playground and Factory*, ed. Trebor Scholz (London and New York: Routledge, 2013), 104.

88. Suzanne Scott, "*Battlestar Galactica*: Fans and Ancillary Content," in *How to Watch Television*, ed. Ethan Thompson and Jason Mittell (New York: New York University Press, 2013), 321.

89. Gérard Genette, *Paratexts: The Thresholds of Interpretation*, trans. Jane E. Lewin (Cambridge: Cambridge University Press, 1997), 1–5.

90. Jonathan Gray, *Show Sold Separately: Promos, Spoilers, and Other Media Paratexts* (New York: New York University Press, 2010), 17.

theatrical release, a four-disc extended edition that added in nearly thirty minutes of additional scenes, together with many hours of elaborate behind-the-scenes documentaries, image galleries, audio commentaries, and other extras. While the movie-only DVD was geared toward the widest possible audience, the more elaborate and much pricier box set was obviously intended for more fannish consumers. The elaborate packaging, the exhaustive background material, the availability of limited-edition collectors' editions, and the inclusion of extra footage were designed to appeal to viewers eager to invest in the films beyond simply (re-)experiencing them at home. But the franchise's skyrocketing popularity helped make a much larger audience receptive to the box set's discursive fandom: DVD sales of the extended editions ended up far exceeding expectations, setting a new benchmark for home video releases and winning many awards for their extra features.[91]

The production company's impactful approach to the films' DVD release strategy thereby provided a new model for "turning fan-friendly publicity material into a revenue-producing stream."[92] This was the result of the producers' skillful negotiation of fan culture throughout the process of marketing, production, and distribution, but perhaps above all because of Jackson's hugely successful appeal to a recognizable fan sensibility. In the many hours of audio commentary and behind-the-scenes material, he positions himself first as a fan of the books struggling valiantly to adapt the source material for another medium. He speaks candidly of his lifelong passion for the material in the register of fandom, reminiscing about the first paperback edition he used to own, and emphasizing many times that his main reason for making the films was his own fannish desire to see Tolkien's storyworld faithfully adapted to the screen.[93] In the narrative that is constructed in these carefully crafted collages of interview footage and behind-the-scenes materials, all the major cast and crew members become characters in their own right, engaged in a portal-quest that finds legitimacy and emotional resonance through its celebration of fandom.

Throughout the other paratextual material contained on those discs, members of cast and crew are consistently presented as a community of friends and creative collaborators driven by their love for the project, while continuously emphasizing the strong personal bonds that were forged between them. Their combined testimonies in interview form establish a parallel narrative to that of the *LOTR* storyworld, with Jackson playing what can only be described as "the Hobbit role": that of the diminutive and unlikely hero who emerges—reluctantly but reliably—from a peripheral agrarian region to fulfill an impossibly ambitious

91. Kristin Thompson, *The Frodo Franchise: The Lord of the Rings and Modern Hollywood* (Berkeley and Los Angeles: University of California Press, 2007), 216.

92. Thompson, *The Frodo Franchise*, 163.

93. "From Book to Vision," disc 3, *The Lord of the Rings: The Fellowship of the Rings*, extended edition, Blu-ray, directed by Peter Jackson (London: Entertainment in Video, 2011).

task.[94] The cast and crew members that surround him make up a supportive and dedicated Fellowship whose efforts resonate at an emotional level, fostering "an intimate bond between cast, crew, and audience, one that combines with their construction of the film as a Work of Art, and with their construction of the DVD audience as discerning and requiring art aficionados."[95]

The extra material on the DVD box sets thereby performed the crucial work of not only framing the films as something more than global Hollywood blockbusters but also constructing the audience as knowledgeable and respected participants in the process. The galleries and documentaries "teach a significant amount of production literacy,"[96] moving far beyond the usual promotional videos to create a bond of intimacy and involvement with the films' global audience. The producers even came up with a way to include the fans in a more literal sense by adding to the extended edition's end credits a listing of all *LOTR* fan club members. This symbolic acknowledgment of fans' involvement with the franchise speaks volumes about the successful cooptation of fans' affective investment and immaterial labor. The inclusion of many thousands of all-but-illegible names as an addition to the end credits guaranteed thousands of sales, while also sending out an important signal: fans are not simply the invisible and passive consumers but also the appreciated and explicitly acknowledged collaborators on this hugely profitable media enterprise.

This dynamic was heightened even further by the time the film trilogy based on *The Hobbit* went into production in 2011. For this project, The One Ring was established from the very start as the primary platform for the films' promotion. Jackson used the site to broadcast weekly video reports from the set, explaining the novel technology that was being used for the films, giving guided tours of the reconstruction of familiar sets, and inviting viewers to engage with the project as intimate participants rather than anonymous consumers. And it is precisely this Althusserian interpellation of audiences as fans and participants that typifies the cultural logic of Empire.[97] The rise of media convergence and participatory culture effectively deterritorializes the striated landscape of mass media, transforming the traditional distinction between "mainstream" and "cult" by making fans the valuable legitimizers and ambassadors of the most valuable transmedia franchises.

Therefore, just as Tolkien's storyworld seemed to anticipate the dissolution of industrial capitalism's imperialist order, the appropriation of fan culture in the

---

94. Peter Jackson's "humble" New Zealand origins uncannily reflect Bilbo and Frodo's remote geographical placement in the Shire, as far away from the high society of Minas Tirith as Wellington is from Hollywood.

95. Gray, *Show Sold Separately*, 103.

96. Gray, *Show Sold Separately*, 98.

97. Louis Althusser, *On the Reproduction of Capitalism: Ideology and Ideological State Apparatuses*, trans. G. M. Goshgarian (London and New York: Verso, 2014), 261–70.

films' promotion and distribution shows how easily capitalist hegemony incorporates and subsumes countercultural practices. In the process, fans' voluntary and immaterial labor is transformed from a set of social relations that operates on the fringes of capitalist culture to an essential component of Empire's biopolitical power. Just as the difference between the cultural mainstream and countercultural elements has been irrevocably altered, twenty-first-century geek culture reterritorializes audiences' affective relationship with imaginary storyworlds, finding in them new forms of value that suit the context of cognitive capitalism.

TRANSITIONING INTO EMPIRE: THE *STAR TREK* FRANCHISE

Just as Tolkien's storyworld became the defining text for the late twentieth-century fantasy genre, *Star Trek* has established itself as one of the main sf paradigms. There is a long and fascinating history of sf fandom that predates the 1966 appearance of the beloved "original series" (*TOS*), which ran for three seasons before its cancellation due to high production costs and middling ratings.[98] But it isn't much of an exaggeration to state that sf and fantasy fandom as it exists today emerged out of the joint popularity of Tolkien and *Star Trek* from the early 1970s onward.[99] Not only was *Star Trek* fandom a foundational force in the establishment of fantastic world-building as a cultural practice, but it has also been the most frequently cited example of fandom's creative, collaborative, and political potential.

Like Tolkien, *Star Trek*'s storyworld is structured by a teleological view of history in which human development is fundamentally interlinked with modernization and technological advancement. The storyworld's organization is derived first from what Luc Boltanski and Eve Chiapello have described as the spirit of industrial capitalism, in which a sense of security and stability was supplied by "a faith in rationality and long-term planning . . . and, above all, by the very gigantism of organizations."[100] But where *LOTR* mobilizes a precapitalist fantasy of static pseudo-medievalism, *Star Trek* presents a postcapitalist technological utopia. And in the same way that Tolkien created a Golden Age of myth and magic by displacing feudalism's internal contradictions onto an external "other," *Star Trek* similarly mobilizes a human future in which the dialectical nature of

---

98. Roberta Pearson and Máire Messenger Davies, *Star Trek and American Television* (Berkeley and Los Angeles: University of California Press, 2014), 41.

99. An important contributing factor in both cases was a linguistic aspect, with *Star Trek* fans developing a Klingon language in the same way that Tolkien fans could attempt to master Elvish. See Karolina Agata Kazimierczak, "'Linguistic Fandom': Performing Liminal Identities in the Spaces of Transgression," *Liminalities: A Journal of Performance Studies* 6, no. 2 (2010).

100. Luc Boltanski and Eve Chiapello, *The New Spirit of Capitalism*, trans. Gregory Elliott (London and New York: Verso, 2005), 18.

human history is displaced onto an endless series of encounters with a wide range of alien species. Both therefore transform the irresolvable contradictions of capitalism into a fantasy in which these tensions can be pleasurably negotiated.

Just as Tolkien's storyworld was easily adopted by countercultural movements in the 1960s, *Star Trek* has been similarly celebrated for its progressive values. The Federation starship *Enterprise*, with its multiethnic crew, represented for many a meaningful ideal of human progress, or what Raymond Williams famously described as utopian sf's "civilizing transformation, beyond the terms of a restless, struggling society of classes."[101] Drawing on the genre's long tradition of teleological liberalism (from Jules Verne to Isaac Asimov), on the one hand, and the 1960s countercultural energies, on the other, the franchise became for many a touchstone of both the sf genre's penchant for liberal-humanist idealism—in Williams's terms, a "willed transformation" of human society—and its dedication to speculative science and technology (or what Williams calls sf's "technological transformation").[102]

It also became the most elaborate and complex transmedia world-building franchise in all of fantastic fiction. The list of official (or "canonical") live-action *Star Trek* primary texts for television and film is in itself overwhelming: three seasons of the original series (1966–1969, 79 episodes); seven seasons each of *Star Trek: The Next Generation* (1987–1994, 178 episodes), *Star Trek: Deep Space Nine* (1993–1999, 176 episodes), and *Star Trek: Voyager* (1995–2001, 172 episodes); four seasons of *Star Trek: Enterprise* (2001–2005, 98 episodes); and twelve feature films (1979–2013).[103] In addition to this already voluminous output, the official franchise has included an animated series (1973–1974, twenty-two episodes), dozens of videogames, and many hundreds of novels, while at the same time inspiring legions of fans to produce truly unfathomable amounts of

---

101. Raymond Williams, *Culture and Materialism* (London and New York: Verso, 2005 [1980]), 201.

102. Williams, *Culture and Materialism*, 199.

103. *Star Trek: The Motion Picture*, directed by Robert Wise (1979; Hollywood: Paramount Home Entertainment, 2010), Blu-ray; *Star Trek: The Wrath of Khan*, directed by Nicholas Meyer (1982; Hollywood: Paramount Home Entertainment, 2010), Blu-ray; *Star Trek III: The Search for Spock*, directed by Leonard Nimoy (1984; Hollywood: Paramount Home Entertainment, 2010), Blu-ray; *Star Trek IV: The Voyage Home*, directed by Leonard Nimoy (1986; Hollywood: Paramount Home Entertainment, 2010), Blu-ray; *Star Trek V: The Final Frontier*, directed by William Shatner (1989; Hollywood: Paramount Home Entertainment, 2010), Blu-ray; *Star Trek VI: The Undiscovered Country*, directed by Nicholas Meyer (1991; Hollywood: Paramount Home Entertainment, 2010), Blu-ray; *Star Trek: Generations*, directed by David Carson (1994; Hollywood: Paramount Home Entertainment, 2010), Blu-ray; *Star Trek: First Contact*, directed by Jonathan Frakes (1996; Hollywood: Paramount Home Entertainment, 2010), Blu-ray; *Star Trek: Insurrection*, directed by Jonathan Frakes (1998; Hollywood: Paramount Home Entertainment, 2010), Blu-ray; *Star Trek: Nemesis*, directed by Stuart Baird (2002; Hollywood: Paramount Home Entertainment, 2010), Blu-ray; *Star Trek*, directed by J. J. Abrams (2009; Hollywood: Paramount Home Entertainment, 2009), Blu-ray; *Star Trek into Darkness*, directed by J. J. Abrams (2013; Hollywood: Paramount Home Entertainment, 2013), Blu-ray. At the time of writing, a thirteenth film, titled *Star Trek Beyond*, is scheduled for release in August 2016.

fan fiction, fan art, costumes, role-playing games, mashups, crossovers, and other creative appropriations. *Star Trek* is therefore one of those unusually expansive imaginary worlds that has become so vast that it is truly unlikely that even the most devoted fan can have experienced the resulting storyworld in its entirety.[104]

Since this expansive imaginary empire has undergone so many changes over its fifty-year history, it makes little sense to try to define *Star Trek*'s ideological values or its politics in precise terms on the basis of textual analysis. Not only are there obviously substantial differences between series from different historical eras, but there also isn't as much internal coherence or consistency as many have assumed within any single *Star Trek* series. Due to the largely episodic nature of nearly all of American television drama in the years that these seasons were broadcast, the abundant variations, alternate timelines, and "retcons"[105] make it difficult to generalize about the storyworld's politics based on the textual analysis of a single episode, or even an entire season of any *Star Trek* TV series. As Roberta Pearson has cautioned, meaningful analysis cannot be achieved by picking any one episode that happens to suit one's ideological paradigm, thereby using highly selective readings to illustrate a preconceived notion of the text's political organization.[106]

As with my earlier discussion of Tolkien, I develop in this chapter's second section a dialectical reading that takes as its point of departure the notion that the storyworld doesn't exist independent of the contradictory set of social relations from which it emerged. Rather than trying to "make sense" of the *Star Trek* storyworld in its entirety, I focus instead on some of its many internal contradictions and how they illustrate larger tensions specific to capitalism's transition from imperialism to Empire. In order to foreground how the development of *Star Trek*'s storyworld can be read as a way to make sense of the cultural and material emergence of global capitalism, my focus in this chapter lies primarily on *Star Trek: The Next Generation* (*TNG*). This series was produced between 1987 and 1994, the years in which the Cold War ended and the world order made its final transition into truly global capitalism. I will argue here that both *LOTR* and *Star Trek* are constructed upon a similar tension between capitalism's residual imperialism and its emergent imperial order. Drawing first on the contradictory narrative and formal logic that has informed the storyworld's decades-long construction, and second on examples from *TNG* episodes that foreground these contradictions, I will show how the storyworld's internal tension results in a productive political ambivalence: while superficially moving beyond capitalism, *Star Trek*'s storyworld simultaneously

---

104. Wolf, *Building Imaginary Worlds*, 134–35.

105. *Retcon* stands for "retroactive continuity," or changes to earlier story events that are made retroactively in order to make them fit in with the storyworld as it has later developed.

106. Roberta E. Pearson, "*Star Trek*: Serialized Ideology," in *How to Watch Television*, ed. Ethan Thompson and Jason Mittell (New York: New York University Press, 2013), 214.

combines a fundamentally imperialist structure with Empire's emerging practices of immaterial labor and imperial administration.

"TO BOLDLY GO":
STAR TREK'S AMBIVALENT IMPERIALISM

The one concept that defines *Star Trek* in all its incarnations is the fantasy of
a peaceful and benevolent imperialism. The iconic closing words from *TOS*'s
opening-credits voiceover have survived intact over the years: "to seek out new
life and new civilizations; to boldly go where no man has gone before." The
world's most famous split infinitive was used not only in *TOS* and its cinematic
spin-offs but also in the opening of every *TNG* episode, and it was more recently
featured to great effect at the very end of the 2009 cinematic reboot.[107] On the
documentary that accompanied the release of *TNG*'s first season on Blu-ray,
screenwriter Morgan Gendel quotes the phrase while explicitly dissociating the
Star Trek storyworld from capitalism:

> You can't call *Star Trek* capitalist. You can call the business model of *Star Trek* cap-
> italist, but you can't call the show itself capitalist. And yet, I think it's very American
> in that it embodies the hope in the individuality of every person: every person can
> contribute to this thing in good spirit and work together and make a difference. It's
> almost like the pioneer spirit of America, which I think Gene Roddenberry originally
> meant as "*Wagon Train* in Space." So I think it's got a lot of that pioneer spirit, very
> American. "To boldly go."[108]

But the imperialist spirit so essential to *Star Trek*'s storyworld is of course impossible to separate from the history of capitalism. And no matter how many other
aspects of the storyworld have been adapted over the course of half a century, the
franchise's specific structure of feeling remains firmly anchored in this colonialist imperative and the "racist Imaginary" it articulates.[109]

   In its first incarnation, the series' narrative formula clearly reflected its 1960s
context of the Cold War and America's "Golden Age of Capitalism."[110] *TOS*
offered an obvious narrative expression of the United States' rapidly growing
military and economic power after World War II, and its futurist fantasy of
intergalactic exploration provocatively articulated an imaginary "end point of

---

107. The only alteration to the phrase occurred when *TNG* first appeared in 1987, in which the words
no man were replaced by the gender-neutral *no one*.

108. *Beyond the Five Year Mission—The Evolution of Star Trek: The Next Generation*, directed by
Roger Lay Jr. (2014; Hollywood: Paramount Home Entertainment, 2014), Blu-ray.

109. David Golumbia, "Black and White World: Race, Ideology, and Utopia in *Triton* and *Star
Trek*," *Cultural Critique* 32 (1995): 91.

110. Harman, *Zombie Capitalism*, 161–90.

American-dominated globalization."[111] Pitched to the networks as an episodic frontier adventure series set in outer space, *TOS* offered an archetypically American type of imperialism grounded in discourses of peace and collaboration rather than military conquest. Some aspects of this first series therefore already seem to anticipate the later development of global capitalism, especially as it relates to Hardt and Negri's emphasis on the United States' governing role as a benevolent peacekeeping force: precisely like Empire, *Star Trek*'s United Federation of Planets "is formed not on the basis of force itself but on the basis of the capacity to present force as being in the service of right and peace."[112]

In the same way that the naval colonialist fiction of the Victorian era aided in the cultural legitimization of imperialism,[113] the Federation's considerable military power is supposedly only meant to defend, not to conquer.[114] Intergalactic empires in *TOS* compete for allies and resources in ways that mirror the precarious postwar balance of power between the United States and the Soviet Union, with the Klingons standing in for the Russians' competing empire. Compared to the later *Star Trek* series, *TOS* is also more explicitly militaristic—especially during its first year. In the episode "Errand of Mercy,"[115] for instance, Captain Kirk famously proclaims, "I'm a soldier, not a diplomat," while the near-constant combat situations the crew finds itself in do indeed tend to come across as "an inadvertent endorsement of militarism."[116] The flagship's attention-grabbing multiethnic crew therefore symbolizes nothing so much as American capitalism's ability to absorb and contain all forms of difference and opposition.

While *TOS* resonates strongly (if perhaps inevitably) with the dominant organization of capitalism of its own historical era, it also established several crucial narrative coordinates that would reflect capitalism's later development. The franchise's "prophetic" futurism gave dramatic form to a dynamic of intensified globalization that would speed up rapidly in the years following the series' first appearance. The show's postcapitalist Earth, only glimpsed a few times in *TOS* but developed in more detail later in the franchise, famously represented "an ideal utopian future without war, poverty, or racial conflict."[117] The most crucial point in understanding *Star Trek*'s utopian politics is the franchise's central fantasy of resolving class conflict by the passage from industrial to immaterial labor.

111. Booker, "The Politics of *Star Trek*," 199.

112. Hardt and Negri, *Empire*, 15.

113. Stefan Rabitsch, "Space-Age Hornblowers, or Why Kirk and Co. Are Not Space Cowboys: The Enlightenment Mariners and Transatlanticism of *Star Trek*," *Networking Knowledge* 5, no. 2 (2012).

114. Pearson and Messenger Davies, *Star Trek and American Television*, 23.

115. "Errand of Mercy," *Star Trek*, National Broadcasting Corporation (New York: NBC, March 23, 1967).

116. Booker, "The Politics of *Star Trek*," 200.

117. Pearson and Messenger Davies, *Star Trek and American Television*, 39.

As I have argued earlier in this chapter, *LOTR* effectively maps out a process of deterritorialization as an imperialist world's striated terrain is smoothed over by the implacable forces of rationalism and modernization. In *Star Trek*, this kind of deterritorialization has already taken place on Earth, yielding a utopia so boringly bereft of conflict that writers have only mustered up interest in it with great difficulty. Gene Roddenberry's celebrated vision of a flawless human future effectively eradicates all forms of cultural difference, absorbing the entire planet in its grand ideal of total modernization. Internal conflict is thereby displaced onto an imaginary exterior space that helpfully stands in for the many forms of struggle that result from imperialist practices.

As intergalactic explorers, the starship *Enterprise* crew thus performs imperialism's familiar ideological work by mobilizing the fantasy of peaceful and benevolent forces of reason and civilization. The tension between the Federation's self-proclaimed peacefulness and others' experience of its imperialist and militaristic tendencies is sometimes even addressed explicitly, as in this exchange from the third-season *TOS* episode "Requiem for Methuselah"[118]:

> *Kirk*: You said something about savagery, Mr. Flint. When was the last time you visited Earth?
>
> *Flint*: You would tell me that it is no longer cruel. But it is, captain. Look at your starship, bristling with weapons. Its mission: to colonize, exploit, destroy, if necessary, to advance Federation causes.
>
> *Kirk*: Our missions are peaceful, our weapons defensive. If we were barbarians, we would not have asked for Ryetalyn [a valuable mineral the Federation wishes to extract from the planet Kirk is visiting]. Indeed, your greeting, not ours, lacked a certain benevolence.

While *TOS*'s negotiated militarism corresponds roughly with its era's triumphant military-industrial complex, its storyworld at the same time seems to anticipate the transition toward Empire in the years directly following the Cold War. And even though the political and cultural differences between humans and aliens often operate as allegories for real-world cultural and geopolitical tensions, the show's narrative foundation in its most literal sense predicts neoliberalism's world without alternatives. In *Star Trek*'s storyworld, it is a precondition for entry into the Federation that worlds have reached an equivalent point of political unification and speak not as Spinoza's diverse multitude but as a unified Hobbesian "people."[119] One of the main contradictions of *Star Trek*'s storyworld is therefore

---

118. "Requiem for Methuselah," *Star Trek*, National Broadcasting Corporation (New York: NBC, February 14, 1969).

119. "The *People* is somewhat that is *one*, having *one will*, and to whom one action may be attributed." Thomas Hobbes, quoted in Paolo Virno, *A Grammar of the Multitude* (Los Angeles: Semiotext(e), 2004), 22.

the way its unifying approach to any given culture coexists somewhat uncomfortably with the overwhelming diversity of interplanetary species.

Starfleet's superficial respect for ethnic and cultural diversity then boils down in political terms to an assumed teleological endpoint of history for each society, in which the total globalization of highly diverse humanoid societies is made equivalent with Empire's discourses of technological and social progress. This effectively transforms imperialist capitalism's inherent forms of racism into what Étienne Balibar has described as global capitalism's "differentialist racism," with culture now filling the role formerly played by biology.[120] Empire's neoracism operates through the displacement of the problematic, as we move "from the theory of races or the struggle between the races in human history, whether based on biological or psychological principles, to a theory of 'race relations' within society, *which naturalizes not racial belonging but racist conduct*."[121] In other words, what appears superficially as a postracial and postcapitalist worldview amounts in fact to a transference of racism from ethnicity onto the hierarchical organization of cultural difference.

This is evident in many episodes in all *Star Trek* incarnations, especially those that take place on planets that have not yet reached the point of "warp capability." Such societies are somewhat patronizingly presented as less developed than the Federation, and are therefore subject to Starfleet's crucial Prime Directive: alien societies may not be interfered with in any way until they have independently reached this point of political and technological "maturity." And while the many episodes that deal with this liberalist principle show that the Prime Directive is in practice broken with almost comical frequency, it remains a primary expression of a political position that effectively camouflages *Star Trek*'s lingering colonialism. For the *Enterprise* crew, "less developed" alien societies exist either as a puzzle to be solved[122] or—more commonly—as a "primitive" community to be assisted on the path toward Eurocentric enlightenment.[123] In either case, they are ultimately to be absorbed within the Federation's homogenizing political structure.

As a guiding principle for the franchise, the Prime Directive functions simultaneously as a form of deterritorialization of *Star Trek*'s fantastic storyworld, assuming an unambiguous humanist ideal to which all humanoid forms of

120. Étienne Balibar, "Is There a 'Neo-Racism'?" in *Race, Nation, Class: Ambiguous Identities*, Étienne Balibar and Immanuel Wallerstein (London and New York: Verso, 1991), 17–28.

121. Balibar, "Is There a 'Neo-Racism'?" 22.

122. "Darmok," *Star Trek: The Next Generation*, Paramount Domestic Television (First-run syndication, September 30, 1991).

123. "Thine Own Self," *Star Trek: The Next Generation*, Paramount Domestic Television (First-run syndication, February 14, 1994).

intelligent life therefore ultimately aspire.[124] This is all the more interesting for the way in which life on board the *Enterprise* is rigidly structured by hierarchical roles. Within the *Enterprise*'s regular crew, these roles are not merely superficial titles that happen to identify individuals within a particular system of power. In every incarnation of *Star Trek*, the narratives demonstrate without exception that these ranks are the natural extensions of individual talents and character traits: Jean-Luc Picard, like Kirk before him, was *born* to be a starship captain; William Riker has the talent and ambition to fulfill a position of leadership but proves repeatedly that he is happier and more comfortable with his role as second-in-command; and Deanna Troi is ideally suited, both in temperament and in genetic makeup, to be the ship's counsellor.

The hierarchical system in which the crew functions so effectively is repeatedly presented as the necessary result of an innate sense of human competition, with the main crew members' authority and "natural" division of labor articulating the perfect balance resulting from this market logic in the absence of alienating wage labor. The android Data is often the character whose questions set up the ideological justification for the franchise's investment in these "common-sense" values, as occurs in the following exchange:

Data: Forever curious, this urge to compete.

Pulaski: Oh, it's a human response. That inborn craving to gauge your capabilities through conflict.

Data: Doctor, there are other ways to challenge oneself.

Pulaski: Well, perhaps, but they all lack a certain thrill.

Troi: Data, humans sometimes find it helpful to have an outsider set the standard by which they're judged.

Data: To avoid deceiving oneself.[125]

This exchange shows once again how thoroughly the capitalist concept of generalized competition remains central to *Star Trek*'s supposedly postcapitalist storyworld. In the same way, the episodes that explore characters' occasional desire to abandon their Starfleet careers and explore a life of leisure and actual

---

124. Infrequent exceptions do occur, though, in most cases, encounters with nonhumanoid alien intelligence are coded as "animal" with patronizing mock-reverence, as in, for instance, the *TNG* episode in which the *Enterprise* accidentally kills a "space whale" and then must shepherd its orphaned young elsewhere. "Galaxy's Child," *Star Trek: The Next Generation*, Paramount Domestic Television (First-run syndication, March 11, 1991).

125. "Peak Performance," *Star Trek: The Next Generation*, Paramount Domestic Television (First-run syndication, July 10, 1989).

self-determination demonstrate the franchise's ideological limits: these interludes are invariably revealed to be less satisfactory and therefore less desirable than their current careers.[126] The hierarchical organization of *TNG*'s command structure thus goes beyond the militarism implicit in the uniforms and insignia: it combines global capitalism's emergent spirit of competitive individualism with imperialism's residual emphasis on continuity, careerism, and clear and stable boundaries.

To be sure, the static makeup of these roles is also part and parcel of a media-industrial context in which substantial changes to a basic narrative formula were uncommon; consider the difference between *Star Trek*'s largely stable cast of characters and the far more unpredictable variety within twenty-first-century franchises like *Battlestar Galactica* or *Game of Thrones*. But, as I will argue in the next chapter, these production practices at the same time express important ideological and political values that reflect and validate capitalism's material organization in a given period. For this reason again, the *Star Trek* franchise—and *TNG* in particular—is best understood as a transitional text between the striated framework of industrial capitalism and cognitive capitalism's postindustrial Empire. Like *LOTR*, it demonstrates a fundamental ambivalence about capitalism and its alternatives—both real and imagined. It offers the pleasurable fantasy of a postcapitalist utopia, while at the same time clinging desperately to the rigidly hierarchical operational structures and narrative conceits associated with capitalism's "pioneering" years of colonialism.

This enlightened imperialism is made more palatable by contrasting the Federation's practices with those of more obviously aggressive competing imperialist forces, like the Klingons, the Romulans, the Cardassians, and the Borg. Similarly, the avaricious and profit-obsessed Ferengi embody capitalism's unsavory association with a generalized ethic of greed, accumulation, and uncontrollable sexual desire, deploying uncomfortable anti-Semitic stereotypes to again dissociate the postcapitalist Federation from capitalism's more "uncivilized" aspects. But this explicit contrast with less attractive forms of imperialism and capitalism masks the extent to which *Star Trek* remains grounded in those very frameworks. Both its emphatically hierarchical organization and its dedication to competition as a fundamental human quality counterbalance the storyworld's supposedly postcapitalist environment: as Raymond Williams has repeatedly argued, capitalism is grounded in the meaningful organization of social relations, which *TNG*'s *Enterprise*—as a workplace of hierarchically organized immaterial labor—presents as natural and unchanging. The franchise's willful dissociation from capitalism

---

126. A provocative exception is the fifth-season episode "The Inner Light," *Star Trek: The Next Generation*, Paramount Domestic Television (First-run syndication, June 1, 1992). In this installment, Captain Picard lives out a lifetime outside Starfleet by having the memories of the member of an extinct preindustrial culture implanted in him. Tellingly, the episode's enduring legacy in the show is the development of Picard's musical abilities, in the same way that global capitalism so eagerly sees "primitive" societies as a source of "authentic" cultural value to be appropriated and commodified.

therefore effectively amounts to a fantasy in which undesirable aspects of the capitalist order are conveniently erased, while capitalism's social relations persist in unaltered form.

This structural disavowal is even more pronounced in the occasional episodes in which we witness alternate timelines, such as the episodes that take place in the "Mirror Universe," in which a more belligerent version of the *Enterprise* is introduced and explored. Such narratives have appeared many times throughout the franchise, from *TOS* episodes "The Tholian Web"[127] and "Mirror, Mirror"[128] to *Enterprise*'s two-part "In a Mirror, Darkly,"[129] as well as in numerous *Star Trek* comics, novels, and videogames. In *TNG*, such an alternate timeline is featured in the third-season episode "Yesterday's *Enterprise*,"[130] in which an unexpected encounter with a spaceship from the past transforms Picard's ship into a military vessel engaged in an all-out war with the Klingons. Only one character realizes that something has changed, and she speaks up to the captain as follows:

Guinan: Families. There should be children on this ship.

Picard: What? Children on the *Enterprise*? Guinan, we're at war!

Guinan: No we're not! At least we're not . . . supposed to be. This is not a ship of war. This is a ship of peace.

While one might say that the Mirror Universe's overt militarism gives us glimpses of a deeper truth behind *Star Trek*'s pacifist façade, Guinan's inexplicable intuition perfectly expresses Empire's ideological work of legitimization. When the status quo is restored and history's linear progression secured, Guinan's reassuring smile confirms that all is well again, and that an "ideal" balance has been restored.

This privileging of one ideological perspective over all others is also communicated and strengthened at the visual level. There is a striking visual contrast between the *Enterprise* as it is usually seen and the alternate timeline's more ostentatiously militarized version. The starship's bridge and corridors are shrouded in shadow, the low-key lighting dominated by red and yellow hues rather than the customary spectrum of brightly lit and "neutral" greens, grays, and pale blues. Contrary to Kirk's earlier claim from *TOS*, the *Enterprise*'s sudden

127. "The Tholian Web," *Star Trek*, National Broadcasting Corporation (New York: NBC, November 15 ,1968).

128. "Mirror, Mirror," *Star Trek*, National Broadcasting Corporation (New York: NBC, October 6, 1967).

129. "In a Mirror Darkly, Part I," *Star Trek: Enterprise*, Paramount Network Television (New York: UPN, April 22, 2005); "In a Mirror Darkly, Part II," *Star Trek: Enterprise*, Paramount Network Television (New York: UPN, April 29, 2005).

130. "Yesterday's *Enterprise*," *Star Trek: The Next Generation*, Paramount Domestic Television (First-run syndication, February 19, 1990).

transformation from exploratory vessel to military warship is here explicitly coded as undesirable, both in the episode's visuals and in the resolution of its plot. Offering a dystopian imaginary instead of the franchise's usual utopianism, the episode's alternate timeline strengthens the sense of inevitability and lack of viable alternatives to its posthistorical present. The difference allows for a displacement of the *Enterprise*'s military function in the same way that Empire creates the illusion that it operates not as an aggressive force but merely "to pacify, mobilize, and control the separated and segmented social forces."[131] In both cases, public support is derived from the ideological justification that Empire's continuous warfare is not the result of a belligerent militarism, but that it successfully maintains the appearance of a Starfleet-like benevolent peacekeeping force in the defense of values it presents as universal.

Therefore, just as *Star Trek*'s liberal political leanings have disguised the storyworld's stubbornly capitalist underpinnings, Empire has also been able to camouflage the degree to which its power is both military and ideological. In the same way that the endless encounters with alien civilizations are designed to demonstrate above all the *Enterprise* crew's openness, tolerance, and matter-of-fact superiority, global capitalism will abide no actual alternative: the *Star Trek* storyworld therefore very precisely illustrates an imaginary empire that is only postcapitalist in the way that Empire is supposedly posthistorical. This may be a seductive and pleasurable illusion, but it is also one that reveals the contradiction between the storyworld's nominal postcapitalism and its inability to move beyond a set of social relations that are purely capitalist.

REPLICATORS, COMMUNICATORS, AND HOLODECKS: IMMATERIAL AND AFFECTIVE LABOR

Immaterial labor is as crucial to *Star Trek*'s storyworld as it is to global capitalism. Earlier in this chapter, we saw it at play in fans' contributions to the publicity surrounding the Tolkien film adaptations, where organized fandom became an invaluable collaborator in the publicity and cultural legitimization surrounding the burgeoning transmedia franchise. Hardt and Negri place particular emphasis on what they call the "affective face" of immaterial labor, constantly producing and reproducing "social networks, forms of community, biopower."[132] These new forms of biopower that inform what they call the postmodernization of the global economy are crucially driven by the "production and manipulation of affect,"[133] a task that is as much sociocultural as it is economic and political. But

---

131. Hardt and Negri, *Empire*, 339.

132. Hardt and Negri, *Empire*, 293.

133. Hardt and Negri, *Empire*, 293.

what distinguishes this global stage of capitalism from the previous one is its de-centered, inherently collaborative nature: "The cooperative aspect of immaterial labor is not imposed or organized from the outside, as it was in previous forms of labor, but rather, *cooperation is completely immanent to the laboring activity itself.*"[134] This is precisely where Hardt and Negri locate the network society's potential for "a kind of spontaneous and elementary communism"[135]: because the creation of value in the networked economies of global capitalism is the result of immaterial cooperative activity, the multitude becomes less dependent upon capital to "valorize itself" in classically Marxian terms.

But within this new environment of cognitive capitalism, the inherently democratic potential of immaterial labor is also countered by an "oligopolistic mechanism" that constantly attempts to construct new centralized forms of power within this rhizomatic network.[136] This process is evident, for instance, in the ongoing privatization of digital communication platforms, as corporations like Facebook, Google, Apple, and Microsoft organize the flow of information in order to limit the multitude's abilities for self-organization and profit from their immaterial labor. Their privatization of shared digital platforms enhances rather than decreases existing lines of global inequality and exclusion, as "the imma-nent relation between the public and the common is replaced by the transcendent power of private property."[137] The radical, even utopian, democratic potential so often ascribed to networked digital platforms is thereby usurped by an ideology "that values hierarchy, competition, and a winner-takes-all mind-set."[138] The same logic applies to the global conglomerates that now dominate the media industry, where businesses have learned to incorporate the once-subversive practices of fan cultures and the "bastard culture" of user participation.[139] This fluctuating tension between fans' affective investment and the hierarchical structure of capitalism is evident both within the *Star Trek* storyworld and outside it.

A helpful example of the limitations of the franchise's self-proclaimed "culture of freedom and self-determination"[140] may be found in the *TNG* episode "Hollow Pursuits."[141] This episode introduces engineer Reginald Barclay, a guest on the show who would become a recurring character in the *Star Trek* storyworld. The

---

134. Hardt and Negri, *Empire*, 294.

135. Hardt and Negri, *Empire*, 294.

136. Hardt and Negri, *Empire*, 298–99.

137. Hardt and Negri, *Empire*, 301.

138. José van Dijck, *The Culture of Connectivity: A Critical History of Social Media* (Oxford: Oxford University Press, 2013), 21.

139. Mirko Tobias Schäfer, *Bastard Culture! How User Participation Transforms Cultural Production* (Amsterdam: Amsterdam University Press, 2011), 77–123.

140. "The Best of Both Worlds," *Star Trek: The Next Generation*, Paramount Domestic Television (First-run syndication, June 18, 1990).

141. "Hollow Pursuits," *Star Trek: The Next Generation*, Paramount Domestic Television (First-run syndication, April 30, 1990).

episode's plot concerns Barclay's inability to function as an effective worker on the engineering team because of his addiction to the imaginary scenarios he plays out on the ship's immersive Holodeck. The normally affable and ingratiating chief engineer Geordi La Forge chastises Barclay repeatedly for arriving late for work and underperforming in his assigned tasks. An exasperated La Forge even asks Captain Picard for permission to transfer the shy and withdrawn Barclay off the ship. But the captain denies the request, suggesting instead that the chief engineer make Barclay his "pet project" and try to transform him into a more effective worker.

Aside from the striking panic the episode expresses toward the suggested effects of media addiction (particularly regarding videogames), the episode is unusual within the series for showing a direct conflict between an individual crew member and his work environment. Throughout the seven seasons of *TNG*, there has been no shortage of episodes that foreground anxieties about the main characters' ability to carry out their work efficiently and effectively. But in nearly all cases, this anxiety involves normally efficient crew members suddenly undergoing a traumatic change that makes them unable to function within the established structure: Captain Picard suddenly deprived of his natural authority,[142] Commander Riker behaving erratically because of sleep deprivation,[143] Counselor Troi losing her empathic abilities,[144] Lieutenant Worf suffering an injury that could leave him permanently disabled,[145] Doctor Crusher unable to rely on her own professional judgment,[146] or Lieutenant Commander Data experiencing homicidal waking dreams.[147] In all of these cases, the crisis is ultimately resolved by the full restoration of the character's original abilities before the episode's ending. In fact, rather than making them question their assigned task, these experiences repeatedly serve to deepen the characters' commitment to their careers in Starfleet.

This basic stability of character and narrative formula expresses the cultural logic of industrial capitalism: with very few exceptions, the main cast members of *TNG* and the other *Star Trek* series remain permanently employed in

142. "Tapestry," *Star Trek: The Next Generation*, Paramount Domestic Television (First-run syndication, February 15, 1993).

143. "Schisms," *Star Trek: The Next Generation*, Paramount Domestic Television (First-run syndication, October 19, 1992).

144. "The Loss," *Star Trek: The Next Generation*, Paramount Domestic Television (First-run syndication, December 31, 1990).

145. "Ethics," *Star Trek: The Next Generation*, Paramount Domestic Television (First-run syndication, March 2, 1992).

146. "Remember Me," *Star Trek: The Next Generation*, Paramount Domestic Television (First-run syndication, October 22, 1990).

147. "Phantasms," *Star Trek: The Next Generation*, Paramount Domestic Television (First-run syndication, October 25, 1993).

unchanging roles, forming a reliable community with strong social ties.[148] But, at the same time, the labor they perform more closely resembles postindustrial Empire's paradigm of managerialism and immaterial labor. They inhabit a world where material goods are no longer the result of human labor, but where they are created by a seemingly magical "replicator" technology that can conjure up full meals and cups of hot Earl Grey tea out of thin air. In this way, *Star Trek* has done some of the vital work of imagining technology not as what Marx called "the organic composition of capital"[149] but as a way of effacing human labor entirely.[150] All of these elements contribute to a utopian postcapitalism where questions of labor, class conflict, and the inherent limitations of physical resources have been resolved, but where capitalism's social relations still remain unchanged. In many ways, *Star Trek* can therefore be seen not only as a reflection of global capitalism's emergent forms but also as a training ground where one learns both to accept global capitalism's basic coordinates and to desire them.

Indeed, Picard and his crew perform work that is not only primarily immaterial but also—like Empire itself—fully preoccupied with the development of subjectivity and biopolitical power. This is especially meaningful in an economic context in which "co-produced services and relationships" have become ever more central, and where production "increasingly means constructing cooperation and communicative commonalities."[151] And although terms such as *cooperation* and *commonality* may sound quite warm and fuzzy, they are at the same time accompanied by new coercive forms of power. While cognitive capitalism thrives on new forms of productivity that seem to stimulate freedom and collaboration, it now must rule the multitude "along internal lines, in production, in exchanges, in culture—in other words, in the biopolitical context of its existence."[152] Thus, even as *Star Trek* retains imperialism's residual top-down hierarchies, it also gives narrative form to Empire's emergent biopolitical forms of control.

One such form is represented by the iconic "communicator": what had been a hugely influential imaginary precursor to the mobile phone[153] on *TOS* became a

---

148. *TNG* is remarkable within the *Star Trek* franchise for pioneering longer story arcs and subtle call-backs to earlier events. The turning point in the series' world-building came toward the end of the third season, when the writers were allowed to have the guest role Sarek reference his son Spock—a character who had never appeared on *TNG* and therefore would require viewers to have knowledge of a larger transmedia storyworld. "Sarek," *Star Trek: The Next Generation*, Paramount Domestic Television (First-run syndication, May 14, 1990).

149. Karl Marx, *Capital: A Critique of Political Economy, Volume One*, trans. Ben Fowkes (Harmondsworth: Penguin Books, 1976), 762–63.

150. The Holodeck, the bridge viewscreen, the replicator, and Picard's iPad-like tablet are other prominent ways in which the series offered provocative, influential, and desirable ways of imagining technology's supposedly liberating role in the post-Fordist era.

151. Hardt and Negri, *Empire*, 302.

152. Hardt and Negri, *Empire*, 344.

153. Martin Cooper, who invented the first mobile phone for Motorola in 1973, cited *Star Trek* as his inspiration.

tiny badge that all crew members in *TNG* carried on their uniform at all times. The key difference resulting from this change is that the entire crew now constituted an interconnected virtual network of constant surveillance and control, in which their interactions are tracked and monitored by a powerful central computer. Going far beyond Foucault's panopticism,[154] the virtual and ubiquitous nature of the communicators' connectivity resonates much more strongly with Deleuze's writing on the society of control, whose central dependence on computers represents an even more alarming "mutation of capitalism."[155] The mutation in this sense involves the shift from a capitalist order focused on the production of physical commodities to a new dominant mode primarily concerned with the production of subjectivity.

Returning, then, to the *TNG* episode centered on the dysfunctional, overly imaginative Barclay, the plot development in this episode offers a provocative illustration of this very process. The daydreaming Holodeck addict is unreceptive to the more traditional Foucauldian form of discipline, as he fails to respond to the threats that result from top-down institutional power and the normative socio-technical machinery of which he is a part. In fact, La Forge's initial response—that the subject who fails to internalize normative self-discipline must therefore be removed from the corresponding environment—is profoundly Foucauldian.[156] But Picard's response to La Forge's exasperated transfer request instead illustrates Empire's emergent biopolitical logic of affective and immaterial labor.

The conflict is therefore resolved not through the imposition of punitive measures but through an elaborate exploration of his imaginary life, which in *TNG*'s storyworld can be visualized and shared using the Holodeck's immersive and immaterial technology. Several crew members in the episode subsequently visit Barclay's Freudian "dream-work" to witness how they are experienced and re-imagined through his "defective" subjectivity, while many of them pressure him to suppress his overactive imagination and reengage with the ship's daily reality of immaterial labor. Predictably, the crew's attempt to stage an intervention is unsuccessful: Barclay's emotional investment in the imaginary lives he leads on the Holodeck is too strong for him to abandon by sheer force of rational argument.

The episode's resolution hinges instead on the dissolution of the traditional boundary between work and leisure. Just as the neoliberal subject is trained by culture, technology, and economic necessity to relinquish this distinction, Barclay learns that his fannish addiction to fantasy gives him abilities that have a use value on the *Enterprise* bridge. Only Barclay, whose Holodeck fantasies

---

154. Michel Foucault, *Discipline and Punish: The Birth of the Prison* (New York: Vintage, 1995), 228.

155. Gilles Deleuze, "Postscript on the Societies of Control," *October* 59 (1992): 6.

156. According to Foucault's disciplinary logic, the inmate's sustained resistance in the face of institutional pressure exerted by "normalizing power" would lead to his movement to another position within the "carceral network." See Foucault, *Discipline and Punish*, 304.

have strengthened his imaginative capabilities, is able to think "outside the box" during the episode's climax, and his intervention is instrumental in avoiding the ship's imminent destruction. What the episode therefore teaches both Barclay and its audience is that work and leisure—the private and the public—should no longer be approached as separate spheres but as a single continuum. In the same way that the media industry has happily accommodated fandom's cultural practices and sensibilities, the commanding officers on the *Enterprise* learn to absorb Barclay's skillset in a mutually beneficial compromise: Barclay may continue to indulge in his Holodeck compulsion, as long as he does so in more moderate ways that no longer impede his functioning as a productive immaterial laborer.

This is one of several moments in *Star Trek* when the limits of the storyworld's nominal postcapitalism are vividly illustrated. The structural coordinates of *TNG*'s storyworld thereby correspond with remarkable precision to those ideological notions that have mythologized and naturalized the "commonsense" history of capitalism[157]: a teleological narrative propelled by "natural" human competition, progress through technological development, all the while guided by the colonialist "pioneering spirit"—though of course presented in a way that is deprived of its essence of exploitation, violence, and oppression. Given *Star Trek*'s political potential, it is remarkable how rarely it has explored the social, economic, and cultural implications of a world beyond capitalism.[158] Instead, the franchise's sustained focus on the *Enterprise*'s leadership ends up celebrating and mythologizing capitalism's core values of individualism, entrepreneurialism, and hierarchical authority. The striking absence of any kind of democratic forms or procedures speaks volumes about *Star Trek*'s actual investment in a truly postcapitalist imaginary. Instead, it offers a fascinating hybrid of familiar imperialist power structures, on the one hand, and emerging postindustrial practices, on the other.

"MAKE IT SO": THE CHAIN OF COMMAND AND IMPERIAL ADMINISTRATION

So far, I have argued that *Star Trek* in general—and *TNG* in particular—combines the rigid boundaries and stable structures of imperialism with Empire's flexible entrepreneurialism. The show's militaristic trappings reinforce capitalism's inherently hierarchical nature, while the characters' and creators' repeated disavowal of this core militarism allows the audience to engage with the crew

---

157. Arun K. Patnaik, "Gramsci's Concept of Common Sense: Towards a Theory of Subaltern Consciousness in Hegemony Processes," *Economic and Political Weekly* 23, no. 5 (1988).

158. *Star Trek: Deep Space Nine* has arguably demonstrated the most interest in examining more complex shifts in social relations within this imagined future, though it, too, has always remained strongly limited by its familiar imperialist "frontier outpost" framework.

as explorers rather than as enforcers of imperialist conquest. But even more important, the social relations among the main characters and the physical environment on board the *Enterprise* confirm the sense that they are first and foremost co-workers, and the episodes tend to follow the coordinates of television's traditional workplace drama. The vessel's brightly lit interior, full of wasted space and recreational facilities, indeed "looks more like a hotel than a spaceship,"[159] and in this sense the weekly episodes come across as no more radical in their politics than an average episode of *The Love Boat*.

The immaterial and managerial labor performed on the *Enterprise* amounts primarily to what Hardt and Negri would call "imperial administration"[160]: the benevolent and completely voluntary work of maintaining peace and order. Tellingly, the bridge of *TNG*'s *Enterprise* resembles nothing so much as a corporate boardroom, complete with luxurious carpeting, elegant woodwork, and an enormous viewscreen offering the once-futuristic equivalent of modern-day Skype calls. It represents the fantasy of entrepreneurial exploration in the postcolonial age, which—like Tolkien—rewrites the horrific history of imperialism and colonialist exploitation. But where Tolkien imagined a medieval Europe threatened by invasion (from the East and the South, of course), *Star Trek* offers a future where imperialism can be practiced without any harmful effects by a sympathetic, reliable, and (more or less) unchanging elite team of professional managers. *TNG*'s *Enterprise* therefore also represents the perfectly efficient intergalactic corporation, the invention of warp capability, and immaterial labor— an uncanny literalization of Marx's famous description of capitalism's tendency to "annihilate space with time."[161]

David Harvey applies this term to the postindustrial reorganization of capital, which he has helpfully phrased as the neoliberal era of *flexible accumulation*.[162] Although Harvey clearly disapproves of Hardt and Negri's rhetorical gestures,[163] his analysis of postindustrial capitalism perfectly matches their theorization of Empire's deterritorializing power. He explains how capitalism's central value system is now "dematerialized and shifting, time horizons are collapsing, and it is hard to tell exactly what space we are in when it comes to assessing causes and effects, meanings or values."[164] In his own book on America's neoliberal Empire, Harvey again emphasizes capitalism's "incessant drive towards the reduction if

---

159. *TNG* story editor André Bormanis, in *To Boldly Go: Launching Enterprise*, directed by Roger Lay Jr. (2013; Hollywood: Paramount Home Video, 2013), Blu-ray.

160. Hardt and Negri, *Empire*, 339–41.

161. Karl Marx, *Grundrisse*, trans. Martin Nicolaus (Harmondsworth: Penguin Books, 1973), 537–44. See also David Harvey, *The Condition of Postmodernity* (Malden: Blackwell, 1990), 293.

162. Harvey, *The Condition of Postmodernity*, 147.

163. David Harvey, *Seventeen Contradictions and the End of Capitalism* (London: Profile Books, 2014), 238.

164. Harvey, *The Condition of Postmodernity*, 298.

not elimination of spatial barriers," arguing that flexible accumulation "is driven remorselessly by round after round of space-time compression."[165] Hardt and Negri add that this sped-up process of deterritorialization under global capitalism has at the same time been accompanied "not by free play and equality, but by the imposition of new hierarchies."[166]

Both of these aspects are fundamental to *Star Trek*'s storyworld. While the franchise's representation of technological progress has facilitated an almost unimaginable degree of space-time compression, we witness at the same time the rise of a new hierarchy of benevolent and peaceful imperial administration. In spite of this technocratic storyworld's superficially progressive ideals, there is therefore hardly any space for actual democracy (as far as we can see), as its postcapitalist future instead maintains so clearly its emphasis on individualism, hierarchical authority, and generalized competition:

> Instead of contributing to social integration, *imperial administration acts rather as a disseminating and differentiating mechanism.* . . . In short, the old administrative principle of universality, treating all equally, is replaced by the differentiation and singularization of procedures, treating each differently.[167]

This reading is supported not only by the show's dedication to centering our attention on characters in positions of authority but also by the captain and crew's perpetually strained relationship with Starfleet's higher leadership.

As Adam Kotsko has pointed out in a perceptive blog article on *Star Trek*'s politics, the captain's authority tends to be absolute, and general trust in his (or, in the case of *Voyager*, her) leadership unconditional. On those occasions when Starfleet admirals or bureaucratic institutions become involved, they are—with remarkably few exceptions—hindrances to the *Enterprise* crew's usual efficiency. The corruption, bureaucratic entropy and destructive authoritarianism that we encounter repeatedly at the level of Starfleet's larger organization play up the neoliberal sentiment that large, statelike institutions are inefficient at best and destructive at worst.[168] Like a corporation's lean, mean board of directors, the *Enterprise* crew should clearly be free to act without interference from "above," and should therefore also be free to interpret rules and regulations without direct supervision from the bureaucratic and cumbersome organization whose ideals they represent.

As an expression of a political position, this fantasy mobilizes a glaring contradiction one encounters over and over in late capitalist culture. In Kotsko's

---

165. David Harvey, *The New Imperialism* (Oxford: Oxford University Press, 2005), 98.

166. Hardt and Negri, *Empire*, 154.

167. Hardt and Negri, *Empire*, 340–41.

168. The most vivid illustration is offered in the unusual but revealing episode "Conspiracy," *Star Trek: The Next Generation*, Paramount Domestic Television (First-run syndication, May 9, 1988), in which three powerful Starfleet admirals are controlled by evil alien parasites.

words, "The central concept that we're going to get liberal outcomes (Federation ideals!) from authoritarian structures (quasi-military command structures!) is, to say the least, difficult to find evidence for in the real world."[169] For many fans, this ideological contradiction is deemed irrelevant, as their engagement is informed by the franchise's inclusive identity politics and the collaborative cultures that developed around the *Star Trek* storyworld. But if we truly wish to think through the franchise's imaginary empire in terms of its ambivalent relationship to capitalism, these tensions are crucial to understanding the contradictory way in which *Star Trek*'s world-building negotiates its historical and material context of postindustrial capitalism.

CONCLUSION

While Tolkien's storyworld and the *Star Trek* franchise appear to occupy opposite ends of the sf/fantasy spectrum, I have argued in this chapter that they in fact have many traits in common. When considered from the perspective of radical political theory, both storyworlds in their own way reject capitalism, either by establishing a precapitalist fantasy of magic and myth or by imagining a postcapitalist future in which class struggle has been transcended and a technocratic utopia is finally realized. Both franchises became genre-defining examples of transmedia world-building, and they each developed and sustained fan cultures with strong ties to countercultural movements and progressive political ideals. Both also grew from sizable cult phenomena into hugely profitable entertainment franchises in the very period in which capitalism entered its postindustrial stage and started paving the way toward Empire.

Hardt and Negri have devoted great attention to the crucial differences between imperialism and Empire, and these two paradigms of fantastic transmedia storyworlds give us helpful illustrations of world-building practices that straddle both of these frameworks. The structure of feeling that pervades Tolkien's imaginary empire expresses nostalgia for imperialism's organizational norm of strong boundaries while mourning the inevitability of capitalism's remorseless deterritorialization. But as reactionary as *LOTR* can be, there is at the same time a vital, radical current to the storyworld that has indeed been appropriated and made meaningful by fans and countercultural activists for decades.

Associating *Star Trek* with radical politics, however, initially seems more obvious, as the franchise has been popularly known from the start as a progressive and intellectually stimulating popular entertainment. When attempting to untangle *Star Trek*'s actual politics, however, there are surprisingly few direct engagements with the storyworld's setting in a postcapitalist future. Indeed, the

---

169. Adam Kotsko, "What Is *Star Trek*'s Vision of Politics?" *An und für sich*, March 16, 2015, accessed February 1, 2016, https://itself.wordpress.com/2015/03/16/what-is-star-treks-vision-of-politics/.

Star Trek franchise has shaped our imagined relationship with global capitalism more than any other entertainment franchise over the past half century. Arriving in the "Golden Age" of American capitalism, its vision of a glorious future of technological progress and post-scarcity plenitude helped pave the way for global capitalism's era of immaterial labor and imperial administration.

These elements became especially prominent in *TNG*, as *Star Trek*'s increasingly elaborate transmedia storyworld negotiated the tension between industrial capitalism's residual imperialism, on the one hand, and post-Fordism's emergent network structures, on the other. While the narratives of individual episodes, films, novels, and comics engaged with a wide range of social concerns, the structure of feeling provided by the franchise's larger storyworld maintained a contradictory relationship to capitalism. Indeed, the franchise's sustained focus on "enlightened colonialism" alongside global capitalism's covert militarism illustrates most vividly Hardt and Negri's thinking on the transition from imperialism to Empire. Both the stability of the TV series' formats and their continuous investment in stability and hierarchical power resemble Tolkien's political conservatism, while the storyworld's technology facilitates the emergence of a Deleuzian society of control while also providing the most dramatic illustration of capitalism's structural annihilation of space through time.

When considered from the perspective of radical political theory, each storyworld in its own way thus simultaneously embraces and rejects capitalism: Tolkien does this by providing a pleasurable fantasy of a precapitalist world of wonders, and *Star Trek* by imagining a postcapitalist future in which class struggle is transcended and a technocratic utopia is realized. As foundational paradigms of transmedia world-building and pioneering fan culture, these storyworlds developed and sustained international communities with strong ties to countercultural movements and radical politics. And as global entertainment franchises, both ultimately developed from cult phenomena into profitable entertainment brands in the very period in which capitalism entered its postindustrial phase and started paving the way toward global capitalism's "postideological" politics.

3

Fantastical Capitalism and Postideological World-Building

In the very first scene of *Game of Thrones*,[1] we follow a group of three men carefully venturing beyond an impossibly high and immeasurably thick wall. Cautiously exploring a snowbound forest wilderness, they soon encounter the gruesome remains of the band of outlaws they were tracking. Dismissing his increasingly anxious men's warnings about the dangers that lurk behind the Wall as ancient superstition, the arrogant young commander orders them to investigate further, with predictably gruesome results: the men are attacked by supernatural beings whose unexpected resurgence will propel the storyworld's main narrative.

The Wall's prominence in the popular TV series' premiere episode established several crucial elements simultaneously: its size and scale, for instance, foreground the storyworld's genre framework of fantasy, while the visual spectacle and immaculate realism emphasize the show's robust production values and cinematic style.[2] But the establishment of the Wall as a crucial geographic marker at the same time introduces a key thematic motif to the *Game of Thrones* storyworld: as we follow the desperate patrol of obviously terrified men into an unknown, desolate landscape, we instantly recognize that they are venturing into unknown territory—a world outside the normal, where rational laws no longer apply. And, as we soon learn, its power is growing.

The Wall's symbolic significance is so great within *Game of Thrones* because fantastic storyworlds clearly require an outside. As elaborate and detailed as the maps of Oz, Middle-earth, or Narnia may be, our fascination inevitably lies just as much with the blank spaces that surround them. By the same token, *Star Trek*'s world-building must constantly expand outward, as the *Enterprise*'s endless mission must constantly venture farther beyond the expanding boundaries of

---

1. "Winter Is Coming," *Game of Thrones*, Home Box Office (New York: HBO, April 17, 2011).

2. Michael Z. Newman and Elana Levine, *Legitimating Television: Media Convergence and Cultural Status* (New York: Routledge, 2012), 5.

its already-vast imaginary empire. Fantastic transmedia world-building is defined by this contradictory logic: constantly pushing beyond its own borders, beyond individual narratives, beyond separate media, beyond limitations of authorship or closure. But, at the same time, there must always remain an outside to explore, to map out, to conquer. The dialectical movement of fantastic world-building therefore obsessively maps out its own imaginary empires but ceases to exist without an outside to discover.

In the same way, capitalism, too, requires an outside. Since it cannot exist without continuous growth, it must always find new areas to colonize, new resources to harvest, new forms of labor to mobilize. Capitalism's "unique drive for self-expansion"[3] defined its imperialist phase, guided and legitimized by Enlightenment values such as progress, civilization, and technological innovation. As the previous chapter has illustrated, these imperialist concepts are dramatized and negotiated in the teleological storyworlds of Tolkien and *Star Trek*, where they interact in complex ways with the emerging context of global capitalism. Where *LOTR* constitutes an attempt to stave off the most destructive effects of capitalist globalization, *TNG* clings to imperialism's clear hierarchies while embracing Empire's focus on immaterial labor and imperial administration. But both of these imaginary empires were able to maintain a crucial sense of outside, even if these surrounding "other" spaces were already undergoing capitalism's inevitable assimilation—to which all forms of resistance would indeed prove to be futile.

The age of global capitalism, however, is defined by the waning of *any* sense of outside. Guided by Margaret Thatcher's infamous neoliberal mantra, "There is no alternative," Empire's cultural logic has no space for a different world, whether real or imaginary. The utopian imaginary that pervades the sf and fantasy genres is now countered by what Mark Fisher has succinctly termed *capitalist realism*: an intensification of Jameson's postmodern condition, defined precisely by the apparent lack of viable political, ideological, or economic alternatives. Where postmodernism's cultural and political effects were derived from the flattening of lived experience and post-Fordism's sweeping financialization, capitalist realism entails the realization of what Fisher calls a "business ontology, in which it is *simply obvious* that everything in society . . . should be run as a business."[4] It constitutes a truly posthistorical structure of feeling in which there are no goals left to accomplish outside of wave upon wave of consumerism, and where the future has nothing to offer but branded gadgets that hasten the looming environmental apocalypse while at the same time distracting us from it.

Genre fiction has increasingly absorbed and reflected this capitalist realism in the twenty-first century: the posthistorical mood is palpable in the cynicism and bleakness that now pervades so many popular franchises. The film industry's successful focus on reboots and prequels can be seen as evidence of gargantuan

---

3. Ellen Meiksins Wood, *Empire of Capital* (London and New York: Verso, 2003), 23.

4. Mark Fisher, *Capitalist Realism: Is There No Alternative?* (Hants: Zero Books, 2009), 17.

media conglomerates' increasing reliance on "guaranteed" properties with a built-in audience. But the creative stasis they imply also connects to a historical moment where a better future is no longer imaginable, let alone possible. So what is left besides obsessing over what came before, in an age when we still had the capacity to imagine how our world might be different? One of the main trends in this cultural moment has been to make these "reimaginings" of popular franchises darker, grittier, and more "realistic" than their earlier pop-cultural incarnations.[5] In this way, they answer both to Empire's posthistorical spirit of endless recycling and to its postideological emphasis on capitalist realism.

The postideological spirit that so obviously grounds these storyworlds expresses a key ingredient of Empire's cultural logic. Hardt and Negri's description of the global capitalist order brings into focus the absent ideological core of neoliberalism: as power is decentered and networked, more and more emphasis is placed on the individual. In their book *The New Way of the World*, Pierre Dardot and Christian Laval have described this as a new existential norm that calls upon every person to conduct themselves as an enterprise.[6] This hypercompetitive paradigm, which has shaped the past decade of austerity and crisis capitalism, finds expression in transmedia storyworlds that exist in a radical state of ongoing precariousness. In this sense, both *Game of Thrones* and *BSG* reflect different aspects of twenty-first-century Empire, minimizing the residual elements of imperialism and industrial capitalism, and articulating in dramatic form the postideological spirit of global capitalism.

A large part of the attraction exerted on audiences by fantastic genres is the imagined alternatives they offer: fantasy, sf, and other forms of speculative fiction develop environments of estrangement, questioning and sometimes challenging the coordinates of our familiar historical context. SF especially has been understood on the basis of the dialectic between estrangement and cognition. As Carl Freedman explains in *Critical Theory and Science Fiction*, estrangement in this sense refers to "the creation of an alternative fictional world that, by refusing to take our mundane environment for granted, implicitly or explicitly performs an estranging critical interrogation of the latter."[7] But, at the same time, the operation of cognition enables the text "to account rationally for its imagined world and for the connections as well as the disconnections to our own empirical world."[8] And while Freedman, like many other sf scholars, still privileges the "rational, unfantastic ways" in which sf produces these forms of cognitive

---

5. Trend-setting examples of this style include Christopher Nolan's *Batman* film trilogy, Zack Snyder's *Superman* movies, and the second cycle of *Spider-Man* adaptations.

6. Pierre Dardot and Christian Laval, *The New Way of the World: On Neoliberal Society* (London and New York: Verso, 2013), 3.

7. Carl Freedman, *Critical Theory and Science Fiction* (Middletown: Wesleyan University Press, 2000), 16–17.

8. Freedman, *Critical Theory and Science Fiction*, 17.

estrangement,[9] more recent scholarship has emphasized the notion that a similar dialectic is often at play in other fantastic genres as well.[10]

In the previous chapter, we have seen this dialectic at play in both *LOTR* and *Star Trek*, each of which creates productive forms of cognitive estrangement that express an ambivalent and contradictory radical potential, irrespective of the difference between fantasy and sf. These paradigmatic storyworlds depend on a central tension between imperialism's tendency to establish clear boundaries, on the one hand, and capitalism's deterritorializing nature, on the other. Most crucially, Tolkien's and Roddenberry's respective visions of history were fundamentally teleological, with the former offering a fantasy of a romanticized premodern past and the latter imagining a more perfect technological future, while both hinge crucially on the utopian fantasy of a society without alienation by wage labor. As world-building practices, they therefore seemed to offer sincere (though thoroughly compromised) alternatives to capitalism.

But as capitalist realism has become more deeply ingrained in our culture, fantastic fiction has absorbed the cynical politics of neoliberalism, structuring fantasies that no longer flee from, but fully embrace, capitalism's "naked, shameless, direct, brutal exploitation."[11] *Fantastical capitalism* seems an appropriate term to describe fantastical storyworlds that give narrative and aesthetic expression to Empire's spirit of capitalist realism: "fantastical" because—superficially at least—they present us with storyworlds totally unlike our own, and "capitalism" because they incorporate and strengthen capitalism's most basic social and cultural logic, while alternatives are systematically rejected as "unrealistic."

Fantastical capitalism doesn't operate on the basis of imperialism's media logic, developing stable entertainment franchises in which a familiar narrative formula is repeated week after week with sometimes-significant variations. Fantastical capitalism instead expresses a worldview in which there is no outside, no future, no alternative. Its storyworlds aren't utopian, because they lack the ability to imagine a future that is fundamentally different, let alone better. But they also aren't traditionally dystopian, because their dark worlds aren't warnings of what is yet to come. Instead, they constantly reiterate what is considered a basic truth of neoliberal capitalism: it's a harsh world out there, and nice guys always finish last.

Fantastical capitalism therefore offers storyworlds that are turned in upon themselves, embracing neoliberalism's cynical business ethic: every individual is looking out for themselves, and those who aren't will inevitably be left behind as a "loser" in the game of capitalism. One of *Game of Thrones*'s most-repeated lines perfectly encapsulates neoliberalism's merciless form of competitive

---

9. Freedman, *Critical Theory and Science Fiction*, 37.

10. See *Historical Materialism* 10, no. 4 (2002), ed. Mark Bould and China Miéville.

11. Karl Marx and Friedrich Engels, *The Communist Manifesto* (London and New York: Verso, 2012), 38.

individualism: "in the game of thrones, you either win or you die."[12] Global capitalism's postideological structure of feeling pervades both *Game of Thrones* and *Battlestar Galactica*, but in different ways. Besides functioning as barometers of ideological sensibilities, these two storyworlds in particular can be considered neoliberal responses to *LOTR* and *Star Trek*. *Game of Thrones* has often been described as "Tolkien crossed with *The Sopranos*,"[13] with HBO capitalizing on the TV show's acclaim among the source novels' niche group of original fans, and on the wider appeal of the adaptation's branded transmedia franchise. Furthermore, each series in its own way defined for a new generation what its genre entailed: sf and fantasy could be topical, edgy, "realistic," and ambiguous, as both *Game of Thrones* and *Battlestar Galactica* rewrote the coordinates of earlier genre paradigms and opened up fantastic world-building to new audiences.

In this chapter, I approach these two storyworlds as key examples of fantastical capitalism: both give us harsh and unrelentingly bleak fictional environments that dramatize "what is left when beliefs have collapsed at the level of ritual or symbolic elaboration."[14] Like capitalism itself, these imaginary empires are increasingly bereft of the utopian impulse. Instead, they are apocalyptic in the sense that the only possible future their world-building offers is either an end of all things (*Game of Thrones*'s constantly intoned prophecy "Winter is coming"[15]) or a perpetual state of postapocalyptic precariousness (*Battlestar Galactica*'s seemingly endless intergalactic odyssey).[16] And yet both also find lines of flight that foreground capitalism's most basic contradictions. But before discussing either of these two case studies, I will first explain in more detail fantastical capitalism's relation to Empire's postideological structure of feeling.

FROM CAPITALIST REALISM
TO FANTASTICAL CAPITALISM

In Hardt and Negri's theory of Empire, they emphasize repeatedly that power is no longer monolithic and identifiable but decentered and rhizomatic: imperial

---

12. George R. R. Martin, *A Game of Thrones* (New York: Bantam Books, 1996), chapter 44 ("Eddard XII"), chapter 46 ("Eddard XIV"), chapter 55 ("Eddard XV"). Chapters in Martin's book series are not numbered but identified by the names of the recurring characters from whose point of view the chapter is narrated. Since my references are drawn from e-books without page numbers, I have indicated the number of the chapter (by my own count) alongside the relevant character name, followed by a Roman numeral. Thus, "chapter 44 ('Eddard XII')" refers to the forty-fourth chapter in the book, being the twelfth chapter titled "Eddard."

13. Sarah Hughes, "'Sopranos Meets Middle-earth': How *Game of Thrones* Took Over Our World," *The Guardian*, March 22, 2014, accessed January 4, 2016, http://www.theguardian.com/tv-and-radio/2014/mar/22/game-of-thrones-whats-not-to-love.

14. Fisher, *Capitalist Realism*, 4.

15. A phrase spoken twelve times in the first book alone.

16. In the same way that *LOTR* and *Star Trek* are perfectly symmetrical in their respective pre- and postcapitalism, *Game of Thrones* and *BSG* are—respectively—pre- and postapocalyptic.

power is not regulated from a clear and identifiable center but "distributed in networks, through mobile and articulated mechanisms of control."[17] The traditional Marxist concept of "dominant ideology" therefore has a very different resonance in the context of global capitalism, where hegemonic power clearly exists, but where it is no longer signposted and delimited by imperialism's stable and recognizable boundaries. Instead, Hardt and Negri speak of "biopower" and "biopolitical production" to describe the contemporary hegemony of immaterial labor. While these terms sound similar and are, in their abstraction, easily confused, they represent two different but complementary aspects of Empire's authority. The shared prefix *bio-* emphasizes how these categories engage social life in its entirety, while the two terms also indicate separate spheres of power in relation to subjectivity:

> Biopower stands above society, transcendent, as a sovereign authority and imposes its order. Biopolitical production, in contrast, is immanent to society and creates social relationships and forms through collaborative forms of labor.[18]

This concept perhaps requires some unpacking before we continue. What Hardt and Negri are getting at is a double logic that maps out a key contradiction that is specific to Empire's reign: first, biopower's ability to produce a form of social life in which hegemonic rule is articulated simultaneously at multiple levels, as culture becomes "both an element of political order and economic production"[19]; second, the increasingly immaterial and therefore biopolitical nature of labor, "aimed not only at the production of goods, but ultimately at the production of information, communication, cooperation."[20] Biopower, in other words, is not created through the top-down imposition of ideological values, but rather through the constant interaction between alienated members of the multitude on one side, and those in charge of imperial administration on the other. The resulting biopolitical reign of Empire is one in which new collaborative forms are continuously created, but also where this "new immaterial and cooperative creativity of the multitude move[s] in shadows, and nothing manages to illuminate our destiny ahead."[21]

One of Empire's key paradoxes is therefore that while the dominant paradigm of immaterial labor and cognitive capitalism stimulates the formation of new collaborative forms, they must operate in constant shadow, without

---

17. Michael Hardt and Antonio Negri, *Empire* (Cambridge, MA: Harvard University Press, 2000), 384.

18. Michael Hardt and Antonio Negri, *Multitude: War and Democracy in the Age of Empire* (London: Penguin, 2005), 94–95.

19. Hardt and Negri, *Multitude*, 334.

20. Hardt and Negri, *Multitude*, 334.

21. Hardt and Negri, *Empire*, 386.

an actual horizon of change. This utopian horizon has evaporated following neoliberalism's blatant assault on once-meaningful classes and communities, global capitalism having taken a path "towards the elimination of the militant particularisms that have traditionally grounded socialist politics—the mines have closed, the assembly lines cut back or shut down, the ship-yards turned silent."[22] This has made it ever more difficult to see oneself as the member of a meaningful community. The post-Fordist economy in which workers now operate is defined by labor relations that are above all flexible, mobile, and precarious: "*flexible* because workers have to adapt to different tasks, *mobile* because workers have to move frequently between jobs, and *precarious* because no contracts guarantee stable, long-term employment."[23] The combination of these three factors results in Empire's deterritorialization of the welfare state, which had been one of the biggest social and political advancements achieved by twentieth-century social and political struggle.

The resulting global system in which Capital itself has "become a world"[24] is best explained via Slavoj Žižek's description of late capitalism and the nonexistence of the "big Other." He describes this Lacanian concept as "the order of symbolic fictions which operate on a level different from that of direct material causality."[25] The big Other operates as a structuring virtual framework, regulating the way in which we see ourselves as subjects in relation to a coherent reality. Without a shared belief in such a coherent symbolic order, it becomes more difficult for the individual to maintain a stable worldview, as beliefs are increasingly moved to the realm of individual "lifestyle choices" and brand cultures.[26] Therefore, while the big Other is strictly an order of symbolic fiction, it is nevertheless necessary in order to maintain the illusion of a real world: "the paradox is that symbolic fiction is constitutive of reality: if we take away the fiction, we lose reality itself."[27]

In the context of Empire and global capitalism, this crucial symbolic order where our conceptions of Meaning and Truth are maintained can no longer be properly accessed and relied upon. Empire's political and economic system without an outside to compete with has dissolved the last remnants of a shared belief in any such big Other: "Not only do we not know what our acts will amount to, there is even no global mechanism regulating our interactions—this is what the

---

22. David Harvey, *Justice, Nature and the Geography of Difference* (Malden: Blackwell, 1996), 41.

23. Hardt and Negri, *Multitude*, 112.

24. Hardt and Negri, *Empire*, 386.

25. Slavoj Žižek, *The Sublime Object of Ideology* (London and New York: Verso, 1996), 389.

26. Sarah Banet-Weiser, *Authentic™: The Politics of Ambivalence in a Brand Culture* (New York: New York University Press, 2012), 188–89.

27. Slavoj Žižek, *Less Than Nothing: Hegel and the Shadow of Dialectical Materialism* (London and New York: Verso, 2014), 92.

properly 'postmodern' nonexistence of the big Other means."[28] What therefore remains is capitalism's ideological void, which Žižek describes as follows:

> Although capitalism is global, encompassing the whole world, it sustains a *stricto sensu* "worldless" ideological constellation, depriving the vast majority of people of any meaningful cognitive orientation. Capitalism is the first socio-economic order which *de-totalizes meaning*: it is not global at the level of meaning. There is, after all, no global "capitalist worldview," no "capitalist civilization" proper.[29]

While the problem Žižek describes here applies to capitalism in general, the contemporary world's state of "ideological disarray" does indeed seem specific to postindustrial capitalism.[30] We are therefore now seeing an increasing number of fantastic storyworlds whose ideological coordinates are defined primarily by the absence of the symbolic order that gave meaning and direction to Tolkien's subcreation of a meaningful Secondary World or to *Star Trek*'s futuristic world-building. Instead, popular fantasy is adopting the paradigm of fantastical capitalism: storyworlds steeped in a form of cynical reason that appears increasingly hostile to the genre's traditional idealism.[31] Just as Empire's fundamental framework of capitalist realism obstructs our ability to imagine political alternatives in the real world, these fantastical narrative environments paradoxically construct elaborate fantasies that ultimately reproduce global capitalism's dominant logic.

These forms of fantastical capitalism may appear on the surface to have developed beyond the quite obvious ideological coordinates of more traditional sf and fantasy: clear-cut moral and ethical distinctions between good and evil now seem impossible to define, and the narratives' larger goals are rarely obvious or predictable. Nevertheless, we must resist the seemingly self-evident notion that these storyworlds are truly "postideological" in the sense that they are no longer the bearers of ideological content. As Žižek would insist, the fundamental level of ideology "is not that of an illusion masking the real state of things, but that of an (unconscious) fantasy structuring our social reality itself."[32] Therefore, in the same way that there is no such thing as a neutral, commonsense social reality that isn't already steeped in ideology, the seemingly postideological worlds of fantastical capitalism should instead be considered—to use a clichéd but appropriate Žižekianism—as an example of ideology at its purest.

---

28. Žižek, *The Sublime Object of Ideology*, 412.

29. Slavoj Žižek, *The Year of Dreaming Dangerously* (London and New York: Verso, 2012), 54–55.

30. Luc Boltanski and Eve Chiapello, *The New Spirit of Capitalism*, trans. Gregory Elliott (London and New York: Verso, 2005), xlii.

31. See Peter Sloterdijk, *Critique of Cynical Reason* (Minneapolis: University of Minnesota Press, 1988).

32. Žižek, *The Sublime Object of Ideology*, 30.

"WINTER IS COMING": THE PRECARIOUS STORYWORLD OF *GAME OF THRONES*

The casting of Sean Bean should, of course, have been a dead giveaway: whatever role he plays, the poor guy always seems to end up dead.[33] But when Ned Stark bit the dust in the penultimate episode of *Game of Thrones*'s first season,[34] it nevertheless caught many viewers—myself included—off guard.[35] As the embodiment of patriarchal gravitas, the honorable "Warden of the North" supplied the high-fantasy series' first season with its moral compass. As the only adult with an explicit and unshakable set of ethics, Stark's rigid code of honor would be unbearably patronizing if he weren't also a clever investigator and a loving dad. Given all these remarkable traits, Ned Stark could easily have provided any given fantasy franchise with its long-term protagonist and anchor of the series' ideological values.

Instead, author George R. R. Martin made Ned Stark's fate emblematic of the saga's unconventional take on the high fantasy genre. In the novel *A Game of Thrones*, the first in Martin's ongoing series *A Song of Ice and Fire*, Ned Stark suffers one indignity after another, culminating in a death sentence for treason. Having first suffered the ultimate humiliation by publicly disavowing his own moral code and confessing to a crime he didn't commit, there turns out to be no last-minute pardon or heroic rescue, and the executioner's axe irreversibly falls on the Stark patriarch's neck. But if high fantasy has in the past mainly been associated with childish and risk-free entertainment, this narrative U-turn represents the equivalent of putting up a sign proclaiming, "Abandon all hope, ye who enter here." And indeed, the transmedia entertainment franchise based on Martin's saga soon became notorious for upsetting audience expectations, above all by the brutal and unexpected killing of popular leading characters.

For the uninitiated: *Game of Thrones*[36] is set in the imaginary continents of Westeros and Essos, both of which are part of a storyworld grounded in high fantasy's familiar pseudo-medievalism. Originally conceived as a trilogy, the book series has become a sprawling saga of power struggles, wars, insurgencies, reversals, dragons, stabbings, and sexual abuse that currently fills five doorstop-

---

33. While Sean Bean has developed a reputation for on-screen deaths, he is in fact surpassed statistically by Vincent Price, Bela Lugosi, and John Hurt. See Kyle Hill, "Does Sean Bean Really Die More Than Other Actors?" *Nerdist*, December 5, 2014, accessed January 14, 2016, http://nerdist .com/does-sean-bean-really-die-more-than-other-actors.

34. "Baelor," *Game of Thrones*, Home Box Office (New York: HBO, June 12, 2011).

35. For first-time viewers of the TV series without knowledge of the books, Ned Stark's featured presence in the promotional materials seemed to confirm his status as the main protagonist.

36. For the sake of consistency, I will refer hereafter to the transmedia storyworld based on Martin's *A Song of Ice and Fire* book series by its shorter and more familiar title *Game of Thrones*, which has been used to brand most other cross-platform expansions.

sized novels,[37] with at least two more expected to fill out the series.[38] The series charts the ongoing power struggles between competing dynasties, each of which has some claim to the Iron Throne that controls the Seven Kingdoms of Westeros. In many ways, it follows fantasy fiction's topofocal tradition, mapping out the many characters' increasingly byzantine trajectories across its imaginary landscape. The geographical organization of this storyworld also reproduces Tolkien's paradigmatic Eurocentrism, with the central continent of Westeros transparently standing in for medieval Europe and the sprawling eastern regions of Essos harboring a variety of less "civilized" societies, most of which feature the usual Orientalist clichés.

Already a book saga with a sizable following among readers of fantasy fiction, Martin's storyworld became one of the most valuable world-building franchises following the success of HBO's high-profile television adaptation. Adopting the first novel's title *Game of Thrones* for the franchise as a whole, the series premiered in 2010 as the boutique cable network's first foray into the fantasy genre, initially leading some critics to sneer at the program's fantasy roots as "boy fiction patronizingly turned out to reach the population's other half."[39] But audiences and critics alike were soon won over, and *Game of Thrones* developed into the biggest hit in HBO's roster of original drama series, with its fourth season easily breaking the network's viewership record previously held by *The Sopranos*.[40] To build awareness for the largely unknown storyworld, the show's introduction was preceded by an ambitious publicity campaign that included games, apps, collectables, and live events. And since that time, the franchise has expanded to include numerous videogames, spin-off novels, comic books, Google Map extensions, role-playing games, board games, cookbooks, and reams of fan fiction. I will return in more detail to the television adaptation, the transmedia campaign, and its reception later in this chapter, but I will now first unpack the storyworld's political and ideological basis as established in Martin's novels.

As a fantastic storyworld, the *Game of Thrones* universe distances itself emphatically from the reassuring Tolkienian mold of high fantasy. *LOTR*'s

37. George R. R. Martin, *A Game of Thrones*; *A Clash of Kings* (New York: Bantam Books, 1998); *A Storm of Swords* (New York: Bantam Books, 2000); *A Feast for Crows* (New York: Bantam Books, 2005); *A Dance of Dragons* (New York: Bantam Books, 2011).

38. At the time of writing, the sixth and most likely penultimate book, *The Winds of Winter*, is expected to be published within a matter of months, while the television series plans to keep moving ahead with annual seasons irrespective of Martin's publication pace. In showrunner David Benioff's words, "The show must go on . . . and that's what we're going to do." Joanna Robinson, "*Game of Thrones* Creators Confirm the Show Will Spoil the Books," *Vanity Fair*, March 22, 2015, accessed January 16, 2016, http://www.vanityfair.com/hollywood/2015/03/game-of-thrones-tv-show-will-spoil-books.

39. Ginia Bellafante, "A Fantasy World of Strange Feuding Kingdoms," *New York Times*, April 14, 2011, accessed December 27, 2015, http://www.nytimes.com/2011/04/15/arts/television/game-of-thrones-begins-sunday-on-hbo-review.html?_r=0.

40. Tim Kenneally, "*Game of Thrones* Becomes Most Popular Series in HBO's History," *The Wrap*, June 5, 2014, accessed January 4, 2016, http://www.thewrap.com/game-of-thrones-becomes-most-popular-series-in-hbos-history.

transitional organization represented the kind of thinning one encounters so often in the genre as magical and mythical elements start making way for a purely rational modernity.[41] But Martin's storyworld moves in the opposite direction: much of the books' primary narrative revolves around the unexpected resurgence of monsters, spirits, and mythical creatures assumed to belong to this storyworld's forgotten past, and an important part of the narrative slowly (indeed, interminably) sets up the reappearance of dragons and other beasts as forces to be reckoned with. Instead of Tolkien's elegiac nostalgia for an older, more innocent world, Martin's fantastic fiction reverses this dynamic to show an emergent modernity in which "all the old numinous powers come roaring to life."[42] Where Tolkien's world-building gave symbolic form to capitalism's inevitable deterritorialization of imperialism's stable boundaries, Martin develops a storyworld in which an arrogant and self-obsessed elite is unwittingly threatened by an unstoppable army of zombies from one side and a trio of ferocious dragons from the other. In *Game of Thrones*, the truly apocalyptic threat thus comes—with considerable irony—from monsters no one believes in any longer.

Unlike the clearly hierarchical organization of human power in *LOTR*, with the vast narrative building up to the fated return of the one true king, power in this storyworld has been virtualized and dissociated from the premodern sovereign's traditional authority.[43] The aforementioned execution of Ned Stark is but the first of many slayings of kings, lords, and other major figures of authority, with no fewer than five contenders in the eponymous game of thrones meeting an untimely end before the fourth book in the series is even over. Where Tolkienian high fantasy associates power explicitly with the Arthurian tradition of a transcendent, godlike monarch, this storyworld marks it instead as purely immanent. This is perfectly illustrated by an exchange that takes place in the second book, *A Clash of Kings*, between duplicitous councilor Varys and the highborn but powerless Tyrion Lannister, as they discuss the question of power in relation to Stark's public execution:

> "Some say knowledge is power. Some tell us that all power comes from the gods. Others say it derives from the law. Yet that day on the steps of Baelor's Sept, our godly High Septon and the lawful Queen Regent and your ever-so-knowledgeable servant were as powerless as any cobbler or cooper in the crowd. Who truly killed Eddard Stark do you think? Joffrey, who gave the command? Ser Ilyn Payne, who swung the sword? Or . . . another?"

---

41. Gerold Sedlmayr, "Fantastic Body Politics in Joe Abercrombie's *The First Law* Trilogy," in *Politics in Fantasy Media: Essays on Ideology and Gender in Fiction, Film, Television and Games*, ed. Gerold Sedlmayr and Nicole Waller (Jefferson: McFarland, 2014), 167–68.

42. Sam Kriss, "*Game of Thrones* and the End of Marxist Theory," *Jacobin*, April 10, 2015, accessed May 28, 2015, https://www.jacobinmag.com/2015/04/game-of-thrones-season-five-marxism.

43. Michel Foucault, *Discipline and Punish: The Birth of the Prison* (New York: Vintage, 1995), 304.

Tyrion cocked his head sideways. "Did you mean to answer your damned riddle, or only to make my head ache worse?"

Varys smiled. "Here, then. Power resides where men *believe* it to reside. No more and no less."

"So power is a mummer's trick?"

"A shadow on the wall." Varys murmured, "yet shadows can kill. And ofttimes a very small man can cast a very large shadow."[44]

If one would expect to encounter yet another return to premodern assumptions about autonomous sovereign power in Martin's pseudo-medieval storyworld, we find here instead a pithy summary of Foucault's key point that power in the modern age is not held but merely exercised.[45] Pablo Iglesias, secretary-general of Spanish left-wing political party Podemos, even went so far as to cite this particular franchise as a narrative example of power's inherent instability: "What is at stake in *Game of Thrones* is a regime crisis, in that the image of the king is not a consolidated institutional figure but a fragile one, which is constantly being put into question and can change at any time."[46] If Tolkien's Middle-earth was already built upon the tension between premodern enchantment and thoroughly modern maps and narrative forms, *Game of Thrones* clearly embraces Empire's framework of decentered biopower to the fullest.

It is also worth pointing out that the above exchange takes place between two characters who are of particular interest in the broader context of biopolitical production and cognitive capitalism. Varys is presented in the narrative as a master of information: through his network of "little birds," he is able to exercise influence through the strategic deployment of rumor and hearsay, to which he has unique and privileged access. As a former slave who was castrated at an early age, Varys's (unreliable and fragmented) backstory marks him as a character whose position of relative power is derived entirely from his preternatural ability to access and coordinate informational networks. And, by the same token, Tyrion, son of powerful lord and patriarch Tywin Lannister, was born into privilege and security but has been excluded from actual positions of authority because of his physical appearance. Having been born a dwarf, he is perceived by his father and many others as an incomplete and defective man, and he is referred to by others as "imp," "halfman," "freak," "boyman," and "Lord Tywin's Bane." Neither Varys nor Tyrion (both of whom are tremendous fan favorites) therefore has direct access to the circuits of power, and both are coded as queer characters who must operate on the basis of their own exclusion from normative processes.[47]

---

44. Martin, *A Clash of Kings*, chapter 8 ("Tyrion II").

45. Foucault, *Discipline and Punish*, 305.

46. Pablo Iglesias, "Spain on Edge," *New Left Review* 93 (May–June 2015), accessed May 28, 2015, http://newleftreview.org/II/93/pablo-iglesias-spain-on-edge.

47. Valerie Estelle Frankel, *Women in* Game of Thrones*: Power, Conformity and Resistance* (Jefferson: McFarland, 2014), part 3, par. "Men in the Gender Biased System."

These two characters most clearly exemplify the storyworld's resonance with Empire's framework of precariousness and immaterial labor. Not only have they been unusually resilient and resourceful within a truly merciless storyworld, where even the most popular characters are always at risk of being killed, maimed, and sexually abused, but they have quite obviously survived the eponymous game of thrones thus far because of their extreme flexibility. Due to their own experience of marginalization, their privileged understanding of the immanent nature of power makes them better able to adapt to changing circumstances. Both Varys and Tyrion thus navigate the treacherous waters of their unstable storyworld with an outsider's perspective that could just as easily be termed a queer subjectivity. This adaptability amidst a constant state of precariousness is most evident in Tyrion, who skillfully navigates a series of life-threatening adventures in the first book, becomes a provisional ruler of the capital city in the second, is framed for murder and imprisoned in the third, and was last seen forging new overseas alliances as his expulsion from the Seven Kingdoms (alongside his occasional ally Varys) forces him to reinvent himself yet again.

In their flexibility, mobility, and precariousness, Tyrion and Varys therefore embody a key aspect of post-Fordism's imperial logic. The other main characters who have survived the many ordeals the storyworld has had in store for them (Arya, Bran, Jaime, Margaery, Petyr Baelish, Ser Davos Seaworth) are similarly defined by these basic "postideological" qualities. On the other hand, those who are defined by a more old-fashioned sense of stability, entitlement, and ideology (both Stark parents, Robb, Robert Baratheon, Viserys Targaryen, Joffrey, Cersei, and Tywin Lannister) have each in different ways run up against a world in which those categories no longer seem relevant. Even Daenerys Targaryen, the character with the strongest claim to the Iron Throne, has survived above all by her ability to adapt to changing and unpredictable situations. Her power is ultimately derived not so much from her "core identity" in a positive sense but from her consistent ability to remain flexible amid fantastical capitalism's bleak, uncertain, and constantly shifting world. Thus, to put it once more in Žižekian terms, those who maintain a residual faith in a coherent symbolic order appear much less likely to survive fantastical capitalism than those who have relinquished their belief in the big Other and no longer have any illusions about the harsh and precarious storyworld they inhabit.

POSTIDEOLOGICAL RELIGION AND THE "BIG OTHER"

In the unstable narrative environment of *Game of Thrones*, organized religion makes up an important element of the storyworld's internal organization. The franchise effectively inverts the coordinates of Middle-earth, where the striking absence of any kind of religion paradoxically but very consciously supports the storyworld's religious implications. Tolkien's process of subcreation is deliberately designed to honor and reflect what the author saw as the divine act of creation: "We make in our measure and in our derivative mode, because we are made: and not only made, but made in the image and likeness of a Maker."[48] The presence of imaginary religious systems in such a Secondary World could distract from or even impede the development of religious allegory within the storyworld[49]—which is precisely what happens in *Game of Thrones*.

In this imaginary empire, there are several coexisting religious systems, some of which are in direct competition with each other, while others function primarily as world-building elements, adding texture and dimension to local cultures.[50] The official religion of the Seven Kingdoms of Westeros is the "Faith of the Seven," a hierarchically organized institution allied with the monarchical power structure and similar in many respects to medieval Roman Catholicism. Until the puritanical sect of "Sparrows" takes power within the church in the fourth novel, *A Feast for Crows*, organized religion is presented primarily as corrupt and inherently complicit with vested political interests. The church and its dignitaries are featured in rituals like weddings, coronations, and executions, but leading characters rarely (if ever) profess a sincere religious sentiment; the Sparrows' swift rise to power is in fact the result of the church's general association with corruption and empty ritual. However, both the pope-like High Septon and the reformist "High Sparrow" are ultimately portrayed on the basis of secular, postmodern assumptions about organized religion: their actions are clearly guided by a pragmatism that is part and parcel of fantastical capitalism's cynical *Realpolitik*.

In contrast with the storyworld's "new gods" of the Faith of the Seven, the "old gods" still revered in the less sophisticated North of Westeros aren't part of any organized form of religion. Without churches, priests, or holy scripture, the old gods are primarily associated with the storyworld's iconic red-and-white weirwood trees, articulating the Northern peoples' enduring ties to an authentic mythical past. The more urban and modernized South, however, has lost its connection to this natural world and traditional life. As one character says, "The old gods have no power in the south. The weirwoods there were all cut down, thousands of years ago."[51] Westeros's religious transition from the old gods to the new thus clearly represents high fantasy's predictable form of thinning, expressing the idea so common to the genre that modernization is inevitably accompanied by alienation from tradition and disenchantment from old beliefs.

---

48. J. R. R. Tolkien, "On Fairy-Stories," in *The Monsters and the Critics and Other Essays*, ed. Christopher Tolkien (London: HarperCollins, 1997 [1983]), 145.

49. *LOTR* is commonly interpreted as a Roman Catholic allegory. See Kristin Kay Johnston, "Christian Theology as Depicted in *The Lord of the Rings* and the Harry Potter Books," *Journal of Religion and Society* 7 (2005), accessed May 29, 2015, http://moses.creighton.edu/jrs/2005/2005-5 .pdf.

50. Examples of simple religious systems include the Drowned God, worshiped by the "Ironborn" of the Iron Islands, and the river goddess Rhoynar, a deity to the "orphans of the Greenblood" in Dorne.

51. Martin, *A Game of Thrones*, chapter 48 ("Bran V").

But both of these belief systems are challenged by the appearance in the third book of a new monotheistic religion that worships R'hlorr, also known as the Lord of Light or the Red God.[52] The cult originates in Essos and is barely practiced in Westeros until the mysterious and seductive "Red Priestess" Melisandre converts lord Stannis Baratheon with her prophetic visions of power and victory. Stannis, as one of several contenders for the Iron Throne, makes the religion mandatory for his sizable army and retinue, and publicly burns sacred artifacts from the Faith of the Seven. Inspired by the ancient religion of Zoroastrianism,[53] the worshipers of R'hllor believe in a single supreme god and maintain an absolute distinction between good and evil. The religion's fundamentalist spirit, its violent rejection of other belief systems, and its Eastern origins align it discursively for a contemporary Western audience with Islam, in spite of the fact that it doesn't share any of its actual characteristics. Melisandre's witchlike supernatural abilities and the ease with which she is able to seduce men sexually add further Orientalist resonance to this upstart belief system. Above all, the conflict between a largely secularized institutional Western religion and a fundamentalist faith that has arrived from the East reproduces Samuel Huntington's deeply offensive but widely embraced "clash of civilizations" argument.[54]

It is obvious from the storyworld's organization of these imaginary religions that none of these belief systems embody a form of absolute truth. Neither the Faith of the Seven, the old gods of the weirwood, the Lord of Light, nor any of the other religions in this storyworld represents an unassailable and transcendent symbolic order. Like global capitalism's secularized perspective on religion, these main belief systems are coded—respectively—as a blatant extension of political power, as the nostalgic remains of a lost connection with the natural world, and as a dangerous fundamentalist threat to Western civilization. In interviews, Martin himself has spoken many times of the way he uses religion primarily as a way to add texture and realism to his fantasy storyworld.[55] The sense that religion is primarily represented within the storyworld as immanent to the world's many diverse cultures rather than a single symbolic order therefore offers another way in which the storyworld's postideological spirit is strengthened.

But if there is no coherent "big Other" to provide a shared and absolute structure for *Game of Thrones*'s many characters, does this mean that the storyworld

---

52. Martin, *A Clash of Kings*, "Prologue."

53. "R'hllor," *A Wiki of Ice and Fire*, accessed January 4, 2016, http://awoiaf.westeros.org/index.php/R'hllor.

54. Samuel P. Huntington, "The Clash of Civilizations?" *Foreign Affairs* 7, no. 3 (1993): 22–49.

55. As Martin has put it in interviews, "I do always try to consider the question of religion, which is important because religion shapes societies and shapes cultures and shapes values, even in our modern world." See "George R. R. Martin's Funny and Insightful Explanation of the Role Religion Plays in *Game of Thrones*," *Business Insider UK* video, 4:38, April 19, 2015, http://uk.businessinsider.com/george-rr-martin-role-of-religion-got-game-of-thrones-westeros-2015-4?r=US&IR=T.

is fundamentally bereft of meaning? Is everything about this world provisional, each plot development designed simply to set up another unexpected narrative U-turn? Is this imaginary empire a quite literal embodiment of what Jameson so famously described as late capitalism's "purely *fungible* present in which space and psyches alike can be processed and remade at will"?[56] Or is there yet some force inside Martin's storyworld that ultimately unifies the narrative's many, seemingly inchoate conflicts? The question, in other words, is whether the absence of a shared symbolic order or belief system renders *Game of Thrones* truly postideological.

The answer is, of course, that what seems on the surface like the absence of ideology in fact represents ideology at its purest. As with global capitalism's similar ideological disavowal, the apparent lack of belief systems strengthens the storyworld's ideological thrust. Just like the characters' competitive individualism, institutions are also presented as social and material forces that influence the storyworld not because they are governed by some larger symbolic order but because fantastical capitalism proscribes that each party will relentlessly pursue its own interest. From this perspective, the Iron Bank of Braavos is worth mentioning as one of the storyworld's crucial structuring elements. The Iron Bank is mentioned only briefly in the first two books as the powerful financial institution to which the Crown is deeply indebted. But it starts affecting the storyworld's development more actively in the fourth volume, *A Feast for Crows*, when the bank ceases to supply credit across Westeros after Queen Cersei defers payment on the court's outstanding loans.[57] This is the first clear indication that there is a larger, more abstract power in this imaginary empire that transcends the many petty feuds and character conflicts.

It is little wonder, then, that this symbolic embodiment of Capital is revealed as a crucial force whose "rational" decisions will end up strongly influencing the central game's outcome. The fact that very few characters within the storyworld are aware of Capital's real influence only strengthens this depiction of financial capitalism's wholly virtualized power, existing only as what Hardt and Negri described as an "ontological lack":

> As it constructs its supranational figure, power seems to be deprived of any real ground beneath it, or rather, it is lacking the motor that propels its movement. The rule of the biopolitical imperial context should thus be seen in the first instance as an empty machine, a spectacular machine, a parasitical machine.[58]

In this sense, it is one of the franchise's clever ironies that even in a nominally precapitalist fantasy saga, the most formidable power does not lie with any of

---

56. Fredric Jameson, "The Antinomies of Postmodernity," in *The Cultural Turn: Selected Writings on the Postmodern, 1983–1998* (London and New York: Verso, 1998), 57.

57. Martin, *A Feast for Crows*, chapter 17 ("Cersei IV").

58. Hardt and Negri, *Empire*, 62.

the strongly individualized familial dynasties, with their charisma, their rivalries, their sigils, their fashions, their dialects, their sexual liaisons, and their constantly shifting alliances. The Iron Bank, with its remote physical location but universal reach, its merciless calculations, and its blandly bureaucratic human representatives, in a sense operates as a "more real" reality than all the courtroom intrigue and spectacular battles that make up the genre's traditional bread and butter.

This makes perfect sense, as this constantly shifting storyworld illustrates so vividly that capitalist realism has effectively made a shared belief in an ideologically defined big Other impossible to sustain. But without some form of symbolic order, our perception of reality itself would effectively collapse, as would the kind of fantastic world-building that is organized in this Tolkienian mode of subcreation. The Iron Bank's increasing importance in the storyworld illustrates how the ideological vacuum left by the collapse of ideology is inevitably filled by a godlike virtual force in which we are all made to believe: that of finance. As the individual micronarratives that provide so much emotional investment are shown to be secondary to the banal machinations of Capital, one "global mechanism"[59] at least is introduced to *Game of Thrones*'s storyworld as a viable (though appropriately unreliable) symbolic order.

But while the Iron Bank operates in *Game of Thrones*'s storyworld as a literal embodiment of Capital's true power, the growing army of walking corpses beyond the Wall at the same time offers an allegorical representation of global capitalism's truly monstrous face. Capitalism's implicit association with the apocalypse has been well documented, especially in relation to climate change and Capital's many inherent forms of "creative destruction."[60] They have established the basis for what we might call capitalism's apocalyptic imaginary, as Žižek sums up toward the end of his book *Living in the End Times*:

> Fredric Jameson's old quip holds today more than ever: it is easier to imagine a total catastrophe which ends all life on earth than it is to imagine a real change in capitalist relations—as if, even after a global cataclysm, capitalism will somehow continue. . . . We may worry as much as we want about global realities, but it is Capital which is the Real of our lives.[61]

The same truth pertains to the storyworlds of fantastical capitalism. In *Game of Thrones*, capitalism's dialectic of creative destruction is neatly divided between the Iron Bank's abstract power and the apocalyptic horizon emerging from be-

59. Slavoj Žižek, *The Ticklish Subject* (London and New York: Verso, 1999), 412.

60. See, for instance, David Harvey, *The Limits to Capital* (London and New York: Verso, 2006), 235–38; Kevin Rozario, *The Culture of Calamity: Disaster and the Making of Modern America* (Chicago: Chicago University Press, 2007); Gerry Canavan and Kim Stanley Robinson, eds. *Green Planets: Ecology and Science Fiction* (Middletown: Wesleyan University Press, 2014); and Naomi Klein, *This Changes Everything: Capitalism vs. the Climate* (New York: Simon & Schuster, 2014).

61. Slavoj Žižek, *Living in the End Times* (London and New York: Verso, 2010), 334.

yond the Wall. To the reader of Martin's books, the real threat faced by the inhabitants of Westeros is certainly that of the mythical monsters slowly reemerging from the frozen world outside its border. Unlike Tolkien, who perceives the unstoppable advance of reason and modernity as a melancholy process of disenchantment, the monsters of Westeros appear to be called forth by the emergence of capitalist realism: it is precisely the dissolution of a shared belief in a coherent symbolic order that seems to have triggered the resurrection of a more monstrous reality.

Together, the Iron Bank and the army of undead "Others"[62] from beyond the Wall therefore operate as an expression of global capitalism's monstrous and elusive dialectical nature: interrupting the rules of the eponymous game by creating a threat that challenges the characters' very conceptions of reality. In brief moments of horror, when previously unimaginable events suddenly occur, we can catch glimpses of the Lacanian Real[63]: an irrational and shapeless void so unsettling that it must instantly be fictionalized and displaced by reasserting some form of symbolic order.[64] Therefore, just as the storyworld's postideological spirit reflects global capitalism's aforementioned ontological lack, the occasional intrusion of the Real paradoxically but necessarily resurrects a symbolic order that can stave off this traumatic abyss, if only provisionally.[65]

The appearance of the Others and the looming apocalypse they embody triggers a paradigm shift that upsets the narrative's high-stakes dramatization of relentless competition between its main characters and foregrounds the systemic monstrousness of fantastical capitalism. What is crucial about the nature of both the Iron Bank and the Others is that neither is grounded by a positive and identifiable center. Unlike Sauron in *LOTR*, the real threat to Westeros comes in the form of networks without a single source of identity or power.[66] The Others mobilize the critical potential contained within the zombie genre (which I will explore in more detail in chapter 5), while the Iron Bank represents the inhuman and implacable abstraction of Capital in all of its cold, monstrous abstraction.

If the central spirit of the *Game of Thrones* storyworld expresses the cultural logic of capitalist realism, where the big Other no longer seems to be operative, the inevitable appearance of this monstrous Real does facilitate a productive form

---

62. In the TV series, they are referred to as "White Walkers."

63. Benjamin Noys, "The Horror of the Real: Žižek's Modern Gothic," *International Journal of Žižek Studies* 4, no. 4 (2010).

64. Žižek, *The Year of Dreaming Dangerously*, 50.

65. Horror author H. P. Lovecraft's Cthulhu mythos is among the best-known fantastic storyworlds commonly associated with the unrepresentable Real, as it revolves around horrific tales in which "no direct contact with the real object is possible." Graham Harman, *Weird Realism: Lovecraft and Philosophy* (Hants: Zero Books, 2012), 238.

66. In the case of the Others, the plot thus far suggests the presence of a "Winter King" leading the assault on Westeros, thus bestowing at least some degree of conscious agency upon the zombie horde. But even if there does turn out to be some presence imparting individual intent, it will be an identity that this threat is given retroactively, again as a necessary retreat from the unrepresentable void of the Real.

of anticapitalist critique. Therefore, without making exaggerated claims about this popular franchise's politics, we can easily recognize in the organization of its storyworld an allegorical depiction of global capitalism's material organization. In the countless think pieces churned out by bloggers and journalists, it has become commonplace to point out that Martin's imaginary empire "chimes perfectly with the destabilized and increasingly non-Western planetary order today."[67] There have even been Marxist critics who have celebrated *Game of Thrones* for its radical potential, suggesting that we enjoy this kind of fantasy so much because it helps explain "our own demon-haunted world"[68] of immaterial labor and radical inequality.

True as this may be, the franchise's most likely outcome will negate the striking elements that gave the franchise this provocative radical edge. If, as Aaron Bady has argued, *Game of Thrones*'s innovation to the genre was to suggest that "goodness" is a tragic flaw and nice guys are doomed to finish last, the expected reversal of this dynamic would return the franchise to Tolkien's teleological world-building, where the apocalypse is avoided through the restoration of authentic monarchic power. In Bady's words:

> If the King returns, and all is well that ends well, then we have returned to the narrative that [Martin] so devilishly skewered in the first three books. If we watched a nightmarish horror, in which good guys finish last, we'll wake up to discover that it was all a dream: actually, good guys finish first![69]

As a rejoinder to Bady's main argument, a politically desirable ending would stay true to the franchise's "winter is coming" mantra, and would see all of Westeros fall to the monstrous Others from beyond the Wall, after which—with any luck—"the peasants string up all the aristocrats and collectivize agriculture and establish a socialist utopia."[70] But of course we know this won't happen, and not because we have privileged access to Martin's closely guarded master plot. It remains one of the most blatant contradictions of popular culture that capitalism's ideological vacuum can only be represented within a larger storyworld whose final outcome refuses to challenge capitalism's triumphalist mythology. In other words, Empire's postideological spirit can find reflection in the makeup of its characters and in its superficial subversions and innovations. But in nearly every case, it remains constrained by bourgeois culture's insistence on narrative outcomes that leave commercial culture's logic of reassurance intact.

---

67. Benjamin Breen, "Why *Game of Thrones* Isn't Medieval—and Why That Matters," *Pacific Standard*, June 12, 2014, accessed June 3, 2015, http://www.psmag.com/books-and-culture/game-thrones-isnt-medieval-matters-83288.

68. Kriss, "*Game of Thrones* and the End of Marxist Theory."

69. Aaron Bady, "When *Game of Thrones* Stopped Being Necessary," *The New Inquiry*, June 15, 2015, accessed January 16, 2016, http://thenewinquiry.com/blogs/zunguzungu/when-game-of-thrones-stopped-being-necessary.

70. Bady, "When *Game of Thrones* Stopped Being Necessary."

In large part, this is because the *Game of Thrones* storyworld doesn't exist in isolation from its media-industrial context. The complex and ambiguous ways in which it generates meaning and value illustrate the contradictory workings of popular culture, politics, and genre fiction in the context of media convergence and participatory culture. In the following section, I will therefore conclude this chapter's discussion of *Game of Thrones* by examining more closely its position as a branded commodity, and its ambiguous relationship with fan culture and immaterial labor.

BRANDED STORYWORLDS AND THE CULTURAL LOGIC OF GENTRIFICATION

The elements of the *Game of Thrones* storyworld that set it apart from most preconceptions about popular fantasy are the very ones that connect it to HBO's framework of "Quality TV." Like the cable network's other influential drama series, from *The Sopranos* to *True Detective*, the television adaptation of Martin's storyworld is one of narrative complexity, moral ambiguity, high production values, cinematic aesthetics, and an explicitly "adult" sensibility.[71] The subscription-based network's famous slogan, "It's not TV, it's HBO," emphatically distances itself from the expectations and assumptions governing our perception of commercial television drama.[72] Where American television in the network era had been defined by its prescriptive emphasis on "Least Objectionable Programming," scripted drama in the age of media convergence thrives on its opposite—and *Game of Thrones* is in many ways an embodiment of "Most Objectionable Programming," notorious for its frequent scenes of simulated sex and (female) nudity, graphic violence, and profanity.[73]

As an HBO production, the *Game of Thrones* TV series predictably sets itself apart from previous fantasy shows on television, such as *The Storyteller* or *Xena: Warrior Princess*, which had contributed to the popular perception of fantasy as an "immature" genre. It does so by foregrounding and even exaggerating those aspects of the books that fit the network's established style and audience. Dean J. DeFino has defined this "HBO effect" as a style that has redefined the general understanding of quality television "by shaking up the conventions of genre, expanding the boundaries of content and form, and injecting an unprecedented

---

71. Jason Mittell, *Complex TV: The Poetics of Contemporary Television Storytelling* (New York: New York University Press, 2015), 17.

72. Robin Nelson, "Quality TV Drama: Estimations and Influences Through Time and Space," in *Quality TV: Contemporary American Television and Beyond*, ed. Janet McCabe and Kim Akass (London and New York: I. B. Tauris, 2007), 38–51.

73. Marc Leverette, "Cocksucker, Motherfucker, Tits," in *It's Not TV: Watching HBO in the Post-Television Era*, ed. Marc Leverette, Brian L. Ott, and Cara Louise Buckley (New York: Routledge, 2008), 123–51.

sense of fatalism into American television."[74] In *Game of Thrones*, DeFino also recognizes the now-familiar elements introduced in series such as *The Wire*, *Six Feet Under*, and *Deadwood*, which bestow upon "quality television" a degree of cultural capital that makes it attractive to the most highly valued audience with abundant disposable income.[75]

I have argued in the previous pages first that the *Game of Thrones* storyworld incorporates several key features of global capitalism, including its ambiguously postideological spirit. I have also shown how the franchise includes a politically productive tension between the nonexistence of global capitalism's big Other and the emergence of a monstrous, unrepresentable Real. But, at the same time, its storyworld circulates globally not just as a successful transmedia franchise but also as an entertainment brand that is a vital part of cognitive capitalism's powerful media industries. As interesting as the storyworld's political implications might be, we could at the same time argue that both HBO and *Game of Thrones* are encapsulated by what Sarah Banet-Weiser has described as a global "brand culture," in which cultural meanings are overdetermined by economic exchange.[76] The recurring paradox in the cultural logic of global capitalism then becomes that brands must find ways of presenting themselves as "authentic" in order to generate exchange value. In this contradictory context, "the authentic and commodity self are intertwined within brand culture," even to the extent that any assumed distinction between authenticity and branded commodities has come to evaporate.[77]

In the case of *Game of Thrones*, the construction of this crucial authenticity relied heavily on fans' immaterial labor and their willingness to contribute actively to the selling of an unfamiliar narrative franchise to a wider audience. As I have discussed in the previous chapter, the fan cultures that first emerged as transformative grassroots communities have by now increasingly come to function as "legitimizers" of transmedia franchises. For individual filmmakers and production companies, establishing forms of "geek credibility" has become a crucial ingredient in the introduction of a fantastic storyworld. Film studios and media conglomerates target fan conventions like Comic-Con with exclusive previews and celebrity appearances in order to draw in the audience members who have the strongest involvement with the storyworld. As former Marvel CEO Avi Arad said about the importance of these overt appeals to fan culture, "If you can make a good impression here, your movie has hope."[78]

74. Dean J. DeFino, *The HBO Effect* (New York and London: Bloomsbury, 2014), 129–30.

75. Jane Feuer, "HBO and the Concept of Quality TV," in *Quality TV: Contemporary American Television and Beyond*, ed. Janet McCabe and Kim Akass (London and New York: I. B. Tauris, 2007), 147.

76. Banet-Weiser, *Authentic™*, 7.

77. Banet-Weiser, *Authentic™*, 14.

78. Scott Bowles, "Comic-Con Illustrates Genre's Rising Influence," *USA Today*, July 25, 2004, accessed June 4, 2015, http://usatoday30.usatoday.com/life/movies/news/2004-07-25-comic-con-side _x.htm.

For this reason, fan conventions have become a vital platform for media corporations like Disney, Fox, and Time Warner subsidiary HBO. Even though genre fans who attend such conventions remain something of a niche group, they have become important media voices whose enthusiasm and approval bestow an essential seal of authenticity upon the franchise in question. In the context of a media landscape that has shifted from broadcasting to narrowcasting, commercial narrative franchises have been made to rely upon this form of legitimation for their "authentic" brand appeal. Marvel's ongoing series of superhero movies, TV series, comic books, and videogames, known collectively as the Marvel Cinematic Universe, is an excellent example of this process, as fans' collaborative efforts have been effectively mobilized to bring in a much larger audience.[79]

Game of Thrones is an even better example of this kind of strategic fan mobilization. When HBO set about publicizing its first outing into the fantasy genre, the company enlisted marketing agency Campfire to develop a campaign that focused specifically on fans, bloggers, and other "influencers" who could help spread the word and make the branded storyworld more visible. As a marketing company, Campfire specializes in creating a customized transmedia experience that, according to its website, "shapes perceptions and enhances brand preference through social storytelling, digital content, and physical experiences." Building on its founding members' earlier experience developing influential transmedia projects like *The Blair Witch Project*,[80] the campaign was designed to appeal especially to the relatively small fan base already familiar with the novels.

The marketing effort consisted of several cross-platform extensions of the *Game of Thrones* storyworld, organized around the concept of "Four Senses." These included a weather app for tablets and smartphones in which local weather reports are integrated into some of the main locations featured in the first season; a mobile game in which players win points by exploring storyworld settings and sharing their findings via social media; handcrafted wooden boxes containing specially created spices from Westeros; and food truck events where celebrity chef Tom Colicchio prepared snacks that reflect the storyworld's culture, handed out for free on the streets of New York City and Los Angeles. The apps and games were available as free downloads for mobile devices and designed to introduce the widest possible audience to the branded *Game of Thrones* storyworld. The latter two elements, on the other hand, were much more exclusive and created with the specific purpose of generating exposure by mobilizing fan labor. The spice boxes were sent to select bloggers and YouTube channels, many of whom recorded elaborate "unboxing" videos that found swift distribution via social media. The food trucks, while obviously also limited in their direct reach,

79. See Derek Johnson, "Cinematic Destiny: Marvel Studios and the Trade Stories of Industrial Convergence," *Cinema Journal* 52, no. 1 (2012): 1–24.

80. *The Blair Witch Project*, directed by Daniel Myrick and Eduardo Sánchez (1999; Santa Monica, CA: Artisan Home Entertainment, 1999), DVD.

contributed strongly to the series' growing buzz, as the events became "miniature fan conventions," where loyal readers were given the opportunity to "congregate and share their passion."[81] By supplying these easily sharable extensions of the *Game of Thrones* storyworld, Campfire therefore succeeded in mobilizing fans' immaterial labor as a crucial component in the franchise's first introduction to a wider audience.

Campfire's participatory marketing is based on a conceptual difference the company identifies between three segments of the audience: Skimmers, Dippers, and Divers. Creative director Steve Coulson assumes that the largest part of the audience is made up of Skimmers, who may become loyal viewers, players, or readers, but who won't invest abundant energy in exploring the storyworld in much depth. They make up what is also often described as a "mainstream" audience of more or less casual consumers for whom the experience typically begins and ends with viewing the product in question. Dippers are a smaller but still substantial audience segment, which may, for instance, purchase a series like *Game of Thrones* on Blu-ray or DVD in order to rewatch a season or view a behind-the-scenes documentary. Finally, the smallest but most highly engaged group is that of the Divers: the true fans who will typically devote enormous amounts of time and energy to a particular franchise or storyworld. Divers will plunge into a storyworld with the ambition of unlocking as many of its secrets as possible, typically using the fan community's collective intelligence to share, organize, and decode these puzzles.[82]

Where media producers and advertising companies traditionally focused their energy on appealing directly to the largest possible group (the Skimmers), contemporary marketing strategies like Campfire's start with the most devoted fans (the Divers) because, as Coulson points out, "Divers can be great evangelists." Relying entirely on audience members' willingness to participate actively in this marketing process, media producers have made fans' immaterial labor a crucial part of the expanding circles for this kind of marketing: "the Divers bring the Dippers down, the Dippers bring the Skimmers, and it becomes a self-propulsive loop." The commercial appeal of branded transmedia storyworlds like *Game of Thrones* therefore first requires a pivotal form of authentication by the much smaller group of devoted Divers. It is difficult indeed to imagine a more vivid illustration of Hardt and Negri's central concept of cognitive capitalism's biopolitical production of affective and immaterial labor.

At the same time, this process bestows upon the show a critical sense of discursive authenticity that aligns itself with what sociologist Sharon Zukin has described as the cultural logic of gentrification. In her book *Naked City*, she

---

81. Quotations in this section are cited from an interview conducted by the author with Campfire's creative director Steve Coulson on February 6, 2014. See Dan Hassler-Forest, "Skimmers, Dippers, and Divers: Campfire's Steve Coulson on Transmedia Marketing and Audience Participation," *Participations* 13, no. 1 (2016).

82. Henry Jenkins, *Convergence Culture: Where Old and New Media Collide* (New York: New York University Press, 2006), 17–18.

describes gentrification as a hegemonic cultural process in which a political and economic elite continuously seeks out both physical spaces and (sub)cultural practices that are specifically associated with a "gritty" sense of authenticity:

> Critics praised gritty novels, plays, and art for their honest aesthetic qualities, their ability to represent a specific space and time, and identified "gritty" with a direct experience of life in the way that we have come to expect of authenticity. . . . Today the use of "gritty" in the media depicts a desirable synergy between underground cultures and the creative energy they bring to both cultural consumption and real estate development.[83]

Game of Thrones's much-discussed "grittiness" and discursive authenticity offers an example of the cultural logic of gentrification, which I have described elsewhere as "the hegemonic appropriation and adaptation of subcultures and genres in ways that are experienced as 'gritty' and 'authentic.'"[84] In the case of *Game of Thrones*, this resides partly in the orchestration of fans' collaboration, as their participation proves (among other things) that the show is indeed perceived as "real" by fans with the authority to provide this kind of legitimization. It is also and perhaps even more visible in its uncompromising dedication to HBO's kind of "most objectionable programming" involving sex and violence. While distancing itself from popular perceptions of the fantasy genre, *Game of Thrones* offers value to those very "hipsters and gentrifiers" who continuously seek out novel but crucially "authentic" experiences,[85] and who of course also make up HBO's most desirable audience.

The show's tendency to court controversy therefore makes more sense once we perceive it from this perspective of gentrification and discursive authenticity, and the way it continuously distinguishes HBO's brand identity from "normal" network television. As the series has developed throughout its first five seasons, it has in fact adapted some of the most violent and controversial moments from the novels by making them even more intense than the already somewhat notorious source texts.[86] For instance, in the third-season episode[87] that adapts the Red

---

83. Sharon Zukin, *Naked City: The Death and Life of Authentic Urban Places* (Oxford: Oxford University Press, 2010), 53.

84. Dan Hassler-Forest, "*Game of Thrones*: The Politics of World-Building and the Cultural Logic of Gentrification," in *The Politics of Adaptation: Media Convergence and Ideology*, ed. Dan Hassler-Forest and Pascal Nicklas (Basingstoke: Palgrave Macmillan, 2015), 192.

85. Zukin, *Naked City*, 7.

86. In the fourth-season episode "Oathkeeper," *Game of Thrones*, Home Box Office (New York: HBO, April 27, 2014), the transformation of an already incestuous sex scene between Jaime and Cersei that was consensual in the book was dramatized as a rape scene in the series, an adaptive choice that follows the same logic but (for once) seemed to overreach in its attempt to be as "gritty" as possible: it resulted in a great deal of negative criticism, which at the same time, of course, brought more free publicity to the franchise as a form of "mature and edgy" fantasy.

87. "The Rains of Castermere," *Game of Thrones*, Home Box Office (New York: HBO, June 2, 2013).

Wedding sequence from the novel *A Storm of Swords*,[88] the mass murder that takes place onscreen involves not only the grisly deaths of popular main characters Robb and Catelyn Stark but also that of Robb's fiancée, whose pregnant belly is graphically stabbed several times before her throat is slit. Beyond making this scene intensely violent, showrunners and screenwriters David Benioff and D. B. Weiss adapted it for television in a way that made an already grisly sequence a great deal more graphic and controversial, resulting in a tremendous amount of desirable media attention that once again emphasized the show's "gritty" and "uncompromising" authenticity.

It also provided an exemplary showcase for the legitimizing powers of collaborative fandom within convergence culture. The episode of late night talk show *Conan* in the week following the Red Wedding episode's broadcast provides a vivid example of the organic way in which media conglomerates effortlessly incorporate fandom's affective and immaterial labor.[89] Author George R. R. Martin was a guest on the show, and after a few minutes of the usual general chitchat with host Conan O'Brien, he was shown a compilation of YouTube videos showing viewers reacting to the instantly notorious sequence. Fans who knew the books had secretly recorded video footage of "newbies" responding to the scene, resulting in a wide range of hugely entertaining emotional responses. Many such compilations had been making the rounds via social media, but the moment when the author was invited to respond on national television, spurred on by one of America's best-known talk show hosts, indicates both the extent and the range of this productive interaction between the media industry and participatory fan culture.[90]

Through such processes, the *Game of Thrones* storyworld is marked as part of a brand culture that results from the biopolitical collaboration between producers and fans eager to participate in ways that also increase the franchise's brand value. While the storyworld includes structural contradictions that resonate with the cultural logic of global capitalism, they are at the same time all too easily overshadowed by two separate processes that nevertheless reinforce each other: first, by the sustained foregrounding of neoliberalism's fantastical capitalism, with its precarious structure, its postideological politics, and its narrative emphasis on individuals engaged in unrelenting competition; and second, by the political economy that has inscribed the franchise with HBO's "authentic" brand and the cultural logic of gentrification.

The successful collaboration between the franchise's producers and marketers, on the one hand, and participatory audiences, on the other, offers a potent

---

88. George R. R. Martin, *A Storm of Swords*, chapter 51 ("Catelyn VII").

89. "The Man Whose Darkest Secret Is That He Kind of Likes the Wallflowers," *Conan*, Turner Broadcasting System (New York: TBS, June 6, 2013).

90. Beside the episode's 1.5 million viewers watching the live broadcast, the segment proved especially popular as a shared item via social media, drawing over four million hits on its YouTube page and many more via the official *Conan* website.

illustration of the deeply ingrained concept of affective and immaterial labor. It shows how canny marketing agencies working on behalf of media conglomerates now commonly employ strategies that have much in common with traditional grassroots movements, and which have absorbed fan culture's inherent focus on constructing affective and long-term relationships between audience and story-world. But in the age of Empire, this relationship revolves as much around brand identity as it does around the storyworld's contents, while the biggest fans have become valuable online "brand ambassadors."

"ALL OF THIS HAS HAPPENED BEFORE": REIMAGINING *BATTLESTAR GALACTICA'S* STORYWORLD

> The Cylons were created by man
> They rebelled
> They evolved
> They look and feel human
> Some are programmed to think they are human
> There are many copies
> And they have a plan

Memorably accompanied by the rhythmic repetition of a single piano note and some moody strings, these now-iconic lines opened the first episodes[91] of the reimagined version of sf series *Battlestar Galactica* (hereafter *BSG*). They effectively and concisely establish the basic structure of the series' storyworld while also emphasizing one of this new version's important differences from the short-lived 1978 series on which it was based. In the original *BSG*, the malevolent race of artificial beings called "Cylons" had been created by a now-extinct alien race, while the twenty-first-century reboot, which ran from 2004 to 2009, makes humanity responsible for creating its own enemy.

This crucial shift facilitates a whole range of transformations and adaptations that dissociate the reboot from the original series and the many preconceptions surrounding twentieth-century sf. The decision to foreground "realist" codes and styles made the reimagined *BSG* resonate strongly—and in ways that are remarkably similar to *Game of Thrones*—with its historical and material context of global capitalism, most notably by the way it foregrounds the destruction of a once-stable symbolic order. As in the previous section's analysis of *Game of Thrones*, my discussion of this transmedia storyworld will be focused on its postideological structure of feeling by examining more closely three central elements: first, its self-proclaimed "naturalism" and the way this ties into a larger context of capitalist realism; second, the ambivalent way in which the franchise

---

91. The lines were tweaked and adapted for later seasons as the narrative developed.

dramatizes daily life as existing under a permanent state of exception; and third, the storyworld's dialectical negotiation of religion.

As a transmedia world-building franchise, *BSG* is a complex multitext that requires a few words of necessary explanation. It first appeared in 1978 as a prime-time TV series on ABC, which was clearly hoping to connect to a wide audience after the blockbuster success of *Star Wars* in the previous year. It introduces a technologically advanced human society that inhabits the "Twelve Colonies of Kobol": an interplanetary group of human settlements living in peace and prosperity in a remote part of the galaxy. This society meets its end in the very first episode,[92] as the artificial race of Cylons nearly wipes out all of existing humanity in a massive sneak attack. Only a small group of human survivors is able to flee on board the famous "ragtag fleet" of spaceships, led and protected by a formidable military vessel, the eponymous "battlestar" *Galactica*. The original series subsequently followed the fleet's adventures across the galaxy in search of the legendary "Thirteenth Colony" named Earth, all the while pursued by the robotic Cylons.

While *BSG* was originally conceived as a series of three made-for-TV movies, the three-hour pilot was instead followed by a season's worth of one-hour episodes. But, as with *Star Trek* in the previous decade, budget overruns and declining ratings led to the series' early cancellation. A year after this first season ended, the network attempted to restart the franchise with *Battlestar 1980*, for which the decision to have the fleet of survivors arrive on contemporary Earth was a convenient cost-cutting measure. But this second attempt was poorly received and cancelled after only ten episodes. The series' storyworld was subsequently explored and expanded in comic books and novels, and the franchise was given wider exposure by the theatrical release of reedited footage from the pilot and other two-part episodes in Canada and Europe.

The *BSG* storyworld combines elements from Greek and Roman mythology with influences from the Book of Mormon and other aspects of Christian theology, building a sf franchise with its own recognizable iconography, technology, and belief system. While often described as cheesy and childish, the original series nevertheless accumulated its own fan culture over the years, and several unsuccessful attempts were made to revive the franchise with a new TV show or movie. Though nowhere near the size of *Star Trek* fandom, *BSG* remained for many genre fans a fondly remembered rarity, if only for the fact that it had brought an ambitious space opera with a complex storyworld and relatively high production values to American network television.

When it finally did resurface on the Sci-Fi (later renamed SyFy) Channel as a so-called backdoor pilot,[93] *BSG* proved to have aspirations far beyond the simple

---

92. "Saga of a Star World," *Battlestar Galactica*, American Broadcasting Company (New York: ABC, September 17, 1978).

93. It was produced as a three-hour miniseries that would be followed by a full season only if it generated sufficient ratings.

revival of a nostalgic sf brand. Showrunner Ronald D. Moore had started his television career as a writer and producer on the *Star Trek* series *TNG* and *Deep Space Nine*, and he wished to expand on his previous work by creating complex and socially relevant sf for television.[94] His franchise reboot ran as a remarkably successful television series from 2004 to 2009 on American basic cable, soon crossing over into other media in the form of interseason webisodes, comic books and novels, card games and videogames, three feature-length films made for cable television and home video,[95] and the prequel series *Caprica*. And while the TV show floundered in its last season, with declining ratings and a notoriously unpopular finale, *BSG* remains an imaginative, ambitious, and intensely beloved imaginary empire that many have come to see as marking "the beginning of a new era in pop culture."[96]

Such was Moore's ambition for the show that the pilot's script was accompanied by a manifesto titled "Naturalistic Science Fiction (or Taking the Opera out of Space Opera)." In this statement of intent, Moore explicitly sets out to dissociate the new *BSG* from traditional preconceptions about the sf genre. As with *Game of Thrones*, *BSG*'s showrunner and his production team wished to connect their entertainment franchise to the emerging meta-genre of Quality TV by foregrounding discursive realism, both in the visual representation of the storyworld and in the depiction of its characters:

> Our characters are living, breathing people with all the emotional complexity and contradictions present in quality dramas like *The West Wing* or *The Sopranos*. In this way, we hope to challenge our audience in ways that other genre pieces do not. We want the audience to connect with the characters of *Galactica* as people. Our characters are not super-heroes. They are not an elite. They are everyday people caught up in an enormous cataclysm and trying to survive it the best they can. They are you and me.[97]

The revived franchise's stated devotion to concepts of realism takes a direction different from the spectacular and immersive visuals of *LOTR*, on the one hand, and *Star Trek*'s squeaky-clean techno-futurism, on the other. While the visual

94. Quoted in Alan Sepinwall, *The Revolution Was Televised: The Cops, Crooks, Slingers and Slayers Who Changed TV Drama Forever* (self-published, 2012), 250.

95. *Battlestar Galactica: Razor*, directed by Félix Enríquez Alcalá (2007; Los Angeles: Universal Studios Home Entertainment, 2007), Blu-ray; *Battlestar Galactica: The Plan*, directed by Edward James Olmos (2009; Los Angeles: Universal Studios Home Entertainment, 2009), Blu-ray; *Battlestar Galactica: Blood & Chrome*, directed by Jonas Pate (2012; Los Angeles: Universal Studios Home Entertainment, 2012), Blu-ray.

96. Arthur Chu, "How *Battlestar Galactica*, *Game of Thrones*, and FanFiction Conquered Pop Culture," *The Daily Beast*, May 6, 2014, accessed June 11, 2015, http://www.thedailybeast.com/articles/2014/05/06/how-battlestar-galactica-game-of-thrones-and-fanfiction-conquered-pop-culture.html.

97. Ronald D. Moore, "Naturalistic Science Fiction (or Taking the Opera out of Space Opera)," *Battlestar Wiki*, accessed June 8, 2015. http://en.battlestarwiki.org/wiki/Naturalistic_science_fiction.

effects are expertly produced and occasionally do take center stage, *BSG* adopts a visual aesthetic of "gritty realism" throughout. It is the kind of aesthetic choice that is fundamentally ideological in the sense that it articulates capitalist realism's basic notion that solutions to society's problems can only be found "within the logic of existing profit-driven structures of production and consumption."[98] In order to achieve this visual style, the series' high-definition digital footage was filtered in postproduction to desaturate the colors and make the image less colorful and more grainy.[99] This resulted in an end product that resembles film shot on 16mm film, its "realism" heightened by the obtrusive use of handheld cameras and zoom lenses. Together, these elements coalesce into an overall style that is strongly associated with the visual realism of documentary and the cinéma vérité movement.[100]

BSG's "vérité-in-space" aesthetic meshes perfectly with the reboot's naturalistic approach to world-building. More specifically, it offers a twenty-first-century sensibility that is postideological in its cynical and wholly pragmatic perspective on politics and ideology. In lieu of the stable imperialist binaries of its own predecessor, the new *BSG* franchise offers instead radical ambiguity and constant negotiation. In Moore's effort to develop an imaginary world that features the aforementioned "emotional complexity and contradictions,"[101] the series' story-world is populated by a range of characters that are once again difficult to divide into a stable good/evil binary. An obvious example is the figure of Gaius Baltar, a character who had been featured in the original series as an irredeemable villain and traitor to mankind. But in the reboot, Baltar's accidental betrayal and strategic duplicitousness is presented not as a fully ontological evil but as ambivalent indications of his all-too-human fallibility. His decisions, many of which are guided by vanity and self-interest, often have disastrous consequences. But the writers go out of their way to make Baltar a relatable figure, whose constant doubts, misgivings, and self-recriminations are the source of interminable discussions and debates with an imaginary Cylon companion, thereby positioning the character as a "realistic" portrait of a complex human being.[102]

Baltar's depiction as a flexible, unpredictable, and deeply ambiguous character typifies *BSG*'s larger storyworld. Its focus on structural ambiguity and the

---

98. Nicole Aschoff, *The New Prophets of Capital* (London and New York: Verso, 2015), 11.

99. Kevin McNeilly, "'This Might Be Hard for You to Watch': Salvage Humanity in 'Final Cut,'" in *Cylons in America: Critical Studies in Battlestar Galactica*, ed. Tiffany Potter and C. W. Marshall (New York: Continuum, 2008), 186.

100. One specific way in which *BSG* conspicuously sought to emulate the visual language of cinéma vérité was through its noticeable use of handheld cameras and zoom lenses—even in computer-generated shots where the zoom lens is purely virtual.

101. Moore, "Naturalistic Science Fiction."

102. Lorna Jowett, "Mad, Bad, and Dangerous to Know? Negotiating Stereotypes of Science," *Cylons in America: Critical Studies of Battlestar Galactica*, ed. Tiffany Potter and C. W. Marshall (New York: Continuum, 2008), 71.

constant deterritorialization of familiar terrain clearly expresses the basic spirit of global capitalism, where every decision is provisional, and where universalizing assumptions and belief systems have been delegitimized. Its fluid and thoroughly unpredictable storyworld therefore forces individuals into neoliberalism's precarious and flexible paradigm of competitive individualism. Kevin J. Wetmore Jr. identifies a crucial change in the transformation from the 1978 *BSG* to its twenty-first-century reboot: whereas the original storyworld allowed for plentiful moments of authentic play (or what Johan Huizinga would call *ludi*), the reimagined *BSG* features only serious forms of competition (*agon*).[103] For while the clear boundaries of Cold War–era imperialism and the security of the welfare state allowed for a more relaxed attitude to one's environment, the deterritorialized world of precarious neoliberalism offers no guarantees whatsoever. Gaius Baltar's constantly shifting role illustrates this fluid sense of precarious identity, as we see him transform with remarkable ease from celebrity scientist to politician to religious leader. And this logic applies to the larger structure of the storyworld as well, which was at its best (and certainly at its most popular) when it seemed most completely dedicated to a process of constant radical reinvention.

*BSG'*S PERMANENT STATE OF EXCEPTION

The general absence of stable structures, identities, or boundaries in *BSG*'s storyworld clearly aligns itself with the dominant framework of fantastical capitalism, in which political alternatives are categorically dismissed as "unrealistic." This is strengthened by the complex serialized narrative's resistance to its own genre traditions, constantly pushing back against the stable, imperialist coordinates of *Star Trek*'s episodic format. But another important way in which *BSG* expresses the tension of fantastical capitalism lies in the reboot's intensified precariousness, where the storyworld's defining characteristic is its productive liminality. As the storyworld is grounded in the notion of an ongoing crisis following a 9/11-like attack, the "in-betweenness" of the fleet's uncertain odyssey focuses our attention on the social, political, and economic structures of global capitalism's permanent state of exception.

The term *state of exception* as global capitalism's new political paradigm is most substantially explored in the work of Giorgio Agamben, who describes it as a modern form of imperial totalitarianism: "The voluntary creation of a permanent state of emergency (though perhaps not declared in the technical sense) has become one of the essential practices of contemporary states, including so-called democratic ones."[104] Neoliberalism's ethos of competitive individualism

---

103. Kevin J. Wetmore Jr., "Pyramid, Boxing, and Sex," *Cylons in America: Critical Studies in Battlestar Galactica*, ed. Tiffany Potter and C. W. Marshall (New York: Continuum, 2008), 77–78.

104. Giorgio Agamben, *State of Exception* (Chicago: University of Chicago Press, 2005), 2.

not only benefits from but also positively hinges on this destabilization of social and economic order, providing endless opportunities for businesses to profit from catastrophe and conflict.[105] Empire's military, political, and economic state of exception has yielded years of destructive austerity policies, and it is also reflected in cultural texts that negotiate this framework of universal precariousness. Increasingly, the fantastic storyworlds that proliferate across Western popular culture embrace this ongoing state of exception, grounded like global capitalism itself in its "permanent structure of juridico-political de-localization and dis-location."[106]

BSG has been rightfully celebrated for its dialogic approach to fantastic world-building, "informed by questions, debate, and analysis, representing the world not merely as it is, or as it should be."[107] And if we approach it as a pop-cultural play on post-9/11 American sociocultural debates, the franchise certainly did much to reestablish sf as a genre with an urgent and quite obvious sense of direct cultural relevance. But interrogating the *BSG* storyworld as an attempt to construct an imaginary representation of a postcapitalist culture and society brings up different kinds of questions. From this perspective, its structural ambivalence, in which every point of view is dialogically countered by its opposite, also tends to yield the kind of balance that "conflates and substitutes 'neutrality' for 'objectivity'"[108]: in other words, it offers compromise in response to every radical challenge to capitalism's default options.

This is articulated most vividly by the storyworld's apocalyptic imaginary, which also looms so strongly over *Game of Thrones*, and which sets *BSG*'s endless series of transformations and reversals in motion. The first episode establishes this apocalyptic motif even in its opening scene, in which the spectacular destruction of a lonely human outpost foreshadows the larger attack on all of existing humanity. Throughout the two-part miniseries, the doomed planet of Caprica is coded as a close approximation of our own global order of advanced capitalism. Caprica's instantly familiar, only slightly futuristic society represents the evaporating stability of imperialism's older world, strongly resembling *Star Trek*'s peaceful ideal of technologically advanced and ethnically diverse futurity. But although there are no visible signs of poverty or class conflict in

---

105. See Anthony Loewenstein, *Disaster Capitalism: Making a Killing Out of Catastrophe* (London and New York: Verso, 2015).

106. Giorgio Agamben, *Homo Sacer: Sovereign Power and Bare Life* (Palo Alto: Stanford University Press, 1998), 28.

107. C. W. Marshall and Tiffany Potter, "'I See the Patterns': *Battlestar Galactica* and the Things That Matter," in *Cylons in America: Critical Studies of Battlestar Galactica*, ed. Tiffany Potter and C. W. Marshall (New York: Continuum, 2008), 6.

108. Chris Dzialo, "When Balance Goes Bad: How *Battlestar Galactica* Says Everything and Nothing," in *Cylons in America: Critical Studies of Battlestar Galactica*, ed. Tiffany Potter and C. W. Marshall (New York: Continuum, 2008), 171–72.

the glimpses we get of Caprica before its destruction,[109] it isn't a postcapitalist world in the way that *Star Trek* explicitly embodies. As we discover during the storyworld's later development, *BSG* is primarily preoccupied with mapping out the cultural, religious, military, political, and social conflicts that develop both among the human survivors during their precarious odyssey and within Cylon society, which develops its own dynamic in the reboot from the end of the second season onward.[110]

Just as *Game of Thrones* is in many ways a storyworld that refashions Tolkienian fantasy for the age of global capitalism, the *BSG* reboot thereby updates the bounded and compartmentalized Cold War context of earlier sf series for a post-9/11 world. Like *Game of Thrones*, its storyworld is marked by its post-ideological structure of feeling: just as the first-season execution of Ned Stark functions as the destruction of a once-reliable symbolic order, the stability associated with the "big Other" in *BSG* is undermined by the genocidal attack that sets the plot in motion.[111] And whereas the Cylon attack in the original series established a clear-cut conflict between good and evil without inflicting noticeable trauma on the survivors, the new *BSG* constantly interrogates its own basic structure—ultimately even to the point of incoherence. But whereas *Game of Thrones* provides a storyworld that exists under the constant (though largely unrecognized) threat of apocalypse, *BSG*'s *post*apocalyptic quest opens up the possibility for a truly different world. And where characters that stand for clear ideological positions are systematically removed from Martin's storyworld, *BSG* desperately clings to the notion of a utopian imaginary even from within its own postideological framework.

Examples of the storyworld's provisional and precarious structure are legion, from the ongoing tension between competing forms of dictatorship[112] to the finale's uncomfortable compromise between religious prophecy and the storyworld's immanent and precarious structure of feeling. But as a more detailed example, the

---

109. The series' preapocalyptic storyworld is explored in more detail in the prequel series *Caprica*, which weds *BSG*'s generic futurism with a film noir–inspired aesthetic sensibility. But although this later series revolves thematically about the development of a mechanical race of slaves, it stubbornly avoids addressing questions of class conflict.

110. The political, ideological, and religious tensions among the Cylons are first explicitly introduced in "Downloaded," *Battlestar Galactica* (Sci-Fi Channel, February 24, 2006).

111. Similarly, the relative stability of the original series, presided over by the immutably patriarchal power of the first Commander Adama, stands in stark contrast with the unpredictable chaos aboard the *Galactica* in the second series, where the later Adama must constantly struggle to maintain his authority.

112. *BSG* fruitfully explores multiple forms of political process, including the implications of living under martial law's explicit state of exception, the role of the media and populist demagogues in a liberal democracy, and the Cylons' literal embodiment of collective intelligence. The most recurrent tension, however, occurs between the benevolent military rule of Commander Adama and the political leadership of President Roslin. Both characters are portrayed sympathetically, but they also constantly make decisions that compromise their respective moral and ethical positions.

micro-conflict in the episode "Black Market"[113] is especially appropriate to this context, as it is one of the rare occasions in which the storyworld engages directly with issues of labor and class identity outside of its central group of characters. Like the *TNG* episodes discussed in the previous chapter, it is also one of the episodes that contributes most conspicuously to the series' world-building, as it is not directed toward developing the main narrative, instead exploring some of the storyworld's less visible areas. While most narratives in the *BSG* storyworld feature the storyworld's central cast of military and political leaders involved in exciting crisis management, "Black Market" demonstrates how the fleet's population will automatically and unavoidably fall back on capitalist practices.

In the episode, the dashing, idealistic young pilot Apollo discovers the existence of a black market ruled by criminals who traffic in illegal goods and services including drugs, medicine, sex work, and child slavery. While Apollo is tasked by President Roslin to put a stop to illegal trade, he becomes convinced that a criminal economy like this is in fact inevitable, and he ultimately manages to persuade the president to allow it to continue on the condition that its worst excesses are curbed. The episode's plot therefore presents the ship's market economy as something unavoidable: criminal and exploitative markets will arise within communities as "a clear inevitability, an arrangement that human society produces simply as a matter of course."[114] Apollo and Roslin's resignation to a compromise that rejects more radical alternatives as "unrealistic" demonstrates the storyworld's basic inability to imagine social relations outside of capitalism's pure market economy.

This position is confirmed by a later episode similarly preoccupied with exploring the storyworld in more detail without advancing the series' main narrative: "Dirty Hands"[115] revolves around a labor dispute, as workers on board the fleet's refinery ship sabotage the production process in order to negotiate for better working conditions. As in "Black Market," a main character in this episode unexpectedly discovers the existence of exploitation and inequality, and then attempts to convince the political and military leadership of the legitimacy of workers' claims. In this case, the conflict focuses on the workers' right to strike, which is denied them by the military and judicial powers because of the storyworld's permanent state of exception. And again, a "balanced" compromise ultimately breaks the stalemate, as the laborers remain prohibited from going on strike, but class mobility is improved by the introduction of a rotation system for high-risk production facilities. And while strikes remain illegal for as long as this ongoing crisis endures, the president at the same time supports and—bizarrely—even

113. "Black Market," *Battlestar Galactica* (Sci-Fi Channel, January 27, 2006).

114. Carl Silvio and Elizabeth Johnston, "Alienation and the Limits of the Utopian Impulse," in *Cylons in America: Critical Studies of Battlestar Galactica*, ed. Tiffany Potter and C. W. Marshall (New York: Continuum, 2008), 43.

115. "Dirty Hands," *Battlestar Galactica* (Sci-Fi Channel, February 25, 2007).

encourages the workers' unionizing. It is one of the many contradictory examples in *BSG* of how the storyworld introduces questions of class conflict and inequality, only to resolve these tensions by having sympathetic leaders offer a compromise solution legitimized by exceptional circumstances.

In this way, real-world social and political issues raised in *BGS*'s storyworld are dealt with on the basis of a state of exception that has become permanent and generalized, just as under Empire's sovereignty in the real world, where "the exception has become the rule, pervading both foreign relations and the homeland."[116] While *BSG* isn't as obviously reactionary in its politics as a TV series such as *24*, the notoriously conservative pop-cultural embodiment of neoliberalism's cultural and political logic,[117] it similarly projects a narrative environment in which all of life is confined to what Hardt and Negri describe as a "general omni-crisis, when the state of war and thus the state of exception become indefinite or even permanent, as they do today."[118] In this sense, *BSG* literalizes the notion that permanent imperial war ultimately becomes a form of biopower in the positive, productive sense: the storyworld's precariously organized "ragtag fleet" provides not only a pleasurable fantasy of high-stakes excitement and adventure but also the utopian possibility of "a large-scale, cooperative, and fully technologized society independent of the alienation created by the wage system."[119] This creates a contradiction that should be instantly familiar to anyone who has reflected on the weird logic of global capitalism: the very system that offers the promise of real change is simultaneously held back by the palpable ideological constraints of capitalist realism.

"SO SAY WE ALL": RELIGION AND IDEOLOGY

One of the most remarkable similarities between *BSG* and *Game of Thrones* is the prominence of religious conflict in both storyworlds—especially because both franchises articulate a near-identical tension between an institutionalized polytheism coded as Western, and a more recent monotheism that is introduced as a threat to normative culture. In both cases, the newer monotheistic religion is associated with excessive devotion and violent fundamentalism, while the older, more secularized polytheism has a social function that is largely ritualistic. But in *BSG*'s storyworld, the older religion's empty but comforting ritual becomes suddenly relevant in the context of an exceptional crisis: at the end of the miniseries, Commander Adama's speech rallies the survivors through the shared repetition

---

116. Hardt and Negri, *Multitude*, 7.

117. Dennis Broe, "Fox and Its Friends: Global Commodification and the New Cold War," *Cinema Journal* 43, no. 4 (2004): 97–102.

118. Hardt and Negri, *Multitude*, 8.

119. Silvio and Johnston, "Alienation and the Limits of the Utopian Impulse," 42.

of the religious mantra "so say we all," which transforms within the scene from hollow phrase to an urgent shared expression of a common cause.[120] Thus, the ingrained knowledge of a cultural code becomes meaningful not necessarily because it ignites religious fervor, but rather because it explicitly reestablishes a sense of continuity and solidarity among the surviving community.

In this way, *BSG*'s use of institutionalized religion differs from the Faith of the Seven that is similarly organized in the *Game of Thrones* storyworld. While both organized religions are enmeshed in structures of government and control, *BSG* foregrounds a range of religious positions, thus offering its audience "a rich tapestry in which degrees of faith and differing doctrinal positions are treated sympathetically and sincerely."[121] The storyworld's inclusive and diverse representation of organized religion is far removed from *Game of Thrones*'s cynical perspective on matters of faith: as I observed earlier in this chapter, the main religious systems in Westeros are presented as opportunistic power hierarchies (the Faith of the Seven), threatening and seemingly malevolent fundamentalist practices (the Lord of Light, the Sparrows), or dwindling relics of ancient traditions (the Old Gods). The most sympathetic characters are meanwhile presented as fully postmodern subjects who are inherently skeptical about all forms of religious belief.

While the more fundamentalist sects within *BSG*'s dominant faith are often similarly demonized, the franchise proceeds to negotiate its own partly inherited, partly improvised mythology in sometimes bizarre but always sincere ways. This is very different from the juxtaposition of competing religions in *Game of Thrones*, where it primarily expresses what Žižek has so often described as "the postmodern disdain for ideological Causes."[122] While religious converts in Martin's storyworld are all too often revealed as power-hungry opportunists (Stannis Baratheon) or gullible zealots (Matthos Seaworth or Lancel Lannister), even Gaius Baltar's transformation into a religious leader is presented in *BSG* with a sincerity that many viewers found off-putting.

The *BSG* storyworld therefore ends up enmeshed in a fascinating ideological contradiction: on the one hand, the franchise's self-proclaimed "naturalism" and ongoing references to current affairs position its storyworld as postideological and therefore in alignment with what I have called fantastical capitalism; on the other hand, its use of prophetic visions as central plot devices and its sincere handling of religious convictions created a tension between sf's traditional cognitive focus and the storyworld's more mystical elements. This contradiction results from the writers' ambition to push beyond the confines of capitalist realism

---

120. "Part II," *Battlestar Galactica* (Sci-Fi Channel, December 9, 2003).

121. C. W. Marshall and Matthew Wheeland, "The Cylons, the Singularity, and God," in *Cylons in America: Critical Studies in Battlestar Galactica*, ed. Tiffany Potter and C. W. Marshall (New York: Continuum, 2008), 101.

122. Slavoj Žižek, *Welcome to the Desert of the Real* (London and New York: Verso, 2002), 85.

and allow for "a tremendous sense of hope,"[123] even as attempts to construct real alternatives are repeatedly frustrated. As the final seasons of the TV series attempted to work toward definitive narrative closure in an increasingly muddled storyworld, this tension between its precarious realism and Moore's ambition to align *BSG*'s utopian aspirations with its patchwork mythology culminated in the notorious final episode.[124]

In the finale, the Cylon civilization, by now locked into a full-fledged civil war, is divided between those who follow what they perceive to be "God's plan" and side with the humans, and those who have turned their backs on religion and are subsequently destroyed in the final battle. The ending thus conclusively resolves the series' long-running conflict with the Cylons, as a spectacular space battle separates the "good" from the "bad," and the true believers on both sides see their prophetic visions fulfilled. The survivors then hand over the remainder of the fleet to the Cylons' newly sentient robot Centurions, as all remaining humans and "good" humanoid Cylons settle on the newly discovered planet Earth.

But in order to make the alien tribes' arrival on Earth even somewhat plausible while also avoiding comparisons with the universally derided *Battlestar 1980*, the *Galactica*'s arrival on Earth occurs in humanity's prehistory: Adama, Roslin, and their followers encounter a virginal planet, thinly populated by scattered tribes of early humans. But instead of colonizing this prehistoric Earth and attempting to re-create it as another "New Caprica,"[125] they decide to "break the cycle" by abandoning their technology and blending in with the existing inhabitants. The surviving Cylons and humans each go their separate ways, and the human-Cylon child Hera, whose existence had been prophesied as crucial to the fate of both races, explicitly embodies a eugenic solution to the storyworld's most basic conflict: the series finale thus offers "a happily-ever-after based on breeding difference out of humanity by breeding in hybridity, an oxymoronic offer of simultaneous inclusion and erasure."[126]

Impossible as it is to make real sense of an ending that has enraged innumerable fans in its desire to bring closure to *BSG*'s sprawling storyworld, there is at least one striking contradiction that is worth pointing out: the mantra "all of this has happened before, and all of this will happen again"[127] is repeated many times from the first season onward, implying a cyclical history in which similar patterns

---

123. Jim Casey, "'All This Has Happened Before': Repetition, Reimagination, and Eternal Return," in *Cylons in America: Critical Studies in Battlestar Galactica*, ed. Tiffany Potter and C. W. Marshall (New York: Continuum, 2008), 249.

124. "Daybreak (Parts 2 & 3)," *Battlestar Galactica* (Sci-Fi Channel, March 20, 2009).

125. An earlier attempt to colonize a habitable planet as "New Caprica" yielded disastrous results, as depicted in the finale of season 2, the first three episodes of season 3, and the webisodes that filled the narrative gap between them.

126. Anne Kustritz, "Breeding Unity: *Battlestar Galactica*'s Biracial Reproductive Futurity," *Camera Obscura* 27, no. 3 (2012): 9.

127. Paraphrased from the opening of Walt Disney's *Peter Pan* (1953).

will recur indefinitely.[128] And at first glance, the fleet's decision to "break the cycle" by resisting the temptation to re-create their old society on Earth has an admirably anticolonial resonance. But, at the same time, it also traps itself in an antimodern dead end that exacerbates the franchise's recurrent technophobic elements. In its attempt to end the *BSG* narrative on a truly utopian note, it ends up taking the concept of the reboot all too literally. As Jameson is fond of pointing out, "Capitalism is at one and the same time the best thing that has ever happened to the human race, and the worst."[129] While *BSG* at times seemed eager to meet the challenge of imagining a world that is able to move *beyond* capitalism, it ends up withdrawing entirely into the contradictory fantasy of a premodern but genetically engineered "purity." And as the final episode's baffling coda clearly suggests,[130] the ending hereby simply reiterates the inevitability of Earth's own inescapable future of global capitalism.

INTERPASSIVITY AND *BSG* FANDOM

The finale's combination of technophobia and religious sincerity baffled and disappointed many fans, including famously vocal *BSG* enthusiast George R. R. Martin, who commented on his blog that "a deus ex machina is a crappy way to end a story." But perhaps even more jarring was the way in which showrunner Ronald D. Moore and his team had decided to end the series in a way that hermetically seals off the storyworld from further exploration. Creative fan culture is fueled to a large extent by the shared desire to expand and embellish any given imaginary universe. After the original *Star Wars* trilogy, for instance, the combination of bottom-up fan fiction and top-down transmedia franchising resulted in the development of the Expanded Universe, a complex and more or less coherent narrative environment that follows major and minor movie characters, develops complex family genealogies that move backward and forward in time, and expands substantially on the events from the films. This enormous amount of creative labor was made possible by the ending of the *Star Wars* films' narratives, which offered not only a firmly established storyworld but also strong potential for the endlessly deferred narrative that is so vital to the cult text.[131]

By supplying a finale that definitively foreclosed any further adventures of the *Galactica* and its crew, Moore and his cowriters established a story canon

---

128. Casey, "'All This Has Happened Before,'" 242–44.

129. Fredric Jameson, *Postmodernism, or, The Cultural Logic of Late Capitalism* (Durham: Duke University Press, 1991), 47.

130. In this bizarre final sequence, we see Gaius Baltar and his Cylon companion (who may or may not be imaginary) walking around twenty-first-century New York City, speculating about whether modern-day humanity will repeat its earlier mistakes.

131. Matt Hills, *Fan Cultures* (London: Routledge, 2000), 143.

that allowed for precious few fruitful options in terms of expansion or embellishment. One might even see this somewhat radical ending as typical for a larger strategy of fan containment that had emerged throughout the reboot series' run. The *BSG* franchise had been resurrected in the context of media convergence and participatory culture, where social, cultural, and technological transformations had reshaped the interaction between producers and consumers of media texts. While fan communities were among the most loyal consumers of such franchises, digitization and convergence culture also introduced new tensions between media corporations and fan communities concerning copyright and questions of intellectual authorship.[132] And while older forms of fan culture tended to operate at a leisurely pace,[133] the digital age saw the introduction of what Matt Hills has called "just-in-time fandom": a form of fan culture organized around broadcast schedules and therefore controlled by the pace with which producers make new installments and other materials available.[134]

In the case of *BSG*, fans wishing to stay abreast of the developing storyworld and its background faced a new kind of challenge. Embracing to the fullest his dual role as a fan and media author, showrunner Moore supervised a formidable onslaught of materials to keep the growing horde of "just-in-time fans" occupied with fannish but fully authorized additions to the TV series. Building on Henry Jenkins's distinction between "prohibitionist" and "collaborationist" corporate approaches,[135] Suzanne Scott has argued that the overwhelming amount of fan-oriented authorized material has—in appropriate *BSG* parlance—"frakked" fan production.[136] The avalanche of authorized podcasts, video blogs, downloadable audio commentaries, deleted scenes, webisodes, interviews, and other materials shifted fans' focus by necessity from production to consumption. The celebrated DIY ethic of fan communities thereby moves, as Scott pithily observes, from "Do-It-Yourself" to "Download-It-Yourself," as "these authorized supplements come at the expense of letting fans explore those narrative fissures through their own textual production."[137]

If the incorporation of fan labor into the promotion of the *LOTR* films first signaled the media industries' growing collaborationist approach, *BSG*'s appeal to fan sensibilities represents a further step in this redefined relationship between fan communities and media producers. Accessing free promotional content and

---

132. Mirko Tobias Schäfer, *Bastard Culture!* (Amsterdam: Amsterdam University Press, 2011), 12.

133. Henry Jenkins, *Fans, Bloggers, and Gamers* (New York: New York University Press, 2006), 141.

134. Hills, *Fan Cultures*, 78–79.

135. Jenkins, *Convergence Culture*, 138.

136. Suzanne Scott, "Authorized Resistance: Is Fan Production Frakked?" in *Cylons in America: Critical Studies in Battlestar Galactica*, ed. Tiffany Potter and C. W. Marshall (New York: Continuum, 2008), 210–11.

137. Scott, "Authorized Resistance," 211.

purchasing transmedia products that explore the *BSG* storyworld in authentically fannish ways plugs fan culture's gift economy and creative subversion back into the circuits of consumerism and commodity circulation. And while *BSG* was one of the first popular storyworlds to explore this strategy of readymade fan fiction, the practice has by now grown explosively. Fans of *The Walking Dead* can spend an hour directly following each episode watching fans geek out about the episode they've just watched with actors, writers, and other crew members on the weekly talk show *The Talking Dead*. Corporate-owned blogs now offer instant recaps and elaborate discussions of new films and TV episodes to attract just-in-time fans, and programs like *The Nerdist* further illustrate the growing ubiquity of authentic fan culture produced and distributed as a commodity for profit.

This incorporation of fan communities' cultural practices exemplifies Robert Pfaller's ingenious notion of *interpassivity*. Building on Žižek's observational remarks about canned laughter in American sitcoms,[138] Pfaller developed his theoretical concept as a way of understanding art spectatorship in the postideological age of global capitalism. Whereas the widely used term *interactivity* presupposes an active audience participating directly in the production of meaning, "interpassivity" offers what Pfaller calls "delegated enjoyment."[139] Just as the audience's taped laughter in a sitcom relieves us of our own duty to laugh, the deluge of consumable *BSG*-related materials relieves fans of the necessity to contribute creatively. And since these materials are doubly legitimized—first by Moore's emphatic author function,[140] and second by his acknowledged standing as an authentic self-identified fan[141]—it quite obviously helps alleviate corporations' anxieties about intellectual ownership and transformative fan appropriation.

As with so many other recent fantastic franchises, the industrial production of material targeted directly at fans encourages this kind of interpassivity. With such a wealth of material constantly available, and with so many media franchises that now cater to fannish sensibilities, the balance within fandom is easily shifted from creative and transformative production to continuous consumption. What is more: this actual interpassivity all too often takes seemingly participatory forms, as we engage with this material by sharing, liking, and commenting on it via commercial social media platforms. A form of immaterial labor that revolved around the creative and collaborative expansion of imaginary worlds is thus refocused on the continuous circulation of authorized promotional materials and the collaborative legitimization of an increasingly powerful media industry's intellectual property.

---

138. Žižek, *The Sublime Object of Ideology*, 35.

139. Robert Pfaller, *On the Pleasure Principle in Culture: Illusions without Owners* (London and New York: Verso, 2014), 18.

140. Michel Foucault, "What Is an Author?" in *The Norton Anthology of Theory and Criticism*, 2nd ed., ed. Vincent B. Leitch et al. (New York: Norton and Co., 2010), 1475–90.

141. Suzanne Scott, "*Battlestar Galactica*: Fans and Ancillary Content," in *How to Watch Television*, ed. Ethan Thompson and Jason Mittell (New York: New York University Press, 2013), 323.

CONCLUSION

In this chapter, I have approached *Game of Thrones* and *BSG* as twenty-first-century responses to the world-building practices established by Tolkien and *Star Trek*. While these older paradigms of fantasy and sf negotiated the tension between industrial capitalism's imperialist framework and the emerging cultural logic of global capitalism, *Game of Thrones* and *BSG* are both obvious examples of Empire's postideological spirit: through embracing an atmosphere and aesthetic of gritty realism and ruthless competition, both resonate strongly with global capitalism's decentered, unstable, and thoroughly precarious organization. They show us storyworlds in which the most popular and enduring characters aren't necessarily the ones that are traditionally heroic: they are above all *flexible* and *adaptable*.

Of course, this is only postideological in the sense that they reject all traditional forms of symbolic order. But what they teach us about politics is at the same time purely ideological: by constructing fantastic storyworlds that actively dissociate themselves from the "quaintness" and ethical clarity of their predecessors, they have gained relevance, popularity, and enormous economic and cultural value. *Game of Thrones* has been especially successful at constructing a sense of quality, urgency, and authenticity that I have related in this chapter to the cultural logic of gentrification and now-ubiquitous brand culture. By absorbing the prestige of edgy, adult-oriented "Quality TV" while at the same time appropriating fandom's immaterial labor, the franchise has developed into a cultural phenomenon that knows few equals. And while the storyworld will clearly not sustain fantastical capitalism's bleak, hollow worldview indefinitely, this is precisely what has made its style and characters resonate so strongly among twenty-first-century audiences.

BSG similarly embraces a style and ethic of capitalist realism, developing a re-imagined version of its storyworld in which the earlier distinction between good and evil is increasingly muddied. But while *BSG*'s overall storyworld remains as precarious as that of *Game of Thrones*, its representation of religion performs a crucially different function. Whereas Empire's competitive individualism consistently rejects the notion of a shared belief in a single symbolic order, *BSG*'s world-building awkwardly tries to reconcile this with a sincere attempt to create a meaningful collective. And while the franchise never found a satisfying way to resolve the tension between capitalist realism and what remains of a utopian impulse, its storyworld and fandom long thrived on this contradiction.

Since both these franchises critique their own genre conventions while at the same time finding new and spectacular forms for them, they illustrate the contradictory political logic of fantastical capitalism: "What seems most utopian about them is the idea that we might reject the generic corpus of which they are a part, disidentify, and simply walk away—and what is most anti-utopian about the texts is the seductive appeal of these works *even in the moment of their own self-denunciation.*"[142] But these two storyworlds didn't just offer influential updates to two of fantastic fiction's most important paradigms. Their effective incorporation of fandom's immaterial labor also illustrates a crucial cultural transition. As the transmedia campaign surrounding the *Game of Thrones* TV series has illustrated, the most devoted fans (the Divers) remain a niche audience. But in the context of participatory culture and media convergence, this relatively small group can offer immense value to media producers as brand ambassadors whose collaborative labor can bring in the much larger groups of Dippers and Skimmers. At the same time, such activity can hardly be classified as creative or subversive, let alone transformative. I have suggested that we qualify this type of collaborationist and consumer-friendly approach as a form of interpassivity: a form that offers the illusion of participation while remaining firmly grounded in the processes of cognitive capitalism's immaterial labor and capital accumulation.

---

142. Gerry Canavan, "You Think You Know the Story: Novelty, Repetition, and Lovecraft in Whedon and Goddard's *The Cabin in the Woods*," in *The Politics of Adaptation: Media Convergence and Ideology*, ed. Dan Hassler-Forest and Pascal Nicklas (Basingstoke: Palgrave Macmillan, 2015), 207.

4

Revolutionary Storyworlds
and Postdemocratic Capitalism

There's a practical joke I once saw described on Facebook that I've always been tempted to try. The idea is simple: You go to your nearest Starbucks coffee shop, you stand in line for an overpriced cup of mediocre coffee, and when the disconcertingly cheerful service worker asks you for your name, you say, "Spartacus." Assuming that this overworked and in all likelihood underpaid employee gets the name right when writing it on the paper cup destined to hold your grande latte, the barista working the other end of the production line will at some point call out the name they see inscribed: "Spartacus? Spartacus?!" The joke, then, is that as you answer—as loudly and clearly as possible—"I'm Spartacus!" other customers will instantly recognize the reference to the iconic film scene and start stepping forward and answering the call. In my admittedly overactive imagination, the execution of this silly prank would result in a moment of delightful pandemonium, as the quiet coffee shop is suddenly filled with voices echoing, "I'm Spartacus!" and resounding with completely spontaneous laughter.

Of course, a gag like this would never work, unless the coffee shop in question happens to be populated entirely by middle-aged cinephiles with a passion for cheesy swords-and-sandals epics.[1] But the fantasy is such a pleasurable one because it imagines a momentary respite from the artificial friendliness of consumerism's service industry: instead of the rigorously scripted smiles and passive-aggressive

---

1. The joke has been performed with hidden cameras by New York comedy troupe Improv Everywhere, but not as an attempt to elicit a spontaneous response: a group of actors was present among the customers, and they were the only ones to answer the call, culminating in the entrance of one final actor dressed up in a gladiator's costume. Tellingly, while the staff and the customers clearly appreciated the brief interruption, none of them actually participated in the gag. "'I Am Spartacus!' Starbucks Prank—Movies in Real Life (Ep 9)," YouTube video, 1:43, posted by Improv Everywhere, November 26, 2013, https://www.youtube.com/watch?v=5_pKKO35Kh4.

consumer friendliness, even the most trivial interruption of this dreary routine would be experienced as a huge relief. But besides its inherent silliness, the practical joke appeals to me not only because it draws on a shared knowledge of popular culture but also because it gains resonance from the specifics of the reference. The Spartacus narrative represents one of the most resilient popular myths of emergent communism, and this scene in particular enacts the kind of spontaneous solidarity and collectivity—albeit a quite obviously gendered one—that is central to resisting capitalism's relentless individualism. As someone who also sees in popular culture a common language that can stimulate the imagination and even inspire collective social and political action, the "Spartacus Starbucks" gag brings together in seemingly frivolous miniature the dream of spontaneous solidarity and the playful exercise of transformative fandom.[2]

It is also a joke that resonates with the tentative blossoming of revolutionary dreams, both in fantastic storyworlds and on the streets. As other critics and scholars have pointed out,[3] a remarkable number of recent sf and fantasy texts have offered allegorical reflections of movements like Occupy Wall Street, the Arab Spring, and Black Lives Matter. What is striking about films like *Snowpiercer*,[4] *In Time*,[5] *Elysium*,[6] and *Rise of the Planet of the Apes*[7] is not so much that they villainize greedy corporations or corrupt political systems—this has, after all, been a regular feature of Hollywood entertainment from *It's a Wonderful Life*[8] to *The LEGO Movie*. More remarkable is the revolutionary spirit that informs these storyworlds: the protagonists in these fantastic narratives somehow find themselves developing a sense of class consciousness that ultimately leads them from emerging solidarity to collective political action. Even in a film like *The Dark Knight Rises*,[9] with its virulent portrayal of the Occupy movement,[10]

---

2. A similar joke is in circulation about *The Hunger Games*: when the barista calls out the name "Primrose Everdeen," customers are supposed to respond with "I volunteer as Tribute!" (Thanks to Richard McCulloch for alerting me to this.)

3. See, for instance, Carl Freedman, "Capitalist Realism in Three Recent Sf Films," *Paradoxa* 26 (2014): 67–80, and Gerry Canavan, "'If The Engine Ever Stops, We'd All Die': *Snowpiercer* and Necrofuturism," *Paradoxa* 26 (2014): 41–66.

4. *Snowpiercer*, directed by Bong Joon-Ho (2013; Beverly Hills: Anchor Bay Entertainment, 2014), Blu-ray.

5. *In Time*, directed by Andrew Niccol (2011; Century City, CA: Twentieth Century Fox Home Entertainment, 2012), Blu-ray.

6. *Elysium*, directed by Neill Blomkamp (2013; Culver City: Sony Pictures, 2013), Blu-ray.

7. *Rise of the Planet of the Apes*, directed by Rupert Wyatt (2011; Century City, CA: Twentieth Century Fox Home Entertainment, 2011), Blu-ray.

8. *It's a Wonderful Life*, directed by Frank Capra (1946; Hollywood: Paramount Home Entertainment, 2009), Blu-ray.

9. *The Dark Knight Rises*, directed by Christopher Nolan (2012; Burbank: Warner Home Video, 2012), Blu-ray.

10. Mark Fisher, "Batman's Political Right Turn," *The Guardian*, July 22, 2012, accessed January 18, 2016, http://www.theguardian.com/commentisfree/2012/jul/22/batman-political-right-turn.

there remains a sincere and deeply felt appreciation for the passionate love that animates revolutionary action.[11]

Popular fantasies like these reflect a historical moment of seemingly universal crisis, which many voices have interpreted as an opportunity for real and lasting political change. In his widely read book *Why It's Still Kicking Off Everywhere*, Paul Mason, for instance, boldly states that we are currently "in the middle of a revolution caused by the near-collapse of free-market capitalism combined with an upswing in technical innovation, a surge in desire for individual freedom and a change in human consciousness about what freedom means."[12] While the still-tentative resurgence of leftist movements is somewhat encouraging, Mason's postcapitalist rhetoric nevertheless smacks of hyperbole, clearly misunderesti-mating[13] both the power and the adaptability of cognitive capitalism in its current form. When he speaks of "a surge in desire for individual freedom," he too easily overlooks the fact that global capitalism has in fact thrived on the "liberation" of the individual, and that digital technology is neither inherently liberating nor fundamentally democratic.

It is precisely this emphasis on individualism, flexibility, and freedom of (consumer) choice that has typified our postdemocratic age of Empire. The shift from industrial to postindustrial capitalism has broken down traditional class for-mations and intensified the cultural, social, and economic focus on competitive individualism. The paradox then becomes that while global capitalism bestows upon privileged Western subjects ever-greater personal freedoms, it at the same time systematically erodes the foundations upon which meaningful political change had previously been achieved. Therefore, if the multitude is indeed going to enact its exodus from capitalism, as Hardt and Negri so bravely suggest, it is not enough to understand Empire's biopolitical logic: we must also develop ways of imagining and enacting this transformation toward a postcapitalist world.

For this reason, I will focus my attention in this chapter on two storyworlds organized around the development of new collective forms and revolutionary political change. As described in the previous two chapters, fantastic storyworlds such as these offer ways of thinking through some of the key contradictions of global capitalism. The paradigms of *LOTR* and *Star Trek* provided a basis for world-building that negotiated imperialism's compartmentalized, teleological worldview, and *Game of Thrones* and *BSG* combined them with Empire's post-ideological spirit of ubiquitous precariousness, flexibility, and capitalist real-ism. In this chapter, I will illustrate my discussion of potentially revolutionary

---

11. Slavoj Žižek, "The Politics of Batman," *New Statesman*, August 23, 2012, accessed December 27, 2015, http://www.newstatesman.com/culture/culture/2012/08/slavoj-žižek-politics-batman.

12. Paul Mason, *Why It's Still Kicking Off Everywhere* (London and New York: Verso, 2013), 3.

13. Undoubtedly the best thing to have come out of the otherwise entirely lamentable George W. Bush presidency is this unintentionally profound neologism, which elegantly combines the meanings of the verbs *misunderstand* and *underestimate*.

storyworlds with two more case studies from the realm of twenty-first-century transmedia world-building.

The Hunger Games is the most obvious contemporary example of this kind of franchise: a massively popular cross-platform entertainment property in which a young woman from the most impoverished background leads a revolution against an oppressive capitalist elite. As a transmedia storyworld constituting three novels, four film adaptations, elaborate transmedia expansions, and overwhelming amounts of fan art and fan fiction, *The Hunger Games* is notable not only for its prominence within the genre but also for the way in which its imaginary empire is, as Mark Fisher has emphasized, "irreducibly political."[14] This is largely the result of the storyworld's indebtedness to the cultural legacy of the Spartacus narrative, with its gladiatorial arena transformed into the media spectacle of reality TV competition and the Roman Empire adapted into a more futuristic dystopian Empire.

My analysis of *The Hunger Games* is therefore preceded by a discussion of the Spartacus mythology as it developed throughout the twentieth century, culminating in a more detailed look at the successful transmedia storyworld that developed around the twenty-first-century *Spartacus* TV show.[15] This series spawned a similarly expansive transmedia franchise that included comic books, videogames, novels, and a board game, while offering a storyworld that is as radical in its politics as it is in its aesthetics. Both of these storyworlds foreground the crucial role of spectacle and mass media as an instrument of global capitalism's biopolitical power, bringing into clearer focus the central problematic of imagining new collective forms that could mobilize anticapitalist action.

While Hardt and Negri at their most utopian see these multitudinous collective forms as inherently transformative, the challenge that must first be overcome is that of global capitalism's deeply ingrained cultural, economic, and political norm of competitive individualism. Extending Hardt and Negri's approach to the problem of democracy within global capitalism, I draw in this chapter on the work of Jeremy Gilbert, Jodi Dean, and Paolo Virno. Their thinking develops in more detail the question of how to understand and overcome the many obstacles of postdemocratic capitalism, and offers suggestions on how to imagine new forms of political subjectivity. What do we make, then, of fantastic storyworlds that seem designed to question and critique the very system of commodified spectacle of which they are such an integral part? Can they be credibly described as forms of anticapitalist popular culture? And—to paraphrase Gilbert—would we even recognize anticapitalist culture if we saw it?[16] Can these storyworlds about

---

14. Mark Fisher, "Precarious Dystopias: *The Hunger Games, In Time*, and *Never Let Me Go*," *Film Quarterly* 65, no. 4 (Summer 2012): 27.

15. Unless noted otherwise, further mentions of *Spartacus* (in italics) will refer to the franchise surrounding the Starz TV series.

16. Jeremy Gilbert, *Anticapitalism and Culture* (London: Bloomsbury, 2008), 98.

revolution truly be understood as revolutionary, or are these successful franchises less radical than they appear to be?[17] And most of all, do they point beyond competitive individualism toward a properly communist horizon?

POSTDEMOCRATIC CAPITALISM
AND THE COMMUNIST HORIZON

The age of global capitalism is fundamentally postdemocratic. This seemingly counterintuitive statement is one of the key points made not only throughout Hardt and Negri's three major works but also across twenty-first-century radical thought and critical theory. In *Commonwealth*, Hardt and Negri reiterate that their critique of globalization is intended to articulate and thus liberate those crucial elements pointing toward a future that might once more be made democratic.[18] The biopolitical hegemony of Empire is sustained by the constant and uncannily successful appropriation of the multitude's creative energy. Only if—though for Hardt and Negri it sometimes appears to be merely a question of *when*—the Spinozist multitude comes to understand and embrace its own irreducibly multiple nature might the spell of cognitive capitalism finally be broken, and the commons at last restored to its rightful collective ownership.

In spite of their frighteningly detailed critical analysis of global capitalism's overwhelming power, Hardt and Negri remain stubbornly optimistic about this utopian destiny. At the same time, they are notoriously vague when it comes down to how exactly such a revolutionary transformation is supposed to take place. They speak blithely of an impending "exodus from capitalism,"[19] while attempting to resurrect love as "an essential concept for philosophy and politics."[20] In his book *Common Ground*, Jeremy Gilbert tackles this issue head on, helpfully simplifying some of the key terms introduced by many theoretical heavyweights, including dynamic duos such as Hardt and Negri, Laclau and Mouffe, and Deleuze and Guattari. Neoliberal doctrine, Gilbert argues, has resulted in a generalized war of all against all, as competitive individualism becomes the one and only yardstick for all forms of social relations. He draws on what Marx described as one of the central contradictions of capitalism, "its tendency to socialize *production* and its tendency to individualize and privatize *consumption*."[21] Under global

---

17. Marlon Lieber and Daniel Zamora, "Rebel Without a Cause," *Jacobin*, January 4, 2016, accessed January 6, 2016, https://www.jacobinmag.com/2016/01/hunger-games-review-capitalism-revolution-mockingjay-suzanne-collins.

18. Michael Hardt and Antonio Negri, *Commonwealth* (Cambridge, MA: Belknap, 2009), 8.

19. Hardt and Negri, *Commonwealth*, 152–53.

20. Hardt and Negri, *Commonwealth*, 179.

21. Jeremy Gilbert, *Common Ground: Democracy and Collectivity in an Age of Individualism* (London: Pluto Press, 2013), 26.

capitalism and its allegedly participatory culture, this results in a fundamental ambivalence that undermines any meaningful kind of democracy:

> Neoliberalism must ensure that this ambivalence is lived, at least by strategically crucial constituencies, as exciting, amusing, liberating, and desirable; and by other constituencies it must at least be experienced as unavoidable, unchangeable, a fact of life. But in all cases it must be experienced as confirming the basic assumption that competitive and individualized social relations are normal, desirable, and inevitable, as the various modulations of capitalist ideology have all done since the seventeenth century. Today, the key challenge for radical democratic forces is surely to activate this ambivalence in a different way, to enable it to be experienced as the condition of possibility of another world, in which the creative potential of the collective is realized beyond the limits set by capital accumulation and individual competition.[22]

When Gilbert sketches out some of the ways in which this ambivalence might indeed be activated, he draws on the crucial distinction Raymond Williams once made between alternative and oppositional tendencies in capitalist culture.[23] He emphasizes that most of the contemporary forms of collaborative and participatory culture celebrated by many fan studies scholars clearly fall into the former category: they have provided alternatives to "mainstream" culture, but without structurally opposing capitalism's basic logic. While the cultural values and identity politics of these groups would traditionally be considered oppositional to a politically conservative "dominant ideology," they are in fact completely at home within the cultural logic of neoliberalism. As Gilbert points out, "Hegemonic neoliberalism is perfectly happy for individuals to undergo personal transformations, so long as they do not aggregate or catalyze any significant social transformation."[24]

For such a significant social transformation, a revolutionary zeal is required that goes beyond a critical and theoretical anticapitalism: neoliberalism's war of all against all can only be overcome by radical solidarity. Where Hardt and Negri ultimately adopt the term *love* as the crucial ingredient in overcoming the dominant structures of Empire, Gilbert similarly suggests "collective joy" as the affective state that defines truly transformative social and cultural forms.[25] For this reason, the Bakhtinian carnivalesque should be embraced, but in a way that makes it more than a momentary escape from the normative environment of competitive individualism.[26] As an institutionalized pressure valve, carnivalesque behavior is easily integrated into the circuits of commodity circulation; the annual rituals of fan conventions like San Diego Comic-Con are a good example of sincere and

---

22. Gilbert, *Common Ground*, 26–27.

23. Raymond Williams, *Marxism and Literature* (Oxford: Oxford University Press, 1977), 114.

24. Gilbert, *Common Ground*, 195.

25. Gilbert, *Common Ground*, 200.

26. Gilbert, *Common Ground*, 193.

relatively spontaneous outbursts of collectivity that fit comfortably within global media conglomerates' logic of endless capital accumulation. A transformative radical politics therefore requires a far more determined effort to foster the love and collective joy that arises from truly collaborative social relations.

While fandom has thus far clearly remained compromised in this regard, it isn't hard to see where a certain enthusiasm for fan culture's political potential comes from. The authentic devotion to fantastic storyworlds' dialectic of cognition and estrangement, together with organized fandom's general atmosphere of mutual tolerance, liberal political and social values, and solidarity, seems like an ideal environment for fostering the kind of new collective Gilbert describes. It is certainly visible in those fan communities surrounding the works of explicitly political sf and fantasy authors such as China Miéville, Octavia E. Butler, and Kim Stanley Robinson, whose novels combine the traditions of weird and speculative fiction with vividly imagined and politically charged alternative worlds. Without exception, works like these emphasize narratives in which the traditional "hero's journey" is either ignored or explicitly ridiculed: their storyworlds are not attractive prosceniums in which the individual subject is made to shine but complex and contingent worlds where actual social change emerges dialectically and unpredictably as the result of collective action.[27]

This brings me then to fantastic storyworlds that imagine a political transformation that goes beyond the reactionary fantasy of returning the world to some imaginary state of former glory. Rather than falling back on a "timeless" struggle between good and evil, storyworlds like *Spartacus* and *The Hunger Games* dramatize a political struggle that takes aim squarely at capitalist social relations. These transmedia franchises do so by foregrounding in the storyworld's structure the key dramatic tension not as interpersonal conflict but as an irreducibly political class struggle, while relating this dynamic explicitly to political economies of media production. Where *The LEGO Movie* poked superficial fun at branding and power-hungry corporations, both *Spartacus* and *The Hunger Games* feature storyworlds whose very structural organization foregrounds the intersection of power, capital, and spectacle. Unlike the overwhelming majority of popular narratives about revolutionary movements,[28] these storyworlds are organized on the basis of class conflict and refuse to be dismissive of collective social forms.

Nightmare visions of collectivity have haunted Anglo-American fantastic fiction for decades, from the emotionless pod people of *Invasion of the Body*

---

27. Williams, *Marxism and Literature*, 86.

28. The acclaimed Hollywood film *Reds*, directed by Warren Beatty (1981; Hollywood: Paramount Home Entertainment, 2010), Blu-ray, is a notorious example of a historical drama in which complex collective movements are constantly collapsed back into individual character development. Mick Eaton, "History to Hollywood: Mick Eaton Talks to Trevor Griffiths," *Screen* 23, no. 2 (1982): 61–70.

Snatchers[29] and the monstrous Borg Collective of *Star Trek: TNG*[30] to the sectarian society of the *Divergent* franchise.[31] In all of these cases, each and every form of collectivity is equated with totalitarianism and the loss of personal liberties, as highly individualistic protagonists struggle heroically to resist the horrors of cooperative organization. Such narratives feed into global capitalism's "meta-individualism,"[32] a current of thought that "tends to imagine itself opposed to a totalitarian collectivism, which would smother the individuality of individuals by incorporating them into a homogeneous and unitary mass."[33] Moving beyond traditional liberalism, the neoliberal glorification of meta-individualism inherently mistrusts all forms of collectivity. Even the apparent collective of something like the Fellowship of the Ring in *LOTR* is approached with obvious paranoia and unease, as what begins as a somewhat diverse (though exclusively straight, white, and male) collaborative team is quickly and inevitably broken up into parallel individual quests. Therefore, while Tolkien's imaginary world can still be viably interpreted along ambivalent anticapitalist lines (see chapter 1), and *Game of Thrones* provides its own joyless form of radicalism (see chapter 2), the power relationships that structure the storyworlds of *Spartacus* and *The Hunger Games* are specifically and even emphatically about capitalist social relations.

In these two storyworlds, we even encounter imagined forms of collectivity that seem to open up what Jodi Dean has described as a communist horizon. For Dean, "communism is reemerging as a magnet of political energy because it is and has been the alternative to capitalism."[34] She sees this horizon becoming visible in places like the Occupy movement, in the radical potential of complex digital networks, in the emerging Leftist politics of Latin America, and increasingly in Western Europe, where the resurgence of left-wing politics can be recognized in movements like Podemos in Spain, Syriza in Greece, Jeremy Corbyn's Labour leadership in the United Kingdom, and Bernie Sanders's US presidential campaign. Between the Right's demonization of socialism and the post-Clinton/Blair embrace of neoliberalism by formerly left-wing parties, what is necessary for this horizon to emerge once more is the reinvigoration of communism.

However, the participatory cultures and technologies that have the potential to facilitate this transformation are also a trap that ensnares users in an environment over which they have little actual control. This trap of what Dean calls

---

29. *Invasion of the Body Snatchers*, directed by Don Siegel (1956; Chicago: Olive Films, 2012), Blu-ray.

30. "The Best of Both Worlds," *Star Trek: The Next Generation* (Paramount Domestic Television; First-run syndication, June 18, 1990).

31. *Divergent*, directed by Neil Burger (2014; Braine L'Alleud: Belga Films, 2014), Blu-ray.

32. Gilbert points out that meta-individualism is not unique to global capitalism but shared by many other currents of thought, including traditional communism, fascism, and most forms of nationalism. Gilbert, *Common Ground*, 70.

33. Gilbert, *Common Ground*, 70.

34. Jodi Dean, *The Communist Horizon* (London and New York: Verso, 2012), 10.

communicative capitalism lies for a large part in the spectacular nature of capitalism's media industries. The considerable attractions of celebrity culture, ostentatious material wealth, and media spectacle fuel the engine of capital accumulation in the postindustrial era. While connective digital media are clearly essential to the modern-day organization of participatory and collective forms, their commercial exploitation also maintains and even increases the obscenely unequal distribution of global wealth. The challenge for anticapitalist activism therefore lies in the political mobilization of the multitude through the development of new collective forms and subjectivities, and the reappropriation of the digital world as a free, democratic, and truly participatory commons.

For Dean, this transformation will not occur spontaneously, as Hardt and Negri sometimes seem to suggest. For the purposes of this book, I find her intervention most useful in the way she connects the radical potential that is latent in communicative capitalism to the rehabilitation of communism as a robust political alternative to neoliberalism's competitive individualism.[35] And while I remain unconvinced by her attempts to resuscitate the Leninist vanguard party[36] alongside her attractive and almost inevitable-sounding notion of a unifying "communist horizon," I see two ways in which this particular work can be helpful in the context of this book's discussion of fantastic world-building and radical politics.

First, the radical potential offered by fantastic storyworlds is their ability to project the organization of social, cultural, and political alternatives in ways that foreground systems, structures, and social relations rather than individual narratives. These storyworlds, while most commonly ambivalent in their ideological representation of capitalism, have the uncanny ability to offer imaginary empires that are perceived as alternatives to our own society while at the same time reflecting critically on our own familiar social and economic totality. They therefore also have the potential of rekindling a utopian imaginary by foregrounding the contradictions of capitalist realism through fantastic fiction's dialectic of cognition and estrangement. Second, these storyworlds—irrespective of their isolated narratives and ideological contradictions—have provided remarkably fertile ground for fan collectives engaged in many different forms of social and political activism. In this context, fan activism has been one of the ways in which capitalism's hegemony over participatory culture has been challenged, and in which productive attempts have been made to reestablish a commons on the basis of a shared love of fantastic storyworlds and the political ideals they articulate.

In the following section of this chapter, I approach the twenty-first-century *Spartacus* franchise as a transmedia storyworld that draws on the character's rich

---

35. Dean, *The Communist Horizon*, 123.

36. As many others have pointed out, the Communist Party as envisioned by Dean remains a rather unhelpful abstraction. See, for instance, Jeffrey C. Isaac, "The Mirage of Neo-Communism," *Dissent* (Summer 2013), accessed January 6, 2016, https://www.dissentmagazine.org/article/the-mirage-of-neo-communism.

legacy as a pop-cultural communist imaginary. The novel by Howard Fast and its popular Hollywood adaptation established influential anticapitalist motifs both by developing potent communist allegories and by their extratextual connections to public debates about politics and ideology in popular art. But the *Spartacus* storyworld also adapts this radical legacy in ways that reflect the contradictions of cognitive capitalism's political economy and of Quality TV's forms of cultural legitimization. A radical text in many ways, *Spartacus* combines the subversive traditions of exploitation cinema with a thoroughly self-reflexive commentary on its own media-industrial position as commodified spectacle.

SPARTACUS AND THE COMMUNIST IMAGINARY

The name *Spartacus* is most commonly associated first with the 1960 Hollywood blockbuster starring Kirk Douglas,[37] and second with the iconic gay travel guidebook that has appeared annually since 1970.[38] In the twenty-first century, the character and its associated iconography comes loaded, on the one hand, with associations of queerness and camp and, on the other, with a tradition of left-wing politics and what can only be termed a communist imaginary. The figure's original historical context is the Third Servile War, which took place in ancient Rome from 73 to 71 BC. It was the only slave rebellion to threaten Roman imperial might directly, with Spartacus emerging as one of the leaders of a growing army of former slaves and gladiators who staged numerous impactful raids across the Italian peninsula.[39] While no evidence exists that the rebellion truly aimed to abolish slavery,[40] the texts that introduced the historical narrative into twentieth-century culture framed the conflict as an explicit allegory for contemporary class struggle. And as one of the rebellion's leaders, the former gladiator Spartacus was singled out as the embodiment of modern revolutionary zeal: a martyr figure whose narrative was carefully molded by several different authors to fit the context of post–World War II anticapitalism.

The specifically twentieth-century politicization of the historical Spartacus narrative began with Arthur Koestler's novel *The Gladiators*, first published in 1939.[41] Koestler, a former member of the German Communist Party, used the figure as a way to express his own disillusionment with the communist movement. In the novel, Spartacus is presented as a charismatic and articulate leader whose grand ideals are instrumental in directing and politicizing a spontaneous slave

---

37. *Spartacus*, directed by Stanley Kubrick (1960; Los Angeles: Universal Studios Home Entertainment, 2015), Blu-ray.

38. See http://www.spartacusworld.com.

39. Barry Strauss, *The Spartacus War* (New York: Simon & Schuster, 2010), chapter 1.

40. Strauss, *The Spartacus War*, chapter 1.

41. Arthur Koestler, *The Gladiators* (New York: Random House, 2011).

rebellion. But his idealism is tainted as soon as Spartacus becomes a political leader who is no longer merely fighting against his own exploitation but espouses his beliefs in the form of an ideology. Like Orwell's similarly organized allegory *Animal Farm*,[42] Koestler's version of the historical narrative thereby firmly articulates the notion that "revolutionary leaders inevitably become tyrants,"[43] thus connecting an episode from ancient Roman history with popular perceptions of twentieth-century communism.[44]

Howard Fast's 1951 novel *Spartacus*[45] further consolidated this relationship between the historical slave rebellion and developing American perceptions of the communist imaginary. As a wartime member of the Communist Party, Fast was called before Senator McCarthy's House Un-American Activities Committee (HUAC) in 1950, and he was subsequently blacklisted and imprisoned after refusing to identify fellow communists. The author started work on his literary dramatization of the slave rebellion while incarcerated, and he self-published the novel as the only way to see it in print under his own name.[46] In the novel, which was successful for a self-published book,[47] Fast also used the Spartacus narrative as an allegorical vessel for his own representation of twentieth-century communism, but with a very different emphasis. While Koestler saw the slave rebellion's defeat as evidence of all politics' inherently corrupting nature, Fast imagined Spartacus as an unimpeachable idealist, a natural leader whose struggle against oppression formed a potent symbol for the struggle against twentieth-century capitalism. As Fast's biographer Gerald Sorin notes, the novel was an attempt to critique the author's own capitalist environment, presenting his main character as a martyr whose legend would ultimately bring about a communist revolution: "For Fast, ancient Rome, with its slaves and factory workers, was a capitalist society, and like the United States, an unjust imperial society in the last stages of decay."[48] His version of the character is portrayed with a reverence that borders on saintliness, a creative decision that is made more palatable by having him appear almost exclusively via other characters' perspectives. More than a historical character, Fast's version of Spartacus is thus presented to us as myth:

---

42. George Orwell, *Animal Farm: A Fairy Story* (Harmondsworth: Penguin Books, 2000 [1945]).

43. John Bokina, "From Communist Ideologue to Postmodern Rebel: Spartacus in Novels," *The European Legacy* 6, no. 6 (2001): 726.

44. Geoffrey Wheatcroft, "The Darkness at Noon for Arthur Koestler Was in His Heart," *New Statesman*, November 20, 1998, accessed December 27, 2015, http://www.newstatesman .com/darkness-noon-arthur-koestler-was-his-heart-yet-his-early-work-inspired-his-disillusionment -communis.

45. Howard Fast, *Spartacus* (New York: Simon & Schuster, 1996 [1951]).

46. Gerald Sorin, *Howard Fast: Life and Literature in the Left Lane* (Bloomington: Indiana University Press, 2012), 237–38.

47. In his memoir, Fast quips that fifty thousand copies were printed, of which forty-eight thousand were sold (see Howard Fast, *Being Red* [Boston: Houghton Mifflin, 1990], 294).

48. Sorin, *Howard Fast*, 238.

a revolutionary specter of radical solidarity and revolutionary passion whose storyworld has come to haunt capitalist modernity.

Fast's novel thus became part of what has been described as "modern communists' appropriation of Spartacus,"[49] a movement that was, paradoxically, both enhanced and diminished by the 1960 release of the popular Hollywood film. A fascinating battleground of politics, star power, genre, and auteur theory, the film was cleverly marketed as "the thinking man's epic,"[50] clearly establishing its intellectual ambition as well as its political sincerity. The script by Dalton Trumbo—himself, like Fast, a well-known victim of HUAC's Hollywood blacklist—remained largely faithful to Fast's ideological commitment, portraying Spartacus as a messianic leader struggling to lead his ragtag group of former slaves to freedom. And while the film is often cited as having broken the blacklist by giving Trumbo screen credit after a decade of forced obscurity, its actual political resonance was simultaneously undercut as the Universal film studio attempted to remove as many subversive elements as possible. The original theatrical version was therefore severely edited by the studio to avoid the suggestion that the script was "designed to foment revolution in America."[51] Not only were the potentially controversial explicit allusions to homosexuality deleted, but, according to actor-producer Kirk Douglas, "any hint that [Spartacus] might have been leading a successful revolution was removed from the film."[52]

But in spite of the many compromises that surrounded the film's release, its association with the breaking of Hollywood's blacklist and the character's growing resonance as a left-wing icon still gave the legend a prominent place among Western fantasies of radical political movements and the communist imaginary. In all of the varied twentieth-century adaptations of the Spartacus narrative, its interpretation is grounded in class conflict: the failed slave rebellion opens up a horizon for imagining resistance in the conflict between hierarchically organized imperial power and a spontaneously emerging collective. Even in the *Star Trek TNG* novel *Spartacus*,[53] the franchise's patronizing and complacent liberalism draws explicitly on the Roman slave rebellion's heritage to dramatize the ethics of violent revolution as a response to systemic exploitation.[54]

---

49. W. Jeffrey Tatum, "The Character of Marcus Licinnius Crassus," in *Spartacus: Film and History*, ed. Martin M. Winkler (Malden: Blackwell, 2007), 137.

50. Martin M. Winkler, "Introduction," in *Spartacus: Film and History*, 3.

51. Kirk Douglas, *I Am Spartacus! Making a Film, Breaking the Blacklist* (New York: Open Road Media, 2012), chapter 11.

52. Douglas, *I Am Spartacus!*, chapter 11. A restoration was undertaken in 1991, and the version currently available on home video is much closer to the film's original cut.

53. T. L. Mancour, *Star Trek: The Next Generation—Spartacus* (London: Titan Books, 1992).

54. Jared, the escaped android slave who functions as the novel's Spartacus figure, explains his motivation for the rebellion in terms that resonate strongly with the twentieth-century labor movement and the exploitative history of capitalism: "I looked at my world, and saw the great hypocrisy in it. In great universities, they talked about the supreme values of civilization and freedom, of the Golden

But in all of these popular incarnations, the class conflict that the Spartacus narrative represents is consistently played out along traditional binaries of class and gender. The revolution as depicted both in Howard Fast's novel and in the Hollywood film is a traditionally masculine and heterosexual movement, in which female characters are primarily nurturers and supporters,[55] and where homosexuality is systematically associated with imperial Roman decadence and moral decay.[56] At the same time, one of the most striking contradictions in both novel and film is the way in which the character of Spartacus is described as a unique and exceptional individual, "the best and bravest of all men,"[57] but also as someone whose personality was inconsequential, since in his absence "the forces which prodded him would simply have turned elsewhere."[58] This contradiction resurfaces in the Starz *Spartacus* TV series and transmedia storyworld in ways that provocatively reflect its postideological and postdemocratic context.

THE *SPARTACUS* TRANSMEDIA FRANCHISE AND TWENTY-FIRST-CENTURY RADICALISM

The twenty-first-century *Spartacus* franchise began in 2010 with the thirteen-episode TV series *Spartacus: Blood and Sand*, commissioned and broadcast by fledgling American cable network Starz. In an increasingly crowded marketplace of scripted drama on premium cable, the hyperviolent swords-and-sandals epic helped the network carve out a niche for itself as a no-holds-barred purveyor of uncompromising pulp fiction. At the same time, the successful series was ambitiously expanded across several other media: a series of comic books[59] focused on characters with a more limited presence in the TV episodes and were themselves

---

Age of men, of the nobility of the human spirit, all the while they were waited on hand and foot by a servile—no, make that a class of slaves. They were treating their own creations worse than they had treated themselves, all the time they were talking about how noble and civilized they were. They had proclaimed their Golden Age . . . and conveniently failed to see the horrors on which it was built" (Mancour, *Spartacus*, 116–17).

55. While Fast's novel does include a moment in which Spartacus's wife Varinia is described as a fierce warrior who was "like a fury," this only occurs in response to a direct physical threat to children, with her representation of maternal care further enhanced by the fact that she battles the Roman soldiers completely naked. See Fast, *Spartacus*, part 5, chapter 7.

56. The most suggestive scene from the film, in which the Roman general Crassus (Laurence Olivier) attempts to seduce his slave Antoninus (Tony Curtis), was removed from the theatrical release.

57. Fast, *Spartacus*, part 6, chapter 10.

58. Fast, *Spartacus*, part 6, chapter 3.

59. Steven S. DeKnight and Adam Archer, *Spartacus—Blood and Sand: Upon the Sands of Vengeance* (Chicago: Devil's Due, 2009); Jimmy Palmiotti and Dexter Soy, *Spartacus—Blood and Sand: Shadows of the Jackal* (Chicago: Devil's Due, 2009); Todd and Aaron Helbing and Jon Bosco and Guilherme Balbi, *Spartacus—Blood and Sand: The Beast of Carthage* (Chicago: Devil's Due, 2009); Miranda Kwok and Allan Jefferson, *Spartacus—Blood and Sand: The Shadow of Death* (Chicago: Devil's Due, 2009).

adapted for online distribution as animated "motion comics"[60]; the novels *Spartacus: Swords and Ashes*[61] and *Spartacus: Morituri*[62] explored the interpersonal dynamics between the gladiators of the first-season arena while offering spectacular set pieces impossible to achieve on the TV show's limited production budget; the board game *Spartacus: A Game of Blood and Treachery* put players in charge of their own *ludus*, strategizing against other players as they "vie for dominance through careful diplomacy, cunning intrigues and the glory of the Arena"[63]; and the free-to-play console videogame *Spartacus Legends* (Moby Games, 2013) invited players to go through gladiatorial training and battle each other in the arena.

The production of a second season was postponed when leading actor Andy Whitfield was diagnosed with non-Hodgkin's lymphoma. To fill the gap left by his absence, the production company instead put together a six-episode miniseries titled *Spartacus: Gods of the Arena*, a prequel to the first season that mapped out the earlier history of the House of Batiatus. With the now fatally ill Whitfield unable to return to the role of Spartacus, his part was recast and continued over two more seasons: *Spartacus: Vengeance* followed the transition from a small band of rebellious slaves and ex-gladiators to the creation of a revolutionary army, and *Spartacus: War of the Damned* concluded the cycle with the climactic battles in which the slave rebellion faces off against the Roman imperial army, led by Senator Crassus and a young Julius Caesar.[64]

With the advantages of an extended running time and an explicit license to experiment, subvert, and offend, the Starz franchise draws on the character's established tradition of radicalism while substantially expanding the storyworld's scope. Throughout the series, the character of Spartacus is systematically dissociated from the saintly martyr and father figure of Fast's novel and its film adaptation. One of the most obvious ways in which the Starz series deviates from the earlier dramatizations involves the circumstances under which Spartacus becomes a gladiator. The earlier texts depict Spartacus as a slave toiling in the mines before he is purchased by Batiatus to join his *ludus* of gladiators, where the character's innocence and purity of spirit is underlined by the revelation of his virginity. In both cases, his rebellion is a direct response to the conditions

---

60. "Upon the Sands of Vengeance," YouTube video, 15:55, posted by Manga Entertainment, March 15, 2010, https://www.youtube.com/watch?v=UHU1yLbD6qM; "Spartacus: Blood and Sand—Motion Comic—Shadows of the Jackal," YouTube video, 15:35, posted by Manga Entertainment, March 15, 2010, https://www.youtube.com/watch?v=G4680pXncvA; "Spartacus: Blood and Sand—Motion Comic—The Beast of Carthage," YouTube video, 9:20, posted by Manga Entertainment, March 15, 2010, https://www.youtube.com/watch?v=DM3h7Vxu3uM; "The Shadow of Death," YouTube video, 12:20, posted by Manga Entertainment, March 15, 2010, https://www.youtube.com/watch?v=h3qewAh7gE0.

61. J. M. Clements, *Spartacus: Swords and Ashes* (London: Titan Books, 2012).

62. Mark Morris, *Spartacus: Morituri* (London: Titan Books, 2012).

63. Promotional text from the board game's website, http://spartacusboardgame.com.

64. Caesar's completely speculative inclusion in the storyworld is one of the TV series' explicit references to the 1960 film, in which John Gavin played Caesar as a young senator.

of oppression and exploitation he witnesses first as a slave and then as a gladiator, and it resonates within a context of clear and obvious boundaries between classes. As Fast puts it in his novel's dedication, *Spartacus* tells "a story of brave men and women," toiled over and published "so that the dream of Spartacus may come to be in our own time."[65] These words sum up the clear binary distinction between "good" workers and "evil" capitalists so typical of older forms of left-wing radicalism.

The creators of the Starz franchise have been much more reluctant to portray Spartacus as an ideologically driven, purely heroic character. In the first season, his motivation hinges on the purely personal: initially isolated and aloof from the community of gladiators in which he finds himself from the second episode onward, he is driven by the desire to return to his wife, who had also been betrayed by Roman forces and sold into slavery. Surrounded by other gladiators whose "code of honor" maintains an ethic of competitive individualism at its purest, Spartacus keeps his distance from his fellow fighters. He only develops a friendship with Varro, a free man who entered voluntarily into an indentured period as a gladiator to provide for his family, while entering into a provisional alliance with Batiatus.

While Spartacus is appalled by the conditions under which the gladiators are made to exist, he is also attracted by the celebrity and relative privilege that follow his victories in the arena, and at first he has faith in a system that seemingly allows him to bargain with his owner Batiatus across class lines, based on his individual abilities. But through a combination of complex plotting and Batiatus's unwillingness to release the human capital in which he has invested, Spartacus ultimately learns that the cruelty and exploitation he witnesses are neither personal nor incidental: the exploitation he faces is the kind that cannot be bargained with, as it is systemic and therefore demands collective action, not individual negotiation. After considerable effort, he is ultimately able to convince the other gladiators that they must learn to see past their ethical code of competitive individualism and recognize that they share a common plight and therefore must unite in common purpose.

With thirteen one-hour episodes devoted entirely to the events leading up to the gladiators' first collective act of rebellion, the TV series invests a great deal of time in developing the various other characters that make up Batiatus's *ludus*. Instead of the relatively homogeneous group of loyal followers depicted in earlier versions of the storyworld, the rich cast of supporting characters is remarkably diverse in ethnicity, gender, personal background, and sexual orientation. Barca, for instance, is a Carthaginian captive who has become a champion of the gladiatorial arena and is saving up his prize money to purchase his own freedom and that of his lover Pietros. Crixus, a captive slave from Gaul, has become a star of the arena as "the undefeated Gaul" and developed into the fiercest defender

---

65. Fast, *Spartacus*, dedication.

of the gladiators' code of honor. This code is taught in a relentless combination of physical and ideological conditioning by Oenamaus, the equivalent of a drill sergeant in a Hollywood film, whose personal background—revealed slowly over the course of three seasons—has blinded him to the contradictions of his own ideological and ethical position. This diverse group of individuals represents a microcosm of subjects whose personal interests have made it overwhelmingly difficult for them to recognize the political nature of their individual predicaments, and whose relative privilege results from their willingness to participate willingly in their own exploitation.

Captured within a system that pits gladiators against each other while offering privilege based on individual achievement, the *Spartacus* storyworld cleverly articulates the schizophrenic nature of capitalist subjectivity. This adaptation therefore becomes meaningful in the context of global capitalism not because it teaches us anything particularly noteworthy about ancient Rome, which the writers and directors readily profess was never a priority. This latest incarnation of the Spartacus storyworld makes for such a fruitful political and ideological feeding ground because of the way it adapts the character's tradition of left-wing allegory to neoliberalism's schizophrenic dynamic of subjection and enslavement.

Many critiques of post-Fordism have been grounded in forms of "schizoanalysis," a theoretical approach to the forms of subjectivity produced under late capitalism grounded in poststructuralist psychoanalytical theory.[66] For Deleuze and Guattari, schizophrenia is inherent in the machinic nature of late capitalism, as the subject becomes an assemblage existing in a state of constant negotiation between multiple competing affective identities.[67] More recently, Maurizio Lazzarato has further developed this theoretical description of the forms of subjectivity produced under global capitalism and what he calls its "machinic tendency." He argues that the schizophrenic direction Deleuze and Guattari identified in the early stages of post-Fordism has grown exponentially as we have entered the twenty-first century's increasingly global, increasingly virtual, and increasingly inescapable capitalism.[68]

As the cultural logic of neoliberalism has come to rule out the very idea of an alternative, machinic enslavement should not be understood as operating topdown, as power or ideology is imposed on the subject through various forms of social, political, and ideological repression. It now takes over from the inside, as the production of subjectivity combines as its fundamental categories of labor both "work on the self" (praxis) and "labor" (production).[69] This results in what

---

66. Gilbert, *Common Ground*, 149–50 and 225n.

67. Gilles Deleuze and Félix Guattari, *A Thousand Plateaus* (New York: Continuum, 2004 [1987]), 38.

68. Maurizio Lazzarato, *Signs and Machines: Capitalism and the Production of Subjectivity* (Cambridge, MA: MIT Press, 2014).

69. Lazzarato, *Signs and Machines*, 51.

Lazzarato describes as a new subjective figure that typifies the combination of subjection and enslavement unique to global capitalism: "the economic subject as 'human capital' or entrepreneur of the self."[70] Empire's affective and immaterial labor hereby no longer defines human capital in terms of a single proletarian group identity but as a vast network of "entrepreneurs of the self," captured within a political and ideological system of machinic enslavement.

This neoliberal subjectivity is therefore in the first place a form of enslavement that—paradoxically—appears to operate voluntarily. What Lazzarato brilliantly recognizes as the machinery of Empire is far removed from the spirit of industrial capitalism, where power is operated more identifiably in a top-down manner.[71] As represented in earlier incarnations of the Spartacus narrative, the organization of power was more visible and more clearly circumscribed in the industrial age. Post-Fordism's machinic enslavement, on the other hand, is biopolitical because of its decentered network form that seems to operate as much from the inside out as it does from the outside in. While this logic is legitimized in part by global capitalism's systemic mythologization of individual forms of freedom, it effectively results in atomized and more completely alienated subjects whose sense of identity is every bit as precarious as the economic conditions they are forced to endure.

The gladiators in the twenty-first-century version of *Spartacus* correspond perfectly with neoliberalism's specific combination of subjection and enslavement: they are introduced not as a group but as a collection of individuals who are each caught up within a vast network of power that has made it difficult to recognize who the common enemy is. Their internal struggle to overcome their differences and establish a meaningful collective is central not only to the first season but also to every part of the franchise. The complex central narrative's many subplots in the first season chart the many ways in which individual characters deploy a variety of tactics to resist, escape, or at least survive their own enslavement, always with fatal results. And even after a moment of crisis causes them to band together in rebellion, the group members' diversity and individualist habits continue to frustrate attempts to remain a unified collective.

This dynamic is further strengthened by the storyworld's representation of Roman characters, most notably that of Batiatus, the gladiators' owner and the first season's ambiguous antagonist. The character was typically portrayed in earlier versions as duplicitous and buffoonish, but also as an ingratiating figure most closely resembling popular performances of Hollywood pimps.[72] But Batiatus as played by John Hannah is granted a complex narrative and set of dramatic

---

70. Lazzarato, *Signs and Machines*, 52.

71. Luc Boltanski and Eve Chiapello, *The New Spirit of Capitalism*, trans. Gregory Elliott (London and New York: Verso, 2005), 19.

72. Especially in Peter Ustinov's Oscar-winning performance in *Spartacus*.

conflicts of his own.[73] Moreover, his role as mediator/antagonist typifies the storyworld's focus on systems of power over and above individual characters' moral and ethical choices. We witness repeatedly that whatever Batiatus's personal motivations and desires might be, his actions are ultimately determined by the political system of which he is a part, a pure—and often strangely sympathetic—embodiment of Foucault's notion that power is never owned but merely exercised.[74] Batiatus's character illustrates most vividly how this scheming opportunist is caught within a political network of power that operates outside of his control. And while he is clearly responsible for a wide variety of nefarious and immoral acts, the narrative goes out of its way to emphasize how he is chiefly the figure of the all-too-human capitalist for whom, as Marx famously put it, personal intentions are always secondary to their function as "bearers of particular class-relations and interests."[75]

Applying the same narrative logic to Roman antagonists who become more prominent later in the series,[76] the storyworld is designed to emphasize that the only effective response to competitive individualism lies in collective political action. Skillfully dramatizing neoliberalism's dual processes of subjection and enslavement, the storyworld provides a fantasy that elegantly articulates one of the key contradictions of postdemocratic capitalism. By emphasizing not only the machinic enslavement of the gladiators but also the way in which Batiatus and the other Roman characters are similarly subjected and enslaved by a decentered network of political power, the new *Spartacus* succeeds in combining the left-wing heritage of its predecessors with narrative variations that resonate strongly with the spirit of global capitalism. And this connection is solidified all the more by the franchise's provocative combination of digital aesthetics and exploitation cinema tropes.

"JUPITER'S COCK!": EXPLOITATION AND THE SOCIETY OF THE MEDIA SPECTACLE

The first time I came across an episode of *Spartacus* on cable TV, I couldn't quite believe I was watching an actual television series. Even after a decade of binge-watching edgy and ground-breaking "Quality TV" full of sex and violence, I wasn't quite prepared for the sheer outrageousness of the Starz network's flagship production. The extravagant bloodletting of *The Sopranos*, the baroque

---

73. While Batiatus is absent from the last two seasons of the TV series, he is featured prominently in the comic books, the various games, and both novels.

74. Michel Foucault, *Discipline and Punish* (New York: Vintage, 1995), 193.

75. Karl Marx, *Capital, Vol. 1*, trans. Ben Fowkes (Harmondsworth: Penguin Books, 1976), 96.

76. Glaber, the chief antagonist of *Spartacus: Vengeance*, and Crassus, the rebellion's final opponent in *Spartacus: War of the Damned*, both perform roles similar to that of Batiatus in the first season and prequel miniseries: while each is certainly a colorful and appropriately villainous antagonist, they are emphatically enmeshed in and constricted by a larger political network.

profanity of *Deadwood*, the nonstop parade of boobs and vaginas in *Game of Thrones*, the flamboyant gruesomeness of *Dexter*—each of these productions flaunted pay channels' freedom from American broadcast restrictions but also went out of its way to justify those aesthetic excesses as mature and tasteful rather than as cheap, gratuitous, or exploitative. HBO and other premium cable TV channels distinguish themselves from "normal" television by offering their privileged viewers valuable cultural capital, primarily by "enclosing the profane in a discourse of historical verisimilitude and saturating it in literary respectability and highly valued performative traditions."[77]

Not so in the cartoonish world of *Spartacus*. Rather than embedding the subversive elements of fantastic world-building in the bourgeois conventions of art cinema and middlebrow literature, *Spartacus* gleefully appropriates the stylistic vocabulary of exploitation cinema and other culturally denigrated forms, including horror, soft-core porn, comics, professional wrestling, and videogames.[78] Scenes of sex and violence are depicted in close-up and slow motion, the frequent orgies and extended depictions of simulated copulation so detailed and vivid that they were all too easily dismissed by early reviewers as purely pornographic, representing "a new low in television narrative."[79] Following the tired old binary opposition between valuable "high" art and disposable "low" exploitation, *Spartacus*'s blatant excess was categorized by many critics as junk, the kind of "pure bad camp"[80] that is structurally devalued in bourgeois culture. But it is precisely exploitation cinema's unruly and "tasteless" register that gives *Spartacus* its subversive potential.

This radical energy is heightened by the franchise's active dissociation from Quality TV's aesthetic and discursive realism. Unlike premium cable drama's usual emphasis on verisimilitude, location shooting, and formidable production values, the *Spartacus* series flaunts its artificiality by relying on obvious CGI backgrounds, cartoonish and ostentatiously unrealistic bloodletting, and an idiosyncratic form of dialogue that constantly draws attention to itself.[81] In terms

---

77. Janet McCabe and Kim Akass, "It's Not TV, It's HBO's Original Programming," in *It's Not TV: Watching HBO in the Post-Television Era*, ed. Marc Leverette, Brian L. Ott, and Cara Louise Buckley (London and New York: Routledge, 2008), 89.

78. These aesthetic and discursive choices are at the same time what renders *Spartacus* fantastic: while the other central case studies in this book can be described as fantastic because their storyworlds contain explicitly futuristic and/or supernatural elements, *Spartacus* aligns itself with the fantastic by aesthetic choices, generic associations, and its dedication to forms and styles associated with the traditions of fantastic fiction.

79. Robert Moore, "Is *Spartacus: Blood and Sand* a Joke?" *PopMatters*, January 22, 2010, accessed December 27, 2015, http://www.popmatters.com/post/119149-spartacus-blood-and-sand.

80. Summarized critics' judgment according to popular review aggregator site *Rotten Tomatoes*, http://www.rottentomatoes.com/tv/spartacus/s01/.

81. Some of the more attention-grabbing stylistic choices in the writing across all media platforms include the prominent substitution of the word *absent* for *without* ("It is never an easy thing to see a friend once loved now absent breath"), the creative and colorful use of storyworld-specific profanity ("Jupiter's cock!"), and the seemingly arbitrary elision of definite and indefinite articles ("Once again the gods spread the cheeks to ram cock in fucking ass!").

of visual style, it resembles the similarly artificial comic book adaptations of *Sin City*,[82] *The Spirit*,[83] and, above all, Zack Snyder's *300*.[84] The franchise's striking aesthetic choices dissociate *Spartacus* from the genre of historical fiction, aligning it much more strongly with the styles, audiences, and media forms of fantastic storyworlds. It draws on the visual and narrative conventions that reference the long history of fantastic fiction, and in this sense it operates in a register much closer to classic pulp literature like Robert E. Howard's Conan stories[85] or Edgar Rice Burroughs's John Carter of Mars cycle[86] than prestigious historical drama, like the multimillion-dollar history lesson *Rome* or even the deeply silly but nominally "realist" *The Tudors*.

This blatant artificiality not only liberates *Spartacus* from the burden of historical accuracy but also facilitates its remarkably radical approach to world-building and politics. Rather than seeming to re-create a narrative from ancient history, the visual style and "gratuitous" use of sex and violence contribute to something resembling sf and fantasy's estrangement effect, immersing the audience in a storyworld that is both alien and quite obviously constructed. As Slavoj Žižek remarked in his notorious reading of the influential comic book adaptation *300*,[87] the striking use of photographed human actors within an artificial green-screen environment creates a claustrophobic effect that results in "a truly autonomous aesthetic space."[88] While Žižek's comments about the comic book's emphatically digital adaptation are as poorly thought through as his myopic ideological reading of an otherwise indefensible film, his point about the political potential of digital aesthetics is worth pursuing further.

While digital cinema in postclassical Hollywood usually strains to re-create the traditional forms of cinematic realism, its postindexical ontology[89] at the same time uncannily reflects "the endlessly modulating financial flows of globalized network capitalism."[90] World-building franchises like *LOTR*, *Star Wars*, *Game*

---

82. *Sin City*, directed by Robert Rodriguez and Frank Miller (2005; Los Angeles: Buena Vista, 2009), Blu-ray.

83. *The Spirit*, directed by Frank Miller (2008; Santa Monica, CA: Lionsgate Home Entertainment, 2009), Blu-ray.

84. *300*, directed by Zack Snyder (2007; Burbank: Warner Home Video, 2007), Blu-ray.

85. Robert E. Howard, *The Coming of Conan the Cimmerian* (New York: Ballantine Books, 2003).

86. Edgar Rice Burroughs, *Mars Trilogy: A Princess of Mars; The Gods of Mars; The Warlord of Mars* (New York: Simon & Schuster, 2012).

87. Many critics have rightfully taken issue with Žižek's contrarian interpretation of the film's politics: see Mark Fisher, "Permissive Hedonism and the Ascesis of Positivity," *k-punk*, May 2, 2007, accessed December 27, 2015, http://k-punk.abstractdynamics.org/archives/009325.html; and Steven Shaviro, "Zizek/Hollywood," *The Pinocchio Theory*, April 30, 2007, accessed December 27, 2015, http://www.shaviro.com/Blog/?p=574.

88. Slavoj Žižek, *In Defense of Lost Causes* (London and New York: Verso, 2008), 71.

89. Lev Manovich, *The Language of New Media* (Cambridge, MA: MIT Press, 2002), 176–212.

90. Steven Shaviro, *Post Cinematic Affect* (Hants: Zero Books, 2010), 30.

of Thrones, BSG, and *The Hunger Games* certainly make abundant use of CGI, but always in ways that aim to produce the illusion of a coherent and self-evident material reality. What Žižek seems to be getting at when he celebrates *300*'s inversion of digital realism, in which photographed human actors are placed in a closed and artificial world, is the acknowledgment of global capitalism's fully machinic reality. If the illusionistic spectacle expresses a nostalgic desire for the stable and mappable boundaries of imperialism, the truly *virtual* reality of *Spartacus* offers a way to confront and perhaps even challenge the spirit of global capitalism more directly. The twenty-first-century adaptation of the Spartacus mythology thereby offers not only a narrative critique of Empire's machinic enslavement and competitive individualism but also an aesthetic that supports and even heightens its radical energy.

But, of course, the *Spartacus* storyworld expresses this energy in a form that is deeply contradictory: while critiquing the spectacle as commodity, it simultaneously gives new form to it as a successful transmedia franchise. The series' thematic focus on the nature of the spectacle, celebrity, and immaterial labor resonates obviously and directly with Guy Debord's critique of the spectacular nature of capitalism in the age of mass media. Debord's theses are by now deeply ingrained in post- and neo-Marxist thinking, and as many others have pointed out, his work has lost none of its relevance in the age of digitization and media convergence. The French situationist's wonderfully provocative thesis that the spectacle forms "the very heart of society's real unreality"[91] has been made more concrete by Marxist authors such as David Harvey, who has described neoliberalism as an economic system of flexible accumulation in which "the need to accelerate turnover time has led to a shift of emphasis from the production of goods (most of which . . . have a substantial lifetime) to the production of events (such as spectacles that have an almost instantaneous turnover time)."[92]

Even more than in Debord's own time, capitalism in the twenty-first century is centered on the creation of immaterial goods, like events, experiences, and personalities. As Jeremy Rifkin has argued in *The Age of Access,* Hollywood and the rest of the entertainment industry have been the real pioneers of this mode of production. Even before developments like outsourcing, automation, and IT-driven financialization facilitated the emergence of post-Fordism in other industrial sectors, the media industries had already adopted a decentered organizational mode that revolved entirely around the production of spectacle in its various forms.[93]

It should therefore hardly be surprising that fantastic storyworlds like *Spartacus* and *The Hunger Games* have foregrounded the political implications of media spectacles in the context of immaterial labor and machinic enslavement. First, the

---

91. Guy Debord, *The Society of the Spectacle* (New York: Zone Books, 1994 [1967]), 13.

92. David Harvey, *The Condition of Postmodernity: An Enquiry into the Origins of Cultural Change* (Malden: Blackwell, 1990), 157.

93. Jeremy Rifkin, *The Age of Access: The New Age of Hyper-Capitalism Where All of Life Is a Paid-for Experience* (New York: Tarcher, 2000), 24–29.

very excess that caused so many viewers and critics to dismiss *Spartacus* as pornographic is crucial to its radical spirit: as with similarly formed underground and exploitation cinema, the franchise's determination to offend bourgeois sensibilities is one way of locating its subversive edge. Linda Williams has argued that the low cultural status of exploitation's sensational *body genres* is reinforced by "the perception that the body of the spectator is caught up in an almost involuntary mimicry of the emotion or sensation of the body on the screen."[94] But this affective and collective physical response is precisely what underlies the multitude's radical potential: the affective turn is derived from our bodies' ability "to form productive relations with other bodies, and it specifically identifies joy itself with such an augmentation of potential and relationality."[95]

This process is dramatized constantly throughout the *Spartacus* franchise across all its media incarnations, from TV series to comic books to videogames. The outrageously violent battle scenes in the arena are emphatically intercut with shots of the spectators, whose physical responses to the spectacle on display seem to be exactly as involuntary as Williams describes. The crowds in the arena react to the fights with hysterical abandon, not only screaming and gesturing like unruly sports fans but also exposing themselves and even engaging in sexual acts:

> The crowd leapt in ecstasy, hurling fruits in excitement. Strangers grabbed each other in delight. In the stands, Successa felt the hard bulge of an erection pressing at her behind.[96]

This depiction of the direct visceral impact of violent and exploitative spectacle is so striking that it begs comment, especially because it is consistently organized along class lines.

While the lower-class commoners in the audience are physically transformed by the spectacle on display, the upper-class aristocrats in their separate viewing space—the Roman equivalent of a sports stadium's exclusive "luxury box"—are only affected when they hold a stake in the fight's outcome: either because a financial investment is unexpectedly in danger[97] or because they have a personal interest in one of the gladiators.[98] The distinction obviously reproduces the traditional middlebrow perception of the working class as irrational/feminine and the bourgeoisie as rational/masculine. But the visual disparity between the two groups also reflects ironically on *Spartacus*'s ambiguous position in relation to the franchise's own ambiguous status within the twenty-first-century media landscape and its shifting cultural hierarchies.

---

94. Linda Williams, "Film Bodies: Gender, Genre, and Excess," *Film Quarterly* 44, no. 4 (1991): 4.

95. Gilbert, *Common Ground*, 147.

96. Clements, *Spartacus: Swords and Ashes*, chapter 10, "Ad Bestias."

97. Batiatus repeatedly sees his desired outcome of a fight thwarted by the unexpected intervention of a more powerful figure who insists a favorite gladiator be killed after surviving a fight.

98. In the first season, for instance, an important subplot involves the sexual relationship between Crixus and Batiatus's wife, Lucretia.

The class-based prejudice about the elite viewers of prestigious Quality TV holds that "pay cable consumers can handle graphic language, sex, and violence in a more thoughtful and productive way than broadcast viewers."[99] The depicted tension between these two radically different ways of responding to such spectacles therefore directly affects the television audience's discursive position. In *Spartacus*, the "gratuitous" emphasis on visceral violence depicted in close-up and slow motion sensationalizes the spectacle, while the shots of audience responses together with the visuals' emphatic comic book artificiality simultaneously alienate us from what we're seeing. This sets up a dialectical tension in our role as spectators outside the storyworld, which simultaneously acknowledges the seductive power of the spectacle while also critiquing its fundamentally political nature.

Rather than offering a choice between the privileged position of ironic detachment and the assumption of involuntary excitement, the dialectics at play here express what Jan Teurlings has described as neoliberalism's "new and enhanced" version of Debord's Society of the Spectacle. Teurlings argues that the twenty-first-century attention economy has made the spectacle more radically self-reflexive, as it has now been "absorbed within the capitalist mode of production, incorporating it in contemporary forms of the spectacle."[100] His point is especially helpful in the context of affective labor and immaterial production because it adds an appropriate layer of media literacy to Debord's implication of a naïve and easily malleable audience. Teurlings's argument extends the reach of Debord's critique, showing how our participation with spectacular forms of entertainment above all makes us complicit with the politics of global capitalism. Rather than rendering the audience immune to the Spectacle's alluring power, our obsession with the mechanics of popular entertainment paradoxically strengthens its hold over us. Like the endless audio commentaries and behind-the-scenes documentaries that accompany major releases like *LOTR* (see chapter 2), the media industries dedicated to revealing how spectacular storyworlds are created serve to celebrate and mythologize the spectacle in its commodity form.[101]

This is precisely what *Spartacus* dramatizes with remarkable sophistication and wit. The first and second season's structural focus on the inner workings of the gladiatorial arena both parodies and reproduces the structure of the media industries' intense focus on the mechanics of the spectacle. Spartacus, like his fellow gladiators, learns slowly that the entertainment he provides is part of a much larger political economy over which he has no control, even after he outcompetes

99. Deborah L. Jaramillo, "The Family Racket: AOL Time Warner, HBO, *The Sopranos*, and the Construction of a Quality Brand," *Journal of Communication Inquiry* 26, no. 1 (2002): 66.

100. Jan Teurlings, "From the Society of the Spectacle to the Society of the Machinery: Mutations in Popular Culture 1960s–2000s," *European Journal of Communication* (2013): 2.

101. "Far from destroying the 'fetishist' illusion, the insight into the production mechanism in fact even strengthens it, in so far as it renders palpable the gap between the bodily causes and their surface effect." Slavoj Žižek, *The Plague of Fantasies* (London and New York: Verso, 1997), 129.

his rival gladiators and achieves a substantial degree of individual wealth and acclaim. As a rather obvious allegory about media production, *Spartacus: Blood and Sand* gives the audience what it supposedly wants—sex, violence, and juicy melodrama—in a wholly appropriate "excessive" form that quite literally expresses Marx's famous point about capital coming into the world "dripping from head to toe, from every pore, with blood and dirt."[102] In addition, its dramatization of the Society of the Spectacle constantly reminds us of the media industry's workings: its corrupting and exploitative nature, its fiendishly addictive depictions of its own backstage drama, and, above all, its ability to thrive commercially even as it indicts the system of which it is a part.

At the same time, the way the franchise foregrounds conflicting modes of spectatorship assumes a knowledgeable audience that is able to negotiate its own viewing position critically and flexibly. Besides its impressive ability to extend itself across media platforms, the confidence with which the TV series combines a wide range of influences and registers results in a style that is as much an assemblage as Deleuze and Guattari's post-Fordist subject: its artificiality liberates the franchise from the stifling constraints of realism, its generic and stylistic fluidity demanding an audience well versed in the mechanics of media production. The storyworld's systemic focus on class conflict and anticapitalist revolution is therefore strengthened, on the one hand, by its dramatization of spectatorship, immaterial labor, and the Society of the Spectacle and, on the other, by the franchise's aesthetic multiplicity and its central dialectic of cognition and estrangement.

"DID YOU EXPECT FREEDOM TO COME ABSENT COST?": *SPARTACUS* FANDOM

Is Starz's *Spartacus* franchise then indeed a radical revolutionary tract cleverly disguised as a flimsy bit of pop-cultural junk? In the preceding sections, I have argued—perhaps counterintuitively—for an interpretive reading that foregrounds those elements of the franchise that resonate with radical anticapitalism and critical theory. And indeed, when sifting through the rich collection of texts that make up the transmedia storyworld of *Spartacus*, there is a great deal of evidence that seems to support such a reading. But, at the same time, we must also be careful not to overlook the internal contradictions that typify pop-cultural entertainment franchises such as this and push it too hard in any single interpretive direction. My interest in world-building and politics throughout this book is in the first place about the question of whether these storyworlds can facilitate and sustain real-world anticapitalism, both in theory and in practice. And while I have outlined its storyworld's theoretical radicalism, a brief discussion of the franchise's

---

102. Marx, *Capital, Vol. 1*, 926.

fandom will shed some light on its actual reception and the degree to which politics may or may not play a role beyond the purely theoretical.

Like so many other TV series in fantastic genres, *Spartacus* has accumulated a lively community of fans with multiple levels of involvement in the franchise. But even though this particular storyworld is in many ways more overtly political than many others, the fandom that surrounds it isn't all that different from other cult television hits. Fan activity surrounding the franchise appears to have grown rather than diminished since the series finale brought an end to the official franchise in April 2013. A first major "Rebels SpartaCon" fan convention was organized at a sports stadium in Waldorf, Maryland, in August 2015, following a smaller-scale event in Paris, France, the previous year. Attended by nearly three thousand participants,[103] the first SpartaCon featured a well-populated roster of prominent cast members speaking on panels and giving out autographs, as with other similar types of cons. Additionally, the sports stadium was used as an arena where fans could engage in workshops and put on performances of mock-gladiatorial combat.

While there is something charming about the creative cosplay and inclusive atmosphere that emanates from SpartaCon's website and Facebook page, it is at the same time striking how apolitical these events appear to be. All the energy at the conference is directed at interaction between cast members and fans, on the one hand, and the reenactment of gladiatorial games, on the other. As the website proclaims, "What makes Rebels SpartaCon so unique and different from any other convention is that it's an interactive con for fans and celebrity guests alike." The most prominently displayed photos show leading actors such as Liam McIntyre (who played Spartacus in the last two seasons) and Manu Bennett (who played Crixus) engaging in workshops and gladiatorial tomfoolery with cosplaying fans. The crowdfunding campaign to make SpartaCon II possible promises more of the same:

> SpartaCon was a success because so many of you saw the vision of what SpartaCon will be. Now that planning for SpartaCon II is well underway, once again, we call upon our rebel brothers and sisters to help make SpartCon II [*sic*] even more bad-dass [*sic*]!!
>
> With SpartaCon II, we hope to finish fulfilling the dream of transforming a baseball stadium into Gladiator arena [*sic*].[104]

While there is nothing necessarily wrong with dreaming about transforming a modern sports arena into a gladiatorial ring just for the sake of it, this particular kind of ambition also doesn't really qualify as a political act—or even as a particularly subversive one. In fact, it is quite obvious both in the organization of these

---

103. Number drawn from the conference organizers' website, http://redserpents.com.

104. From the Indiegogo crowdfunding campaign website for SpartaCon II: https://www.indiegogo.com/projects/spartacon-ii#/.

conventions and in the franchise's other visible forms of fandom (on Facebook, on the Starz website, on the *Spartacus* wiki pages, and on online fan forums) that actual fan activity is derived not from the storyworld's politics but from a sincere enthusiasm for the spectacle the series has offered, and from an individual sense of connection with the characters. In other words, despite the storyworld's subversive edge and left-wing legacy, there is no evidence that the most visible forms of organized fandom read *Spartacus* along similar lines.

Of course, this doesn't mean that *Spartacus* isn't interpreted and experienced in political terms, or that this new adaptation has abandoned the character's long-standing association with radical politics and the communist horizon its revolutionary storyworld suggests. It simply shows once again how a certain type of ideological content doesn't translate automatically into class consciousness or political action. Like the genres of exploitation cinema and fantastic fiction from which *Spartacus* borrows so liberally, the sociocultural rituals that coalesce around cult texts usually don't find their first or main expression in political movements or the formation of radical new social relations: people become fans of *Spartacus* because the story-world is personally meaningful to them, not because they respond to it as some kind of political manifesto. And while one does recognize in these fans' initiatives the infectious joy of collaborative and collective experience, organized fandom's reception of the franchise has not taken an explicitly political direction.

In those relatively rare cases in which forms of social or political activism have emerged out of organized fandom, this has been a much longer-term development. When fan activism did emerge in such forms, it has generally required a certain critical mass in order to translate into something resembling a social or political movement. From the "Frodo Lives!" campaign during the Vietnam War to the social and political activism of radical-minded Harry Potter fans,[105] characters and icons from fantastic storyworlds have only become meaningful political symbols after penetrating or even saturating the mainstream pop-cultural vocabulary. Assuming—if only for the sake of argument—that most viewers approach *Spartacus* in the first place as what showrunner Steven S. DeKnight mockingly describes as nothing more than a "gladiators-gone-wild-and-killing-everybody show,"[106] the franchise at the most superficial level simply delivers its outrageous thrills to a premium cable audience. As a decidedly minor pop-cultural phenomenon,[107] *Spartacus* simply had the advantage of being able to push the boundaries of television content, offering both an aesthetic and a politics that can easily be described as radical.

---

105. Some of the projects undertaken by the Harry Potter Alliance are explored in more detail later in this chapter.

106. Steven S. DeKnight, Peter Mensah, and Katrina Law, "Commentary," disc 4, *Spartacus: Blood and Sand—The Complete First Season* (Beverly Hills: Anchor Bay Entertainment, 2010), Blu-ray.

107. The franchise's highest-rated episode (the prequel series finale "The Bitter End") drew 1.72 million viewers during its original broadcast, while the final season averaged just over one million subscription viewers per episode.

But, at the same time, the franchise's niche appeal can be considered a limitation if we consider it from the perspective of translating its radical energy to real-life politics and anticapitalist activism. Like so many "disreputable" genre texts produced outside of the mainstream, the *Spartacus* franchise is a thoroughly subversive storyworld, but in contradictory ways that aren't automatically seen as political, and targeted at an audience that is neither mainstream nor part of a cultural elite. But while a close analysis of the *Spartacus* transmedia storyworld is rewarding, the fan culture that surrounds it has clearly responded to other aspects of the text than the ones I have foregrounded here. It appears therefore that both the franchise's cultural status and its degree of visibility play crucial roles in an entertainment franchise's political potential. Therefore, as an illustration of a similar kind of storyworld that did indeed become a much larger cultural, commercial, and political phenomenon, the last part of this chapter will turn to the revolutionary storyworld of *The Hunger Games*.

THE HUNGER GAMES: DRAMATIZING COMPETITIVE INDIVIDUALISM

As a trilogy of novels aimed at an audience of YA (young adult) readers, *The Hunger Games* was a smash hit from the moment the first book was published in 2008. But before long, it became a cultural phenomenon with a significance that swept far beyond its initial primary audience. By 2012, editorials and think pieces were being published that approached a large variety of topics from the storyworld's allegorical perspective, from comical *BuzzFeed* collages of animated GIFs giving fifteen reasons why the London Underground is exactly like *The Hunger Games*[108] to critical analyses of the increasingly competitive and exploitative organization of the academic job market.[109] Not only has the franchise become a cultural phenomenon, but its storyworld was also swiftly embraced as a form of narrative shorthand for the hypercompetitive cultural logic of global capitalism. Where *Spartacus* remained a niche property with provocative radical implications, *The Hunger Games*'s visibility has helped give its ambiguous political allegory a very real and wide-ranging symbolic power.

Appearing in annual installments from 2008 to 2010, Suzanne Collins's novels *The Hunger Games*,[110] *Catching Fire*,[111] and *Mockingjay*[112] introduced readers

---

108. Sabrina Barr, "15 Ways the London Underground Is Exactly Like *The Hunger Games*," *BuzzFeed*, October 9, 2015, accessed February 7, 2016, http://www.buzzfeed.com/sabrinabarr/15 -ways-the-london-underground-is-literally-the-h-1qpyv?utm_term=.pjpe2AbGG#.aa71Egmvv.

109. Carolyn Foster Segal, "Academic Hunger Games," *Inside Higher Education*, October 18, 2012, accessed December 27, 2015, https://www.insidehighered.com/views/2012/10/18/new-academic -underclass-adjunct-committee-member-essay.

110. Suzanne Collins, *The Hunger Games* (New York: Scholastic Press, 2008).

111. Suzanne Collins, *Catching Fire* (New York: Scholastic Press, 2009).

112. Suzanne Collins, *Mockingjay* (New York: Scholastic Press, 2010).

to the fantastic storyworld of Panem: a dystopian society organized into twelve numbered districts after a sketchily defined apocalypse has laid waste to the United States. These districts are organized into a rigid hierarchy, with the mining community of District 12 populated by the poorest inhabitants and the privileged citizens of District 1 (producers of jewelry and other luxury items) enjoying the degree of leisure and relative wealth associated with the twenty-first-century upper middle class. All are ruled by the Capitol, a fortified metropolis for the true elite, headed by the tyrannical President Snow.

Snow's government ruthlessly exploits Panem's media to maintain complete authority across all districts, with the media spectacle's power to indoctrinate and pacify epitomized by the eponymous annual Hunger Games ritual. This media event takes the form of an orchestrated spectacle of mass murder, as twenty-four teenaged "Tributes" (two lottery-drawn participants from each district) fight each other to the death on live television until only one is left standing. The victor is then assured the privilege of celebrity, material wealth, and freedom from labor for the rest of their lifetime. Certainly contributing to the books' appeal among their target audience, all three novels are narrated by protagonist Katniss Everdeen, the heroine from District 12 whose symbolic defiance of the Capitol's absolute power makes her the figurehead of a complex and ambiguous revolution.

Collins's storyworld is thus an instantly familiar pastiche of well-worn elements drawn not only from the Spartacus narrative of gladiatorial games and slave rebellion but also from Orwellian dystopia, Stephen King's similarly conceived sf novel *The Running Man*[113] and its 1987 film adaptation,[114] the Japanese cult film *Battle Royale*,[115] and the female-centered romance adventure genre that had previously made the fantastic YA franchise *Twilight* a cultural phenomenon. Throughout the narrative, Katniss must constantly negotiate her unexpected (and unwanted) status as a universally recognized and beloved celebrity. Her cynicism about her newly won privilege is fueled by her intimate knowledge of the inequality and brutality that the Hunger Games maintain—and which therefore also make her unwillingly complicit in their political oppression. And while she certainly isn't portrayed as the average, unexceptional Mary Sue stereotype for which this genre is so often criticized,[116] Katniss is also far removed from seemingly predestined Hero's Journey characters such as Luke Skywalker in *Star Wars* or Neo in *The Matrix*.

113. Richard Bachman, *The Running Man* (Harmondsworth: Penguin Books, 1996).

114. *The Running Man*, directed by Paul Michael Glaser (1987; Chicago: Olive Films, 2015), Blu-ray.

115. *Battle Royale*, directed by Kinji Fukasaku (2000; Beverly Hills: Anchor Bay Entertainment, 2012), Blu-ray.

116. Beth E. Bonnstetter and Brian L. Ott, "(Re)Writing Mary Sue: *Écriture Féminine* and the Performance of Subjectivity," *Text and Performance Quarterly* 31, no. 4 (2011): 343.

As played by Jennifer Lawrence in the first book's film adaptation, Katniss became an instant cultural icon, whose image in the smash hit resonated both socially and politically: as a female action hero in a male-dominated genre, as a rebel against capitalism's grossly asymmetrical distribution of wealth and power, and as a figurehead for a generation that has been robbed of its future.[117] The second film, *The Hunger Games: Catching Fire*,[118] was an even bigger commercial success, and the adaptation of the third novel, *Mockingjay*, was subsequently split up into two separate films, released in 2014[119] and 2015.[120] The films expand substantially on the books' original storyworld not only by their spectacular visualization of Panem but also by granting the film audience access to characters, subplots, and locations that are only hinted at in the books. The movies' blockbuster success and uncanny sense of topical relevance thus paved the way for a wealth of corporate transmedia world-building, as the storyworld would be opened up and further explored in games, magazines, billboards, and websites.

Across all these different platforms and media, *The Hunger Games*'s central concept hammers home the specific combination of cognitive capitalism and competitive individualism. For Hardt and Negri, as for Gilbert, Dean, and many other critics of postdemocratic capitalism, the key struggle faced by collective anticapitalism in the age of Empire lies in overcoming these two interlocking mechanisms, which together make up the core of neoliberalism's cultural logic. And while *The Hunger Games*'s storyworld in many ways does critique an oppressive political system in which a small elite enjoys massive wealth and privilege, it is at the same time fully immersed in the very system of celebrity culture and commodified spectacle the storyworld seemingly denounces. It is in fact more than a little unsettling to watch footage of the publicity tour that preceded the first film's release, as the crowds of seemingly hysterical fans straining to get a glimpse of the movie stars visiting an American mall bear an uncanny resemblance to the storyworld's own subject matter.

But even if the seemingly obvious irony is lost on these fans, there are still important ways in which the storyworld attempts to move beyond the confines

---

117. Noreena Hertz coined the term *Generation K* to describe the millennials who see their own lack of options reflected in Katniss's storyworld: "For Generation K the world is less oyster, more Hobbesian nightmare. This is the generation who've had Al Qaeda piped into their living rooms and smartphones and seen their parents and other loved ones lose their jobs. A generation for whom there are disturbing echoes of the dystopian landscape Katniss encounters in *The Hunger Games*' District 12. Unequal, violent, hard." Noreena Hertz, "Generation K: Who Are They, and What Do We Know About Them?" *New York Times*, April 21, 2015, accessed February 7, 2016, http://nytlive.nytimes .com/womenintheworld/2015/04/21/generation-k-who-are-they-and-what-do-we-know-about-them.

118. *The Hunger Games: Catching Fire*, directed by Francis Lawrence (2013; Santa Monica CA: Lionsgate Home Entertainment, 2014), Blu-ray.

119. *The Hunger Games: Mockingjay Part I*, directed by Francis Lawrence (2014; Santa Monica, CA: Lionsgate Home Entertainment, 2014), Blu-ray.

120. *The Hunger Games: Mockingjay Part II*, directed by Francis Lawrence (2015; Santa Monica, CA: Lionsgate Home Entertainment, 2016), Blu-ray.

of fantastical capitalism. Mark Fisher has been one of the most vocal champions of the franchise's political potential, describing his own response to the film version of *Catching Fire* as "genuinely delirious."[121] He suggests that Collins's storyworld offers nothing less than "a counter-narrative to capitalist realism," and sees in the film a punk immanence that miraculously manages to "corrode the commodity culture that frames it."[122] When talking about the film's transmedia publicity campaign, Fisher notes with infectious enthusiasm how the fact that even the advertising appears to belong *inside* the text translates into a sophisticated self-reflexivity that succeeds in deconstructing our own social reality. Thus, by embracing the contradiction inherent in its allegorical critique of commodified entertainment and its own circulation as a branded commodity, *The Hunger Games* supposedly short-circuits the ideological impasse Fisher himself has described in relation to "anticapitalist capitalist culture."[123]

It is indeed tempting to interpret the massively popular franchise from this point of view, especially since *The Hunger Games*'s deceptively simple storyworld is a lot more sophisticated than the yawn-inducing zero-calorie Marxism of similarly themed films such as *Elysium*[124] or *Oblivion*.[125] But, at the same time, we must recognize that the anticapitalist aspects of this storyworld are counterbalanced not only by the franchise's own status as an important instrument of capital accumulation but also by the contradictions contained within its own storyworld. As Jason Dean has pointed out, the revolutionary energy that gives the series its momentum also reverses itself rather abruptly, eventually descending into "the cliché of rebels becoming oppressors (pigs becoming farmers and all that)."[126] At the same time, the storyworld's initial emphasis on Panem's societal structure as a way to map out class conflict increasingly shifts over to a much more personal focus on the diabolical President Snow. As in Koestler's *Spartacus* novel, the revolutionary movement Katniss joins thus follows the predictable trajectory of ideologues being inevitably corrupted by power, suggesting a cyclical form of history that renders all radical political action futile.

This lack of specificity in *The Hunger Games*'s political allegory has fueled an interpretive debate on the franchise, with voices from both sides of the political spectrum laying claim to the storyworld's "polymorphous perversity of solidarity

---

121. Mark Fisher, "Remember Who the Enemy Is," *k-punk*, November 25, 2013, accessed December 27, 2015, http://k-punk.org/remember-who-the-enemy-is/.

122. Fisher, "Remember Who the Enemy Is."

123. Mark Fisher, *Capitalist Realism* (Hants: Zero Books, 2009), 14.

124. *Elysium*, directed by Neill Blomkamp (2013; Culver City: Sony Pictures, 2013), Blu-ray.

125. *Oblivion*, directed by Joseph Kosinski (2013; Los Angeles: Universal Studios Home Entertainment, 2013), Blu-ray.

126. Jason Dean, "Primers for the Post-Apocalypse: *The Hunger Games* Trilogy," *Unemployed Negativity*, September 5, 2011, accessed December 27, 2105, http://www.unemployednegativity .com/2011/09/primer-for-post-apocalypse-hunger-game.html.

and outrage."[127] For those on the Left, the power of the Capitol gave dramatic form to the Occupy movement's "We Are the 99%" mantra and was read as a striking dramatization of capitalism's minority ownership.[128] Deliberately fueling this interpretive perspective, Donald Sutherland, the actor whose performance as President Snow ironically works against some of the franchise's revolutionary momentum, added to the burgeoning wave of publicity by expressing the hope that it would help politicize what he sees as a passive generation of overly complacent millennials: "Hopefully they will see this film and the next film and the next film and then maybe organize. Stand up."[129]

Conversely, many on the Right have found in Katniss a staunch defender of conservative values in the face of "Big Government" and the media-savvy dictator they see in Obama, while the Capitol's autocratic regime was read as a compelling indictment of centralized power.[130] From this point of view, Sutherland's vague and patronizing call to arms could apply equally to Tea Party members, 9/11 truthers, survivalists, UKIP extremists, and any number of other radical right-wing groups who recognize their own concerns in the storyworld's oblique allegory. But this structural ambiguity doesn't automatically mean that the storyworld's political potential is thereby irretrievably contaminated or altogether lost. As in most forms of popular genre fiction, there is a dialectical tension within this complex multitext that is in a very real sense at war with itself. Just as Tolkien's subcreation of Middle-earth moves in opposite political and ideological directions simultaneously, *The Hunger Games* presents us with a similar basic contradiction, as the dialectical organization of this particular storyworld reflects Empire's inherent ideological tension.

Approaching the storyworld not as an expression of a single ideological perspective or contemporary political organization, I will instead focus on how the storyworld's internal contradictions resonate with similar tensions in postdemocratic capitalism. The first of these contradictions lies in the storyworld's representation of state sovereignty that is—weirdly—both pre- and postdemocratic. This central tension is clearly visible in the Capitol's power over the twelve Districts, which succeeds the United States' formally democratic organization temporally, while its backward-looking dystopian dictatorship is at the same time

---

127. Jedediah Purdy, "Teenage Riot: A Sentimental Education," *N+1*, December 5, 2014, accessed December 27, 2015, https://nplusonemag.com/online-only/online-only/teenage-riot/.

128. Ben Child, "How *The Hunger Games* Inspired the Revolutionary in All of Us," *The Guardian*, October 12, 2015, accessed January 21, 2016, http://www.theguardian.com/film/filmblog/2015/oct/12/hunger-games-mockingjay-part-2.

129. Rory Carroll, "Donald Sutherland: 'I Want *Hunger Games* to Stir Up a Revolution,'" *The Guardian*, November 19, 2013, http://www.theguardian.com/film/2013/nov/19/donald-sutherland-hunger-games-catching-fire.

130. Stella Morabito, "The Strange-Bedfellow Politics of *The Hunger Games*," *The Federalist*, December 15, 2015, accessed December 27, 2015, http://thefederalist.com/2014/12/15/the-strange-bedfellow-politics-of-the-hunger-games/.

"most obviously read in terms of colonial domination."[131] In the storyworld's quite literal postdemocratic sense, *The Hunger Games* presents a political order that has moved beyond even the empty rituals of participatory democracy. Instead, it offers a social totality in which a powerful elite rules over labor, resources, and culture in a fully imperial mode. As in *Spartacus*, a variation on the popular imagination of the Roman Empire thus provides a provocative and appealing allegory for global capitalism's twenty-first-century organization, and especially its palpable lack of actual democratic participation.

The second key contradiction is derived from global capitalism's pervasive focus on immaterial and affective labor. While I have suggested earlier that the narrative's main dramatic conflict is that between Katniss and President Snow, one recognizes a more productive tension in Katniss's constant negotiation between her own sense of self, on the one hand, and her transformation into a media celebrity, on the other. Starting with her compulsory makeover as a Tribute in the first installment, she discovers repeatedly that competitive individualism is not limited to the gaming arena, where we encounter it in its most strikingly brutal form. Instead, Katniss finds that she is immersed in it from the moment she enters public life by taking her sister's allotted place as a Tribute in the Games. The appropriation of her image as its own form of media spectacle in cognitive capitalism's biopolitical arena instantly creates the ongoing situation where "everyone wants to be Katniss, except Katniss herself."[132]

This constant negotiation of performative identity is one of the key features of *The Hunger Games*'s storyworld. The anxiety Katniss undergoes throughout the installments resonates strongly with the precarious and unstable forms of subjectivity produced under global capitalism. Once she is removed from her poor but "authentic" home in District 12's rural mining community, she quickly learns that her survival hinges on her performative abilities: paired up with her fellow Tribute, the kind but inscrutable Peeta, she is told repeatedly by her coaches, sponsors, and stylists that her odds of success will increase if she feigns a romantic involvement with him. As their mentor and coach Haymitch explains to Katniss in the first film, "You really want to know how to stay alive? You get people to like you." Peeta seems eager to go along with this approach, but both the novels and the films make it difficult to tell whether Peeta's romantic feelings for Katniss are genuine, or whether he, too, is performing strategically for the ubiquitous cameras that keep them under constant surveillance.

The constant and unrelenting "work on the self" that Katniss and Peeta are made to perform, both by the Capitol and by the resistance, foregrounds once again how Empire's dominant form of labor is fundamentally *immaterial*. While the film posters show actress Jennifer Lawrence taking aim with her bow and arrow like the long-overdue female action hero she is, the most crucial work she

---

131. Fisher, "Precarious Dystopias," 30.
132. Fisher, "Remember Who the Enemy Is."

must perform in order to survive is nevertheless that of affective labor and per-petual self-transformation. From the moment they enter the arena, Katniss's and Peeta's survival hinges on their ability to play the familiar roles of "star-crossed lovers" because they will only receive the assistance on which their lives depend if viewers find their performances appealing.[133] In other words, the immaterial and affective labor that typifies global capitalism trumps not only Katniss's own physical skills but also the superior prowess of her competitors.

This constant pressure to become an entrepreneur of the self creates a palpable gap between perception and reality, which is experienced as a structural impedi-ment to overcoming the competitive individualism that has taken such extreme forms in Panem's oppressive society. Katniss's ultimate disillusionment with the rebellion results from this same frustration. Unlike the romanticized rebels of *Star Wars* or *The Matrix*, whose quite obvious authenticity offers their protago-nists an exciting escape from a more artificial world, Katniss remains a pawn in a larger media game even after she joins the resistance. Moving from the direct competition of the Games into organized rebellion and its "arena of rebel pro-paganda films,"[134] her audiovisual likeness is modified, circulated, and weapon-ized in ways that are again fundamentally outside of her control. And while she proves to be remarkably skilled at adapting to a constantly shifting and precarious environment, there is a huge difference between her flexibility and that of char-acters like Tyrion or Varys in the far more obviously postideological storyworld of *Game of Thrones*. Where the examples in the previous chapter embraced or even celebrated fantastical capitalism's spirit of competitive individualism, *The Hunger Games* foregrounds the mental anxiety, unease, and depression that un-avoidably accompany capitalist realism's world without alternatives.[135]

This contradiction manifests itself both inside and outside the storyworld's nested series of lethal gaming arenas. Throughout the first installment's central competition, the narrative is far more invested in the collaborative partnerships Katniss develops than in her personal abilities or individual heroism. The instant rapport she establishes with her young female co-competitor Rue is a sentimental but effective illustration of her intuitive solidarity, providing a stark contrast with the highly competitive "Careers" from the upper districts, whose partnerships are purely and cynically based on tactical convenience. After trying but failing to keep Rue safe from attack, a grief-stricken Katniss openly defies the Capitol's political might for the first time, raising her arm to the cameras in District 12's

---

133. *The Hunger Games*'s narrative in this regard follows the opposite trajectory of the *Spartacus* TV series: while Katniss and Peeta initially function as subversive deconstructions of heteronormativity in media spectacles, the series' ending collapses back into this very logic. And while *Spartacus* begins as a tedious revenge narrative grounded in traditional heteronormative discourses, the franchise develops into an explicit celebration of queerness and gender neutrality.

134. Purdy, "Teenage Riot."

135. Mark Fisher, *Ghosts of My Life: Writings on Depression, Hauntology and Lost Futures* (Hants: Zero Books, 2014), 50–63.

"three-finger salute." In the film version, this symbolic gesture of solidarity instantly sets off a first wave of public protest in Rue's home district, sparking the rebellion that will develop throughout the franchise.

The Capitol's response constitutes an attempt to reduce to the personal an inherently political act of defiance: within the storyworld's hyperbolic form of postdemocratic capitalism, the threat of mutual suicide is ultimately the only way for Katniss and Peeta to truly resist Empire's power. As Fisher writes, paraphrasing Franco Berardi, "In a world where domination is total, where power has unquestioned dominion over life and death, then the last recourse for the oppressed is to die on their own terms, to use their deaths as—symbolic as well as literal—weapons."[136] Seemingly bereft of alternatives, the only way to create one is to opt out entirely, an act that may paradoxically open up a path toward political resistance. In this sense, the revolutionary energy contained within this storyworld resonates so strongly with radical anticapitalism because it shows how collective forms of resistance can take shape by a seemingly minor and spontaneous act of defiance.

However, Katniss's potent gesture of resistance does not maintain its revolutionary potential as the storyworld develops toward its narrative resolution. After her experience of global capitalism's compulsory immaterial labor is represented so negatively throughout the franchise's storyworld, the last installment ends with Katniss's retreat from political life and her return to domesticity and female reproductive labor. Approaching the series as a narrative, an ideological critique of *The Hunger Games* would certainly and justifiably point out that its radical potential is fatally compromised by this boringly heteronormative ending.[137] If we choose to approach the storyworld from the perspective that narrative closure is decisive when interpreting a text's ideological meaning, it is difficult indeed to avoid the conclusion that its politics are thoroughly reactionary.

But in the contemporary context of media convergence and fan culture, one could equally argue that the tensions and contradictions that define the construction of its storyworld are ultimately much more important. From this perspective, the author's choices on how to bring some of these tensions to a narrative resolution—and those made in the novels' many adaptations in other media—represent *possible worlds* rather than definitive conclusions. Indeed, the wealth of fan fiction offering more imaginative endings to the books' narrative climax indicates that there is no shortage of ways in which active readers envision alternatives that embrace the storyworld's coordinates but reject specific narrative, ideological, and political choices that make up the storyworld's canon. The different directions in which various forms of transmedia world-building have taken this franchise therefore illustrate more clearly the competing interpretive readings of the franchise's politics.

---

136. Fisher, "Precarious Dystopias," 30.

137. See, for instance, Riley McGuire, "Queer Children, Queer Futures: Navigating Lifedeath in *The Hunger Games*," *Mosaic* 48, no. 2 (2015): 63–76.

"ANY ACT OF REBELLION WAS PURELY COINCIDENTAL": SELLING THE STORYWORLD

Already a vivid and sharply drawn fantastic storyworld on the page, *The Hunger Games* expanded significantly as it crossed over into other media. The first film noticeably embellished the novels' limited-perspective narrative, offering not only a richly designed visualization of Panem but also the kind of narrative embroidery resulting from the obvious decision to break free from the books' first-person focalization. Without this limited point of view, we experience much more of the storyworld than we do in the novels. And as fandom surrounding the franchise proliferated, the storyworld was expanded even further by a number of spin-off games, several of which were produced exclusively for play on social media platforms like Facebook, and by the elaborate publicity campaigns that accompanied the later films' releases. The world-building practices that developed around the books and films illustrate the tension that underlies not only this specific storyworld but also any commercial world-building franchise with such an obviously anticapitalist spirit.

The transmedia work that accompanied the release of *Catching Fire* in summer 2013 is an excellent example, as it explored the culture, fashion, and lifestyles of the Capitol far beyond anything in the novels or films. The decision to focus specifically on this part of the storyworld can be understood pragmatically because it is one of the elements that can be developed in ways left untapped by the books or films, foregrounding spectacular design elements that simultaneously function as effective advertising for the franchise and its brand. The free-to-play games as well as the film's elaborate transmedia advertising campaign were designed to immerse the audience in the Panem storyworld: online games like *The Tribute Trials* and *Trial by Fire*[138] took the form of aptitude tests that introduced the player to the rules of the storyworld's central games, while billboards and online banners appeared to advertise the Capitol's fashions and luxury items from within the storyworld. After the first film had introduced the larger public to this environment, the games and publicity campaign appealed both to fans already intimately familiar with the story events and to a larger audience that was reluctant to encounter spoilers of the franchise's overarching plot.

The most ambitious element of this campaign was the *Capitol Couture* Tumblr site,[139] an online magazine situated within *The Hunger Games*'s storyworld. But although the magazine functioned as a playful paratext that seemed to have somehow escaped its own storyworld, the campaign also deliberately blurred the line between the diegetic world of Panem and the audience's real-world environment of brand culture and global capitalism. Writers for existing fashion and lifestyle periodicals such as *Elle*, *Marie Claire*, and *Harper's Bazaar* contributed

---

138. See https://www.scholastic.com/thehungergames/games/play.htm.

139. See http://capitolcouture.pn.

articles written under their own names, while familiar high-end brands such as Giorgio Armani participated in glossy "advertorials." Their names and logos were featured alongside fictional brands that gave fans an elaborate expansion of the franchise's increasingly immersive storyworld. Like Campfire's transmedia work for *Game of Thrones* (as discussed in chapter 3), the successful campaign surrounding *Catching Fire* thus offered paratextual expansions that contributed to the franchise's world-building while also functioning as spreadable and participatory advertising.

At the same time, the *Catching Fire* campaign raised a number of political and ideological issues: where the *Game of Thrones* expansions were focused on establishing the storyworld as a richly organized entertainment property and a recognizable member of the HBO brand, the paratextual work done for *The Hunger Games* also formed alliances with global corporations in the development of its storyworld. The prominence afforded fashion brands such as Armani in the imaginary magazine was an ambiguous strategic move that could—like the storyworld itself—be interpreted in contradictory ways. On the one hand, it could be read as a critique of commodity culture, as the campaign associates these brands with the decadent citizens of the Capitol who are complicit with a system of brutal oppression and gross inequality. On the other hand, the eagerness with which corporations entered into partnerships with the campaign indicates the commodity value of association with *The Hunger Games*'s established brand: the benefits of the franchise's enormous visibility clearly far outweigh the risk that some viewers will indeed see these brands more negatively.

In fact, the campaign's strategic use of established brands and commodities illustrates with crystal clarity that both interpretive readings (as critique or as legitimation) are made irrelevant by the franchise's primary function *as spectacle*. Adding to Debord's definition, Paolo Virno has more recently emphasized what he describes as the spectacle's double nature: as "a specific product of a particular industry, but also, at the same time, the quintessence of the mode of production in its entirety."[140] This is why the spectacle has become so fundamental to Empire's dominant paradigm of immaterial production: because, unlike money, it articulates in experiential form cognitive capitalism's basic productive process. Its political power transcends and collapses traditional forms of ideology critique because it continues to function even when its contents criticize or attack the system of which it is a fundamental part. Since global capitalism is a system that has come to function without an outside, without an alternative, it can therefore also increasingly allow forms of mass culture that illuminate its most critical contradictions.

But it still doesn't take into account the multitude's ability to turn cognitive capitalism's parasitical nature against itself. Virno has adopted the term *virtuosity* to describe this element in his vital elaboration of Hardt and Negri's theoretical

---

140. Paolo Virno, *A Grammar of the Multitude* (Los Angeles: Semiotext(e), 2004), 60.

work on the multitude.[141] For Virno, virtuosity perfectly describes global capitalism's creation of subjects preoccupied with work upon the self: virtuosic labor is labor without an end product, transforming all forms of wage labor into a kind of performing art.[142] But in the same way that global capitalism's decentered networks of immaterial and affective labor are ultimately also the key to its final demise, Virno sees virtuosity as a similarly double-edged sword. As "the intermingling of virtuosity, politics and labor has extended everywhere,"[143] the resulting collapse of the traditional divisions between earlier conceptions of class can also function as the single most vital conceptual tool to organize the multitude into new collective forms.

In the final section of this chapter on revolutionary storyworlds and postdemocratic capitalism, I will therefore supplement my previous discussion of *The Hunger Games*'s transmedia world-building as spectacle with an example of a different kind of virtuosity: fan activism that erupts spontaneously as the virtuosic expression of a collective love not only for fantastic storyworlds but also for the social and political ideals they articulate.

"FIRE IS CATCHING":
FAN ACTIVISM AND POLITICAL WORLD-BUILDING

> Economic inequality knows no boundaries—it is pervasive and persistent, and it affects every city, region, and country across the world. The gap between the wealthy and the poor grows wider every day. The ladder of opportunity is nearly gone. The middle class shrinks and more people find themselves short of what they need to get by. These are our Hunger Games.[144]

While many admired the elaborate *Catching Fire* transmedia campaign for its playful and creative spirit, some of the most devoted fans of the franchise were more critical. They described the clever and immersive world-building that expanded the Capitol's world of decadence and high fashion as "tone-deaf at best and deeply cynical at worst."[145] Arguing that the campaign's collusion with global fashion brands endorsed capitalist values that the storyworld as a whole attacked, fan activist group the Harry Potter Alliance (HPA) responded by launching its own campaign, *Odds in Our Favor*. For fans who responded strongly to

---

141. Virno, *A Grammar of the Multitude*, 52–59.

142. Virno, *A Grammar of the Multitude*, 68.

143. Virno, *A Grammar of the Multitude*, 59.

144. From the *Odds in Our Favor* website: http://oddsinourfavor.org.

145. Christopher Zumski Finke, "The Hunger Games Are Real: Teenage Fans Remind the World What Katniss Is Really Fighting For," *Yes! Magazine*, November 2013, http://www.yesmagazine.org/happiness/the-hunger-games-are-real.

the radical spirit they had recognized in *The Hunger Games*'s storyworld, this countercampaign constituted an explicit attempt to "take back the narrative" and foreground what they saw as the storyworld's true anticapitalist spirit.[146]

The Harry Potter Alliance already had an impressive track record of appropriating icons, characters, and narratives from the culture industry and mobilizing them for political ends. In his book *Convergence Culture*, Henry Jenkins describes how "the group reads the books' magical events as allegories for real-world issues,"[147] drawing on fans' collective love for the storyworld to expand its reach into social and political activism. Working from a more radical and more emphatically political perspective than most other fan organizations, the HPA made productive use of fans' social networks while interpreting the storyworlds in ways that foreground their resonance with the cultural, social, and economic contradictions of global capitalism. The group thus performs a self-described form of "cultural acupuncture,"[148] providing interventions that leverage the visibility of popular franchises like Harry Potter and *The Hunger Games* to organize new forms of social and political activism.

The HPA's first *Hunger Games* campaign had been a food drive titled "Hunger Is Not a Game," coorganized with OxFam to coincide with the first film's release in 2012. This initiative made use of the momentum provided by the franchise's growing popularity to create awareness and encourage collective action in response to global capitalism's poverty epidemic. As the HPA website indicates, "The economy has hit us all hard, and many more people than before have been going hungry, people from all walks of life and people who would never have dreamed of using social services before." The popular franchise thus functioned not only as a way to mobilize existing fan networks and engage in collective activism but also as a means of foregrounding an interpretive perspective on *The Hunger Games*'s storyworld that emphasized its anticapitalist resonance. While the campaign wasn't particularly complex or robust, it soon gained the support of several prominent celebrities on social media, and at the time it was the fastest petition on civic activism website Change.org to reach its projected goal.[149] While it didn't embellish or expand the storyworld itself, the food drive demonstrated how quickly and effectively organized fandom could contribute to anticapitalist activism.

As the franchise continued to gain momentum and exposure after the first film's box office success, the HPA developed a campaign to accompany the second film's appearance that was more ambitious and also more politically

---

146. See http://oddsinourfavor.org.

147. Henry Jenkins, *Convergence Culture* (New York: New York University Press, 2006), 206–7.

148. Henry Jenkins, "'Cultural Acupuncture': Fan Activism and the Harry Potter Alliance," *Transformative Works and Fan Activism*, ed. Henry Jenkins and Sangita Shresthova, *Transformative Works and Cultures* 10 (2012), doi:10.3983/twc.2012.0305.

149. An important source of information for this section was an interview with the HPA's communications director Jackson Bird conducted by the author on September 28, 2015.

radical than a food drive. The campaign attempted to provide an alternative to the studio's official transmedia blitz for *Catching Fire*, using many of the same commercial social media platforms—like Facebook, Twitter, and Tumblr. *Odds in Our Favor* drew upon fans' immaterial labor not as a source of free publicity and public ambassadorship for the franchise but as a means toward community building and class consciousness. Using one of the key symbols from *The Hunger Games*'s storyworld, users were called upon to participate in the action by posting a selfie in which they made Panem's iconic three-finger salute. These photos would be accompanied by personal narratives documenting individuals' precarious economic positions and could be circulated via social media using the hashtag #MyHungerGames. The movement's website, meanwhile, became a living archive where all the crowdsourced photos and stories were collected.

The movement quickly caught on not only among the HPA's ninety thousand subscribers but also far beyond. Mimicking film studio Lionsgate's ongoing campaign of posting news, messages, and advertising "in character" as the ruling elite of Panem, Bird explains that the fans put together "street teams" made up of core members who were given tasks to perform online. Thus, in response to the official franchise's immersive transmedia campaign, fan communities were able to respond instantly, using the storyworld's own visual and rhetorical language to critique real-world forms of social and economic inequality. As the campaign continued into the next year's release of *Mockingjay Part I*, the HPA developed partnerships with unions and workers' rights organizations, all of which embraced the online hashtag #MyHungerGames as a way to draw attention to the destructive impact of neoliberal austerity policies. As the campaign grew to include Facebook pages for the various Districts of Panem, the HPA's political world-building campaign combined creative storyworld expansions with a playful but quite radical anticapitalist energy.

The *Odds in Our Favor* movement thus developed into a very real, very successful attempt to forge a direct link between the radical energy of fantastic world-building and anticapitalist activism. Like the "Frodo Lives!" campaign that emerged out of a countercultural interest in Tolkien's radical potential (as discussed in chapter 2), elements from a popular storyworld were projected onto a geopolitical reality to generate attention for a political cause and foreground one particular interpretation of the franchise. It marked the kind of spontaneous effort to organize and activate new forms of collectivity that Hardt and Negri see as the multitude's inevitable counterrevolution against neoliberalism's global Empire. Like the international anticapitalist movements of Occupy; the student protests in Quebec, Montreal, and Amsterdam; and the Arab Spring, the fan activists made productive use of the same networks that are fundamental to cognitive capitalism's immaterial circuits of production. If Hardt and Negri can be maddeningly vague about how and under what circumstances the multitude will indeed use its creative energy to cast off the imperial shackles, this kind of activism gives a small but remarkably potent real-world example of the multitude's creative capabilities.

CONCLUSION

Fantastic storyworlds in which characters must compete ruthlessly for mere survival don't seem that far removed from global capitalism's precarious material reality. And for *Spartacus* and *The Hunger Games*, this resonance is made even more urgent by presenting neoliberalism's competitive individualism in the form of a popular media spectacle. In both cases, the storyworld's organization emphasizes not only the brutally exploitative nature of Empire's biopolitical regime but also the media audience's complicity with the Spectacle's political power. If fan culture represents the promise of collective appropriation, subversion, and resistance, fandom is at the same time similarly complicit in the media industries' increasingly frightening hold over us within our global attention economy.

The twenty-first-century revival of the historical Spartacus narrative gives a specifically contemporary direction to the character's communist imaginary: the new franchise's storyworld rejects earlier versions' binaries of class and gender, offering instead a thrillingly subversive allegory of media spectacle and biopolitical power in the age of Empire. Its remarkable aesthetic choices reproduce fantastic fiction's dialectic of cognition and estrangement, rejecting fantastical capitalism's discursive realism while fully embracing an inclusive and appropriately multitudinous politics of difference. And in its enthusiastic incorporation of exploitation cinema's "body genres," the transmedia franchise pushes beyond Quality TV's seemingly progressive identity politics to create a refreshingly tasteless radicalism. But this radicalism is limiting in two important ways: first, the franchise's focus on the sensational has limited both its audience and its cultural capital; second, the fandom that has developed around it has foregrounded these sensational aspects far more strongly than the series' ideological and political implications.

The Hunger Games has developed a similar storyworld grounded in class conflict, exploitative media industries, immaterial labor, and competitive individualism. But as a YA book series and blockbuster film franchise, its focus on realist aesthetics and more obvious-seeming allegorical nature helped make it a popcultural phenomenon. As a universally recognizable brand name, *The Hunger Games* has become a kind of shorthand for neoliberalism's fundamentalist paradigm of ruthless competition. But, at the same time, the franchise's oblique and contradictory ideological organization has rendered its symbolic representation of Empire deeply ambiguous, especially since the central narrative retreats from the communist horizon its storyworld so obviously seems to suggest. Clearly, the franchise's overwhelming popularity is derived at least in part from this ambivalence, as antigovernment libertarians have recognized their own worldview in it as much as anticapitalists have.

But the combination of *The Hunger Games*'s storyworld and its cultural ubiquity also makes it useful as both a helpful simplification of cognitive capitalism's exploitative nature and a tool for social justice movements and anticapitalist activism. The work done on this front by the Harry Potter Alliance is a helpful example not only of fandom's political potential but also of fantastic storyworlds' ideological resonance—irrespective of their internal narrative and political contradictions. While *Spartacus* cannot claim the same kind of popular appeal or cultural saturation, it makes the most of its subversive edge by combining its narrative's political legacy with exploitation cinema's radical potential. As fantastic storyworlds with an irrepressibly radical undercurrent, both *Spartacus* and *The Hunger Games* can therefore still serve as helpful reminders of who the enemy is in the age of postdemocratic capitalism.

5

Beyond Capitalism

Posthuman Storyworlds

Zombies and cyborgs: two ubiquitous tropes of fantastic fiction that neatly reflect global capitalism's cultural and political ambivalence in the posthuman age. The zombie, as the uncanny bearer of colonialism's horrific legacy, is one of the most potent symbols of capitalism's machinic dynamic of subjection and enslavement. Both its actions and its method of reproduction are entirely mechanical, and the zombie's apocalyptic emergence is always a harbinger of capitalism's inglorious end. The cyborg, as the zombie's dialectical counterpart,[1] ushers in a different kind of ending, with the organic and the technological merging into a hybrid that upsets and transforms traditional notions of subjectivity and agency. Each in its own way collapses the binary distinction between subject and object that formed the basis for post-Enlightenment Western philosophy, and which has legitimized and perpetuated capitalism's long and brutal history of exploitation and barbarism.

Since both of these figures subvert our very definition of human subjectivity, they hold a powerful potential for critical theory. If the previous chapter offered a discussion of storyworlds built upon a revolutionary promise of radical political change, the zombie and the cyborg make us ponder what kinds of worlds might be possible *beyond* capitalism. Neither trope is anchored to a specific political agenda, as both zombie and cyborg have articulated a wide range of ideological positions, from the fully reactionary to the most radical critiques of capitalism. But whatever any given text's philosophical inclinations, both figures force us to consider the many ways in which capitalism's relentless forward drive must surely reach its breaking point, even if this postcapitalist future can only be imagined in negative terms.

---

1. Within the horror genre, the vampire is the zombie's most frequently mentioned dialectical counterpart. But from the point of view of posthumanism and technological hybridity, the more obvious contradiction is between zombie and android.

The key theoretical concept driving my concluding chapter's discussion of fantastic storyworlds is that of the posthuman. The storyworlds inhabited by zombies and cyborgs are posthistorical in the sense that they lie not only beyond capitalism but also beyond traditional conceptions of human agency. Approaching the zombie and the cyborg from the theoretical perspective of critical posthumanism, I map out some of the contradictions that underlie their various storyworlds: how these posthuman tropes embody both the constraints that impede our ability to imagine alternatives to capitalism and the infinite possibilities of the radical political imagination. Taken together, they embody the contradictory logic of Empire, in which the multitude's growing desire for an alternative to capitalism is matched by a stultifying inability to imagine such a thing. By giving pop-cultural form to the inextricably interwoven feelings of fear and desire that underlie any form of postcapitalist imaginary, the zombie and the cyborg thereby provide productive and meaningful dialectical signifiers for a posthuman world.

CRITICAL POSTHUMANISM
AND THE ANTICAPITALIST IMAGINARY

Posthumanism is no longer a science-fictional concept: ours is already a truly posthuman age. The cyborg's hybridization of the organic and the technological, once a signifier of remote futurity in films such as *Metropolis* and *Blade Runner*, has quietly embedded itself in our daily routines. Our cities are populated by weird human-technological hybrids whose intense engagement with mobile devices is both familiar and alarming: familiar, because we have all come to rely on mobile technology for every aspect of our lives, spending our waking hours connected to an infinite and completely immaterial network; and alarming, because this reliance brings with it not only new connections but also an experience of time, space, and identity that is far removed from earlier conceptions of human subjectivity. At the same time, our reliance on wireless data transfer, smartphones, tablets, and other consumer gadgets is only the tip of the iceberg, as developments in medicine, genetically modified organisms, prosthetics, and quantum mechanics have thoroughly destabilized liberal humanism's anthropocentric worldview on a much larger scale. Therefore, even for the massive global population without privileged access to smartphones, wifi, and ubiquitous computing, the dawn of this posthuman age has become incontrovertible.

Our ambivalence about this fluid world of constant transformations finds expression in fantasies and anxieties that are specific to this posthuman condition. On the one hand, we find some degree of comfort in the popular fantasy that this development merely represents the next step in a longer history of human progress, and that humanity's mastery of technology will ultimately help us overcome our "natural" (organic) limitations. On the other hand, the technological maelstrom that envelops us has also made us question the assumptions that underlie such fundamental Enlightenment-era concepts as "progress," "identity," and the countless binary distinctions that have been fundamental to the Western philosophical tradition. From the latter perspective, the posthuman condition challenges many traditional conceptions of the human-centric worldview: "posthuman bodies are not slaves to masterdiscourses [*sic*] but emerge at nodes where bodies, bodies of discourse, and discourses of bodies intersect to foreclose any easy distinction between actor and stage, between sender/receiver, channel, code, message, context."[2] In short, the radical potential of posthumanism lies in its ability to disrupt and transform the hierarchies that underlie the entire history of capitalism.

Within the rapidly expanding field of posthuman theory, I draw for the purposes of this chapter on Robert Pepperell's definition of the term in his book *The Posthuman Condition*, which helpfully simplifies the main terms of the debate without losing the concept's radical political edge. Pepperell emphasizes the need to move beyond the assumptions of the liberal humanist intellectual and philosophical tradition:

> What is meant by the "posthuman condition"? First, it is not about the "End of Man" but about the end of a "man-centred" universe or, put less phallocentrically, a "human-centred" universe. In other words, it is about the end of "humanism," that long-held belief in the infallibility of human power and the arrogant belief in our superiority and uniqueness.[3]

Echoing key elements of poststructuralist theory, posthumanism demands an acceptance of the idea that "human beings do not exist in the sense in which we ordinarily think of them, that is as separate entities in perpetual antagonism with a nature that is external to them."[4] Instead, a radical redefinition of boundaries is necessary, relating not only to the distinction between human and nonhuman but also to that between subject and object, male and female, straight and queer, white and nonwhite, and so forth. This theoretical shift is in the first place the necessary acknowledgment of a transformation that has in fact already occurred: "The posthuman condition is upon us and that lingering nostalgia for a modernist or humanist philosophy of self and other, alien and human, normal and queer is merely the echo of a discursive battle that has already taken place."[5]

Acknowledging the posthuman condition, therefore, is not so much about the end of humankind as it is about the end of a fundamental belief in humanism. The posthuman body is no longer conceived as singular, rational, and coherent but as a multiplicity: a fluid and uncontainable assemblage that operates as a site

---

2. Judith Halberstam and Ira Livingston, *Posthuman Bodies* (Bloomington: Indiana University Press, 1995), 2.

3. Robert Pepperell, *The Posthuman Condition* (London: Intellect Books, 2003), 20.

4. Pepperell, *The Posthuman Condition*, 22.

5. Halberstam and Livingston, *Posthuman Bodies*, 19.

of constant negotiation.[6] In this sense, the posthumanist framework has utopian implications that open up a horizon for thinking outside the restrictive categories of global capitalism's biopolitical power. It is precisely at this point that Hardt and Negri embrace the concept of the posthuman as a crucial element of their theoretical concept of the multitude.[7] In no uncertain terms, they call for the subject to enter the posthuman realm of radical freedom by sacrificing the self. As they point out, "This does not mean that liberation casts us into an indifferent sea with no objects of identification, but rather the existing identities will no longer serve as anchors."[8]

The radical transformation that is required if we truly want to move beyond the blinkered worldview of global capitalism is therefore a *posthuman turn*, in which "conventional norms of corporeal and sexual relations between and within genders are increasingly open to challenge and transformation."[9] What Hardt and Negri emphasize here is that this is not merely an issue of identity politics or media representation in which social justice warriors establish tactical "sites of resistance" within and against the hegemonic strategies of a larger dominant power.[10] A truly radical politics can only be constructed on the basis of "the recognition that human nature is in no way separate from nature as a whole, that there are no fixed and necessary boundaries between the human and the animal, the human and the machine, the male and the female, and so forth; it is the recognition that nature itself is an artificial terrain open to ever new mutations, mixtures, and hybridizations."[11]

The main contradiction concerning these "new mutations" is that they are both the result of global capitalism's new forms of machinic enslavement and the tools that can ultimately facilitate the multitude's exodus from Empire's biopower. The imperial power that feeds off the multitude's "new productive practices" is by its very nature an unstable and constantly modulating network that also provides "greater possibilities for creation and liberation."[12] The hybrid, fluid, and endlessly adaptable concept of the posthuman is therefore the very thing that will make it possible for us to "push through Empire to come out the other side."[13]

---

6. Gilles Deleuze and Félix Guattari, *A Thousand Plateaus* (New York: Continuum 2004 [1987]), 38.

7. While they rarely use the term *posthuman* itself, their definition of the multitude as a radically diverse category hinges upon posthumanism's explicit disruption of traditional humanist definitions of the subject.

8. Michael Hardt and Antonio Negri, *Commonwealth* (Cambridge, MA: Belknap, 2009), 339–40.

9. Michael Hardt and Antonio Negri, *Empire* (Cambridge, MA: Harvard University Press, 2000), 215.

10. Michel de Certeau, *The Practice of Everyday Life* (Berkeley and Los Angeles: University of California Press, 2002).

11. Hardt and Negri, *Empire*, 215.

12. Hardt and Negri, *Empire*, 218.

13. Hardt and Negri, *Empire*, 218.

But what, then, would this other side look like? Certainly not like Paul Mason's well-intentioned but wafer-thin technotopia, in which postcapitalism can be achieved with minimal effort simply by embracing the connective networks of information capitalism.[14] It also couldn't be something as quaintly nostalgic as Marinaleda, the Spanish village that exists as a precarious island of socialist collectivity amid the rising tide of neoliberal Europe.[15] Perhaps it might be something like the truly participatory democracy that Jeremy Gilbert sketches out, with everyone spending a lot more time in meetings and a lot less time at work.[16] Or, as Nick Srnicek and Alex Williams have proposed in their treatise about a feasible postcapitalist future, a counterhegemonic movement could be constructed as a "post-work imaginary" organized "on the basis of fully automating the economy, reducing the working week, implementing a basic universal income, and achieving a cultural shift in the understanding of work."[17]

Of course, the postcapitalist world in the zombie genre is none of the above. The storyworlds that have typified the walking dead across all media accumulate into a bleak postapocalyptic landscape in which society's complete social, political, and economic collapse is a given. The zombie storyworld, pioneered in Richard Matheson's 1954 novel *I Am Legend*[18] and crystallized for the modern era in *Night of the Walking Dead*,[19] is not merely postcapitalist but fully postapocalyptic.[20] In its most familiar form, the zombie narrative articulates the intense vulnerability of the body—both the physical human body and the immaterial body politic—in the age of late capitalism, where rabid consumerism and the eradication of social structures has yielded a wasteland in which once-privileged human beings are reduced to a state of radical precarity.

But while the zombie genre clearly doesn't offer viable models for constructing a more sustainable world after capitalism, it does provide us with valuable conceptual tools that help understand the contradictory relationship between posthumanism and postcapitalism. At the same time, this most radical form of popular culture also illustrates Hardt and Negri's insistence that the idea of a postcapitalist world is an inherently terrifying one: "Revolution is not for the faint of heart. It is for monsters. You have to lose who you are to discover what

---

14. Paul Mason, *Postcapitalism: A Guide to Our Future* (Harmondsworth: Penguin Books, 2015).

15. Dan Hancox, *The Village Against the World* (London and New York: Verso, 2014).

16. Jeremy Gilbert, *Common Ground* (London: Pluto Press, 2013), 210–12.

17. Nick Srnicek and Alex Williams, *Inventing the Future: Postcapitalism and a World without Work* (London and New York: Verso, 2015), 108.

18. Richard Matheson, *I Am Legend* (London: Gollancz, 1999 [1954]).

19. *Night of the Living Dead*, directed by George A. Romero (1968; London: Network, 2008), Blu-ray.

20. Dan Hassler-Forest, "Zombie Spaces," in *The Year's Work at the Zombie Research Center*, ed. Edward Comentale and Aaron Jaffe (Bloomington: Indiana University Press, 2014), 120–23.

you can become."[21] Therefore, in this chapter's following section, I will discuss posthumanism's radical political potential by directing our attention to the figure of the zombie. By looking in more detail at the popular transmedia franchise *The Walking Dead* and a few key films directed by George A. Romero, I shall perform a brief anatomical investigation of the zombie's radical potential.

THE ZOMBIE'S RADICAL POTENTIAL

The zombie has developed in recent years from a movie monster that appeared primarily in American underground cinema and Italian horror films to a ubiquitous trope in global popular culture. Instantly recognizable to general audiences, yet flexible enough to serve both as a legitimate monster and as the punchline to a bad joke, the figure of the undead has clearly found resonance in late capitalist culture and has been connected to a wide range of political,[22] cultural,[23] and economic[24] frameworks. In the same way that Marx and Engels related the system of industrial capitalism to the figure of the vampire, many critics have pointed out that our postindustrial obsession with zombies is no coincidence. This zombie-theoretical perspective is summarized by Steven Shaviro, who remarked that global capitalism's networked and decentered society is "characterized by a plague of zombies."[25]

The rise of the zombie as what Deleuze and Guattari have described as our culture's "only modern myth"[26] has been accompanied by a simultaneous and insistent foregrounding of convergence culture's many networked and rhizomatic multitexts. Contemporary media are no longer dominated primarily by the classical cause-and-effect chain of narrative, instead engaging in an increasingly layered textual web that extends not only beyond any single individual text but also across many different media. This postmodern convergence of popular media reflects the complex, networked structure of urban experience that dominates contemporary consciousness, just as it does the "space of flows"[27] that makes up finance capitalism, and the posthuman hybridity of ubiquitous computing.

21. Hardt and Negri, *Commonwealth*, 340.

22. Daniel W. Drezler, *Theories of International Politics and Zombies* (Princeton, NJ: Princeton University Press, 2011).

23. Edward P. Comentale and Aaron Jaffe, ed., *The Year's Work at the Zombie Research Center* (Bloomington: Indiana University Press, 2014).

24. Chris Harman, *Zombie Capitalism: Global Crisis and the Relevance of Marx* (London: Bookmarks Publications, 2009).

25. Steven Shaviro, "Capitalist Monsters," *Historical Materialism* 10, no. 4 (2002): 282.

26. Deleuze and Guattari, *A Thousand Plateaus*, 386.

27. Manuel Castells, *The Rise of the Network Society*, 2nd ed. (Chichester: Wiley-Blackwell, 2010), 408–9.

As the examples in my previous chapters have illustrated, many of these trans-media storyworlds have developed knowable and mappable storyworlds across multiple media platforms, joining together fantasy's topofocal tendency and sf's cognitive tradition. In this sense, the commercial development of complex transmedia storyworlds and their respective canons also serves the important purpose of obsessively establishing the exact contours of media corporations' "intellectual property," including the brands, logos, characters, sounds, locations, creatures, and narratives they claim as their own. While the zombie genre has also been preoccupied in its own way with the mapping out of space, this has taken forms quite different from most fantastic world-building franchises. Instead, it has emphasized the role played by space as an active category, operating not as a stable backdrop to human action but giving narrative form to the "spatial turn" that has destabilized the traditional dichotomy between space and time.[28]

The zombie genre is one of the clearest pop-cultural embodiments of this spatial shift and the remarkable effects it has had on narrative structure. In many ways, the zombie genre even represents a form of antinarrative that relies much more strongly on the continuous negotiation of unstable spatial coordinates than it does on the causal chain of classical narrative continuity. The situational paradigm of the zombie genre maps out an environment in which a desperate group of indi-vidual survivors must constantly navigate spaces where "simplistic renderings of inside as familiar/safe and outside as unknown/dangerous are disrupted by the creation of bodies with new identities."[29] Narrative closure arrives neither through the successful resolution and containment of this ontological crisis nor by the establishment of a rational explanation of its key events. Instead, the storyworld's narrative focus is traditionally organized around a series of zombie encounters that challenge and disrupt the traditional uses of public and domestic space.

In their essay "A Zombie Manifesto: The Nonhuman Condition in the Era of Advanced Capitalism," Sarah Juliet Lauro and Karen Embry develop the figure of the zombie as a theoretical tool that can help unpack the "irreconcilable ten-sion between global capitalism and the theoretical school of posthumanism."[30] Their intervention presents the position of the zombie not as a *solution*—for the zombie narrative allows for no rational explanation or narrative closure—but as the embodiment of a negative dialectic that illustrates how "the only way to get posthuman is to become antisubject."[31] Echoing Hardt and Negri's call to allow for new, "monstrous" forms of subjectivity that move far beyond humanism's

---

28. "Space was treated as the dead, the fixed, the undialectical, the immobile. Time, on the the contrary, was richness, fecundity, life, dialectic." Michel Foucault, *Power/Knowledge: Selected Interviews and Other Writings*, ed. Colin Gordon (New York: Pantheon Books, 1980), 70.

29. Jeff May, "Zombie Geographies and the Undead City," *Social & Cultural Geography* 11, no. 3 (2010): 293.

30. Sarah Juliet Lauro and Karen Embry, "A Zombie Manifesto: The Nonhuman Condition in the Era of Advanced Capitalism," *Boundary* 2 (2008): 86–87.

31. Lauro and Embry, "A Zombie Manifesto," 87.

constraints, they celebrate the zombie as "a consciousless being that is a swarm organism, and the only imaginable specter that could really be posthuman."[32]

The zombie made its first appearance in global popular culture in the 1930s as American adaptations of the occult Caribbean *zombi* articulated a range of imperialist colonial anxieties.[33] In these early incarnations, the zombie was an external threat that embodied the terrifying specter of "slave uprisings and re-verse colonization."[34] But as it shambled into the postwar age of late capitalism, the zombie plague was no longer presented as an intruding body, but in terms of its internal presence: from *I Am Legend* and *Night of the Living Dead* onward, the monstrous undead are no longer associated explicitly with black bodies, nor do they emerge from outside the safety of imperialism's "safe" borders. As a thoroughly postmodern horror trope, the zombie is fundamentally uncontainable, allowing its own colonialist legacy to contaminate and destabilize everything it infects. The zombie figure's radical potential therefore lies in its ability to disrupt and reveal: by bringing the banal routines of capitalist society to a shrieking halt, the bodies of the undead present a fundamental challenge to our shared notions of biopolitics and subjectivity. The zombie in this context speaks directly to global capitalism's "episteme of biopolitics in which the boundary between the living and the dead is precisely what is at issue politically and philosophically."[35]

As a literal assemblage of contradictions, the zombie provides a simplified but most effective expression of Marx's appropriation of Hegelian dialectics, which David Harvey describes succinctly as a "process in which the Cartesian separa-tions between mind and matter, between thought and action, between conscious-ness and materiality, between theory and practice have no purchase."[36] This way of thinking, which "emphasizes the understanding of processes, flows, fluxes, and relations over the analysis of elements, things, structures, and organized systems,"[37] allows us to address internal contradictions without attempting to resolve them at the same time. It is exactly the tension inherent in the coexistence of incommensurable opposites that creates the zombie's unique attraction as well as its critical potential: it dialectically expresses both the fear of capitalism's seemingly inevitable self-destruction and the desire to finally break free from the stifling unreality of privilege for a diminishing global elite.

---

32. Lauro and Embry, "A Zombie Manifesto," 88.

33. Jamie Russell, *Book of the Dead: The Complete History of Zombie Cinema* (Surrey: Fab Press, 2005), 15.

34. Kyle William Bishop, *American Zombie Gothic: The Rise and Fall (and Rise) of the Walking Dead in Popular Culture* (Jefferson: McFarland, 2010), 12.

35. Sherryl Vint, "Abject Posthumanism: Neoliberalism, Biopolitics, and Zombies," in *Monster Culture in the 21st Century: A Reader*, ed. Marina Levina and Diem-My T. Bui (London: Bloomsbury, 2013), 135.

36. David Harvey, *Justice, Nature and the Geography of Difference* (Malden: Blackwell, 1996), 48.

37. Harvey, *Justice, Nature and the Geography of Difference*, 49.

Many theoretical approaches to the horror genre foreground this contradictory desire to escape capitalism's superficial "reality" and access a level of experience that is somehow more "real." Zombie narratives strive to create an affective response described by Noël Carroll as *art-horror* by staging a confrontation with frightening monsters that pose a threat "compounded by revulsion, nausea, and disgust."[38] The nature of this threat is always redoubled in the monster's simultaneous representations of our own mirror image or monstrous Other: "Audiences taking in a monster story aren't horrified by the creature's otherness, but by its uncanny resemblance to ourselves."[39] The horror genre, more than any other type of popular narrative, thus provides a relatively safe environment in which viewers can navigate the tension between fear and prohibited desire, charting the gap between the Lacanian realms of the Symbolic and the Real.

This is where Robin Wood's psychoanalytical description of the horror genre as the archetypal mode of expression of repressed fears and desires is helpful. The dialectical structure of the horror narrative requires the reader to continuously navigate between two opposite positions, moving back and forth between the nominal (human) protagonist and the monstrous (nonhuman) Other that embodies the threat to our "natural" order: "Central to the effect and fascination of horror films is their fulfillment of our nightmare wish to smash the norms that oppress us and which our moral conditioning teaches us to revere."[40] The lack of narrative resolution that typifies the horror genre thus aligns it once again with posthumanism's negative dialectic, its ongoing tension between incommensurable points of identification infinitely deferring a final point of closure.

Raymond Williams uses the same kind of dialectical method to map out the historical relationship between the country and the city under capitalism, which should not be understood as the clear opposition between one set of terms (rural, archaic, undeveloped, natural, innocent) in relation to another (urban, modern, sophisticated, artificial, decadent).[41] Like the zombie itself, neither the country nor the city has a true center that defines its meaning independently of other categories; instead, they exist only in relation to each other in a complex process of mutual and internal contradiction. Those discursive formations have no positive existence as transcendent and internally coherent objects in and of themselves: they are simultaneously defined and contradicted by their counterpart, functioning dialectically as a "union of two or more internally related processes that are

---

38. Noël Carroll, "The Nature of Horror," *Journal of Aesthetics and Art Criticism* 46, no. 1 (1987): 54.

39. Annalee Newitz, *Pretend We're Dead: Capitalist Monsters in American Pop Culture* (Durham: Duke University Press, 2006), 2.

40. Robin Wood, "An Introduction to the American Horror Film," in *Planks of Reason: Essays on the Horror Film*, ed. Barry Keith Grant and Christopher Sharrett (London: Scarecrow Press, 1984), 177.

41. Raymond Williams, *The Country and the City* (Nottingham: Spokesman Books, 2011 [1973]).

simultaneously supporting and undermining each other."[42] In this way, the posthuman zombie becomes both self and other, both desirable and terrifying, both
dream and nightmare.

THE WALKING DEAD'S FLUID
TRANSMEDIA STORYWORLD

The opening scenes of many classic zombie films are marked by the sudden appearance of the undead within a supposedly safe and enclosed space: the grave-
yard in *Night of the Living Dead*, the hospital ward in *28 Days Later . . . ,*[43] the
suburban bedroom in the *Dawn of the Dead* remake,[44] the pastoral farmhouse in
28 Weeks Later,[45] and the domestic backyard in *Shaun of the Dead.*[46] Like the
dialectical relationship in Williams's description of country and city, this should
again not be misunderstood as a clear and absolute difference between the safety
of interior space and the danger associated with exterior "otherness."[47] Instead, it
demonstrates a more general worldview in which the very existence of difference
has been eradicated, as global capitalism's biopolitical network has deterritorialized all previously existing boundaries.

In all these films, the survivors' response to the zombie's ontological threat
is the creation of a fortress-like safe house in which the protagonists attempt to
withdraw: the archetypal farmhouse in *Night of the Living Dead*, the shopping
mall in *Dawn of the Dead*,[48] the underground bunker in *Day of the Dead*,[49] the
luxurious high-rises in *Land of the Dead*,[50] London's militarized financial district
in *28 Weeks Later*, and the abandoned pub in *Shaun of the Dead*. The individual's
inability to safeguard against the zombies' posthuman onslaught is played out
across the genre with endless variations on a single theme: if the small groups of

42. Bertell Ollman, "Putting Dialectics to Work: The Process of Abstraction in Marx's Method," *Rethinking Marxism* 3, no. 1 (1990): 49.

43. *28 Days Later . . .* , directed by Danny Boyle (2002; Century City, CA: Twentieth Century Fox Home Entertainment, 2010), Blu-ray.

44. *Dawn of the Dead*, directed by Zack Snyder (2004; Universal City: Universal Studios Home Entertainment, 2008), Blu-ray.

45. *28 Weeks Later*, directed by Juan Carlos Fresnadillo (2007; Universal City: Universal Studios Home Entertainment, 2007), Blu-ray.

46. *Shaun of the Dead*, directed by Edgar Wright (2004; Universal City: Universal Studios Home Entertainment, 2009), Blu-ray.

47. Williams, *The Country and the City*, 96.

48. *Dawn of the Dead*, directed by George A. Romero (1978; Beverly Hills: Anchor Bay Entertainment, 2004), DVD.

49. *Day of the Dead*, directed by George A. Romero (1985; Los Angeles: Shout! Factory, 2013), Blu-ray.

50. *Land of the Dead*, directed by George A. Romero (2005; Universal City, CA: Universal Studios Home Entertainment, 2008), Blu-ray.

struggling human protagonists can be read as an enfeebled humanism's pointless resistance to the advent of a posthuman age, the predictable outcome is always their crushing defeat by the zombie horde.[51] In this sense, the figure's critical potential is derived once again from the negative dialectic, as the zombie forces us to think "precisely in its aversion and hostility to all thought."[52]

This dynamic is played out repeatedly across the many different incarnations of *The Walking Dead*, by far the most commercially successful zombie franchise in the genre's relatively short history. The series began as a monthly comic book published by Image Comics, in which writer Robert Kirkman and artists Charlie Adlard and Tony Moore set out to create a "zombie movie that never ends."[53] In his introduction to the first issue, published in 2003, Kirkman explains that he has always loved the genre but has felt frustrated by zombie films' limited running time and abrupt endings. The idea behind his serialized comic book narrative was therefore to stay with its main character, Rick Grimes, "for as long as humanly possible."[54] And true to Kirkman's promise, *The Walking Dead* has indeed continued to explore its postcapitalist storyworld in monthly issues for over a decade.[55]

As a comic book series, *The Walking Dead* slowly but surely developed a respectable following among fans of the genre. But its high-profile adaptation into a hit TV series by American cable network AMC turned it into a pop-cultural phenomenon. Premiering on Halloween in 2010, the six-episode pilot series attracted an audience of over five million viewers per episode, and its popularity has skyrocketed since then, becoming the first drama series on basic cable to attract more viewers than competing drama shows on American broadcast networks.[56] As a novelty item in the increasingly popular Quality TV meta-genre, *The Walking Dead* has developed into a worldwide commercial sensation, with the franchise

---

51. This narrative logic applies to the zombie narrative in its most traditional form in the horror genre. Many more recent zombie pastiche films incorporate zombies into generic frameworks that also allow for more "happy endings"—for example, the road movie in *Zombieland*, directed by Ruben Fleischer (2009; Culver City: Sony Pictures, 2010), Blu-ray; the romantic comedy in *Warm Bodies*, directed by Jonathan Levine (2013; Universal City, CA: Summit Entertainment, 2013), Blu-ray; or the action-adventure film in *World War Z*, directed by Marc Forster (2013; Hollywood: Paramount Home Entertainment, 2013), Blu-ray.

52. Edward P. Comentale and Aaron Jaffe, "Introduction: The Zombie Research Center FAQ," in *The Year's Work at the Zombie Research Center*, ed. Edward P. Comentale and Aaron Jaffe (Bloomington: Indiana University Press, 2014), 48.

53. Robert Kirkman, quoted in Henry Jenkins, "*The Walking Dead*: Adapting Comics," in *How to Watch Television*, ed. Ethan Thompson and Jason Mittell (New York: New York University Press, 2013), 375.

54. Kirkman, quoted in Jenkins, "*The Walking Dead*," 375.

55. At the time of writing, 150 monthly issues had been published, collected in twenty-five trade paperbacks.

56. Graeme McMillan, "*Walking Dead* Smashes Cable Ratings Records, Beats Broadcast Networks," *Wired*, February 12, 2013, accessed December 27, 2015, http://www.wired.com/2013/02/walking-dead-ratings-record/.

quickly expanding onto a wide variety of other media platforms, including several videogames (some of which have themselves been serialized), a series of novels, online webisodes, and the spin-off TV series *Fear the Walking Dead*.

These adaptations of the comic book storyworld into other media have been unusually flexible in their relationship to the source text. While every effort was made by the producers to reassure fans of the comics that the TV show would remain faithful to its source, the adaptation moved away from the comic books' narrative from the very beginning. Counter to most commercial fantastic storyworlds, in which "canonical" plot details are frequently considered inviolable, the endlessly deferred narrative of the original series here allows for a more flexible approach to adaptation that emphasizes discontinuity and fragmentation.[57] In a promotional feature for the second season, writer and producer Robert Kirkman attempts to legitimize these potentially controversial changes to the original narrative:

> One of the most important aspects of *The Walking Dead* that makes the comic book so successful . . . is the fact that you never know what's going to happen at any time. Anyone could die, anyone can leave, new people come in; and it's a very volatile comic that you can never really expect what's coming [*sic*]. If we were to adapt the show directly, be extremely faithful to the comic, we would lose that key component.

As Kirkman helpfully explains, the core of this undead storyworld is not a particular sequence of events or characters, nor does it lie in the detailed mapping out of a particular physical space.[58] When discussing these changes in publicity materials, the writers and producers continuously emphasize the supposed benefits for the audience. In Kirkman's words, the television series will give you "exactly what you would get from the comic book, but it's so different that you can enjoy them both separately."

This strategy has obvious benefits for a transmedia storyworld that is also a commercial entertainment brand, as each incarnation can develop its own audience without having to rely on any previous familiarity with other versions. Even those paratexts that seem like the most obvious spin-offs are also organized and presented as semiautonomous works. The novel *The Walking Dead: Rise of the Governor*,[59] for instance, is advertised on Amazon with the following pull quote: "This book stands alone and is a compelling read for fans of the series or just fans of zombies. Watch out though, because once you get a taste of the particular Kirkman brand of zombie mayhem, catching up on past issues is just around the

---

57. See Dan Hassler-Forest, "*The Walking Dead*: Quality Television, Transmedia Serialization and Zombies," in *Serialization in Popular Culture*, ed. Thijs van den Berg and Rob Allen (London and New York: Routledge, 2014), 91–105.

58. The franchise's geographical details, apart from its starting point in Atlanta, Georgia, are notoriously obscure.

59. Robert Kirkman and Jay Bonansinga, *The Walking Dead: Rise of the Governor* (New York: St. Martin's Press, 2013).

corner." While the many different versions across multiple media platforms thus each provide possible entry points to the larger franchise, they remain unified by their shared use of a central brand and a common set of aesthetic and narrative conventions. This clever approach to transmedia storytelling demonstrates how convergence culture's fluid and indeterminate nature corresponds perfectly with the immaterial and decentered logic of cognitive capitalism.

But even within this lucrative and hugely commercial entertainment brand, the storyworld's contents continue to resonate with the zombie genre's tradition of radicalism and antiestablishment satire. As its own form of world-building, *The Walking Dead* shows remarkably little investment in the coherent mapping out of a single canonical storyworld across different media, offering instead a variety of ways to explore the remains of a world that has outlasted capitalism—if just barely. At the same time, many aspects of the franchise reflect a structure of feeling that can be read as postideological: the genre obviously provides an all-too-easy metaphor for global capitalism's "zombie zeitgeist" of ubiquitous austerity, precarity, and relentless drive.[60] Therefore, if we read *The Walking Dead*'s storyworld as an attempt to imagine a world beyond capitalism, we inevitably run up against the genre's fundamentally nihilistic disposition: any attempt to stave off the end of the world or rebuild civilization will be met by this precarious society's inevitable defeat.

While this kind of textual analysis would doubtlessly offer further illustration of global capitalism's postideological spirit (as discussed in chapter 3), *The Walking Dead* does at the same time offer a more obvious radical potential when approached from the perspective of critical posthumanism. More specifically, in the franchise's provocative intersection of the zombie narrative and the Western genre, its ubiquitous and highly mutable transmedia form aligns itself perfectly with its unmappable, indeterminate, and intensely fluid storyworld. Somewhat sadistically, author Robert Kirkman has doomed series protagonist Rick Grimes to the Sisyphean labor of erecting one precarious posthistorical society after another, only to see them doomed by the community's inevitable descent into chaos amid the unstoppable tide of a new posthuman consciousness.

"IT'S NEVER, EVER GOING TO BE OKAY": UNDERMINING PHALLOCENTRIC POWER[61]

The Walking Dead opens with a violent encounter between small-town sheriff Rick Grimes and a gang of armed criminals that leaves the protagonist comatose

---

60. Comentale and Jaffe, "Introduction," 54.

61. The following section is based on a longer article previously published elsewhere. See Dan Hassler-Forest, "Cowboys and Zombies: Destabilizing Patriarchal Discourse in *The Walking Dead*," *Studies in Comics* 2, no. 2 (2011): 339–55.

in the hospital. Awaking with a start some time later, he finds the city overrun by zombies and makes his escape to the countryside. His first concern, rather than discovering what caused the outbreak, is seeking out his wife and child, who have miraculously escaped the zombie onslaught. The character's initial lack of interest in locating the cause or finding a solution for the zombie epidemic is maintained throughout the franchise,[62] keeping the narrative's focus on the more immediate concern of how to survive in this postcapitalist world, which—in true dialectical fashion—is presented as both horrific and deeply pleasurable.

The pleasurable fantasy offered by this type of storyworld lies in its puncturing of our Baudrillardian "hyperreality" as we are moved back from a world of artificial simulations into one of urgent necessity with life-and-death stakes.[63] For an uncannily precise illustration of this idea, consider the text that adorns the back cover of every issue of the comic book:

> How many hours are in a day when you don't spend half of them watching television?
> When is the last time any of us REALLY worked to get something we wanted?
> How long has it been since any of us really NEEDED something that we WANTED?
> The world we knew is gone.
> The world of commerce and frivolous necessity has been replaced by a world of survival and responsibility.
> An epidemic of apocalyptic proportions has swept the globe causing the dead to rise and feed on the living.
> In a matter of months society has crumbled,
> no government,
> no grocery stores,
> no mail delivery,
> no cable TV.
> In a world ruled by the dead, we are forced to finally start living.

Clearly, the structure of feeling that this fantasy provides is not only the fear of an apocalyptic event that will bring about the end of human civilization but also the fact that we are libidinally invested in just such an event: a delight taken in the removal of all "unnecessary" and "unnatural" modern preoccupations, thereby allowing the individual subject to reengage with "a world of survival and responsibility." One of the most disturbing fantasies the zombie genre therefore invests in is that of neoliberalism's world of urgent necessity, in which a permanent state of exception excuses socially unacceptable behavior:

---

62. The only exception to this rule is the first-season finale "TS-19," *The Walking Dead* (New York: AMC, December 5, 2010), in which a surviving scientist encountered at the Centers for Disease Control and Prevention explains the outbreak's medical origins. As Henry Jenkins has pointed out, this plot thread was widely rejected by fans for breaking the established "rules" of the storyworld. See Jenkins, "*The Walking Dead*: Adapting Comics," 377–78.

63. Jean Baudrillard, *Simulacra and Simulation* (Ann Arbor: University of Michigan Press, 1995).

Here we find the darkest, and simultaneously most joyous, heart of the zombie film: the consummate bad faith of the savagery you've wanted to inflict all along. It is bad faith because it veils the real desire under the sign of necessity: I had to kill her, she was going to "turn." It is the misanthropy of everyday life, the common urge to just stop talking things through, to stop biting your tongue, to unload on your friends, neighbors, siblings, and parents. And even more, on the stranger, the human body we don't know.[64]

This attraction runs through many of the classic zombie texts, in which only those characters who are physically fit, practical-minded, and ethically flexible will ultimately survive. In *The Walking Dead* comic books,[65] protagonist Rick Grimes functions as the ambiguous embodiment of these qualities: On the one hand, he must be completely adaptable to survive in an environment entirely bereft of stability. On the other, his natural authority and his social position as a police officer make him the bearer of white, straight, male authority, and therefore "a synecdoche for the pre-zombie social order."[66] Just as the traditional cowboy hero enjoyed a position of natural (if seemingly reluctant) authority in any community he chose to join, the invitation with which Rick is invited to take on leadership of the group speaks volumes: "We need someone to look up to . . . to make us feel safe, especially the women. I talked to everyone earlier. . . . We think that someone is you."[67] Rick then continues to pursue his original goal of establishing a safe haven for his family, with his role as patriarch quickly becoming more largely inclusive of the whole community. From that point in the comic books' narrative, the important decisions are left to him, the group in all its increasing diversity implicitly supporting Rick's postapocalyptic enactment of capitalism's white, patriarchal traditions.

Remarkably, the first substantial challenge to Rick's authority comes from the character of Tyreese, the first black man to join Rick's community. Initially Rick's most faithful ally and physically the strongest member of the group, Tyreese's role as a competing figure of similar power and authority is soon weakened by the gruesome murder of his children. In contrast to Rick, Tyreese is thereby proved unable to maintain his position as father and therefore his hold over patriarchal power, the primary function of which is the innate ability to safeguard one's own progeny.[68] Soon after this symbolic emasculation, Tyreese

---

64. Evan Calder Williams, *Combined and Uneven Apocalypse* (Winchester: Zero Books, 2011), 83.

65. Rick is characterized along similar lines in the TV series, but my discussion in the following pages will focus on the comic books, where the franchise's basic "rules" took shape.

66. Gerry Canavan, "'We *Are* the Walking Dead': Race, Time, and Survival in Zombie Narrative," *Extrapolation* 51, no. 3 (2010): 436.

67. Robert Kirkman, Charlie Adlard, Tony Moore, and Cliff Rathburn, *The Walking Dead: Compendium 1* (Berkeley: Image Comics, 2009), chapter 2, "Miles Behind Us."

68. While Rick does fail to safeguard his wife, Lori, and infant daughter later in the narrative, his emasculation is mitigated by her earlier unfaithfulness and the revelation that Rick wasn't the child's biological parent. Rick's "real" son, Carl, however, thus far continues to survive even the most lethal circumstances, including—miraculously—a direct gunshot to the head.

explicitly challenges Rick's role as leader, culminating in a bloody fistfight that ends in an uncomfortable impasse. But not long thereafter, Tyreese is captured and killed by the series' first major villain, thus again consolidating Rick's position of absolute authority over the group.[69]

While it may be unfair to level charges of outright racism at a series that features a high number of nonwhite characters among its ensemble cast, it must be remarked that the way the narrative ultimately deals with black male characters does seem to stack the deck in favor of Rick as the specific embodiment of residual white hegemony. In his article on race, time, and survival in the zombie genre, Gerry Canavan has argued that the zombie genre must be understood as an expression of a lingering Western imperialism that transforms the undead into "completely realized colonial objects."[70] While the zombie in and of itself is a walking contradiction, its appearance in fantastic storyworlds also establishes new distinctions between subject and object that helpfully "repackage the violence of colonial race war in a form that is ideologically safer."[71] In this sense, the most obvious reading of *The Walking Dead* clearly reproduces the genre's fundamentally colonial fantasy of racist violence: the pleasurable idea that an inevitably apocalyptic postcapitalist world will serve as a stage for acting out American Empire's cowboy narratives within neoliberalism's "differentialist racism."[72]

But, at the same time, *The Walking Dead* has actively disrupted the objectifying colonial gaze that privileges white patriarchy's traditional forms of power. Although Rick Grimes certainly has no difficulty establishing himself as the group's leader, the narrative reveals repeatedly that the communities that develop under his leadership remain fundamentally unsustainable. While Rick obviously functions as the residual embodiment of imperialist power and its colonial gaze, his leadership isn't justified in the ways one might expect. Many times over, he makes obvious and crucial errors of judgment that frequently cause the deaths of other members of the various communities he leads. Perpetually insecure about his own abilities and prone to outbursts of violent rage, Rick Grimes is as much an indictment of the centered, humanist subject as he is a celebration of it.

His unreliability is vividly illustrated in the early stages of the comic books' prison narrative,[73] during which his leadership is threatened first from within, by other members of his precarious community, and then from without, by his

---

69. In the first forty-eight issues of *The Walking Dead*, the only black character to survive alongside Rick is the samurai-sword-wielding "tough chick" Michonne, and this is only after her having suffered through an astonishingly brutal extended rape sequence. Of the two black males who constitute a viable threat to Rick's central leadership position, one is executed by Rick, while Tyreese ends up sacrificing himself after a failed attempt to take over while Rick lies wounded.

70. Canavan, "We *Are* the Walking Dead," 437.

71. Canavan, "We *Are* the Walking Dead," 439.

72. Étienne Balibar, "Is There a 'Neo-Racism'?" in *Race, Nation, Class: Ambigious Identities*, Étienne Balibar and Immanuel Wallerstein (London and New York: Verso, 1991), 17–28.

73. Kirkman, Adlard, Moore, and Blackburn, *The Walking Dead: Compendium 1*, chapters 3–8.

monstrous mirror image, The Governor. The internal conflict is resolved in a sequence that shows Rick legitimizing his leadership of the group in spite of the fact that he repeatedly leaps to the wrong conclusion and must resort to physical force to maintain his dominance over the community. The sequence then ends with the establishment of the first explicit law Rick articulates in the storyworld's emergent postapocalyptic society: "You kill, you die."[74]

Rick's deceptively simple first commandment is a literal expression of his phallocentric authority: by making this pronouncement, Rick inscribes his patriarchal power on the group, thus explicitly extending his position beyond that which he holds over his more literal family. In Lacan's psychoanalytical vocabulary, this act therefore perpetuates the figure of the father as symbolic Law-Giver, his power over others sustained by a threat of violence that is normally merely implied but which is in this context completely explicit.[75] But, as Lacan states, this violence that supposedly maintains social order by punishing transgressors is ultimately irrational and even uncontrollable. Since it must be exercised in order to reassure the male figure of authority that his phallic power is intact, Lacan's definition of the phallus proposes instead that neither man nor woman can ever in fact achieve this, as the phallus functions as a symbolic *objet petit a* that will always elude one's direct grasp: "Man cannot aim at being whole while ever the play of displacement and condensation to which he is doomed in the exercise of his functions marks his relation as subject to the signifier."[76] Or, to put it in simpler terms, any actual attempt to exercise phallic power is doomed to failure, as it constitutes an attempt to fill a gap that is essentially unfillable. In the context of *The Walking Dead*, this means that Rick's appropriation of patriarchal power will inevitably collide with the generic structure of a storyworld in which no stable symbolic order can be maintained.

It is therefore hardly surprising that the first character to break this primal "Law of the Father" is the leader figure himself. Directly after first proclaiming his first commandment, Rick ruthlessly executes a competing male character during the chaos of a zombie assault, thus resolving yet another threat to his leadership and securing the group's residence in the prison. But, of course, another character has witnessed Rick's act, and before long everyone in the prison knows what Lacan (or Freud, for that matter) would have predicted—namely, that the Father is not only the Law-Giver but also its original transgressor. Nor is Rick himself oblivious to the contradiction inherent in his position: when the truth is revealed to the whole group, he confronts the community with the reality of their situation as he now sees it, articulated in a lengthy and dramatically staged monologue. Flippantly reversing his earlier position, he now dismisses his

74. Kirkman, Adlard, Moore, and Blackburn, *The Walking Dead: Compendium 1*, chapter 3.

75. Jacques Lacan, *Écrits: A Selection*, trans. Bruce Fink (London and New York: Routledge, 2001), 67–84.

76. Lacan, *Écrits*, 287.

first law as "the most naïve thing I've ever said."[77] During his speech, in which the panels provide a montage of images of the group members listening intently while the zombies crowd around the gates, he builds toward his big announcement, which is climactically presented across a two-page splash panel: "We *are* the walking dead!"[78]

Within the zombie genre, a statement like this isn't exactly a groundbreaking moment of profound insight: from *Night of the Living Dead* onward, a conclusion along these lines has been at the core of these nihilistic narratives.[79] Nevertheless, true to the zombie genre's radical spirit, Rick's words clearly acknowledge the fact that the world they inhabit is a truly posthuman one. The many different groups' countless attempts to construct a viable society on the basis of human history, including the phallocentric authority Rick struggles to embody, are doomed from the outset. In a thoughtful commentary on the comic books, Peter Y. Paik has observed that these central myths are portrayed in this storyworld as "exhausted, as incapable of carrying out the functions formerly accorded to them of building a society in what was once a wild and hostile territory."[80] For Paik, who also acknowledges the franchise's attempt to offer "a thought experiment about the reconstitution of community life,"[81] the storyworld's political potential is undercut by its simultaneous "repudiation of the possibility of any alternative."[82]

In a way, this will no doubt remain true: for as long as the series might continue to run, Rick's attempts to forge durable alternatives will surely be defeated by the posthuman world they inhabit, no matter how high they build their walls. After all, in the zombie genre as elsewhere, "the *telos* of the fortress, like the *telos* of empire, is always, in the end, to fall."[83] But, by the same token, the storyworld's political potential lies not in its ability to resolve the contradictions it raises but in its dialectical approach to the dramatic specter of the posthuman condition. Even though *The Walking Dead* constantly and quite brutally undermines its own utopian potential, its storyworld also stubbornly insists on the possibility of a postcapitalist future where "there is no distinction between rich and poor, resources are shared equally among the major characters, and human beings rediscover the value of duty and mutual obligation."[84]

---

77. Kirkman, Adlard, Moore, and Blackburn, *The Walking Dead: Compendium 1*, chapter 4.

78. Kirkman, Adlard, Moore, and Blackburn, *The Walking Dead: Compendium 1*, chapter 4.

79. Romero's *Dawn of the Dead* features this motif's most literal and iconic articulation: *Francine Parker*: What the hell are they? *Peter*: They're us, that's all.

80. Peter Y. Paik, "Doing What Comes Unnaturally: The Gnostic Zombie in Robert Kirkman's *The Walking Dead*," Eric Voegelin Society Meeting 2011, Seattle, WA, 9, http://wearethewalkingdead .weebly.com/survival-tools/doing-what-comes-unnaturally-the-gnostic-zombie-in-robert-kirkmans -the-walking-dead-by-peter-paik.

81. Paik, "Doing What Comes Unnaturally," 4.

82. Paik, "Doing What Comes Unnaturally," 9.

83. Canavan, "'We *Are* the Walking Dead,'" 445.

84. Paik, "Doing What Comes Unnaturally," 10.

Therefore, *The Walking Dead* remains above all an expression of global capitalism's deep ambivalence regarding the posthuman condition. While there is a recognizably utopian impulse in the series' continuous attempts to flesh out meaningful forms of collective living in a postcapitalist world, the groups' inevitable demise also results from their inability to embrace the zombie's posthuman implications. The main problem with these precarious communities is therefore that they are clearly not radical enough: in order to allow for a truly postcapitalist imaginary, it is not enough for human communities merely to survive the zombie epidemic. One must learn to embrace the zombie's implicit collapse of all humanist definitions of the self that underlie capitalism's forms of subjectivity. To quote "A Zombie Manifesto" once more:

> Capitalism depends on our sense of ourselves as having individual consciousnesses to prohibit the development of a revolutionary collective and to bolster the attitude that drives it: every man for himself. Appositely, posthumanity can only really be attained when we pull the trigger on the ego. To kill the zombie, you must destroy the brain, and to move posthuman [*sic*], to lay humanism and its legacy of power and oppression in the grave, we have to undo our primary systems of differentiation: subject/object, me/you. In fact, these terms cannot be separated—like the deathlife of the zombie, the capitalist superstructure and the posthuman fantasy have been yoked together in a monstrous body, the existence of one state prohibits the presence of the other.[85]

Thus, in its continued resistance to the undead as a figure of spectacular monstrosity, *The Walking Dead* also structurally rejects its own radical potential. This is even more so in the TV series and serialized videogames developed by Telltale, where the focus has been more strongly than in the comic books on the visually spectacular encounters between the human survivors and the undead "walkers." But even if the structural organization of this multilayered transmedia storyworld diminishes the zombie's posthuman implications, it has at the same time made the walking dead a more robust part of a widely shared pop-cultural vocabulary, giving fans and activists new opportunities to appropriate the zombie as a figure of transformation and resistance on their own terms.

ZOMBIES, OCCUPY, AND THE RIGHT TO THE CITY

If Marx's oft-cited metaphor of capital as a vampiric force remains intact,[86] we might continue to perceive the zombie as the embodiment of (un)dead labor. Capitalist alienation is grounded in coercive social relations that force wage-laborers

---

85. Lauro and Embry, "A Zombie Manifesto," 106.
86. Karl Marx, *Capital, Vol. 1*, trans. Ben Fowkes (Harmondsworth: Penguin Books, 1976), 915.

Chapter 5

to fragment and sell their time for money, leading to "a sort of death-in-life."[87] Little wonder, then, as David McNally has pointed out, that "images of the living dead proliferate so widely in the capitalist culture-industry."[88] But this logic applies only if we take the phrase literally and emphasize the notion that labor in the postindustrial world has indeed—to quote Monty Python's famous "Dead Parrot" sketch—run down the curtain and joined the choir invisible.[89] The zombie figure's appeal to Western audiences makes more sense if we interpret it as the phantasmic resurrection of a labor force that has been increasingly disenfranchised, ignored, and marginalized in postindustrial capitalism: the legions of the unemployed, homeless, and destitute that have become the horrific by-product of neoliberal globalization.[90]

This conception of the zombie as industrial capitalism's undead residue also corresponds with the genre's obsession with private property and domestic security. Global capitalism's urban centers have been transformed in recent years into increasingly privatized and militarized carceral archipelagoes held together by "technologies of violence and social control, fostered by capital and the state."[91] Beginning with the Western urban centers of concentrated capital, but swiftly spreading to major cities worldwide, this development has now resulted in the dramatic gap between the increasingly isolated ghettoes, shantytowns, and favelas of the poor existing side by side with the spectacular and rigidly guarded gated communities of the obscenely wealthy. While the guilty desire to join the ranks of the aristocratic vampire permeates the Gothic horror genre tradition,[92] the zombie's status as racialized and ghettoized Other supposedly made it a purely negative trope: no one in their right mind dreams of marrying—let alone becoming—a zombie.

And yet, we have more recently seen an increasing number of zombie narratives in which forms of undead consciousness have been explored, and even some fictions in which the zombie body can become desirable: the suburban comedy

---

87. David McNally, *Monsters of the Market: Zombies, Vampires and Global Capitalism* (Chicago: Haymarket Books, 2012), 147.

88. McNally, *Monsters of the Market*, 147.

89. This metaphorical image also incorporates Chris Harman's fiercely argued point that labor in the postindustrial age has become more invisible than absent—not just globally but also locally within advanced capitalist countries. He warns us not to exaggerate the purely "immaterial" nature of labor in postindustrial capitalism, especially in a context where "the common sense among philosophers has departed from empirical reality." See Harman, *Zombie Capitalism*, 331.

90. As Steven Shaviro has helpfully described these "capitalist monsters," "In contrast to the inhumanity of vampire-capital, zombies present the 'human face' of capitalist monstrosity. This is precisely because they are the dregs of humanity: the zombie is all that remains of 'human nature,' or even simply of a human scale, in the immense and unimaginably complex network economy." Shaviro, "Capitalist Monsters," 288.

91. Edward W. Soja, "Six Discourses on the Postmetropolis," in *The Blackwell City Reader*, 2nd ed., ed. Gary Bridge and Sophie Watson (Malden: Blackwell, 2010), 379.

92. See Nina Auerbach, *Our Vampires, Ourselves* (Chicago: University of Chicago Press, 1995).

Fido[93] imagines the zombie as a man-servant and (even more provocatively) domestic pet, foregrounding and destabilizing the relationship not only between master and servant but also between human and animal; Isaac Marion's popular YA novel *Warm Bodies*[94] and its film adaptation[95] feature a zombie as both first-person narrator and the romantic lead in an undead variation on *Romeo and Juliet*; and several European television series, including *In the Flesh* and *Les Revenants*, have used the zombie framework to explore ways in which interactions between "real" human survivors and posthuman zombies challenge and disrupt existing social and cultural boundaries.

Prior to these twenty-first-century forms of undead consciousness, "zombie auteur" George A. Romero explored the posthuman potential contained within the zombie trope his independent films had popularized. Certainly the most celebrated example of the zombie as a hybrid posthuman subject is that of "Bub" in the underrated third film in his original "Living Dead Trilogy," *Day of the Dead*. As the test subject for a scientist's experimental work on zombie brains, Bub is conditioned to respond to stimuli and soon becomes the most purely sympathetic character amid the film's rapidly deteriorating community of human survivors. As a zombie who develops a form of (post)human consciousness, Bub signaled a movement toward embracing the zombie as a productive liminal figure.[96]

Bub's pioneering zombie subjectivity was developed further in Romero's first and only studio-financed zombie film, *Land of the Dead*, in which the previous film's tangential thread becomes the narrative's guiding force. Unlike *The Walking Dead*, where the zombie catastrophe forces survivors to construct precarious alternatives in a postcapitalist world, the apocalypse in *Land of the Dead* only intensifies global capitalism's already obscene levels of inequality. In the film, the inner city has been fenced in to create a gated community that keeps its wealthy inhabitants safe from the undead hordes roaming the suburbs and the countryside. In the skyscraper district of Fiddler's Green, the rich continue to live in opulent luxury, while the ordinary citizens are reduced to the barest levels of subsistence. Everything beyond the city limits has been abandoned and left to the zombies, while only a new class of armed free-agents ventures outside in search of increasingly scarce resources, the bulk of which is claimed by the wealthy capitalists.

The film's central allegory of class conflict is compounded by its specific representation of zombie bodies, which are introduced in the first scene as they are being sadistically taunted and butchered by the corporate-sponsored raiders.

---

93. *Fido*, directed by Andrew Currie (2006; Santa Monica, CA: Lionsgate Home Entertainment, 2007), DVD.

94. Isaac Marion, *Warm Bodies* (New York: Atria Books, 2010).

95. *Warm Bodies*, directed by Jonathan Levine (2013; Universal City: Summit Entertainment, 2013), Blu-ray.

96. Bub's enduring popularity among zombie fans led to a cameo appearance among the "walkers" in "Us," *The Walking Dead* (AMC, March 23, 2014).

Observing the violence inflicted for no apparent reason on these disposable bodies, the zombified gas station attendant known only as "Big Daddy" develops a first inkling of consciousness and becomes the leader of a massive "suburban to urban zombie migration."[97] Strategically directing his more feeble-minded brethren, Big Daddy is able to recognize a weakness in the city's security system. And in the film's climax, he leads a mass of the living dead into the heart of the city, where the monstrous capitalists finally meet their just desserts at the hands of their own redundant workforce.

What sets this film apart not only from the other Romero films but also from most other previous zombie films is its development of an obviously allegorical class system specific to Empire's social totality: the rich occupants of Fiddler's Green represent capitalism's minority ownership, the impoverished inhabitants of the city are the precarious remainder of a disenfranchised middle class, and the zombies outside the city's nested gated communities represent the stubborn remainder of unwanted and unemployable labor. Amid this ham-fisted metaphor of class conflict, the raiders represent cognitive capitalism's new entrepreneurial class that mediates between these different worlds, providing crucial access to information and resources while profiting from the injustices of the status quo. Although this small group of mercenaries includes the film's protagonists and is superficially guided by good intentions, they are at the same time completely alienated by the endemic greed and corruption that defines the system of which they are a reluctant part. Their mercantilist cynicism flows directly from their obvious detachment from everything around them, while their postideological mercenary work exemplifies the neoliberal notion that only the most completely self-reliant entrepreneurs of the self will thrive in this world.

This careful layering of characters, none of whom are able to break free of the system's basic cycle of exploitation and accumulation, makes *Land of the Dead* one of the most ambitious attempts to use a zombie film for an explicitly anticapitalist critique. Moving beyond the effective but simple-minded satire of consumerism in *Dawn of the Dead*, this film shows how neoliberal capitalism would not only survive a zombie epidemic but also seem to be completely at home in this apocalyptic environment. At the same time, the film foregrounds the systemic horrors that global capitalism inevitably produces. As the bland protagonists finally concede the city to Big Daddy and his zombie legion, *Land of the Dead* effectively reverses the traditional dynamic of the zombie genre. Remarkably, the living dead are no longer represented as the monstrous threat of a postindustrial, postideological, and fully posthuman world: they are instead shown as the sympathetic victims of a ruthless economic system that offers immense privilege to a small and underserving minority. Thus, as the zombies finally bear down on

---

97. Jeff May, "Zombie Geographies and the Undead City," *Social & Cultural Geography* 11, no. 3 (2010): 295.

the capitalists of Fiddler's Green, we see "capitalist ideology annihilated by the racialized working-class anti-hero."[98]

This reversal of the zombie-human dialectic, in which the audience is encouraged to cheer on the living dead as they invade the private mansions of capital, connects the zombie directly to recent social movements and the increasingly robust anticapitalist struggle. Zombies in the neoliberal age can just as easily be portrayed as the victims of a totalizing framework that systematically alienates and destroys every form of human community. Combining this recent trend of zombie rehabilitation with the anticonsumerism of earlier zombie texts, factions of the Occupy Wall Street movement took to dressing up as zombies while reclaiming the city streets as a form of political and social commons. These carnivalesque dress-up parties succeeded in establishing substantial visibility for the movement via reports in the mainstream press, and the appropriation of the zombie motif also resonated with Occupy's own ambiguous program. In one protester's words, "I like the fact that you can take it two ways: Are we saying they are the zombies for serving corporate masters? Or are we saying the rest of us—the 99 percent—are the zombies for putting up with this mess we're in?"[99]

This emergence of what Slavoj Žižek has described as "an international protest movement without a coherent program" reflects a deeper crisis that must first be acknowledged before possible solutions can even be imagined.[100] Occupy's call for change without any single clear conception of a preferred alternative is indicative of our postideological framework in which the traditional Left has been hollowed out by its own inability to formulate a political alternative to neoliberalism.[101] It makes the movement's occasional tactic of applying zombie makeup all the more appropriate: the attempt to challenge and subvert the coordinates of public space perfectly fits the many ways in which the zombie genre expresses the breakdown of seemingly stable barriers and the radical transformation of physical space. Occupy's zombie parades therefore not only strengthen the movement's attempt to draw attention to the neoliberal organization of urban space but also implicitly endorse the idea that a postcapitalist world first requires a real embrace of the zombie's posthuman promise: "To become a zombie is in this way to risk becoming 'disposable' ourselves; to do it would mean forsaking the zombie gaze for the zombie embrace."[102]

---

98. May, "Zombie Geographies and the Undead City," 292.

99. Mitch Potter, "Occupy Wall Street 'Zombies' Keep Streets Alive," *Toronto Star*, October 3, 2011, accessed December 27, 2015, http://www.thestar.com/news/world/2011/10/03/occupy_wall_street_zombies_keep_protest_alive.html.

100. Slavoj Žižek, "Occupy Wall Street: What Is to Be Done Next?" *The Guardian*, April 24, 2012, accessed December 27, 2015, http://www.guardian.co.uk/commentisfree/cifamerica/2012/apr/24/occupy-wall-street-what-is-to-be-done-next.

101. Srnicek and Williams, *Inventing the Future*, 16–22.

102. Canavan, "We *Are* the Walking Dead," 450.

But although the zombie's radical potential helps us confront and interrogate the concept of the posthuman, its dialectical form still remains entirely negative: while it is helpful to explore the zombie as a kind of antisubject, it is still at the same time a "vacant and incessant sign of a breakdown both of historical thought and of history's prospects of going differently."[103] Like Occupy itself, the zombie remains stuck in what Srnicek and Williams have described as *folk politics*: frothing with anticapitalist energy, but lacking any kind of program for a postcapitalist alternative. If we wish to imagine a postcapitalist world that offers something other than a systemic breakdown, we require more than mere resistance: we will also need—among other things—"the creation of new cognitive maps, political narratives, technological interfaces, economic models, and mechanisms of collective control."[104] In summary, while the zombie has tremendous potential to illuminate and critique some of capitalism's basic contradictions, the walking dead are clearly less helpful if we want to think beyond the limitations imposed by Occupy's folk politics and self-satisfied Apocalypticism.

If the zombie's anticapitalist potential is indeed its "dystopic promise . . . that it can only assure the destruction of a corrupt system without imagining a replacement,"[105] we must therefore turn to another kind of fantastic worldbuilding for a more productive take on a postcapitalist future. In this chapter, I have adopted the theoretical framework of posthumanism in order to identify a productive intersection between fantastic storyworlds and a postcapitalist imaginary. In the book's final section, I will now turn to the figure of the cyborg as the zombie's dialectical counterpart: an ambiguous posthuman figure with more obviously utopian implications. While the zombie remains firmly anchored by its negative dialectics, the cyborg can give us posthumanism's full political potential by embracing the multitude's radical hybridity.

JANELLE MONÁE'S "METROPOLIS SAGA"[106]

Approaching the concept of world-building from the perspective of radical politics, I have dealt throughout this book with popular and commercially exploited fantastic storyworlds. Many earlier studies of fan culture's relationship with fantastic fiction have focused on fandom's transformative and subversive powers. But the cultural logic of neoliberalism has enveloped once-radical identity politics with remarkable ease, moving too many debates about gender, race, and

---

103. Williams, *Combined and Uneven Apocalypse*, 146.

104. Srnicek and Williams, *Inventing the Future*, 16.

105. Lauro and Embry, "A Zombie Manifesto," 96.

106. The following section is expanded from a previously published essay. See Dan Hassler-Forest, "The Politics of World-Building: Heteroglossia in Janelle Monáe's Afrofuturist WondaLand," *Paradoxa: Studies in Literary Genres* 26 (2015): 284–303.

sexuality into a framework from which "capitalist market forces are treated as unassailable nature."[107]

In the political economy of corporate convergence culture and ubiquitous social media, active engagement with this type of brand culture is more than creative and transformative appropriation: it has become media corporations' overriding goal. And this strategic approach merges all too well with the cultural practices of fantastic world-building, as the systematic nature of these worlds' spatial and temporal organization perfectly fits the objectifying framework of managerial neoliberal culture. The key political issue about fantastic world-building therefore concerns not so much the ways in which the narrative contents of any given storyworld articulate ideological values that could be described as either conservative or progressive. The question we need to ask is whether its organization helps destabilize the governing framework of capitalist realism. In other words, in a context where even the most subversive counternarratives can be effortlessly appropriated and recycled within the very system they attack, the important work of imagining alternatives and creating productive resistance expands to the larger sphere of world-building.

Janelle Monáe's creative work offers a provocative example of world-building that structurally resists capitalism's neutralizing and objectifying framework. As a musician working with sf tropes, her "Metropolis Saga" is far more loosely organized than the fantastic worlds in media more preoccupied by narrative, such as literature, film, comic books, or even videogames. While her concept albums, music videos, and stage performances contain obvious narrative elements, they simultaneously remain open to a wide variety of alternative readings. By the same token, individual tracks can mean different things outside the context of an album or when experienced as a music video or live performance.

By looking at some of the tensions this multiplicity creates throughout Monáe's work, both within individual media and in the intertextual spaces between them, I argue in this final section that her world-building is best understood through Bakhtin's concept of *heteroglossia*. This term indicates the politically productive coexistence of multiple competing meanings within a single signifying system that destabilizes any central conception of "unity" or single meaning.[108] Bakhtin introduces heteroglossia as a way to describe the novel's radical and uncontainable difference, which stands in contrast to scientific discourse or religious dogma. He describes these discourses as "authoritative" in the sense that the reader must yield to a single and centered "centripetal" meaning. The cultural and political role of the novel, or, by extension, Monáe's eclectic transmedia storyworld, should be to

---

107. Adolph Reed Jr., "From Jenner to Dolezal: One Trans Good, the Other Not So Much," *Common Dreams*, June 15, 2015, accessed December 27, 2015, http://www.commondreams.org/views/2015/06/15/jenner-dolezal-one-trans-good-other-not-so-much.

108. Mikhail Bakhtin, *The Dialogic Imagination: Four Essays*, ed. Michael Holquist (Austin: University of Texas Press, 1981), 263.

draw the very concept of the authoritative into question by foregrounding its own hybrid nature and "centrifugal" multiplicity of meaning.[109]

These Bakhtinian terms are especially helpful when we turn our attention to transmedia world-building as a practice that is defined by this very tension between the authoritative desire to unify, on the one hand, and the hybrid nature of "heteroglot" texts, on the other. So much of the energy deployed by writers, producers, and critics in relation to world-building has been directed toward the centripetal notion of the authoritative: the ways in which imaginary worlds become mappable, measurable, and navigable spaces with coherent chronologies, characters, and events, even when they cross over into other media. Transmedia storyworlds such as Tolkien's Middle-earth or the *Star Wars* franchise have established elaborate canons that identify clearly which texts are considered part of the "real" imaginary world, and which are to be consigned to the margins.[110]

This desire for coherence and measurability has been central to most academic work on world-building as well, even when the authors take into account not only the profusion of these narratives across media but also the contributions made by active audiences through fan fiction and mashup culture. Jonathan Gray's book *Show Sold Separately* rightfully emphasizes the importance of more or less peripheral "paratexts" such as trailers, spoilers, and other intertexts that John Fiske described as "secondary" and "tertiary."[111] But Gray's focus on the narrative coherence across media consistently privileges texts that add to the development of an authoritative and explicitly *narrative* storyworld. For instance, Gray strongly privileges fan-created material that contributes to the narrative's thematic coherence by producing a mashup video that "invites viewers to contemplate [a] character" by adding "the time and reflective space . . . that the films never truly provide."[112] In contrast, the paratextual existence of a "Gotham City

---

109. Jason Mittell has made a similar distinction between centripetal and centrifugal modes of transmedia storyworld expansion, but he is more interested in narrative structure than in their political implications. See Jason Mittell, "Strategies of Storytelling on Transmedia Television," in *Storyworlds Across Media: Toward a Media-Conscious Narratology*, ed. Marie-Laure Ryan and Jan-Noël Thon (Lincoln: University of Nebraska Press, 2014), 253–77.

110. To illustrate this notion, a crisis erupted among *Star Wars* fans when the announcement was made by LucasFilm that the "Expanded Universe" would henceforth no longer be part of the "canonical" storyworld in order to make room for new film sequels and spin-offs. See Chris Taylor, "Star Wars Rewrites History: Books, Comics No Longer Official," *Mashable*, April 25, 2014, accessed December 27, 2015, http://mashable.com/2014/04/25/star-wars-expanded-universe-gone/-RqsqQXCRmuqo.

111. See John Fiske, *Television Culture* (London and New York: Routledge, 1987), 117–26. While the clear difference Fiske describes here between secondary texts (promotional materials, professional reviews, and other "producerly" paratexts) and tertiary texts (letters, discussions, and other materials produced by media audiences) is far more difficult to make in the context of participatory culture and media convergence, it remains a useful conceptual distinction that helps us question the various functions of specific paratexts.

112. Jonathan Gray, *Show Sold Separately: Promos, Spoilers, and Other Media Paratexts* (New York: New York University Press, 2010), 156.

pizza" in relation to the film *The Dark Knight* is dismissed as a "mere marketing tool" whose sole function is to "signal the size of the film."[113] Thus, the further any given paratext is removed from centripetal notions of narrative coherence, character development, and thematic consistency, the less it is valued as a paratextual expansion of the storyworld.

But as Philip K. Dick articulated so memorably in his short essay "How to Build a Universe That Doesn't Fall Apart Two Days Later," this exclusive focus on centripetal coherence has far-reaching political implications. The desire to create, navigate, or otherwise engage with an imaginary world that is stable and coherent expresses a desire to understand what Wolf describes as the Primary World in similar terms. By contrast, an approach like the one Dick favors, of "building universes that *do* fall apart,"[114] shifts our focus to a posthuman environment defined by multiplicity, transformation, fluidity, and irresolvable internal contradictions. Such a form of world-building rejects the post-Enlightenment foundations organized around a metaphysics of presence in favor of the posthuman realm of Hardt and Negri's multitude. Only the most radical approach to fantastic transmedia world-building can express this thoroughly posthuman ontology by providing storyworlds that are constantly "becoming unglued"[115] not just at the level of narrative and storyworld but also in the cultures of fandom and activism that surround them. For an example of this type of radical world-building, I now turn to the cultural practices of Afrofuturism and Janelle Monáe's centrifugal storyworld.

AFROFUTURISM AND CENTRIFUGAL WORLD-BUILDING

While the paradigmatic imaginary worlds of *LOTR* and *Star Trek* have resulted in a tendency in fantastic fiction toward forms of world-building that are easily integrated into global capitalism, alternatives have also emerged that take world-building in radical new directions. One such phenomenon has been the twenty-first-century revival of Afrofuturism, the cultural movement that emerged among black artists, authors, and musicians in the 1960s and 1970s as "speculative fiction that treats African-American themes and addresses African-American concerns in the context of 20th-century technoculture."[116] The Afrofuturist movement appropriated sf imagery, which had been overwhelmingly white in

---

113. Gray, *Show Sold Separately*, 209–10.

114. Philip K. Dick, "How to Build a Universe That Doesn't Fall Apart Two Days Later," in *I Hope I Shall Arrive Soon* (New York: Doubleday, 1985), 5 (emphasis added).

115. Dick, "How to Build a Universe That Doesn't Fall Apart Two Days Later," 4.

116. Mark Dery, "Black to the Future: Interviews with Samuel R. Delany, Greg Tate, and Tricia Rose," in *Flame Wars: The Discourse of Cyberculture*, ed. Mark Dery (Durham: Duke University Press, 1994), 180.

its mainstream cultural representations, and used it to reimagine a past, present, and future in which people of color play central roles rather than the marginal ones foisted upon them by Eurocentric capitalism. From the elaborate mythology articulated by avant-garde jazz musician Sun Ra to the spectacular stage shows of 1970s bands such as Funkadelic, Parliament, and Earth, Wind and Fire, Afrofuturist culture gleefully absorbed, transformed, and rearticulated familiar sf tropes with people of color in leading roles.

When compared to a more conventional sf franchise like *Star Trek*, Afrofuturism mobilized forms of world-building that are fundamentally similar in their desire to question the present by speculating about the future. Roddenberry's utopian vision of humanity's destiny has been heralded for its incorporation of ethnic and cultural diversity, but, as I argued in chapter 1, it remained at the same time a vision "based on a thoroughly Western vision of the importance of material wealth and technological modernization."[117] Afrofuturism rejects the incorporation of people of color into such a larger framework of liberal capitalist humanism, offering instead a radical reenvisioning of the past in which capitalism's Eurocentric dynamic is reversed, rethought, and rewritten.

This alternative framework is strengthened by Afrofuturist sf's far more obviously centrifugal form: while most mainstream sf storyworlds have been driven by linear narrative media like episodic TV drama, cinema, comic books, and literature, musicians have been the primary guiding force for the multiple "sonic fictions" of Afrofuturism.[118] By practicing what Kodwo Eshun describes as *chronopolitics*, Afrofuturists use world-building not as a way to reinforce the coordinates of existing reality but as "a means through which to preprogram the present."[119] Therefore, the forms within which Afrofuturism was articulated and circulated have been as destabilizing as the speculative pasts and futures they expressed.[120]

Sun Ra's elaborate "MythScience," for instance, offers an account of black history in which ancient Egypt was created by a technologically advanced race of black aliens from the planet Saturn, while claiming an identity for himself as a time-traveling deity who has returned from the past via the future to liberate people of color from our oppressive historical present. The mythology constructed by Sun Ra thus presents itself to us not in terms of secondariness to a single shared

117. M. Keith Booker, "The Politics of *Star Trek*," in *The Essential Science Fiction Television Reader*, ed. J. P. Telotte (Lexington: University Press of Kentucky, 2008), 198.

118. See Kodwo Eshun, *More Brilliant Than the Sun: Adventures in Sonic Fiction* (London: Quartet Books, 1998).

119. Kodwo Eshun, "Further Considerations of Afrofuturism," *CR: The New Centennial Review* 3, no. 2 (2003): 290.

120. Other key influences on Afrofuturism have been novelists such as Octavia E. Butler and Samuel R. Delany, whose work is no less centrifugal than that of Afrofuturist musicians: in both content and form, their work constantly subverts, contradicts, and transforms teleological Eurocentric historiography.

Primary World but as a challenge to "the invisible paradigm of unquestioned reality" of historical white supremacy,[121] allowing the artist's performative role as a black musician to resonate on multiple registers simultaneously. It thus explicitly operates in the centrifugal register of Bakhtinian heteroglossia rather than in sf's dominant mode of centripetal, "rational" world-building.

The fact that so much Afrofuturist world-building has been developed by musicians rather than writers, filmmakers, and game designers is therefore very meaningful. As Jeremy Gilbert and Ewan Pearson have argued in their book *Discographies*, music has the remarkable potential to collapse the post-Renaissance distinction between body and mind, opening up a space in which existing subjectivities can be negotiated and even dissolved. Dance music in particular tends to challenge the dominant logocentric tradition that "privileges modes of thought and experience which occur in the medium of verbal language, which thereby have clearly identifiable and analyzable meanings."[122] The forms of music most strongly associated with Afrofuturism, such as "the intergalactic big-band jazz churned out by Sun Ra's Omniverse Arkestra, Parliament-Funkadelic's Dr. Seussian astrofunk, and Lee 'Scratch' Perry's dub reggae,"[123] each in their own way resist this logocentric tradition, embracing instead the collective, the improvisational, the nonverbal, and the ephemeral. These groups' long, improvisational, and highly collaborative jams are direct precursors of the electronic dance grooves that Gilbert and Pearson describe as bypassing and transforming "the acceptable channels of language, reason and contemplation."[124] Afrofuturist music therefore destabilizes mainstream sf's shameful exclusion of people of color, but it does so in forms that practice an innate ability to upset the implicit hierarchies of Western culture and philosophy.

In this way, Afrofuturism presented an important and influential challenge to the authoritative white discourses of fantastic fiction while implicitly providing an alternative to centripetal and logocentric modes of world-building. George Clinton's P-Funk Collective[125] was especially ambitious in its development of an elaborate transmedia storyworld: fictional characters like the heroically funky StarChild, his wise mentor Dr. Funkenstein, and the nefarious Sir Nose D'VoidofFunk were performed as on-stage characters during P-Funk's spectacular stage shows and on Parliament's series of concept albums. They also came

---

121. Tobias C. Van Veen, "Vessels of Transfer: Allegories of Afrofuturism in Jeff Mills and Janelle Monáe," *Dancecult: Journal of Electronic Dance Music Culture* 5, no. 2 (2013): 11.

122. Jeremy Gilbert and Ewan Pearson, *Discographies: Dance Music, Culture and the Politics of Sound* (London and New York: Routledge, 1999), 57.

123. Dery, "Black to the Future," 182.

124. Gilbert and Pearson, *Discographies*, 42.

125. Clinton's two recording and performing groups, Parliament and Funkadelic, were both made up of former members of James Brown's backing band and featured many of the same musicians. Together with the later P-Funk All Stars and Bootsy's Rubber Band, these groups of overlapping contributors are now commonly referred to as the P-Funk Collective.

to life in many other ways: as narrative figures first introduced on the album *Mothership Connection*[126]; as comic book characters designed by artist Overton Loyd in the publication that was included with the 1977 album *Funkentelechy vs. the Placebo Syndrome*[127]; as illustrations and cardboard cut-outs on the numerous album cover variations for *Motor Booty Affair* (1978)[128]; and even in a little-seen but beautifully animated TV commercial meant to publicize the latter.

Offering a more accessible elaboration of Sun Ra's experimental Afrofuturist jazz music, P-Funk's creative work in this era virtually exploded across a variety of media platforms, combining the iconography of ancient Egyptian civilization and elements of the African American gospel tradition with a hypermodern and radically inclusive futurist sound and vision. Clinton and his "Afronauts" disseminated a new kind of black mythology that would usher in a utopian and deeply funky new age through the irresistible power of music and performance. Using motifs strongly indebted to Sun Ra's MythScience, Clinton's collective also had an explicitly political direction that sought to "liberate consciousness from the trappings of an alienating, technocratic society."[129] P-Funk's 1970s transmedia Afrofuturism was therefore a movement directed toward helping those who are trapped in oppressive capitalism's "Zone of Zero Funkativity," using dance music's transformative power to collapse divisive particularisms and achieve a universal and wholly utopian "Funkentelechy."

Within this ambitious and politically charged storyworld, the P-Funk Collective did much of the heavy lifting that established a popular tradition of musical Afrofuturism. Their music provided emerging hip-hop artists with a seemingly inexhaustible supply of hooks, beats, and samples, and their flexible and astonishingly playful negotiation of masculinity also upended the normative models of patriarchy.[130] At the same time, their approach to identity continued Sun Ra's movement away from the Black Arts Movement's separatist vision in the 1960s,[131] transcending racial difference through the universal and wholly inclusive category of "Funkativity." Thus, even though Clinton's increasingly misogynistic lyrics and album covers in the 1980s illustrated how strongly the group's work still reinforced rock music's inherent phallocentrism and heteronormativity,[132]

---

126. George Clinton, Bootsy Collins, and Bernie Worrell, *Mothership Connection*, Parliament, © 2003, 1975 by Mercury Records, UMG 440-077-032-2, Compact disc.

127. George Clinton, Bootsy Collins, and Bernie Worrell, *Funkentelechy vs. The Placebo Syndrome*, Parliament, © 1977 by Polygram Records, Casablanca 824-501-2, Compact disc.

128. George Clinton, Bootsy Collins, and Bernie Worrell, *Motor Booty Affair*, Parliament, © 1978 by Mercury Records, UICY-77156, Compact disc.

129. Daniel Kreiss, "Performing the Past to Claim the Future: Sun Ra and the Afro-Future Underground, 1954–1968," *African American Review* 45, no. 1–2 (2012): 200.

130. Francesca T. Royster, *Sounding Like a No-No: Queer Sounds and Eccentric Acts in the Post-Soul Era* (Ann Arbor: University of Michigan Press, 2013), 102–3.

131. Kreiss, "Performing the Past to Claim the Future," 201.

132. Gilbert and Pearson, *Discographies*, 85.

their flexible and highly centrifugal world-building provided an important step toward a radical posthuman aesthetic.

The cultural work of Afrofuturists has survived in many forms within mainstream pop music, where its transformative and subversive influence is profoundly felt even in places as unlikely as the oeuvre of "King of Pop" Michael Jackson.[133] But it has more recently resurfaced as "neo-Afrofuturism," most notably in the work of Janelle Monáe. Unlike the P-Funk Collective's "Afrocentric, masculinist, and messianic overtones,"[134] Monáe's collection of on- and off-stage android and human personas playfully negotiates the tightrope of celebrity culture and performativity in a fully posthuman age. Her ongoing series of concept albums together with her growing collection of music videos (or "emotion pictures"), stage performances, and media appearances offer a new, more radical perspective on worldbuilding that builds on Afrofuturism as much as it does on twenty-first-century convergence culture and fantastic fiction. While certain elements across these media cohere loosely into narrative patterns and recognizable structures, they are also constantly interwoven with innumerable lines of flight that frustrate any attempt to separate fictional characters, locations, and events from a contemporary social and political context that insistently infects them. In this sense, Monáe's "Wondaland," both as a description of a (possibly imaginary) location within her storyworld and as the name of her Atlanta-based arts collective and record label, takes on forms that are even more fluid than the loosely constructed *The Walking Dead* franchise.

The storyworld Monáe develops across her transmedia work has mostly evaded straightforward storytelling, instead weaving seemingly contradictory strands of autobiography, social commentary, and fantastic world-building into a radically heterogeneous multitext.[135] Initially, her storyworld's sf premise appears simple and straightforward: the lavishly illustrated booklet that accompanies Monáe's first official release, *Metropolis: The Chase Suite* (2008),[136] includes a brief primer on the artist's futuristic storyworld and its primary character, Monáe's android alter ego Cindi Mayweather.[137] When read intertextually alongside the

---

133. See Erik Steinskog, "Michael Jackson and Afrofuturism: *HIStory*'s Adaptation of Past, Present and Future," in *The Politics of Adaptation: Media Convergence and Ideology*, ed. Dan Hassler-Forest and Pascal Nicklas (Basingstoke: Palgrave Macmillan, 2015), 126–40.

134. Daylanne K. English and Alvin Kim, "Now We Want Our Funk Cut: Janelle Monáe's Neo-Afrofuturism," *American Studies* 52, no. 4 (2013): 220.

135. For a detailed chronological breakdown of Monáe's concept albums and music videos, see Phil Sandifer, "A Short Guide to Janelle Monáe and the Metropolis Saga," *Your New Problematic Ninth Favorite*, June 2015, accessed November 25, 2015, http://www.philipsandifer.com/blog/a-short-guide-to-janelle-monáe-and-the-metropolis-saga/.

136. Janelle Monáe, *Metropolis: The Chase Suite—Special Edition*, © 2008, Bad Boy Records, Wondaland 7567-89932-8. Compact disc.

137. This EP was originally released as a collection of five tracks, the first four of which tell a fairly straightforward narrative. A later "Special Edition" rerelease expands the original version with the two bonus tracks "Mr. President" and "Smile," neither of which is clearly connected to the larger sf storyworld.

booklet illustrations, liner notes, and the singer's many published interviews on the project, her storyworld takes shape along patterns that are broadly familiar from countless dystopian sf tales while poking playful fun at them: a postapocalyptic high-tech city ruled by "evil Wolfmasters," an oppressed class of androids sold to and exploited by "partying robo-zillionaires," and heroic android protagonist Cindi Mayweather, the "slave girl without a race" whose "programming includes a rock-star proficiency package and a working soul."[138]

Cindi Mayweather, also known as Android No. 57821, is a celebrity in this future Metropolis as "the leading voice of a rebellious new form of pop music known as cybersoul" when she is forced to go on the run, chased by colorful bounty hunters, for having committed the crime of falling in love with a human being. This is the point in the narrative where the album begins, the opening track, "March of the Wolfmasters," summarizing the most crucial plot points in its rousing proclamation of Cindi's newly decreed outlaw status:

> Goooo-oo-ood morning, cy-boys and cyber-girls. I am happy to announce that we have a star-crossed lover in today's Heartbreak Sweepstakes: android number 57821, otherwise known as Cindi Mayweather, has fallen desperately in love with a human named Anthony Greendown. And you know the rules: she is now scheduled for immediate disassembly. Bounty hunters, you can find her in the Neon Valley Street district, on the fourth floor at the Leopard Plaza apartment complex. The Droid Control Marshals are full of fun rules today: no phasers, only chainsaws and electro-daggers! Remember: only card-carrying bounty hunters can join our chase today. And as usual, there will be no reward until her cyber-soul is turned in to the Star Commission. Happy hunting!

The next two tracks, "Violent Stars Happy Hunting" and "Many Moons," then offer a relentless musical chase sequence in which sound effects and occasional bursts of spoken dialogue add a quite obvious narrative dimension to the songs' propulsive rhythms, after which the narrative sequence concludes with Cindi's disembodied imprisonment in the track "Cybertronic Purgatory."

But while this first suite in her still-unfinished "Metropolis Saga" offers the most obviously narrative episode in the cycle, the elaborate music video that accompanied the album's single "Many Moons" at the same time depicts a sequence of events very different from the narrative events on the album. Thus, even as the tracks on this first album establish the straightforward narrative of a fugitive android, the storyworld as introduced on the album is both complemented and contradicted by the music video: the lyrical content is relegated to background noise in the video's entirely different representation of Cindi Mayweather as a performer and commodity at an android auction-cum-fashion show.

---

138. All direct quotations in this paragraph and the next are taken from the explanatory liner notes in the digital booklet that accompanies Monáe's album *Metropolis: The Chase Suite*.

This radically centrifugal storyworld, moving in multiple directions simultaneously, is developed further on Monáe's first full-length album, *The ArchAndroid*.[139] Rather than providing a direct continuation of the first suite's narrative sequence, *The ArchAndroid* instead sketches out the contours of a futuristic storyworld in which the enslaved class of androids has come to perceive Cindi as their leader and savior because of her symbolic resistance to authority. The album's two suites of eclectic pop songs preceded by orchestral overtures demonstrate the wide range of Monáe's musical influences and abilities,[140] incorporating arrangements, rhythms, and harmonies that sometimes seem like an attempt to bring together as wide a range of different genres and styles as possible.[141] Storytelling threads and world-building elements are woven throughout the album, ranging from heartsick ballads addressed to Cindi's love interest like "Sir Greendown" to the futuristic techno-soundscapes of "Neon Gumbo" or the more obviously narrative interlude "57821."

Throughout this second album, Mayweather/Monáe's celebrity as the eponymous ArchAndroid plays upon the messianic status claimed by earlier Afrofuturists such as Sun Ra and George Clinton, while at the same time rendering her predecessors' Afrocentrism thoroughly ambiguous. As a black woman attempting to work autonomously within the twenty-first-century culture industries, she must constantly "tip on the tightrope of a cultural logic of late capitalism,"[142] in which neither her storyworld nor her own musical career allows for an easy escape from what Jameson has described as the "massive Being of capital."[143] Unlike her precursors in the 1970s, whose music was meant to offer a "narrative of ascension" that led the way to a better, brighter future,[144] Monáe's storyworld neither ignores nor evades the contradictions of global capitalism. By organizing her futuristic storyworld on the basis of commodification, machinic enslavement, and class struggle, Monáe's world-building offers a productive confrontation with capitalism's oppressive power rather than an escape from it. But where the zombie genre fails to escape a purely negative dialectic, Monáe's centrifugal storyworld mobilizes posthumanism's inherently contradictory nature.

This dialectical tension is not only recognizable in the organization of the storyworld she has developed over the course of her concept albums but also strengthened and expanded in the paratextual materials that accompany and

---

139. Janelle Monáe, *The ArchAndroid*, © 2010, Bad Boy Records, Wondaland 512256-2, Compact disc.

140. The "Metropolis Saga" was originally planned to consist of five such suites, but the next album's release expanded the total expected number to seven.

141. Amid the incorporation of traditionally black musical genres such as R&B, funk, soul, gospel, and hip-hop, Monáe also effortlessly includes numerous "white genres," including show tunes, acoustic folk, pop, electronica, and rock.

142. English and Kim, "Now We Want Our Funk Cut," 218.

143. Frederic Jameson, *Postmodernism* (London and New York: Verso, 1991), 48.

144. English and Kim, "Now We Want Our Funk Cut," 220.

frame them. In the liner notes accompanying *The ArchAndroid*'s CD release, for instance, we learn that Monáe herself is a time traveler from the year 2719 whose stolen DNA was used for the creation of her android alter ego. In interviews, she has embellished this idea further, explaining that there is a hidden "time traveling machine" in her adopted city of Atlanta, through which many influential black musicians have passed, herself and hip-hop duo OutKast included.[145] This playful, self-reflexive, and thoroughly fluid relationship to her alter ego demonstrates not only her authorial claim upon her imaginary world but also the way her artificial alter ego is also inseparable from the "real" persona she performs as a twenty-first-century pop artist.

This contradictory logic reaches new heights on her third concept album, *The Electric Lady*,[146] containing suites 4 and 5 of what is currently projected to be a total of seven. Again, the latest installment in her ongoing series of concept albums declines to provide a clear narrative successor to the previous album. Perfectly in line with her established centrifugal method, the album moves backward, forward, and sideways at the same time: some tracks function as a prequel to earlier story events, others clearly continue on from *The Arch-Android*, while scripted "talk radio" interludes add world-building texture by drawing explicit parallels between the futuristic storyworld and contemporary social justice movements. This radical heteroglossia is further expanded in the four "emotion pictures" that accompanied the release, each of which simultaneously expands the existing storyworld while also undermining our earlier understanding of it.

Her music and persona thus deliberately blur the lines between her many "selves," as celebrity, as artist, as author, as performer, as producer, and as a black woman who is also a media spectacle, a role model, and a celebrity. In short, Monáe's world-building makes it impossible to separate her Secondary World of "androids, cyborgs, and d-boys" from our own Primary World of global capitalism. Indeed, her central figure of the android as an oppressed worker class of "othered" bodies not only relates back to capitalism's horrific Afrodiasporic history of slavery and institutionalized racism but also provides a remarkably slippery signifier that can be related back to gender, sexuality, class, and religion. In the way that Monáe presents them both inside and outside her fluid transmedia storyworld, "androids are the ultimate exploitable 'other,' a human-like being who does not need to be afforded the rights of humanity."[147] Or, as Monáe explains her posthuman symbolism herself in emphatically political terms, "When

---

145. Paul Lester, "Janelle Monae: 'It's True. I Am Part-Android,'" *The Guardian*, April 2, 2014, accessed January 26, 2016, http://www.theguardian.com/culture/2014/apr/02/janelle-monae-interview-david-bowie-prince.

146. Janelle Monáe, *The Electric Lady*, © 2013 by Bad Boy Records, Wondaland 536210-2, Compact disc.

147. Marissa Brandt, "Janelle Monáe's Liberationist Posthuman Pop," *Difference Engines*, March 5, 2014, accessed July 2014, http://www.differenceengines.com/?p=1021.

I'm talking about the android, I'm not talking about an avant-garde art concept or a science-fiction fantasy; I'm talking about the 'other': women, the negroid, the queer, the untouchable, the marginalized, the oppressed."[148]

"POWER UP": POSTCAPITALISM AND SYNTHETIC FREEDOM

The general tendency in many forms of Afrofuturism, as well as in hip-hop, pan-Africanism, and black nationalism, has been to insist on "keeping it real" by rejecting whiteness and "adhering to the standards of the 'black community.'"[149] But the problem of "keeping it real," even in the context of the worthy cause of antiracist activism, is that this strategy too easily collapses back into a form of identity politics that loses sight of capitalism's own fundamentally oppressive and exploitative nature. As Srnicek and Williams argue forcefully in their postcapitalist manifesto *Inventing the Future*, the way forward lies not in a return to a state of organic "authenticity" but in constructing what they term a "synthetic freedom":

> The full development of synthetic freedom . . . requires a reconfiguration of the material world in accordance with the drive to expand our capacities for action. It demands experimentation with collective and technological augmentation, and a spirit that refuses to accept any barrier as natural and inevitable. Cyborg augmentations, artificial life, synthetic biology and technologically mediated reproduction are all examples of this elaboration.[150]

The high-tech form of postcapitalism they envision therefore crucially relies on overcoming the endless particularisms of identity politics, as only the construction of a new "expansionary and inclusive universal" can unite the multitude in its resistance to capitalism.[151] Race and gender should therefore never be seen as an alternative to class politics: the only way to defeat capitalism is by uniting in common cause against this one shared enemy.[152] Or, to put it in other words, our only hope of overcoming neoliberalism's focus on competitive individualism and its endless array of possible identities is through the elaboration of a truly *posthuman* subject as anticapitalism's new universal category.

---

148. Quoted in Geoffrey Himes, "Janelle Monáe: Imagining Her Own Future," *Paste*, September 9, 2013, accessed January 26, 2016, http://www.pastemagazine.com/articles/2013/09/janelle-monae-imagining-her-own-future.html.

149. Howard Rambsy II, "Beyond Keeping It Real: OutKast, the Funk Connection, and Afrofuturism," *American Studies* 52, no. 4 (2013): 205.

150. Srnicek and Williams, *Inventing the Future*, 88, 279.

151. Srnicek and Williams, *Inventing the Future*, 78.

152. Reed, "From Jenner to Dolezal."

This concept leads us back to Donna Haraway's now-classic theorization of the cyborg, offering a fundamentally impure and artificial "hybrid of organism and technology"[153] as a productive replacement for humanism's restrictive binaries of gender, race, and sexual identity. But as exciting and provocative as Haraway's manifesto was, the cyborg figure has remained an ambiguous and continuously contested figure in the decades since it was first published.[154] The many cyborg and android figures in late capitalist popular culture, including the Terminator, RoboCop, *Star Trek TNG*'s Data, and Iron Man, hardly provided embodiments of the radical posthuman fluidity that Haraway suggested. Instead, their most noticeable features have more commonly tapped into the emerging discourse of *transhumanism*[155]: a framework that does not move beyond the basic assumptions of the Cartesian subject, constructing instead a techno-utopian future in which "humans and technologies merge into a new entity, which is sometimes even considered to be the successor of Homo sapiens."[156] But while so many popular incarnations of the cyborg figure have been easily absorbed by capitalism's transhumanist imaginary, Haraway's original vision remains a potent deconstruction of humanism's hierarchical binaries.

Monáe's posthuman android figure so precisely matches both Haraway's conception of the cyborg and Srnicek and Williams's notion of synthetic freedom because it constantly teases out the socially and biopolitically constructed nature of neoliberal subjectivity. Her android alter ego is first a performance that allows a (black, female, working-class) human to foreground questions of race, class, gender, and sexual orientation. For instance, in an interview with *The Guardian* she will insist that she is "part-android," while countering the reporter's suggestion that she is "the lovechild of Fritz Lang and David Bowie" with the retort that her mother is "a Black woman from Kansas."[157] Her first album cover demonstrates the inherent fluidity of this grounding concept most clearly, calling out pop music's ubiquitous eroticization of women's bodies by shedding not just her clothing but also her very skin, revealing beneath it the "robotic ultra-whiteness" of Cindi's androidal endoskeleton.[158] It is Monáe's constant state of becoming, as she moves back and forth between her "real" self and her "synthetic" alter

153. Donna Haraway, "A Manifesto for Cyborgs: Science, Technology, and Socialist Feminism in the 1980s," in *The Gendered Cyborg: A Reader*, ed. G. Kirkup, L. Janes, K. Woodward, and F. Hovenden (London: Routledge, 2000), 50.

154. Carol Mason, "Terminating Bodies: Toward a Cyborg History of Abortion," in *Posthuman Bodies*, ed. Judith Halberstam and Ira Livingston (Bloomington: Indiana University Press, 1995), 227.

155. Dan Hassler-Forest, "Of Iron Men and Green Monsters: Superheroes and Posthumanism," in *The Palgrave Handbook of Posthumanism in Film and Television*, ed. Michael Hauskeller, Thomas D. Philbeck, and Curtis D. Carbonell (Basingstoke: Palgrave Macmillan, 2015), 66–76.

156. Peter-Paul Verbeek, "Cyborg Intentionality: Rethinking the Phenomenology of Human-Technology Relations," *Phenomenology and the Cognitive Sciences* 7, no. 3 (2008): 391.

157. Lester, "Janelle Monae: 'It's True. I Am Part-Android.'"

158. English and Kim, "Now We Want Our Funk Cut," 222.

ego, that renders her performance of the cyborg properly dialectical and therefore more radically posthuman.[159]

Just as her centrifugal storyworld is constantly infected and contaminated by obtrusive elements from the Primary World, the twenty-eighth-century android Cindi Mayweather becomes inseparable from Monáe's (ambiguously) human twenty-first-century public persona. While this productive tension is evident throughout her transmedia work, the most compelling illustration of posthumanism's radical potential in Monáe's oeuvre thus far is the "emotion picture" for the track "Cold War,"[160] the second single that preceded *The ArchAndroid*'s release. Unlike most of her other music videos, "Cold War" includes no overtly futuristic elements or elaborate visual effects; instead, it consists of a single close-up of her face as she lip-synchs the track's lyrics. The form brings to mind similarly minimalistic music videos that focus the viewer's attention entirely on the artist's affective performance—most notably Sinéad O'Connor's 1990 hit "Nothing Compares 2 U."[161] But where the single tear famously running down O'Connor's cheek signaled a performance of genuine intimacy and emotional sincerity, this illusion is disturbed and complicated on multiple levels in Monáe's emotion picture.

The "Cold War" video begins with Monáe's face in close-up, a time-code visible in the screen's bottom-right corner as we see her say something to someone off camera, while taking off a black bathrobe to reveal her bare shoulders. The image is then interrupted by a black title screen with white text that reads "Janelle Monáe, 'Cold War,' Take 1," suggesting that we are viewing the first attempt to record this video. As the music then begins, we return to the close-up of her face, now staring straight into camera, the visible time-code "emphasizing both the constructedness of the art and its unmediated genuineness."[162] Throughout the first two verses and up to the song's bridge, her face moves expressively but also mechanically, slowly panning back and forth laterally and tilting up and down while keeping her eyes fixed on the camera at all times, the movement's artificial-seeming precision enhanced by a wide range of obviously choreographed and rehearsed facial expressions. It's a startlingly precise performance, the rare spectacle of a long, unbroken close-up creating a sense of engagement and immediacy that her robotic performance carefully yet paradoxically maintains.

---

159. Monáe's performance of the android both acknowledges and subverts cinema's long history of associating femininity with eroticized and objectified mechanical bodies, from Fritz Lang's *Metropolis* via *Blade Runner* to *Ex Machina*, directed by Alex Garland (2015; Universal City, CA: Universal Studios Home Entertainment, 2015), Blu-ray.

160. Janelle Monáe, "Cold War," YouTube video, 3:43, posted by "janellemonae," August 5, 2010, https://www.youtube.com/watch?v=lqmORiHNtN4.

161. Sinéad O'Connor, "Nothing Compares 2 U," YouTube video, 5:47, posted by "Rafael Silveira," November 26, 2012, https://www.youtube.com/watch?v=dq2K4jHs92A.

162. Robert Loss, "Power Up: Janelle Monáe, Afrofuturism, and Plurality," *PopMatters*, October 29, 2013, accessed January 26, 2016, http://www.popmatters.com/column/176055 -power-up-janelle-monae-afrofuturism-and-plurality/.

The first fracture in the video's uncanny sense of "liveness" occurs at time-code A:01:06:25, where the last line of the bridge overlaps with the first line of the next verse. Hearing the singer's voice redoubled is nothing unusual on a pop record, but in the video, the moment draws attention to the fact that she is lip-synching to a prerecorded song—something the viewer would tacitly assume but that the precisely disciplined and carefully honed performance has successfully camouflaged up to this point. It is the text's first overt indication that we are not actually watching a performance or even an actual person; instead, the combination of Monáe's playful negotiation of human/robotic personas and the immaterial nature of digital video underline the idea that "there is no original, or Platonic idea, of a celebrity: all instances are generated through the same process of composition and modulation, and therefore any instance is as valid (or 'authentic') as any other."[163]

Then, just two lines further into this verse, the lyric "And it hurts my heart" sees Monáe suddenly stumbling in her performance as her emotional response to the preceding line, "I was made to believe there was something wrong with me," appears to disrupt her flawless lip-synching. Her attempt to blink away erupting tears leads her to express a sudden burst of seemingly unscripted movements and emotions: she turns away briefly from the camera, moves her head momentarily out of focus, speaks a few words that aren't registered by the audio track, and passes from brief nervous laughter into a tearful breakdown that halts her performance. Then, after a brief attempt to continue her lip-synching, she hangs her head for several seconds, attempts to continue, breaks down again, appears to yell out in frustration, and finally, from time-code A:01:06:47, rejoins the lyrics once again without further interruption.

But this seemingly spontaneous interruption has radically transformed the nature of the performance. While the first part's choreographed and immaculately lip-synched performance is an expression of the android's synthetic perfection, the illusion—like Monáe's constantly shifting storyworld itself—is punctured and contaminated by another reality that comes to inhabit the same space. Released from the initial tension produced by the single-take form and the singer's disciplined but artificial acting out of an illusory "liveness," the pleasurable spectacle of celebrity performance is unexpectedly interrupted and transformed into a site of struggle. The tension we then witness becomes meaningful on many levels simultaneously, in the first place because of its profound impact on the illusion of immediacy. The spectacle of the flawless female face, so thoroughly familiar from the advertising industry and its objectifying male gaze, becomes a subject through the performer's perceived failure: Monáe's apparent breakdown disrupts the illusion that maintains a clear division between subject and object, and like fellow posthumanist Grace Jones has done many times before, her performance subsequently begins to transgress "the very sense of what it means to be a self or a subject at all."[164]

---

163. Steven Shaviro, *Post Cinematic Affect* (Hants: Zero Books, 2010), 18.

164. Shaviro, *Post Cinematic Affect*, 20.

Monáe's appropriation of the android figure has therefore given her a way not only to develop a complex fantastic storyworld but also to willfully present herself to us *as a thing*. When Cindi chants the lines "I'm a product of metal / I'm a product of the man," Monáe implicitly forces the listener to confront the nature of capitalist objectification: "the ways that slavery and racism turn black people into things, that patriarchy turns women into things, and that capitalism turns all of us into commodities, or strangely animated things."[165] Instead of witnessing a preprogrammed and ultimately artificial performance of a song designed to stimulate a pleasurable emotional response in the viewer, the video's unique affective structure transforms Monáe's act of pure performance into a fully reactive text: reacting both to the lyrics of the song itself and to what Walter Benjamin memorably described as "a test performance of the highest order,"[166] the video uses the contradiction between the synthetic and the real as a productive dialectic rather than as a pitfall to be avoided. Just like the similarly disruptive *no hay banda* moment in the film *Mulholland Dr.*,[167] the "Cold War" video cleverly blurs the boundary between subject and object, yielding new lines of flight that embrace posthumanism's destabilized dichotomies and radically fluid and contingent subjectivity.

As with her larger world-building project, the centrifugal logic that underlies Monáe's posthuman hybridization in this music video is ultimately not about the mere displacement of an artificial persona by a more authentic one. The disruption of the initial performance does not offer in its place a superior, more "real" reality; instead, the rupture of illusionism itself creates a *mise-en-abyme* that disrupts the false and arbitrary hierarchical organization of the authentic-artificial binary. Repeated viewings of this endlessly fascinating video simply strengthen the sense that each of its parts is both authentic *and* artificial, but in different and mutually reinforcing ways. At the same time, the video's conceptual power is strengthened by the deceptively simple lyric in which the repeated phrase "It's a cold war / Do you know what you're fighting for?" reflects the immaterial nature of biopolitical power while resonating with capitalism's specific histories of racism, sexism, homophobia, and objectification.[168]

As this video demonstrates, Janelle Monáe provides such a compelling cyborg figure because of her constant embrace of posthumanism's logic of "both/and"

---

165. Shaviro, *Post Cinematic Affect*, 20.

166. Walter Benjamin, *The Work of Art in the Age of Its Technological Reproducibility and Other Writings on Media*, ed. Michael W. Jennings, Brigid Doherty, and Thomas Y. Levin (Cambridge, MA: Belknap, 2008), 31.

167. In the film, an emotionally powerful on-stage performance of Roy Orbison's "Crying" ("Llorando" in Spanish) is disrupted when the singer faints, but her voice on the soundtrack continues uninterrupted: what both the audience and the main characters had perceived as authentic liveness is revealed to be staged performance. *Mulholland Dr.*, directed by David Lynch (2001; New York: The Criterion Collection, 2015), Blu-ray.

168. Monáe's visible presence throughout the video as a naked androgynous woman of color further fuels all of these categories simultaneously.

and "neither/nor": she is both Janelle Monáe and Cindi Mayweather, human and android, real and synthetic, which thereby of course also makes her none of those things. The video represents in miniature the centrifugal logic that simultaneously holds together and pulls apart the storyworld she is in the process of erecting and tearing down. Like Philip K. Dick, the prophetic sf author whose work is repeatedly referenced in her lyrics,[169] Monáe has hereby invested above all in building storyworlds that deliberately fall apart: the interweaving of perspectives, constantly shifting back and forth between her own contemporary persona and her twenty-eighth-century alter ego, creates a fully dialectical tension between past, present, and future that makes her work so fundamentally political.

To use another helpful and appropriate Bakhtinian term, her work is in this sense profoundly dialogical: by embracing two identities that both strengthen and contradict each other, she develops an internal tension that "cannot fundamentally be dramatized or dramatically resolved."[170] Her transmedia world-building is constantly in dialogue both with itself and with the shifting sociocultural terrain around it, as it mutates and transforms within and between tracks, albums, performances, and media. It includes a sometimes overwhelming range of intertextual references that not only includes her productive appropriation of "the best memories of the last fifty years of black musical performance" but also uses her androgynous stage persona as an intertextual vessel that spins elastically "from David Bowie's high-concept theatrics to Prince's loose-spined, funky splits and squeals . . . to Grace Jones's coolly imperious robot."[171]

At the same time, her storyworld is also constantly engaged in dialogue with its audience, including not only the many varieties of participatory fan art, like the online comic book project *Cindi Mayweather: The Cyber-Graphic Novel*,[172] but also Monáe's own investment in community building and political activism. This creates a productive collision of genres, forms, styles, and temporalities that gives a creative form to critical posthumanism: never resorting to any single particular race, gender, or identity, but fully embracing the fluidity and multiplicity of Hardt and Negri's transformative multitude.

"SOUND IS OUR WEAPON": SONIC ANTICAPITALISM

Janelle Monáe's transmedia storyworld is complex and slippery, but her world-building strategy based on dialogism, heteroglossia, and radical eclecticism also

---

169. Among Monáe's many references to science fiction texts, the explicit mention of "electric sheep" on each of her albums further reinforces her intertextual association with this particular author's perspective.

170. Bakhtin, *The Dialogic Imagination*, 326.

171. Royster, *Sounding Like a No-No*, 187.

172. See the work by "CanalesComics" on the *Deviant Art* website: http://canalescomics.deviantart .com/art/Cindi-Mayweather-cover-fan-art-411569180.

doesn't result in any breakdown of meaning. Instead, the fictional Wondaland described in verse on *The ArchAndroid*, the dreamlike "world inside / Where dreamers meet each other," is made more meaningful by the Wondaland Arts Society, the Atlanta-based collective and record label of which Monáe's own projects are among the most visible products. On her website, in interviews, and in the credits for her albums and music videos, she consistently emphasizes not only her own membership of this larger collective but also the fact that her work is the result of collaborative creative work rather than purely individual accomplishment. As with her best-known Afrofuturist predecessors Sun Ra and George Clinton, the most utopian elements in her fantastic world-building thus also connect back to a real-world counterpart that is similarly inclusive, collective, and transformative in its aspirations. At the same time, the heteroglossia of her storyworld is more than just a multiplicity of voices and styles contained therein: it is also a platform for collaborative creative work and social and political activism.

On its website, Monáe's Wondaland Arts Society expounds its fundamental belief in "something futuristic and ancient that we call WISM," a force made up of wisdom, sex, magic, love, and wonder. This mantra resonates not only with the various progressive cultural movements that emerged in the post-'68 moment of emerging countercultures and progressive politics but also with twenty-first-century anticapitalism and its insistence on love and hope as radical forces. While moving beyond the essentialist humanism and technocratic frameworks of traditional sf, Monáe's project can be read in alignment with Hardt and Negri's utopian description of joyful "multitudinous energies":

> The path of joy is constantly to open new possibilities, to expand our field of imagination, our abilities to feel and be affected, our capacities for action and passion. In Spinoza's thought, in fact, there is a correspondence between our power to affect (our mind's power to think and our body's power to act) and our power to be affected. The greater our mind's ability to think, the greater its capacity to be affected by the ideas of others; the greater our body's ability to act, the greater its capacity to be affected by other bodies. And we have greater power to think and to act, Spinoza explains, the more we interact and create common relations with others. Joy, in other words, is really the result of joyful encounters with others, encounters that increase our powers, and the institution of these encounters such that they last and repeat.[173]

While most of the forms Monáe's work has taken obviously lend themselves to cognitive capitalism's immaterial forms of capital accumulation, her collaborative networks and centrifugal world-building at the same time open up important spaces for critique, debate, activism, and new collectives. A good example is the track "Hell You Talmbout,"[174] a reworked version of a song first released as a

---

173. Hardt and Negri, *Commonwealth*, 379.

174. Wondaland Records, "Hell You Talmbout," streaming audio, August 13, 2015, https://soundcloud.com/wondalandarts/hell-you-talmbout.

bonus track on *The Electric Lady*. The track, attributed this time not to Monáe herself but to the Wondaland Arts Collective, was not released commercially but made available in August for free streaming and download via the music-sharing platform SoundCloud. The six-and-a-half minute track was produced and released to support and strengthen Black Lives Matter, the social justice movement that erupted on the streets and via social media in response to the unconscionable killings of people of color in urban areas most deeply victimized by neoliberalism's disastrous effects on welfare, unemployment, and social services.

The track consists of a single propulsive central drum line and the phrase "Hell You Talmbout" as a repeated chorus, while the verses are made up of the names of black men, women, and children killed by police violence and other forms of institutional racism. Each name is repeated several times by alternating members of the collective, followed by the words "Say his/her name." Following a folk music tradition, "Hell You Talmbout" was designed to be easily reproduced by large groups with little more than a drum rhythm and one or two easily remembered lines. It thus swiftly became a widely shared anthem that mobilized resistance at marches and street protests, while also circulating online as a universal expression of protest, outrage, and solidarity. On her Instagram account, Monáe posted the following statement about the song when it was first released:

> This song is a vessel. It carries the unbearable anguish of millions. We recorded it to channel the pain, fear, and trauma caused by the ongoing slaughter of our brothers and sisters. We recorded it to challenge the indifference, disregard, and negligence of all who remain quiet about this issue. Silence is our enemy. Sound is our weapon. They say a question lives forever until it gets the answer it deserves. . . . Won't you say their names?

The track, described in the press as "an unadorned, visceral, undeniably earthbound piece of protest music,"[175] stands in sharp contrast with the polished surfaces of Monáe's other musical output. But just as the "Cold War" music video's formal minimalism seems to run counter to the larger scale of her futuristic world-building, the protest song foregrounds the radical and subversive energy that underlies even her most fantastic work. In the same way, her involvement with the Black Lives Matter movement plays into a longer social and musical history of activism and civil protest,[176] which her allegorical approach to politics, ideology, and biopower incorporates into its world-building.

Therefore, just as the Black Lives Matter movement has been a fruitful way of fueling solidarity and political activism by disrupting the obvious particularism of

---

175. Katie Presley, "Janelle Monáe Releases Visceral Protest Song, 'Hell You Talmbout,'" *NPR*, August 18, 2015, accessed December 27, 2015, http://www.npr.org/sections/allsongs/2015/08/18/385202798/janelle-mon-e-releases-visceral-protest-song-hell-you-talmbout.

176. Craig Werner, *A Change Is Gonna Come: Music, Race and the Soul of America* (Edinburgh: Canongate, 2000), 11–15.

institutional racism, Monáe's radical posthumanism resides in her uncanny ability to dissolve the particular into a new universal. Her use of an android alter ego provides a way of moving beyond the restrictive debates of identity politics and connects to Srnicek and Williams's call for a "new heterogeneous universalism"[177] that could give the Left a more solid common basis in the anticapitalist struggle. As part of a revived Afrofuturism, Monáe's world-building resonates with this movement, as it ties the hope of a better future to "a radical critique of existing structures of oppression and a remembrance of past struggles."[178] Her storyworld offers no utopian escape from the increasingly desperate reality of global capitalism, but it does maintain a stubborn optimism and a resilient faith in the multitude's revolutionary potential.

Moreover, while incorporating Afrofuturism's critical and subversive approach to fantastic storyworlds, her world-building mobilizes an imaginative form that can not only challenge and question these traditions but also engage with them joyfully and productively. Her immaculately produced, highly accessible, and commercially viable music is both a collection of branded commodities and an explicit celebration of "non-productive" creative and collaborative activity. While popular culture will quite obviously never change the political organization of postdemocratic capitalism by itself, it can still contribute to the vital work of imagining alternative futures without simultaneously avoiding or suppressing the very contradictions it would dissolve.[179] By placing her contagious call to dance, enjoyment, and creative collaboration in a storyworld that frames it as an act of political resistance, her music becomes an expression of defiance within neoliberalism's "relentless capture and control of time and experience."[180]

While the experience of joy is clearly among the primary goals of Janelle Monáe's blissfully eclectic neo-Afrofuturist pop, the inclusiveness of her approach to style, genre, and identity does indeed seem to facilitate and even organize what Hardt and Negri describe as the "joyful encounters with others"[181] that are so crucial to collective action. Of course, there is nothing inherently political in the momentary communal release of infectious dance music. But when experienced in the context of her unstable imaginary world, it may still provide an entrance point toward more radical political perspectives. Both her imaginary world-building practices and their real-life community-building counterparts, meanwhile, give structural shape to "the institution of these encounters such that they last and repeat,"[182] even in their supposedly low-impact pop-cultural forms.

---

177. Srnicek and Williams, *Inventing the Future*, 78.

178. Srnicek and Williams, *Inventing the Future*, 141.

179. Fredric Jameson, *Archaeologies of the Future* (London and New York: Verso, 2005), 265.

180. Jonathan Crary, *24/7: Late Capitalism and the Ends of Sleep* (London and New York: Verso, 2013), 40.

181. Hardt and Negri, *Commonwealth*, 379.

182. Hardt and Negri, *Commonwealth*, 379.

In this sense, at least, Monáe's work does contribute to the development of forms, narratives, subjectivities, and collaborative practices that help us think beyond the confines of neoliberalism's competitive individualism and move toward a posthuman future that opens up a world beyond capitalism.

CONCLUSION

Fantastic storyworlds give us structured and coherent-seeming "Secondary Worlds" that provide provocative alternatives to our own "Primary" reality. A large part of my argument throughout this book has been that these imaginary empires have a radical potential that reflects some of the most basic contradictions of capitalism. The way these contradictions are negotiated, both within the texts and in their reception, teaches us a great deal about the contradictory logic of immaterial labor, participatory culture, and the imperial nature of global capitalism.

But one of the problems with these highly lucrative commercial storyworlds is that they are hardly ever radical enough. All too often, what appears on the surface to be a world of unlimited creative possibility and collaborative potential simply reproduces the cultural logic of capitalist realism. With the increasing absorption of a once-unruly fan culture by the commercial media industries, corporate-produced and aggressively marketed fan fiction now dominates the media landscape, from the tiresome Marvel Cinematic Universe to the unrelenting *Star Wars* juggernaut. Many popular storyworlds thus become a form of fantastical capitalism as neoliberalism's structure of feeling is reproduced in ways that mostly illustrate how difficult it has become to imagine alternatives to capitalism.

Posthumanism's contribution to this dynamic is that it gives us deceptively simple concepts that can actually move *beyond* capitalism's focus on the individual subject as an entrepreneur of the self. By recognizing that liberal humanist notions of identity are inextricably interwoven with many forms of capitalist alienation, objectification, and exploitation, we open up a path toward the kind of collective and collaborative forms that a postcapitalist world will require. Posthumanism's dissolution of artificial and oppressive binaries not only casts aside the many existing hierarchical divisions within humanity but also rejects the anthropocentric privileging of human life above all others. The only way for fantastic storyworlds to express a truly radical anticapitalism would therefore be to embrace the posthuman turn and move from liberal humanism's stifling individualism to the multitude's infinite diversity.

In this chapter, I have discussed the zombie and the cyborg as fantastic fiction's most obvious embodiments of our own increasingly irrefutable posthuman condition. Zombies have proliferated across popular culture under global capitalism, and zombie theory has developed into a lively and productive form of radical thinking. As a literal embodiment of late capitalism's negative dialectic, the zombie resonates so strongly with posthumanism because it disrupts the system of "progress" and accumulation as we know it. The undead are the walking proof of capitalism's deeply unsustainable, ultimately catastrophic nature. As an ongoing collection of narratives exploring a postcapitalist world, *The Walking Dead* offers productive ways of negotiating some of the tensions inherent in our response to this posthuman condition. Therefore, while the zombie genre has great difficulty imagining a postcapitalist future in a positive sense, it resonates so strongly with posthuman theory because it makes starkly visible our ambivalence in the face of posthumanism's most radical implications.

In the cyborg, fantastic fiction finds a posthuman trope with truly utopian potential. And in the hands of Janelle Monáe, the intersection between the organic and the artificial becomes a site of potential liberation. Her use of the android trope firmly acknowledges the many ways in which capitalist history has used discourses of hybridization, miscegenation, and technological innovation for exploitation and oppression. But, at the same time, her Afrofuturist world-building follows a radically centrifugal logic that playfully challenges and disrupts boundaries of gender, ethnicity, class, and sexual identity. Her fluid, flexible, participatory, and thoroughly political world-building therefore demonstrates provocatively how fantastic fiction can also be used as a powerful anticapitalist weapon.

6

"Post"script

Throughout this book, I have discussed transmedia world-building as a way of negotiating the contradictions of global capitalism. I have argued that fantastic storyworlds provide us with valuable ways to challenge and interrogate the cultural logic of capitalism while at the same time imposing serious limits on their radical political potential. These endlessly expansive and immersive imaginary empires reflect the cultural logic that Hardt and Negri have identified in global capitalism: both are developed and sustained by creative and collaborative immaterial labor, while they also incorporate this participatory and affective energy into cognitive capitalism's new forms of circulation and accumulation.

Looking back on the case studies in the four preceding chapters, this correspondence between Empire and fantastic world-building breaks down into a short list of "posts": the postimperialist spirit of Tolkien and *Star Trek*; the postideological sensibility of *Game of Thrones* and *BSG*; the postdemocratic empires of *Spartacus* and *The Hunger Games*; and the posthuman hybrids of *The Walking Dead* and Janelle Monáe's "Metropolis Saga." I shall close, then, by reflecting briefly on each of these "posts" and their cumulative expression of global capitalism's contradictory logic in fantastic world-building.

POSTIMPERIALISM

The Empire of global capitalism is postimperialist because it no longer allows for any outside. The deterritorialization and space-time compression inherent in capitalism's endless accumulation have eradicated what long seemed like durable boundaries of all kinds. Globalization, neoliberalism, and convergence culture therefore make it increasingly difficult to maintain an understanding of social, cultural, and political order. Fantastic world-building translates this process of global deterritorialization into fantasy's generic convention of thinning, with imaginary empires in the process of losing magic, myth, and mystery as they undergo inevitable modernization.

This postimperialist dynamic is cause for celebration as well as concern: Empire's dissolution of violently oppressive colonial rule, rigidly hierarchical systems, destructive military conflict, and stultifying standardization has allowed for some valuable forms of liberation—especially for those in the Global North. But in doing so, it has neither acknowledged nor resolved capitalism's most basic contradictions: postindustrial capitalism has appeared to make labor invisible by disenfranchising workers, unions, and minorities and by proletarianizing populations outside the most advanced capitalist countries on a massive scale. While a rapidly decreasing elite gets to enjoy the privileges of cognitive capitalism's immaterial labor, Empire's power is still based on new cycles of primitive accumulation on a global scale.

This truly global framework results in a general sense of a world without an outside, as the rapid eradication of imperialist boundaries has made it much more difficult to see ourselves as anything other than atomized and competitive individuals. The crucial challenge in a postimperialist world is therefore to embrace the fluid, decentered, and completely networked structure of Empire's deterritorialized terrain, but to use this flexibility to develop new collective forms of political organization. Throughout this book, I have demonstrated some of the ways in which fantastic world-building functions not only as a narrative embodiment of globalization but also as a productive way of imagining alternatives and organizing participatory collective forms that question the cultural logic of neoliberalism.

POSTIDEOLOGY

Along with global capitalism's deterritorialization of imperialism's striated terrain, it has become increasingly difficult to maintain stable communities and offer organized resistance to neoliberalism's rising tide. The endlessly repeated mantra "there is no alternative" leaves no space for ideological debate, therefore stranding us in a postideological no-man's-land of capitalist realism. This ontological paradigm has translated with remarkable ease to fantastic franchises, which have found new cultural currency by moving away from the genre's "childish" idealism and developing into hard-edged and adult-oriented forms of what I have described as fantastical capitalism: seemingly fantastic storyworlds that have fully absorbed global capitalism's commonsense logic, rejecting ideological alternatives as fundamentally unrealistic.

But the central contradiction of Empire's postideological condition is that what appears as the absence of ideology is, of course, ideology at its purest: there still remain plentiful ideological goals, structures, and beliefs, just as there exist numerous alternatives to capitalism. The key issue is therefore to recognize the ideological hegemony of global capitalism for what it is, just as we can see it plainly reflected in the fantastic storyworlds that give this sentiment commonsense validity. What we recognize in the "gritty," "realistic" storyworlds of fantastical capitalism is our own social reality, with its intensified precarity, mandatory flexibility, and unrelenting competition. Only by recognizing how these imaginary empires both legitimize *and* challenge the basic logic of Empire's own internal contradictions will we be able to leverage this postideological spirit to illuminate capitalism's own internal contradictions.

POSTDEMOCRACY

The rapid dissolution of ideological debate under global capitalism has badly damaged the political ideal of participatory democracy. While the formal procedures of democratic elections are fetishized as periodic rituals and media spectacles, neoliberal rule is in practice purely technocratic, acknowledging no other reality than that of the Market. Little wonder, therefore, that global capitalism operates as an Empire, with national governments devoted in the first place to facilitating wealthy corporations' unfettered accumulation of profit.

In the world of popular culture and fantastic storyworlds, global capitalism's postdemocratic nature is most obvious in the unprecedented power of media conglomerates like Disney and Time Warner, whose seemingly effortless incorporation of once-subversive fan culture now feeds greedily off the multitude's immaterial and affective labor. With bitter irony, the democratic potential of participatory culture has been casually absorbed by the global hegemony of media conglomerates.

But, at the same time, the drawing power of many fantastic storyworld's is derived from their *critical* reflection of postdemocratic rule. While fantastic storyworlds increasingly circulate as branded media spectacles, their representation of politics and social relations also expresses postdemocratic capitalism's oppressive biopower and stifling lack of alternatives. The communist horizon that becomes visible in these storyworlds gives imaginative form to the multitude's revolutionary potential, especially in the forms of political activism they sometimes inspire.

POSTHUMANISM

If the overarching goal of radical anticapitalism is to move *beyond* capitalism, the first and most important step is to move beyond the comfortable traditions of liberal humanism. Global capitalism's biopolitical power depends in the first place on us thinking of ourselves not as members of a class or group but as distinct individuals who cherish their singularity above all else. The cultural logic of neoliberalism thus teaches us to be an entrepreneur of the self while systematically demonizing all forms of collective organization. Therefore, only by ridding ourselves of the binaries of anthropocentric subjectivity can we move beyond capitalism's exploitative forms of oppression.

The tension that informs the posthuman turn is felt especially strongly in the figure of the zombie: it expresses both our anxiety about the radically fluid and contradictory posthuman subject and the desire to move beyond a capitalist system that is so obviously unsustainable. But even though these "undead" storyworlds theoretically open up a space in which one might construct postcapitalist alternatives, the zombie's negative dialectic also tends to defeat such utopian impulses. The cyborg, however, fully embodies the posthuman in its productive hybridization of the organic and the artificial. It helps us think outside humanism's restrictive and hierarchical categories and enables both a politics of difference and a type of truly democratic freedom. Inherently deconstructing binaries of gender, race, class, and sexual orientation, the cyborg is therefore a valuable theoretical tool and a fundamentally political trope that can fuel radical anticapitalism in fantastic world-building.

Reflecting, then, on the importance of these various "posts" to fan culture and fantastic world-building, they only become truly meaningful in connection with the larger ideal of postcapitalism. My discussion of several fantastic storyworlds in this book has approached them as expressions of alternatives in a historical period in which capitalism seems to have enveloped our entire horizon. All too often, we see this reflected in the organization and reception of commercial storyworlds, as even the most imaginative and fantastical franchises see resistance to capitalism's deterritorialization as pointless and—ironically—"unrealistic."

But, at the same time, even the most ambivalent storyworlds are more than mere fantastical capitalism. By their very nature, fantastic transmedia storyworlds provide a type of estrangement that encourages critical reflection on the social and political nature of the world, whether real or imaginary. And while there are many ways in which such immersive and collaborative "Secondary Worlds" become meaningful to individual users, I am firmly convinced that their fundamental and ultimately irresistible attraction lies in this basic truth: whatever shape they take, whatever aspects of social reality they reflect, whatever ideological bias they reveal, and whatever way they are incorporated and commodified by capitalism itself, they remain grounded in the common hope and desire for a different, better world.

Bibliography

Adorno, Theodor. *The Culture Industry*. London and New York: Routledge, 1991.

Agamben, Giorgio. *Homo Sacer: Sovereign Power and Bare Life*. Palo Alto: Stanford University Press, 1998.

———. *State of Exception*. Chicago: University of Chicago Press, 2005.

Althusser, Louis. *On the Reproduction of Capitalism: Ideology and Ideological State Apparatuses*. Translated by G. M. Goshgarian. London and New York: Verso, 2014.

Arnold, Matthew. *Culture and Anarchy*. New York: Oxford's World Classics, 2009.

Aschoff, Nicole. *The New Prophets of Capital*. London and New York: Verso, 2015.

Attebery, Brian. *Strategies of Fantasy*. Bloomington: Indiana University Press, 1992.

Auerbach, Nina. *Our Vampires, Ourselves*. Chicago: University of Chicago Press, 1995.

Bachman, Richard. *The Running Man*. Harmondsworth: Penguin Books, 1996.

Bady, Aaron. "When *Game of Thrones* Stopped Being Necessary." *The New Inquiry*, June 15, 2015. Accessed January 16, 2016. http://thenewinquiry.com/blogs/zunguzungu/when-game-of-thrones-stopped-being-necessary.

Bakhtin, Mikhail. *The Dialogic Imagination: Four Essays*. Edited by Michael Holquist. Translated by Caryl Emerson and Michael Holquist. Austin: University of Texas Press, 1981.

Balibar, Étienne. "Is There a 'Neo-Racism'?" In *Race, Nation, Class: Ambiguous Identities*, Étienne Balibar and Immanuel Wallerstein, 17–28. London and New York: Verso, 1991.

Banet-Weiser, Sarah. *Authentic™: The Politics of Ambivalence in a Brand Culture*. New York: New York University Press, 2012.

Barr, Sabrina. "15 Ways the London Underground Is Exactly Like *The Hunger Games*." *BuzzFeed*, October 9, 2015. Accessed February 7, 2016. http://www.buzzfeed.com/sabrinabarr/15-ways-the-london-underground-is-literally-h-1qpyv?utm_term=.pjpe2AbGG#.aa71Egmvv.

Barthes, Roland. *Image, Music, Text*. London: Fontana Press, 1977.

Baudrillard, Jean. *Simulacra and Simulation*. Ann Arbor: University of Michigan Press, 1995.

Beaumont-Thomas, Ben. "*Game of Thrones* Fans Create an Interactive Map of Westeros . . . via Google Maps." *The Guardian: TV & Radio Blog*, April 15, 2014. Accessed December 27, 2015. http://www.theguardian.com/tv-and-radio/tvandradioblog/2014/apr/15/game-of-thrones-interactive-map-google.

Bellafante, Ginia. "A Fantasy World of Strange Feuding Kingdoms." *New York Times*, April 14, 2014. Accessed December 27, 2015. http://www.nytimes.com/2011/04/15/ arts/television/game-of-thrones-begins-sunday-on-hbo-review.html?_r=0.

Benjamin, Walter. *The Work of Art in the Age of Its Technological Reproducibility and Other Writings on Media*. Edited by Michael W. Jennings, Brigid Doherty, and Thomas Y. Levin. Cambridge, MA: Belknap, 2008.

Bishop, Kyle William. *American Zombie Gothic: The Rise and Fall (and Rise) of the Walking Dead in Popular Culture*. Jefferson: McFarland, 2010.

Bobbitt, Philip. *Terror and Consent: The Wars for the Twenty-First Century*. New York: Alfred A. Knopf, 2008.

Bokina, John. "From Communist Ideologue to Postmodern Rebel: Spartacus in Novels." *The European Legacy* 6, no. 6 (2001): 725–30.

Boltanski, Luc, and Eve Chiapello. *The New Spirit of Capitalism*. Translated by Gregory Elliott. London and New York: Verso, 2005.

Bolter, Jay David, and Richard Grusin. *Remediation: Understanding New Media*. Cambridge, MA: MIT Press, 2000.

Bonnstetter, Beth E., and Brian L. Ott. "(Re)Writing Mary Sue: *Écriture Féminine* and the Performance of Subjectivity." *Text and Performance Quarterly* 31, no. 4 (2011): 342–67.

Booker, M. Keith. "The Politics of *Star Trek*." In *The Essential Science Fiction Television Reader*, edited by J. P. Telotte, 195–208. Lexington: University Press of Kentucky, 2008.

Bould, Mark. "The Ships Landed Long Ago: Afrofuturism and Black SF." *Science Fiction Studies* 34, no. 2 (2007): 177–86.

Bould, Mark, and China Miéville, eds. *Red Planets: Marxism and Science Fiction*. London: Pluto Press, 2009.

Bourdieu, Pierre. *Distinction*. London and New York: Routledge, 2000 (1984).

Boutang, Yann Moulier. *Cognitive Capitalism*. Translated by Ed Emery. Cambridge: Polity Press, 2011.

Bowles, Scott. "Comic-Con Illustrates Genre's Rising Influence." *USA Today*, July 25, 2004. Accessed June 4, 2015. http://usatoday30.usatoday.com/life/movies/news/2004 -07-25-comic-con-side_x.htm.

Brandt, Marissa. "Janelle Monáe's Liberationist Posthuman Pop." *Difference Engines*, March 5, 2014. Accessed December 27, 2015. http://www.differenceengines .com/?p=1021.

Breen, Benjamin. "Why *Game of Thrones* Isn't Medieval—and Why That Matters." *Pacific Standard*, June 12, 2014. Accessed June 3, 2015. http://www.psmag.com/ books-and-culture/game-thrones-isnt-medieval-matters-83288.

Broe, Dennis. "Fox and Its Friends: Global Commodification and the New Cold War." *Cinema Journal* 43, no. 4 (2004): 97–102.

Brooker, Will. *Batman Unmasked: Analyzing a Cultural Icon*. New York: Continuum, 2000.

———. *Hunting the Dark Knight: Twenty-First Century Batman*. London: I. B. Tauris, 2012.

———. *Using the Force: Creativity, Community and Star Wars Fans*. New York: Continuum, 2002.

Burroughs, Edgar Rice. *Mars Trilogy: A Princess of Mars; The Gods of Mars; The Warlord of Mars*. New York: Simon & Schuster, 2012.

Caldwell, J. T. *Televisuality: Style, Crisis and Authority in American Television*. New Brunswick: Rutgers University Press, 1995.

Canavan, Gerry. "'If the Engine Ever Stops, We'd All Die': *Snowpiercer* and Necrofuturism," *Paradoxa* 26 (2014): 41–66.

———. "'We *Are* the Walking Dead': Race, Time, and Survival in Zombie Narrative." *Extrapolation* 51, no. 3 (2010): 431–53.

———. "You Think You Know the Story: Novelty, Repetition, and Lovecraft in Whedon and Goddard's *The Cabin in the Woods*." In *The Politics of Adaptation: Media Convergence and Ideology*, edited by Dan Hassler-Forest and Pascal Nicklas, 201–13. Basingstoke: Palgrave Macmillan, 2015.

Canavan, Gerry, and Kim Stanley Robinson, eds. *Green Planets: Ecology and Science Fiction*. Middletown: Wesleyan University Press, 2014.

Cardwell, Sarah. "Is Quality Television Any Good?" In *Quality TV: Contemporary American Television and Beyond*, edited by Janet McCabe and Kim Akass. New York: I. B. Taurus, 2007.

Carr, Nicholas. *The Shallows: What the Internet Is Doing to Our Brains*. New York: W. W. Norton and Company, 2011.

Carroll, Noël. "The Nature of Horror." *Journal of Aesthetics and Art Criticism* 46, no. 1 (1987): 51–59.

Carroll, Rory. "Donald Sutherland: 'I Want Hunger Games to Stir Up a Revolution.'" *The Guardian*, November 19, 2013. Accessed December 27, 2015. http://www.theguardian.com/film/2013/nov/19/donald-sutherland-hunger-games-catching-fire.

Casey, Jim. "'All This Has Happened Before': Repetition, Reimagination, and Eternal Return." In *Cylons in America: Critical Studies of Battlestar Galactica*, edited by Tiffany Potter and C. W. Marshall, 237–50. New York: Continuum, 2008.

Castells, Manuel. *The Rise of the Network Society*. 2nd edition. Chichester: Wiley-Blackwell, 2010.

Chance, Jane. *The Lord of the Rings: The Mythology of Power*. Revised edition. Lexington: Kentucky University Press, 2001.

Child, Ben. "How *The Hunger Games* Inspired the Revolutionary in All of Us." *The Guardian*, October 12, 2015. Accessed January 21, 2016. http://www.theguardian.com/film/filmblog/2015/oct/12/hunger-games-mockingjay-part-2.

Chu, Arthur. "How *Battlestar Galactica*, *Game of Thrones*, and FanFiction Conquered Pop Culture." *The Daily Beast*, May 6, 2014. Accessed June 11, 2015. http://www.thedailybeast.com/articles/2014/05/06/how-battlestar-galactica-game-of-thrones-and-fanfiction-conquered-pop-culture.html.

Clements, J. M. *Spartacus: Swords and Ashes*. London: Titan Books, 2012.

Clute, John. "Thinning." In *The Encyclopedia of Fantasy*, edited by John Clute and John Grant, 942–43. New York: St. Martin's Griffin, 1999.

Collins, Hattie. "Janelle Monáe Walks the Tightrope between Conceptual Art Weirdness and Robo-Pop Stardom." *The Guardian*, July 9, 2010. Accessed December 27, 2015. http://www.theguardian.com/music/2010/jul/09/janelle-monae-tightrope-archandroid.

Collins, Jim. *Bring on the Books for Everybody: How Literary Culture Became Popular Culture*. Durham: Duke University Press, 2010.

Collins, Suzanne. *Catching Fire*. New York: Scholastic Press, 2009.

———. *The Hunger Games*. New York: Scholastic Press, 2008.

———. *Mockingjay*. New York: Scholastic Press, 2010.

Comentale, Edward P., and Aaron Jaffe. "Introduction: The Zombie Research Center FAQ." In *The Year's Work at the Zombie Research Center*, edited by Edward P. Comentale and Aaron Jaffe, 1–58. Bloomington: Indiana University Press, 2014.

Coren, Michael. *J. R. R. Tolkien: The Man Who Created* The Lord of the Rings. London: Boxtree, 2001.

Crary, Jonathan. *24/7: Late Capitalism and the Ends of Sleep*. London and New York: Verso, 2013.

Csicsery-Ronay, Istvan. "Science Fiction and Empire." *Science Fiction Studies* 30, no. 2 (2003): 231–45.

Curry, Patrick. *Defending Middle-earth: Tolkien: Myth and Modernity*. Boston: Houghton Mifflin, 2004.

Dardot, Pierre, and Christian Laval. *The New Way of the World: On Neoliberal Society*. London and New York: Verso, 2013.

David, Marlo. "Afrofuturism and Post-Soul Possibility in Black Popular Music." *African American Review* 41, no. 4 (2007): 695–707.

De Certeau, Michel. *The Practice of Everyday Life*. Berkeley and Los Angeles: University of California Press, 2002.

De Kosnik, Abigail. "Fandom as Free Labor." In *Digital Labor: The Internet as Playground and Factory*, edited by Trebor Scholz, 98–111. London and New York: Routledge, 2013.

Dean, Jason. "Primers for the Post-Apocalypse: *The Hunger Games* Trilogy." *Unemployed Negativity*, September 5, 2011. Accessed December 27, 2015. http://www.unemployednegativity.com/2011/09/primer-for-post-apocalypse-hunger-game.html.

Dean, Jodi. *The Communist Horizon*. London and New York: Verso, 2012.

Debord, Guy. *The Society of the Spectacle*. New York: Zone Books, 1994 (1967).

———. *Comments on the Society of the Spectacle*. London and New York: Verso, 1998 (1990).

DeFino, Dean J. *The HBO Effect*. London and New York: Bloomsbury, 2014.

DeKnight, Steven S., and Adam Archer. *Spartacus—Blood and Sand: Upon the Sands of Vengeance*. Chicago: Devil's Due, 2009.

Deleuze, Gilles. "Postscript on the Societies of Control." *October* 59 (1992): 3–7.

Deleuze, Gilles, and Félix Guattari. *Anti-Oedipus: Capitalism and Schizophrenia*. New York: Continuum, 2004 (1983).

———. *A Thousand Plateaus*. New York: Continuum, 2004 (1987).

Dena, Christy. "Transmedia Practice: Theorising the Practice of Expressing a Fictional World across Distinct Media and Environments." PhD diss., University of Sydney, 2009.

Derrida, Jacques. *Of Grammatology*. Baltimore: Johns Hopkins University Press, 1976.

———. *Specters of Marx*. Translated by Peggy Kamuf. New York: Routledge, 1994.

———. *Writing and Difference*. Chicago: University of Chicago Press, 1978.

Dery, Mark. "Black to the Future: Interviews with Samuel R. Delany, Greg Tate, and Tricia Rose." In *Flame Wars: The Discourse of Cyberculture*, edited by Mark Dery, 179–222. Durham: Duke University Press, 1994.

Deuze, Mark. *Media Life*. London: Polity Press, 2012.

Dick, Philip K. "How to Build a Universe That Doesn't Fall Apart Two Days Later." In *I Hope I Shall Arrive Soon*, 4–5. New York: Doubleday, 1985.

Doležel, Lubomír. *Heterocosmica: Fiction and Possible Worlds*. Baltimore: Johns Hopkins University Press, 2000.

Douglas, Kirk. *I Am Spartacus! Making a Film, Breaking the Blacklist*. New York: Open Road Media, 2012.

Dowling, William C. *Jameson, Althusser, Marx: An Introduction to the Political Unconscious*. London: Routledge, 1984.

Drezler, Daniel W. *Theories of International Politics and Zombies*. Princeton, NJ: Princeton University Press, 2011.

Dyer-Witherford, Nick, and Greig de Peuter. *Games of Empire: Global Capitalism and Video Games*. Minneapolis: Minnesota University Press, 2009.

Dzialo, Chris. "When Balance Goes Bad: How *Battlestar Galactica* Says Everything and Nothing." In *Cylons in America: Critical Studies of Battlestar Galactica*, edited by Tiffany Potter and C. W. Marshall, 171–84. New York: Continuum, 2008.

Eaton, Mick. "History to Hollywood: Mick Eaton Talks to Trevor Griffiths." *Screen* 23, no. 2 (1982): 61–70.

Ebiri, Bilge. "*The LEGO Movie* Is Practically Communist." *Vulture*, February 7, 2014. Accessed December 27, 2015. http://www.vulture.com/2014/02/lego-movies-antidote -to-kids-movie-clichs.html.

Eco, Umberto. *Faith in Fakes: Travels in Hyperreality*. London: Vintage, 1986.

———. "The Myth of Superman." *Dialectics* 2, no. 1 (1972): 14–22.

Eder, Jens. "Transmediality and the Politics of Adaptation: Concepts, Forms, and Strategies." In *The Politics of Adaptation: Media Convergence and Ideology*, edited by Dan Hassler-Forest and Pascal Nicklas, 66–81. Basingstoke: Palgrave Macmillan, 2015.

Ekman, Stefan. *Here Be Dragons: Exploring Fantasy Maps and Settings*. Middletown: Wesleyan University Press, 2013.

English, Daylanne K., and Alvin Kim. "Now We Want Our Funk Cut: Janelle Monáe's Neo-Afrofuturism." *American Studies* 52, no. 4 (2013): 217–30.

Eshun, Kodwo. "Further Considerations of Afrofuturism." *CR: The New Centennial Review* 3, no. 2 (2003): 287–302.

———. *More Brilliant Than the Sun: Adventures in Sonic Fiction*. London: Quartet Books, 1998.

Eyerman, Ron. "False Consciousness and Ideology in Marxist Theory." *Acta Sociologica* 24, no. 1/2 (1981): 43–56.

Fast, Howard. *Being Red*. Boston: Houghton Mifflin, 1990.

———. *Spartacus*. New York: Simon & Schuster, 1996 (1951).

Fawaz, Ramzi. "'Where No X-Man Has Gone Before!' Mutant Superheroes and the Cultural Politics of Popular Fantasy in Postwar America." *American Literature* 83, no. 2 (2011): 355–88.

Feuer, Jane. "HBO and the Concept of Quality TV." In *Quality TV: Contemporary American Television and Beyond*, edited by Janet McCabe and Kim Akass, 145–57. London and New York: I. B. Tauris, 2007.

———. "The MTM Style." In *MTM "Quality Television"*, edited by Jane Feuer, Paul Kerr, and Tise Vahimagi, 32–60. London: BFI, 1984.

Fisher, Mark. "Batman's Political Right Turn." *The Guardian*, July 22, 2012. Accessed January 18, 2016. http://www.theguardian.com/commentisfree/2012/jul/22/batman -political-right-turn.

———. *Capitalist Realism: Is There No Alternative?* Hants: Zero Books, 2009.

———. *Ghosts of My Life: Writings on Depression, Hauntology and Lost Futures*. Hants: Zero Books, 2014.

———. "The Metaphysics of Crackle: Afrofuturism and Hauntology." *Dancecult: Journal of Electronic Dance Music Culture* 5, no. 2 (2013): 32–55.

———. "Permissive Hedonism and the Ascesis of Positivity." *k-punk*, May 2, 2007. Accessed December 27, 2015. http://k-punk.abstractdynamics.org/archives/009325.html.

———. "Precarious Dystopias: *The Hunger Games*, *In Time*, and *Never Let Me Go*." *Film Quarterly* 65, no. 4 (2012): 27–33.

———. "Remember Who the Enemy Is." *k-punk*, November 25, 2013. Accessed December 27, 2015. http://k-punk.org/remember-who-the-enemy-is/.

———. "SF Capital." *Transmat: Resources in Transcendental Materialism*, 2001. Accessed November 12, 2014. http://www.cinestatic.com/trans-mat/Fisher/sfcapital.htm.

Fiske, John. "The Cultural Economy of Fandom." In *The Adoring Audience: Fan Culture and Popular Media*, edited by Lisa A. Lewis, 30–49. London and New York: Routledge, 1992.

———. *Television Culture*. London and New York: Routledge, 1987.

Foucault, Michel. *Discipline and Punish: The Birth of the Prison*. New York: Vintage, 1995.

———. *The History of Sexuality: 1—The Will to Knowledge*. London: Penguin, 1981.

———. *Power/Knowledge: Selected Interviews and Other Writings*. Edited by Colin Gordon. New York: Pantheon Books, 1980.

———. "What Is an Author?" In *The Norton Anthology of Theory and Criticism*, 2nd edition, edited by Vincent B. Leitch et al., 1475–90. New York: Norton and Co., 2010.

Frankel, Valerie Estelle. *Women in* Game of Thrones*: Power, Conformity and Resistance*. Jefferson, NC: McFarland, 2014.

Freedman, Carl. *Art and Idea in the Novels of China Miéville*. Canterbury: Gylphi Books, 2015.

———. "Capitalist Realism in Three Recent Sf Films." *Paradoxa* 26 (2014): 67–80.

———. *Critical Theory and Science Fiction*. Middletown: Wesleyan University Press, 2000.

Fuchs, Christian. "Against Henry Jenkins: Remarks on Henry Jenkins' ICA Talk." *Christian Fuchs Blog*, May 30, 2011. http://fuchs.uti.at/570/.

Fukuyama, Francis. "The End of History?" *National Interest* 16 (1989): 3–18.

Galloway, Alexander R. "*Warcraft* and Utopia." CTheory.net, February 16, 2006. http://www.ctheory.net/articles.aspx?id=507.

Genette, Gérard. *Paratexts: The Thresholds of Interpretation*. Translated by Jane E. Lewin. Cambridge: Cambridge University Press, 1997.

Gilbert, Jeremy. *Anticapitalism and Culture*. London: Bloomsbury, 2008.

———. *Common Ground: Democracy and Collectivity in an Age of Individualism*. London: Pluto Press, 2013.

Gilbert, Jeremy, and Ewan Pearson. *Discographies: Dance Music, Culture and the Politics of Sound*. London and New York: Routledge, 1999.

Gilroy, Paul. *Between Camps: Nations, Cultures and the Allure of Race*. London: Allen Lane, 2000.

———. *The Black Atlantic: Modernity and Double-Consciousness*. Cambridge, MA: Harvard University Press, 1993.

Goldman, D. P. "Tolkien's *Ring*: When Immortality Isn't Enough." *Asia Times Online*, January 5, 2004. http://www.atimes.com/atimes/Front_Page/FA05Aa01.html.

Golumbia, David. "Black and White World: Race, Ideology, and Utopia in *Triton* and *Star Trek.*" *Cultural Critique* 32 (1995): 75–95.

Gomery, Douglas, "Hollywood Corporate Business Practice and Periodizing Contemporary Film History." In *Contemporary Hollywood Cinema*, edited by Steve Neale and Murray Smith, 47–57. New York: Routledge, 1998.

Gray, Jonathan. *Show Sold Separately: Promos, Spoilers, and Other Media Paratexts.* New York: New York University Press, 2010.

Halberstam, Judith, and Ira Livingston. *Posthuman Bodies.* Bloomington: Indiana University Press, 1995.

Hancox, Dan. *The Village Against the World.* London and New York: Verso, 2014.

Haraway, Donna. "A Manifesto for Cyborgs: Science, Technology, and Socialist Feminism in the 1980s." In *The Gendered Cyborg: A Reader*, edited by G. Kirkup, L. Janes, K. Woodward, and F. Hovenden, 50–57. London: Routledge, 2000.

Hardt, Michael, and Antonio Negri. *Commonwealth.* Cambridge, MA: Belknap, 2009.

———. *Empire.* Cambridge, MA: Harvard University Press, 2000.

———. *Multitude: War and Democracy in the Age of Empire.* London: Penguin, 2005.

———. "Take Up the Baton." *Jacobin*, May 5, 2012. https://www.jacobinmag .com/2012/05/take-up-the-baton/.

Harman, Chris. *Zombie Capitalism: Global Crisis and the Relevance of Marx.* London: Bookmarks, 2009.

Harman, Graham. *Weird Realism: Lovecraft and Philosophy.* Hants: Zero Books, 2012.

Harvey, Colin. *Fantastic Transmedia: Narrative, Play and Memory Across Science Fiction and Fantasy Storyworlds.* Basingstoke: Palgrave Macmillan, 2015.

Harvey, David. *A Brief History of Neoliberalism.* Oxford: Oxford University Press, 2006.

———. *The Condition of Postmodernity: An Enquiry into the Origins of Cultural Change.* Malden: Blackwell, 1990.

———. *Justice, Nature and the Geography of Difference.* Malden: Blackwell, 1996.

———. *The Limits to Capital.* London and New York: Verso, 2006.

———. *The New Imperialism.* Oxford: Oxford University Press, 2005.

———. *Rebel Cities: From the Right to the City to the Urban Revolution.* London and New York: Verso, 2012.

———. *Seventeen Contradictions and the End of Capitalism.* London: Profile Books, 2014.

Hassler-Forest, Dan. "Cowboys and Zombies: Destabilizing Patriarchal Discourse in *The Walking Dead.*" *Studies in Comics* 2, no. 2 (2011): 339–55.

———. "*Game of Thrones*: The Politics of World-Building and the Cultural Logic of Gentrification." In *The Politics of Adaptation: Media Convergence and Ideology*, edited by Dan Hassler-Forest and Pascal Nicklas, 187–200. Basingstoke: Palgrave Macmillan, 2015.

———. "Of Iron Men and Green Monsters: Superheroes and Posthumanism." In *The Palgrave Handbook of Posthumanism in Film and Television*, edited by Michael Hauskeller, Thomas D. Philbeck, and Curtis D. Carbonell, 66–76. Basingstoke: Palgrave Macmillan, 2015.

———. "The Politics of World-Building: Heteroglossia in Janelle Monáe's Afrofuturist WondaLand." *Paradoxa: Studies in Literary Genres* 26 (2015): 284–303.

———. "Skimmers, Dippers, and Divers: Campfire's Steve Coulson on Transmedia Marketing and Audience Participation." *Participations* 13, no. 1 (2016).

———. "*The Walking Dead*: Quality Television, Transmedia Serialization and Zombies." In *Serialization in Popular Culture*, edited by Thijs van den Berg and Rob Allen, 91–105. London and New York: Routledge, 2014.

———. "Zombie Spaces." In *The Year's Work at the Zombie Research Center*, edited by Edward Comentale and Aaron Jaffe, 116–49. Bloomington: Indiana University Press, 2014.

Helbing, Todd, Aaron Helbing, Jon Bosco, and Guilherme Balbi. *Spartacus—Blood and Sand: The Beast of Carthage*. Chicago: Devil's Due, 2009.

Hertz, Noreena. "Generation K: Who Are They, and What Do We Know About Them?" *New York Times*, April 21, 2015. Accessed February 7, 2016. http://nytlive.nytimes.com/womenintheworld/2015/04/21/generation-k-who-are-they-and-what-do-we-know-about-them.

Hill, Kyle. "Does Sean Bean Really Die More Than Other Actors?" *Nerdist*, December 5, 2014. Accessed January 14, 2016. http://nerdist.com/does-sean-bean-really-die-more-than-other-actors.

Hills, Matt. *Fan Cultures*. London: Routledge, 2000.

———. "Realising the Cult Blockbuster: *The Lord of the Rings* Fandom and Residual/Emergent Cult Status in 'the Mainstream.'" In *The Lord of the Rings: Popular Culture in Context*, edited by Ernest Mathijs, 160–71. London: Wallflower, 2006.

Himes, Geoffrey. "Janelle Monáe: Imagining Her Own Future." *Paste*, September 9, 2013. Accessed January 26, 2016. http://www.pastemagazine.com/articles/2013/09/janelle-monae-imagining-her-own-future.html.

Hoberman, J. *Film After Film*. London and New York: Verso, 2013.

Horkheimer, Max, and Theodor Adorno. *Dialectic of Enlightenment: Philosophical Fragments*. Palo Alto: Stanford University Press, 2002.

Howard, Robert E. *The Coming of Conan the Cimmerian*. New York: Ballantine Books, 2003.

Hughes, Sarah. "'Sopranos Meets Middle-earth': How *Game of Thrones* Took Over Our World." *The Guardian*, March 22, 2014. Accessed January 4, 2016. http://www.theguardian.com/tv-and-radio/2014/mar/22/game-of-thrones-whats-not-to-love.

Huntington, Samuel P. "The Clash of Civilizations?" *Foreign Affairs* 7, no. 3 (1993): 22–49.

Iglesias, Pablo. "Spain on Edge." *New Left Review* 93 (May–June 2015). Accessed May 28, 2015. http://newleftreview.org/II/93/pablo-iglesias-spain-on-edge.

Isaac, Jeffrey C. "The Mirage of Neo-Communism." *Dissent* (Summer 2013). Accessed January 6, 2016. https://www.dissentmagazine.org/article/the-mirage-of-neo-communism.

Jackson, Rosemary. *Fantasy: The Literature of Subversion*. New York: Methuen, 1981.

Jameson, Fredric. *Archaeologies of the Future: The Desire Called Utopia and Other Science Fictions*. London and New York: Verso, 2005.

———. "Cognitive Mapping." In *Marxism and the Interpretation of Culture*, edited by Cary Nelson and Lawrence Grossberg, 347–60. Champaign: University of Illinois Press, 1990.

———. *The Cultural Turn: Selected Writings on the Postmodern, 1983–1998*. London and New York: Verso, 1998.

———. *The Geopolitical Aesthetic*. Bloomington: Indiana University Press, 1992.

———. *The Political Unconscious: Narrative as a Socially Symbolic Act*. Ithaca: Cornell University Press, 1981.

———. *Postmodernism, or, The Cultural Logic of Late Capitalism*. Durham: Duke University Press, 1991.

———. "Reification and Utopia in Mass Culture." *Social Text* 1 (1979): 130–48.

Jaramillo, Deborah L. "The Family Racket: AOL Time Warner, HBO, *The Sopranos*, and the Construction of a Quality Brand." *Journal of Communication Inquiry* 26, no. 1 (2002): 59–75.

Jenkins, Henry. *Convergence Culture: Where Old and New Media Collide*. New York: New York University Press, 2006.

———. "'Cultural Acupuncture': Fan Activism and the Harry Potter Alliance." In *Transformative Works and Fan Activism*, edited by Henry Jenkins and Sangita Shresthova, special issue, *Transformative Works and Cultures* 10 (2012). doi:10.3983/twc.2012.0305.

———. *Fans, Bloggers, and Gamers: Exploring Participatory Culture*. New York: New York University Press, 2006.

———. *Textual Poachers: Television Fans and Participatory Culture*. London: Routledge, 1992.

———. "*The Walking Dead*: Adapting Comics." In *How to Watch Television*, edited by Ethan Thompson and Jason Mittell, 373–81. New York: New York University Press, 2013.

Jenkins, Henry, Sam Ford, and Joshua Green. *Spreadable Media: Creating Value and Meaning in a Networked Culture*. New York: New York University Press, 2013.

Jenkins, Henry, Mizuko Ito, and danah boyd. *Participatory Culture in a Networked Era: A Conversation on Youth, Learning, Commerce, and Politics*. Cambridge: Polity Books, 2015.

Jenson, Joli. "Fandom as Pathology." In *The Adoring Audience: Fan Culture and Popular Media*, edited by Lisa A. Lewis, 9–29. London and New York: Routledge, 1992.

Johnson, Catherine. "Tele-Branding in TVIII: The Network as Brand and the Programme as Brand." *New Review of Film and Television Studies* 5, no. 1 (2007): 5–24.

Johnson, Derek. "Cinematic Destiny: Marvel Studios and the Trade Stories of Industrial Convergence." *Cinema Journal* 52, no. 1 (2012): 1–24.

———. *Media Franchising: Creative License and Collaboration in the Culture Industries*. New York: New York University Press, 2013.

Johnston, Kristin Kay. "Christian Theology as Depicted in *The Lord of the Rings* and the Harry Potter Books." *Journal of Religion and Society* 7 (2005). Accessed May 29, 2015. http://moses.creighton.edu/jrs/2005/2005-5.pdf.

Jowett, Lorna. "Mad, Bad, and Dangerous to Know? Negotiating Stereotypes of Science." In *Cylons in America: Critical Studies of Battlestar Galactica*, edited by Tiffany Potter and C. W. Marshall, 64–75. New York: Continuum, 2008.

Kazimierczak, Karolina Agata. "'Linguistic Fandom': Performing Liminal Identities in the Spaces of Transgression." *Liminalities: A Journal of Performance Studies* 6, no. 2 (2010): 1–16.

Kenneally, Tim. "*Game of Thrones* Becomes Most Popular Series in HBO's History." *The Wrap*, June 5, 2014. Accessed January 4, 2016. http://www.thewrap.com/game-of-thrones-becomes-most-popular-series-in-hbos-history.

Kirkman, Robert, Charlie Adlard, Tony Moore, and Cliff Rathburn. *The Walking Dead: Compendium 1*. Berkeley: Image Comics, 2009.

Kirkman, Robert, and Jay Bonansinga. *The Walking Dead: Rise of the Governor*. New York: St. Martin's Press, 2013.

Klastrup, Lisbeth. "The Worldness of EverQuest: Exploring a 21st Century Fiction." *Game Studies* 9, no. 1 (2009).

Klastrup, Lisbeth, and Susana Tosca. "Transmedial Worlds—Rethinking Cyberworld Design." In *Proceedings International Conference on Cyberworlds 2004*. IEEE Computer Society, Los Alamitos, California, 2004.

Klein, Naomi. *This Changes Everything: Capitalism vs. the Climate*. New York: Simon & Schuster, 2014.

Koestler, Arthur. *The Gladiators*. New York: Random House, 2011.

Kotsko, Adam. "What Is *Star Trek*'s Vision of Politics?" *An und für sich*, March 16, 2015. Accessed February 1, 2016. https://itself.wordpress.com/2015/03/16/what-is-star-treks -vision-of-politics/.

Kreiss, Daniel. "Performing the Past to Claim the Future: Sun Ra and the Afro-Future Underground, 1954–1968." *African American Review* 45, no. 1–2 (2012): 197–203.

Kriss, Sam. "*Game of Thrones* and the End of Marxist Theory." *Jacobin*, April 10, 2015. Accessed May 28, 2015. https://www.jacobinmag.com/2015/04/game-of-thrones -season-five-marxism.

Kuipers, Giselinde, and Jeroen de Kloet. "Spirituality and Fan Culture around the *Lord of the Rings* Film Trilogy." *Fabula* 48, no. 3–4 (2007): 300–319.

Kustritz, Anne. "Breeding Unity: *Battlestar Galactica*'s Biracial Reproductive Futurity." *Camera Obscura* 27, no. 3 (2012): 1–37.

Kwok, Miranda, and Allan Jefferson. *Spartacus—Blood and Sand: The Shadow of Death*. Chicago: Devil's Due, 2009.

Lacan, Jacques. *Écrits: A Selection*. Translated by Bruce Fink. London and New York: Routledge, 2001.

Laclau, Ernesto, and Chantal Mouffe. *Hegemony and Socialist Strategy: Towards a Radical Democratic Politics*. London and New York: Verso, 2014 (1985).

Landa, Ishay. "Slaves of the Ring: Tolkien's Political Unconscious." *Historical Materialism* 10, no. 4 (2002): 113–33.

Landow, George. *Hypertext: The Convergence of Contemporary Critical Theory and Technology*. Baltimore: Johns Hopkins University Press, 1991.

Lauro, Sarah Juliet, and Karen Embry. "A Zombie Manifesto: The Nonhuman Condition in the Era of Advanced Capitalism." *Boundary* 2 (2008): 85–108.

Lawrence, John Shelton, and Robert Jewett. *The Myth of the American Superhero*. Grand Rapids: Eerdmans, 2002.

Lazzarato, Maurizio. *Signs and Machines: Capitalism and the Production of Subjectivity*. Cambridge, MA: MIT Press, 2014.

Lester, Paul. "Janelle Monae: 'It's True. I Am Part-Android.'" *The Guardian*, April 2, 2014. Accessed January 26, 2016. http://www.theguardian.com/culture/2014/apr/02/ janelle-monae-interview-david-bowie-prince.

Leverette, Marc. "Cocksucker, Motherfucker, Tits." In *It's Not TV: Watching HBO in the Post-Television Era*, edited by Marc Leverette, Brian L. Ott and Cara Louise Buckley, 123–51. New York: Routledge, 2008.

Lévi-Strauss, Claude. *The Savage Mind*. Chicago: University of Chicago Press, 1966.

Lewis, George E. "Foreword: After Afrofuturism." *Journal of the Society for American Music* 2, no. 2 (2008): 139–53.

Lieber, Marlon, and Daniel Zamora. "Rebel Without a Cause." *Jacobin*, January 4, 2016. Accessed January 6, 2016. https://www.jacobinmag.com/2016/01/hunger-games -review-capitalism-revolution-mockingjay-suzanne-collins.

Loewenstein, Anthony. *Disaster Capitalism: Making a Killing Out of Catastrophe.* London and New York: Verso, 2015.

Lorey, Isabell. *State of Insecurity: Government of the Precarious.* London and New York: Verso, 2015.

Loss, Robert. "Power Up: Janelle Monáe, Afrofuturism, and Plurality." *PopMatters*, October 29, 2013. Accessed January 26, 2016. http://www.popmatters.com/column/176055-power-up-janelle-monae-afrofuturism-and-plurality/.

Lyotard, Jean-François. *The Postmodern Condition: A Report on Knowledge.* Minneapolis: Minnesota University Press, 1984.

Mancour, T. L. *Star Trek: The Next Generation—Spartacus.* London: Titan Books, 1992.

Manovich, Lev. *The Language of New Media.* Cambridge, MA: MIT Press, 2002.

Marion, Isaac. *Warm Bodies.* New York: Atria Books, 2010.

Marshall, C. W., and Tiffany Potter. "'I See the Patterns': *Battlestar Galactica* and the Things That Matter." In *Cylons in America: Critical Studies of Battlestar Galactica*, edited by Tiffany Potter and C. W. Marshall, 1–10. New York: Continuum, 2008.

Marshall, C. W., and Matthew Wheeland. "The Cylons, The Singularity, and God." In *Cylons in America: Critical Studies of Battlestar Galactica*, edited by Tiffany Potter and C. W. Marshall, 91–104. New York: Continuum, 2008.

Martin, George R. R. *A Clash of Kings.* New York: Bantam Books, 1998.

———. *A Dance of Dragons.* New York: Bantam Books, 2011.

———. *A Feast for Crows.* New York: Bantam Books, 2005.

———. *A Game of Thrones.* New York: Bantam Books, 1996.

———. *A Storm of Swords.* New York: Bantam Books, 2000.

Marx, Karl. *Capital: A Critique of Political Economy, Volume 1.* Translated by Ben Fowkes. Harmondsworth: Penguin Books, 1976.

———. *Grundrisse.* Translated by Martin Nicolaus. Harmondsworth: Penguin Books, 1973.

Marx, Karl, and Friedrich Engels. *The Communist Manifesto: A Modern Edition.* London and New York: Verso, 2012.

Mason, Carol. "Terminating Bodies: Toward a Cyborg History of Abortion." In *Posthuman Bodies*, edited by Judith Halberstam and Ira Livingston, 225–43. Bloomington: Indiana University Press, 1995.

Mason, Paul. *Postcapitalism: A Guide to Our Future.* Harmondsworth: Penguin Books, 2015.

———. *Why It's Still Kicking Off Everywhere.* London and New York: Verso, 2013.

Matheson, Richard. *I Am Legend.* London: Gollancz, 1999 (1954).

May, Jeff. "Zombie Geographies and the Undead City." *Social & Cultural Geography* 11, no. 3 (2010): 285–98.

McCabe, Janet, and Kim Akass. "It's Not TV, It's HBO's Original Programming." In *It's Not TV: Watching HBO in the Post-Television Era*, edited by Marc Leverette, Brian L. Ott, and Cara Louise Buckley, 83–93. New York: Routledge, 2008.

McGuigan, J. "The Coolness of Capitalism Today." *tripleC* 10, no. 2 (2012): 425–38.

McGuire, Riley. "Queer Children, Queer Futures: Navigating Lifedeath in *The Hunger Games*." *Mosaic* 48, no. 2 (2015): 63–76.

McMillan, Graeme. "*Walking Dead* Smashes Cable Ratings Records, Beats Broadcast Networks." *Wired*, February 12, 2013. Accessed December 27, 2015. http://www.wired.com/2013/02/walking-dead-ratings-record/.

McNally, David. *Monsters of the Market: Zombies, Vampires and Global Capitalism.* Chicago: Haymarket Books, 2012.

McNeilly, Kevin. "'This Might Be Hard for You to Watch': Salvage Humanity in 'Final Cut.'" In *Cylons in America: Critical Studies in Battlestar Galactica*, edited by Tiffany Potter and C. W. Marshall, 185–97. New York: Continuum, 2008.

Merrifield, Andy. *Magical Marxism: Subversive Politics and the Imagination*. London: Pluto Press, 2011.

Miéville, China. "There and Back Again: Five Reasons Tolkien Rocks." *Omnivoracious*, June 15, 2009. Accessed December 27, 2015. http://www.omnivoracious.com/2009/06/there-and-back-again-five-reasons-tolkien-rocks.html.

———. "Tolkien—Middle Earth Meets Middle England." *Socialist Review* 259 (January 2002). Accessed December 27, 2015. http://www.socialistreview.org.uk/article.php?articlenumber=7813.

Mittell, Jason. *Complex TV: The Poetics of Contemporary Television Storytelling*. New York: New York University Press, 2015.

———. "*Lost* in a Great Story: Evaluation in Narrative Television (and Television Studies)." In *Reading* Lost, edited by Roberta Pearson, 119–38. London: I. B. Tauris, 2009.

———. "Strategies of Storytelling on Transmedia Television." In *Storyworlds Across Media: Toward a Media-Conscious Narratology*, edited by Marie-Laure Ryan and Jan-Noël Thon, 253–77. Lincoln: University of Nebraska Press, 2014.

Moore, Robert. "Is *Spartacus: Blood and Sand* a Joke?" *PopMatters*, January 22, 2010. Accessed December 27, 2015. http://www.popmatters.com/post/119149-spartacus-blood-and-sand/.

Moore, Ronald D. "Naturalistic Science Fiction (or Taking the Opera out of Space Opera)." *Battlestar Wiki*. Accessed June 8, 2015. http://en.battlestarwiki.org/wiki/Naturalistic_science_fiction.

Morabito, Stella. "The Strange-Bedfellow Politics of *The Hunger Games*." *The Federalist*, December 15, 2014. Accessed December 27, 2015. http://thefederalist.com/2014/12/15/the-strange-bedfellow-politics-of-the-hunger-games/.

Morris, Mark. *Spartacus: Morituri*. London: Titan Books, 2012.

Nelson, Robin. "Quality TV Drama: Estimations and Influences Through Time and Space." In *Quality TV: Contemporary American Television and Beyond*, edited by Janet McCabe and Kim Akass, 38–51. London: I. B. Tauris, 2007.

Newitz, Annalee. "A Fantastically Detailed Geological History for *Game of Thrones*." *io9*, August 4, 2014. Accessed December 27, 2015. http://io9.com/a-fantastically-detailed-geological-history-for-game-of-1561092800.

———. *Pretend We're Dead: Capitalist Monsters in American Pop Culture*. Durham: Duke University Press, 2006.

Newman, Michael Z., and Elana Levine. *Legitimating Television: Media Convergence and Cultural Status*. New York: Routledge, 2012.

Nicolay, Theresa Freda, ed. *Tolkien and the Modernists: Literary Responses to the Dark New Days of the 20th Century*. Jefferson, NC: McFarland, 2014.

Noys, Benjamin. "The Horror of the Real: Žižek's Modern Gothic." *International Journal of Žižek Studies* 4, no. 4 (2010).

Ollman, Bertell. "Putting Dialectics to Work: The Process of Abstraction in Marx's Method." *Rethinking Marxism* 3, no. 1 (1990): 26–74.

Orwell, George. *Animal Farm: A Fairy Story*. Harmondsworth: Penguin Books, 2000 (1945).

Paik, Peter Y. "Doing What Comes Unnaturally: The Gnostic Zombie in Robert Kirkman's *The Walking Dead*." Eric Voegelin Society Meeting 2011, Seattle, WA. Accessed

December 27, 2015. http://wearethewalkingdead.weebly.com/survival-tools/doing -what-comes-unnaturally-the-gnostic-zombie-in-robert-kirkmans-the-walking-dead -by-peter-paik.

————. *From Utopia to Apocalypse: Science Fiction and the Politics of Catastrophe.* Minneapolis: Minnesota University Press, 2010.

Palmiotti, Jimmy, and Dexter Soy. *Spartacus—Blood and Sand: Shadows of the Jackal.* Chicago: Devil's Due, 2009.

Panitch, Leo, and Sam Gindin. *The Making of Global Capitalism: The Political Economy of American Empire.* London and New York: Verso, 2013.

Parody, Clare. "Franchising/Adaptation." *Adaptation* 4, no. 2 (2011): 210–18.

Patnaik, Arun K. "Gramsci's Concept of Common Sense: Towards a Theory of Subaltern Consciousness in Hegemony Processes." *Economic and Political Weekly* 23, no. 5 (1988): 2–7.

Pearson, Roberta E. "*Lost* in Transition: From Post-Network to Post-Television." In *Quality TV: Contemporary American Television and Beyond*, edited by Janet McCabe and Kim Akass, 239–56. London: I. B. Tauris, 2007.

————. "*Star Trek*: Serialized Ideology." In *How to Watch Television*, edited by Ethan Thompson and Jason Mittell, 213–22. New York: New York University Press, 2013.

Pearson, Roberta E., and Máire Messenger Davies. *Star Trek and American Television.* Berkeley and Los Angeles: University of California Press, 2014.

Pearson, Roberta E., and William Uricchio, eds. *The Many Lives of the Batman: Critical Approaches to a Superhero and His Media.* London and New York: Routledge, 1991.

Pepperell, Robert. *The Posthuman Condition.* London: Intellect Books, 2003.

Pfaller, Robert. *On the Pleasure Principle in Culture.* London and New York: Verso, 2014.

Piketty, Thomas. *Capital in the Twenty-First Century.* Cambridge, MA: Harvard University Press, 2014.

Potter, Mitch. "Occupy Wall Street 'Zombies' Keep Streets Alive." *Toronto Star*, October 3, 2011. Accessed December 27, 2015. http://www.thestar.com/news/world/2011/10/03/occupy_wall_street_zombies_keep_protest_alive.html.

Presley, Katie. "Janelle Monáe Releases Visceral Protest Song, 'Hell You Talmbout.'" *NPR*, August 18, 2015. Accessed December 27, 2015. http://www.npr.org/sections/allsongs/2015/08/18/385202798/janelle-mon-e-releases-visceral-protest-song-hell-you -talmbout.

Proctor, William. "Beginning Again: The Reboot Phenomenon in Comic Books and Film." *Scan: Journal of Media Arts Culture* 9, no. 1 (2012). http://scan.net.au/scn/journal/vol9number1/William-Proctor.html.

Pullen, Kirsten. "*The Lord of the Rings* Online Blockbuster Fandom: Pleasure and Commerce." In *The Lord of the Rings: Popular Culture in Context*, edited by Ernest Mathijs, 172–88. London: Wallflower, 2006.

Purdy, Jedediah. "Teenage Riot: A Sentimental Education." *N+1*, December 5, 2014. Accessed December 27, 2015. https://nplusonemag.com/online-only/online-only/teenage-riot/.

Rabitsch, Stefan. "Space-Age Hornblowers, or Why Kirk and Co. Are Not Space Cowboys: The Enlightenment Mariners and Transatlanticism of *Star Trek*." *Networking Knowledge* 5, no. 2 (2012): 27–54.

Rambsy, Howard, II. "Beyond Keeping It Real: OutKast, the Funk Connection, and Afrofuturism." *American Studies* 52, no. 4 (2013): 205–16.

Reed, Adolph, Jr. "From Jenner to Dolezal: One Trans Good, the Other Not So Much." *Common Dreams*, June 15, 2015. Accessed December 27, 2015. http://www.common dreams.org/views/2015/06/15/jenner-dolezal-one-trans-good-other-not-so-much.

Reynolds, Richard. *Super Heroes: A Modern Mythology*. Jackson: Mississippi University Press, 1992.

Rifkin, Jeremy. *The Age of Access: The New Age of Hyper-Capitalism Where All of Life Is a Paid-For Experience*. New York: Tarcher, 2000.

Robbins, Bruce. "Multitude, Are You There?" *n+1* 10 (Fall 2010). Accessed December 27, 2015. https://nplusonemag.com/issue-10/reviews/multitude-are-you-there/.

Robinson, Joanna. "*Game of Thrones* Creators Confirm the Show Will Spoil the Books." *Vanity Fair*, March 22, 2015. Accessed January 16, 2016. http://www.vanityfair.com/hollywood/2015/03/game-of-thrones-tv-show-will-spoil-books.

Rose, Frank. *The Art of Immersion: How the Digital Generation Is Remaking Hollywood, Madison Avenue, and the Way We Tell Stories*. London and New York: W. W. Norton and Co., 2011.

Royster, Francesca T. *Sounding Like a No-No: Queer Sounds and Eccentric Acts in the Post-Soul Era*. Ann Arbor: University of Michigan Press, 2013.

Rozario, Kevin. *The Culture of Calamity: Disaster and the Making of Modern America*. Chicago: Chicago University Press, 2007.

Russell, Jamie. *Book of the Dead: The Complete History of Zombie Cinema*. Surrey: Fab Press, 2005.

Said, Edward W. *Orientalism*. 25th anniversary edition. New York: Vintage Books, 1994.

Saler, Michael. *As If: Modern Enchantment and the Literary Prehistory of Virtual Reality*. Oxford: Oxford University Press, 2012.

Salmon, Christian. *Storytelling: Bewitching the Modern Mind*. Translated by D. Macey. London and New York: Verso, 2010.

Sandifer, Phil. "A Short Guide to Janelle Monáe and the Metropolis Saga." *Your New Problematic Ninth Favorite*, June 2015. Accessed November 25, 2015. http://www.philipsandifer.com/blog/a-short-guide-to-janelle-monáe-and-the-metropolis-saga/.

Santo, Avi. "Para-Television and Discourses of Distinction: The Culture of Production at HBO." In *It's Not TV: Watching HBO in the Post-Television Era*, edited by Marc Leverette, Brian L. Ott, and Cara Louise Buckley, 19–45. New York: Routledge, 2008.

Schäfer, Mirko Tobias. *Bastard Culture! How User Participation Transforms Cultural Production*. Amsterdam: Amsterdam University Press, 2011.

Scholz, Trebor, ed. *Digital Labor: The Internet as Playground and Factory*. London and New York: Routledge, 2013.

Schürer, Norbert. "Tolkien Criticism Today." *Los Angeles Review of Books*, November 13, 2015. Accessed January 12, 2016. https://lareviewofbooks.org/essay/tolkien-criticism-today.

Scott, Suzanne. "Authorized Resistance: Is Fan Production Frakked?" In *Cylons in America: Critical Studies in Battlestar Galactica*, edited by Tiffany Potter and C. W. Marshall, 210–23. New York: Continuum, 2008.

———. "*Battlestar Galactica*: Fans and Ancillary Content." In *How to Watch Television*, edited by Ethan Thompson and Jason Mittell, 320–29. New York: New York University Press, 2013.

Sedlmayr, Gerold. "Fantastic Body Politics in Joe Abercrombie's *The First Law* Trilogy." In *Politics in Fantasy Media: Essays on Ideology and Gender in Fiction, Film, Television and Games*, edited by Gerold Sedlmayr and Nicole Waller, 165–78. Jefferson: McFarland, 2014.

Segal, Carolyn Foster. "Academic Hunger Games." *Inside Higher Education*, October 18, 2012. Accessed November 12, 2015. https://www.insidehighered.com/views/2012/10/18/new-academic-underclass-adjunct-committee-member-essay.

Sepinwall, Alan. *The Revolution Was Televised: The Cops, Crooks, Slingers and Slayers Who Changed TV Drama Forever*. Self-published, 2012.

Sharkey, Rodney. "'Being' Decentered in *Sandman*: History, Dreams, Gender, and the 'Prince of Metaphor and Allusion.'" *ImageTexT: Interdisciplinary Comics Studies* 4, no. 1 (2008).

Shaviro, Steven. "Capitalist Monsters." *Historical Materialism* 10, no. 4 (2002): 281–90.

——. *Post Cinematic Affect*. Hants: Zero Books, 2010.

——. "Zizek/Hollywood." *The Pinocchio Theory*, April 30, 2007. Accessed December 5, 2015. http://www.shaviro.com/Blog/?p=574.

Shepherd, Julianne Escobedo. "Janelle Monáe: The Billboard Cover Story." *Billboard*, June 7, 2013. Accessed December 27, 2015. http://www.billboard.com/articles/columns/the-juice/1566282/janelle-monae-the-billboard-cover-story.

Silvio, Carl, and Elizabeth Johnston. "Alienation and the Limits of the Utopian Impulse." In *Cylons in America: Critical Studies of Battlestar Galactica*, edited by Tiffany Potter and C. W. Marshall, 40–51. New York: Continuum, 2008.

Skipper, Ben. "Fox News Takes Aim at *The LEGO Movie* for Being 'Anti-Capitalist.'" *International Business Times*, February 10, 2014. Accessed January 29, 2015. http://www.ibtimes.co.uk/fox-news-takes-aim-lego-movie-being-anticapitalist-video-1435808.

Sloterdijk, Peter. *Critique of Cynical Reason*. Minneapolis: University of Minnesota Press, 1988.

Soja, Edward W. "Six Discourses on the Postmetropolis." In *The Blackwell City Reader*, 2nd edition, edited by Gary Bridge and Sophie Watson, 374–81. Malden: Blackwell, 2010.

Sorin, Gerald. *Howard Fast: Life and Literature in the Left Lane*. Bloomington: Indiana University Press, 2012.

Srnicek, Nick, and Alex Williams. *Inventing the Future: Postcapitalism and a World without Work*. London and New York: Verso, 2015.

Steinskog, Erik. "Michael Jackson and Afrofuturism: *HIStory*'s Adaptation of Past, Present and Future." In *The Politics of Adaptation: Media Convergence and Ideology*, edited by Dan Hassler-Forest and Pascal Nicklas, 126–40. London: Palgrave Macmillan, 2015.

Strauss, Barry. *The Spartacus War*. New York: Simon & Schuster, 2010.

Suvin, Darko. *Metamorphoses of Science Fiction: On the Poetics and History of a Literary Genre*. New Haven, CT: Yale University Press, 1979.

Tatum, W. Jeffrey. "The Character of Marcus Licinnius Crassus." In *Spartacus: Film and History*, edited by Martin M. Winkler, 128–43. Malden: Blackwell, 2007.

Taylor, Chris. "Star Wars Rewrites History: Books, Comics No Longer Official." *Mashable*, April 25, 2014. Accessed December 27, 2015. http://mashable.com/2014/04/25/star-wars-expanded-universe-gone/ - RqsqQXCRmuqo.

Teurlings, Jan. "From the Society of the Spectacle to the Society of the Machinery: Mutations in Popular Culture 1960s–2000s." *European Journal of Communication* (2013): 1–13.

Thompson, Kristin. *The Frodo Franchise: The Lord of the Rings and Modern Hollywood*. Berkeley and Los Angeles: University of California Press, 2007.

Tolkien, J. R. R. *The Fellowship of the Ring: Being the First Part of the Lord of the Rings*. 2nd edition. Boston: Houghton Mifflin Company, 1965.

——. *The Hobbit (or There and Back Again)*. Boston: Houghton Mifflin Books for Children, 1973.

———. "On Fairy-Stories." In *The Monsters and the Critics and Other Essays*, edited by Christopher Tolkien, 109–62. London: HarperCollins, 1997 (1983).

———. *The Return of the King: Being the Third Part of the Lord of the Rings*. 2nd edition. Boston: Houghton Mifflin Company, 1965.

———. *The Silmarillion*. Boston: Houghton Mifflin Company, 1977.

———. *The Two Towers: Being the Second Part of the Lord of the Rings*. 2nd edition. Boston: Houghton Mifflin Company, 1965.

———. *Unfinished Tales*. Boston: Houghton Mifflin Company, 1980.

Van Dijck, José. *The Culture of Connectivity: A Critical History of Social Media*. Oxford: Oxford University Press, 2013.

Van Veen, Tobias C. "Vessels of Transfer: Allegories of Afrofuturism in Jeff Mills and Janelle Monáe." *Dancecult: Journal of Electronic Dance Music Culture* 5, no. 2 (2013): 7–41.

Verbeek, Peter-Paul. "Cyborg Intentionality: Rethinking the Phenomenology of Human-Technology Relations." *Phenomenology and the Cognitive Sciences* 7, no. 3 (2008): 387–95.

Vercellone, Carlo. "From Formal Subsumption to General Intellect: Elements for a Marxist Reading of the Thesis of Cognitive Capitalism." *Historical Materialism* 15 (2007): 13–36.

———. "The Hypothesis of Cognitive Capitalism." Paper presented at "Towards a Cosmopolitan Marxism," Historical Materialism Annual Conference, Birkbeck College and School of Oriental and African Studies, November 4–6, 2005.

Vint, Sherryl. "Abject Posthumanism: Neoliberalism, Biopolitics, and Zombies." In *Monster Culture in the 21st Century: A Reader*, edited by Marina Levina and Diem-My T. Bui, 133–45. London: Bloomsbury, 2013.

Virno, Paolo. *A Grammar of the Multitude*. Los Angeles: Semiotext(e), 2004.

Voigts, Eckart. "Bastards and Pirates, Remixes and Multitudes: The Politics of Mash-Up Transgression and the Polyprocesses of Cultural Jazz." In *The Politics of Adaptation: Media Convergence and Ideology*, edited by Dan Hassler-Forest and Pascal Nicklas, 82–96. Basingstoke: Palgrave Macmillan, 2015.

Werner, Craig. *A Change Is Gonna Come: Music, Race and the Soul of America*. Edinburgh: Canongate, 2000.

Wetmore, Kevin J., Jr. "Pyramid, Boxing, and Sex." In *Cylons in America: Critical Studies in Battlestar Galactica*, edited by Tiffany Potter and C. W. Marshall, 76–87. New York: Continuum, 2008.

Wheatcroft, Geoffrey. "The Darkness at Noon for Arthur Koestler Was in His Heart." *New Statesman*, November 20, 1998. Accessed December 27, 2015. http://www.newstatesman.com/darkness-noon-arthur-koestler-was-his-heart-yet-his-early-work-inspired-his-disillusionment-communis.

Wheeler, Brian. "Why Are Fantasy World Accents British?" *BBC.com*, March 30, 2012. Accessed December 27, 2015. http://www.bbc.com/news/magazine-17554816.

Wiki of Ice and Fire. "R'hllor." Accessed January 4, 2016. http://awoiaf.westeros.org/index.php/R'hllor.

Williams, Evan Calder. *Combined and Uneven Apocalypse*. Winchester: Zero Books, 2011.

Williams, Linda. "Film Bodies: Gender, Genre, and Excess." *Film Quarterly* 44, no. 4 (1991): 2–13.

Williams, Mary Elizabeth. "'Hobbit' Controversy: When Is Casting Racism?" *Salon*, November 30, 2010. Accessed January 13, 2016. http://www.salon.com/2010/11/30/racism_the_hobbit.

Williams, Raymond. *The Country and the City*. Nottingham: Spokesman Books, 2011 (1973).

———. *Culture and Materialism*. London and New York: Verso, 2005 (1980).

———. *Keywords*. London: Fontana Press, 1983 (1976).

———. *Marxism and Literature*. Oxford: Oxford University Press, 1977.

Winkler, Martin M. "Introduction." In *Spartacus: Film and History*, edited by Martin M. Winkler, 1–13. Malden: Blackwell, 2007.

Wolf, Mark J. P. *Building Imaginary Worlds: The Theory and History of Subcreation*. London and New York: Routledge, 2012.

Wood, Ellen Meiksins. *Empire of Capital*. London and New York: Verso, 2003.

Wood, Robin. "An Introduction to the American Horror Film." In *Planks of Reason: Essays on the Horror Film*, edited by Barry Keith Grant and Christopher Sharrett, 164–200. London: Scarecrow Press, 1984.

Yaszek, Lisa. "Afrofuturism, Science Fiction, and the History of the Future." *Socialism and Democracy* 20, no. 3 (2006): 41–60. doi: 10.1080/08854300600950236.

Young, Iris Marion. "The Ideal of Community and the Politics of Difference." In *The Blackwell City Reader*, 2nd edition, edited by Gary Bridge and Sophie Watson, 228–36. Chichester: Wiley-Blackwell, 2010.

Zielinski, Siegfried. *Audiovisions: Cinema and Television as Entr'Actes in History*. Amsterdam: Amsterdam University Press, 1999.

Žižek, Slavoj. *First as Tragedy, Then as Farce*. London and New York: Verso, 2009.

———. *The Fragile Absolute*. London and New York: Verso, 2000.

———. *In Defense of Lost Causes*. London and New York: Verso, 2008.

———. *Less Than Nothing: Hegel and the Shadow of Dialectical Materialism*. London and New York: Verso, 2014.

———. *Living in the End Times*. London and New York: Verso, 2010.

———. "Occupy Wall Street: What Is to Be Done Next?" *The Guardian*, April 24, 2012. Accessed December 27, 2015. http://www.guardian.co.uk/commentisfree/cifamerica/2012/apr/24/occupy-wall-street-what-is-to-be-done-next.

———. *The Parallax View*. Boston: MIT Press, 2006.

———. *The Plague of Fantasies*. London and New York: Verso, 1997.

———. "The Politics of Batman." *New Statesman*, August 23, 2012. Accessed December 27, 2015. http://www.newstatesman.com/culture/culture/2012/08/slavoj-žižek-politics-batman.

———. *The Sublime Object of Ideology*. London and New York: Verso, 1996.

———. *The Ticklish Subject*. London and New York: Verso, 1999.

———. *Welcome to the Desert of the Real*. London and New York: Verso, 2002.

———. *The Year of Dreaming Dangerously*. London and New York: Verso, 2012.

Zukin, Sharon. *Naked City: The Death and Life of Authentic Urban Places*. Oxford: Oxford University Press, 2010.

Zumski Finke, Christopher. "*The Hunger Games* Are Real: Teenage Fans Remind the World What Katniss Is Really Fighting For." *Yes! Magazine*, November 2013. Accessed December 27, 2015. http://www.yesmagazine.org/happiness/the-hunger-games-are-real.

FILMS

28 Days Later . . . Directed by Danny Boyle. 2002. Century City, CA: Twentieth Century Fox Home Entertainment, 2010. Blu-ray.

28 Weeks Later. Directed by Juan Carlos Fresnadillo. 2007. Universal City, CA: Universal Studios Home Entertainment, 2007. Blu-ray.

300. Directed by Zack Snyder, 2007. Burbank, CA: Warner Home Video, 2007. Blu-ray.

Batman. Directed by Tim Burton. 1989. Burbank, CA: Warner Home Video, 2011. Blu-ray.

Battle Royale. Directed by Kinji Fukasaku. 2000. Beverly Hills: Anchor Bay Entertainment, 2012. Blu-ray.

Battlestar Galactica: Razor. Directed by Félix Enríquez Alcalá. 2007. Los Angeles, CA: Universal Studios Home Entertainment, 2007. Blu-ray.

Battlestar Galactica: The Plan. Directed by Edward James Olmos. 2009. Los Angeles, CA: Universal Studios Home Entertainment, 2009. Blu-ray.

Battlestar Galactica: Blood & Chrome. Directed by Jonas Pate. 2012. Los Angeles, CA: Universal Studios Home Entertainment, 2012. Blu-ray.

Beyond the Five Year Mission—The Evolution of Star Trek: The Next Generation. Directed by Roger Lay Jr. 2014. Hollywood: Paramount Home Entertainment, 2014. Blu-ray.

Blade Runner. Directed by Ridley Scott. 1982. Burbank, CA: Warner Home Video, 2013. Blu-ray.

The Blair Witch Project. Directed by Daniel Myrick and Eduardo Sánchez. 1999. Santa Monica, CA: Artisan Home Entertainment, 1999. DVD.

Comic-Con Episode IV: A Fan's Hope. Directed by Morgan Spurlock. 2011. Antwerp: Remain in Light, 2013. Blu-ray.

The Dark Knight. Directed by Christopher Nolan. 2008. Burbank, CA: Warner Home Video, 2008. Blu-ray.

The Dark Knight Rises. Directed by Christopher Nolan. 2012. Burbank: Warner Home Video, 2012. Blu-ray.

Dawn of the Dead. Directed by George A. Romero. 1978. Beverly Hills: Anchor Bay Entertainment, 2004. DVD.

Dawn of the Dead. Directed by Zack Snyder. 2004. Universal City, CA: Universal Studios Home Entertainment, 2008. Blu-ray.

Day of the Dead. Directed by George A. Romero. 1985. Los Angeles: Shout! Factory, 2013. Blu-ray.

Divergent. Directed by Neil Burger. 2014. Braine L'Alleud: Belga Films, 2014. Blu-ray.

Elysium. Directed by Neill Blomkamp. 2013. Culver City: Sony Pictures, 2013. Blu-ray.

Ex Machina. Directed by Alex Garland. 2015. Universal City, CA: Universal Studios Home Entertainment, 2015. Blu-ray.

Fido. Directed by Andrew Currie. 2006. Santa Monica, CA: Lionsgate Home Entertainment, 2007. DVD.

"From Book to Vision." Disc 3. *The Lord of the Rings: The Fellowship of the Rings*, extended ed. Blu-ray. Directed by Peter Jackson. London: Entertainment in Video, 2011.

The Hobbit: An Unexpected Journey. Directed by Peter Jackson. 2012. Burbank, CA: Warner Home Video, 2013. Blu-ray.

The Hobbit: The Desolation of Smaug. Directed by Peter Jackson. 2013. Burbank, CA: Warner Home Video, 2014. Blu-ray.

The Hobbit: The Battle of the Five Armies. Directed by Peter Jackson. 2014. Burbank, CA: Warner Home Video, 2015. Blu-ray.

The Hunger Games. Directed by Gary Ross. 2012. Santa Monica, CA: Lionsgate Home Entertainment, 2012. Blu-ray.

The Hunger Games: Catching Fire. Directed by Francis Lawrence. 2013. Santa Monica, CA: Lionsgate Home Entertainment, 2014. Blu-ray.

The Hunger Games: Mockingjay Part I. Directed by Francis Lawrence. 2014. Santa Monica, CA: Lionsgate Home Entertainment, 2014. Blu-ray.

The Hunger Games: Mockingjay Part II. Directed by Francis Lawrence. 2015. Santa Monica, CA: Lionsgate Home Entertainment, 2016. Blu-ray.

In Time. Directed by Andrew Niccol. 2011. Century City, CA: Twentieth Century Fox Home Entertainment, 2012. Blu-ray.

Invasion of the Body Snatchers. Directed by Don Siegel. 1956. Chicago: Olive Films, 2012. Blu-ray.

It's a Wonderful Life. Directed by Frank Capra. 1946. Hollywood: Paramount Home Entertainment, 2009. Blu-ray.

Land of the Dead. Directed by George A. Romero. 2005. Universal City, CA: Universal Studios Home Entertainment, 2008. Blu-ray.

The LEGO Movie. Directed by Phil Lord and Christopher Miller. 2014. Burbank, CA: Warner Home Video, 2014. Blu-ray.

The Lord of the Rings: The Fellowship of the Rings. Directed by Peter Jackson. 2001. London: Entertainment in Video, 2011. Blu-ray.

The Lord of the Rings: The Return of the King. Directed by Peter Jackson. 2003. London: Entertainment in Video, 2011. Blu-ray.

The Lord of the Rings: The Two Towers. Directed by Peter Jackson. 2002. London: Entertainment in Video, 2011. Blu-ray.

The Matrix. Directed by Lana and Lilly Wachowski. 1999. Burbank, CA: Warner Home Video, 2010. Blu-ray.

Metropolis. Directed by Fritz Lang. 1927. London: Eureka Video, 2010. Blu-ray.

Mulholland Dr. Directed by David Lynch. 2001. New York: The Criterion Collection, 2015. Blu-ray.

Night of the Living Dead. Directed by George A. Romero. 1968. London: Network, 2008. Blu-ray.

Oblivion. Directed by Joseph Kosinski. 2013. Los Angeles, CA: Studios Home Enterainment, 2013. Blu-ray.

Reds. Directed by Warren Beatty. 1981. Hollywood: Paramount Home Entertainment, 2010. Blu-ray.

Rise of the Planet of the Apes. Directed by Rupert Wyatt. 2011. Century City, CA: Twentieth Century Fox Home Entertainment, 2011. Blu-ray.

The Running Man. Directed by Paul Michael Glaser. 1987. Chicago: Olive Films, 2015. Blu-ray.

Shaun of the Dead. Directed by Edgar Wright. 2004. Universal City, CA: Universal Studios Home Entertainment, 2009. Blu-ray.

Sin City. Directed by Robert Rodriguez and Frank Miller. 2005. Los Angeles: Buena Vista, 2009. Blu-ray.

Snowpiercer. Directed by Bong Joon-Ho. 2013. Beverly Hills: Anchor Bay Entertainment, 2014. Blu-ray.

Spartacus. Directed by Stanley Kubrick. 1960. Los Angeles, CA: Universal Studios Home Entertainment, 2015. Blu-ray.

The Spirit. Directed by Frank Miller. 2008. Santa Monica, CA: Lionsgate Home Entertainment, 2009. Blu-ray.

Star Trek: The Motion Picture. Directed by Robert Wise. 1979. Hollywood: Paramount Home Entertainment, 2010. Blu-ray.

Star Trek II: The Wrath of Khan. Directed by Nicholas Meyer. 1982. Hollywood: Paramount Home Entertainment, 2010. Blu-ray.

Star Trek III: The Search for Spock. Directed by Leonard Nimoy. 1984. Hollywood: Paramount Home Entertainment, 2010. Blu-ray.

Star Trek IV: The Voyage Home. Directed by Leonard Nimoy. 1986. Hollywood: Paramount Home Entertainment, 2010. Blu-ray.

Star Trek V: The Final Frontier. Directed by William Shatner. 1989. Hollywood: Paramount Home Entertainment, 2010. Blu-ray.

Star Trek VI: The Undiscovered Country. Directed by Nicholas Meyer. 1991. Hollywood: Paramount Home Entertainment, 2010. Blu-ray.

Star Trek: Generations. Directed by David Carson. 1994. Hollywood: Paramount Home Entertainment, 2010. Blu-ray.

Star Trek: First Contact. Directed by Jonathan Frakes. 1996. Hollywood: Paramount Home Entertainment, 2010. Blu-ray.

Star Trek: Insurrection. Directed by Jonathan Frakes. 1998. Hollywood: Paramount Home Entertainment, 2010. Blu-ray.

Star Trek: Nemesis. Directed by Stuart Baird. 2002. Hollywood: Paramount Home Entertainment, 2010. Blu-ray.

Star Trek. Directed by J. J. Abrams. 2009. Hollywood: Paramount Home Entertainment, 2009. Blu-ray.

Star Trek Into Darkness. Directed by J. J. Abrams. 2013. Hollywood: Paramount Home Entertainment, 2013. Blu-ray.

Star Wars IV: A New Hope. Directed by George Lucas. 1977. Century City, CA: Twentieth Century Fox Home Entertainment, 2005. DVD.

To Boldly Go: Launching Enterprise. Directed by Roger Lay Jr. 2013. Hollywood: Paramount Home Video, 2013. Blu-ray.

V for Vendetta. Directed by James McTeigue. 2005. Burbank, CA: Warner Home Video, 2008. Blu-ray.

Warm Bodies. Directed by Jonathan Levine. 2013. Universal City, CA: Summit Entertainment, 2013. Blu-ray.

World War Z. Directed by Marc Forster. 2013. Hollywood: Paramount Home Entertainment, 2013. Blu-ray.

Zombieland. Directed by Ruben Fleischer. 2009. Culver City: Sony Pictures, 2010. Blu-ray.

TELEVISION EPISODES

"Baelor." *Game of Thrones*. Home Box Office. New York: HBO, June 12, 2011.

"The Best of Both Worlds." *Star Trek: The Next Generation*. Paramount Domestic Television. First-run syndication, June 18, 1990.

"Black Market." *Battlestar Galactica*. Sci-Fi Network, January 27, 2006.

"Darmok." *Star Trek: The Next Generation*. Paramount Domestic Television. First-run syndication, September 30, 1991.

"Daybreak (Parts 2 & 3)." *Battlestar Galactica*. Sci-Fi Network. March 20, 2009.

DeKnight, Steven S., Peter Mensah, and Katrina Law. "Commentary." Disc 4, *Spartacus: Blood and Sand—The Complete First Season*. Beverly Hills: Anchor Bay Entertainment, 2010. Blu-ray.

"Dirty Hands." *Battlestar Galactica*. Sci-Fi Network. February 25, 2007.

"Downloaded." *Battlestar Galactica*. Sci-Fi Network. February 24, 2006.

"Errand of Mercy." *Star Trek*. National Broadcasting Corporation. New York: NBC, March 23, 1967.

"Ethics." *Star Trek: The Next Generation*. Paramount Domestic Television. First-run syndication, March 2, 1992.

"Fantasy Nerdist." *The Nerdist*. BBC America, April 20, 2013.

"Galaxy's Child." *Star Trek: The Next Generation*. Paramount Domestic Television. First-run syndication, March 11, 1991.

"Hollow Pursuits." *Star Trek: The Next Generation*. Paramount Domestic Television. First-run syndication, April 30, 1990.

"In a Mirror Darkly, Part I." *Star Trek: Enterprise*. Paramount Network Television. New York: UPN, April 22, 2005.

"In a Mirror Darkly, Part II." *Star Trek: Enterprise*. Paramount Network Television. New York: UPN, April 29, 2005.

"The Inner Light." *Star Trek: The Next Generation*. Paramount Domestic Television. First-run syndication, June 1, 1992.

"The Loss." *Star Trek: The Next Generation*. Paramount Domestic Television. First-run syndication, December 31, 1990.

"The Man Whose Darkest Secret Is That He Kind of Likes the Wallflowers." *Conan*. Turner Broadcasting System. New York: TBS, June 6, 2013.

"Mirror, Mirror." *Star Trek*. National Broadcasting Corporation. New York: NBC, October 6, 1967.

"Oathkeeper." *Game of Thrones*. Home Box Office. New York: HBO, April 27, 2014.

"Part II." *Battlestar Galactica*. Sci-Fi Network. December 9, 2003.

"Peak Performance." *Star Trek: The Next Generation*. Paramount Domestic Television. First-run syndication, July 10, 1989.

"Phantasms." *Star Trek: The Next Generation*. Paramount Domestic Television. First-run syndication, October 25, 1993.

"The Rains of Castermere." *Game of Thrones*. Home Box Office. New York: HBO, June 2, 2013.

"Remember Me." *Star Trek: The Next Generation*. Paramount Domestic Television. First-run syndication, October 22, 1990.

"Requiem for Methuselah." *Star Trek*. National Broadcasting Corporation. New York: NBC, February 14, 1969.

"Saga of a Star World." *Battlestar Galactica*. American Broadcasting Company. New York: ABC, September 17, 1978.

"Sarek." *Star Trek: The Next Generation*. Paramount Domestic Television. First-run syndication, May 14, 1990.

"Schisms." *Star Trek: The Next Generation*. Paramount Domestic Television. First-run syndication, October 19, 1992.

"Tapestry." *Star Trek: The Next Generation*. Paramount Domestic Television. First-run syndication, February 15, 1993.

"Thine Own Self." *Star Trek: The Next Generation*. Paramount Domestic Television. First-run syndication, February 14, 1994.

"The Tholian Web." *Star Trek*. National Broadcasting Corporation. New York: NBC, November 15, 1968.

"TS-19." *The Walking Dead*. AMC. New York: AMC, December 5, 2010.

"Us." *The Walking Dead*. AMC. New York: AMC, March 23, 2014.

"Winter Is Coming." *Game of Thrones*. Home Box Office. New York: HBO, April 17, 2011.

"Yesterday's *Enterprise*." *Star Trek: The Next Generation*. Paramount Domestic Television. First-run syndication, February 19, 1990.

ONLINE VIDEOS

"George R. R. Martin's Funny and Insightful Explanation of the Role Religion Plays in *Game of Thrones*." *Business Insider* UK video, 4:38. April 19, 2015. http://uk.businessinsider.com/george-rr-martin-role-of-religion-got-game-of-thrones -westeros-2015-4?r=US&IR=T.

"'I Am Spartacus!' Starbucks Prank—Movies in Real Life (Ep 9)." YouTube video, 1:43. Posted by "Improv Everywhere." November 26, 2013. https://www.youtube.com/ watch?v=5_pKKO35Kh4.

Monáe, Janelle. "Cold War." YouTube video, 3:43. Posted by "janellemonae." August 5, 2010. https://www.youtube.com/watch?v=lqmORiHNtN4.

O'Connor, Sinéad. "Nothing Compares 2 U." YouTube video, 5:47. Posted by "Rafael Silveira." November 26, 2012. https://www.youtube.com/watch?v=dq2K4jHs92A.

"The Shadow of Death." YouTube video, 12:20. Posted by Manga Entertainment. March 15, 2010. https://www.youtube.com/watch?v=h3qewAh7gE0.

"Spartacus: Blood and Sand—Motion Comic—The Beast of Carthage." YouTube video, 9:20. Posted by Manga Entertainment. March 15, 2010. https://www.youtube.com/ watch?v=DM3h7Vxu3uM.

"Spartacus: Blood and Sand—Motion Comic—Shadows of the Jackal." YouTube video, 15:35. Posted by Manga Entertainment. March 15, 2010. https://www.youtube.com/ watch?v=G4680pXncvA.

"Upon the Sands of Vengeance." YouTube video, 15:55. Posted by Manga Entertainment. March 15, 2010. https://www.youtube.com/watch?v=UHU1yLbD6qM.

MUSIC

Clinton, George, Bootsy Collins, and Bernie Worrell. *The Clones of Dr. Funkenstein*. Parliament. © 1976 by Polygram Records. Casablanca 842-620-2. Compact disc.

———. *Funkentelechy vs. The Placebo Syndrome.* Parliament. © 1977 by Polygram Records. Casablanca 824-501-2. Compact disc.

———. *Mothership Connection.* Parliament. © 2003, 1975 by Mercury Records. UMG 440-077-032-2. Compact disc.

———. *Motor Booty Affair.* Parliament. © 1978 by Mercury Records. UICY-77156. Compact disc.

Monáe, Janelle. *The ArchAndroid.* © 2010 by Bad Boy Records. Wondaland 512256-2. Compact disc.

———. *The Electric Lady.* © 2013 by Bad Boy Records. Wondaland 536210-2. Compact Disc.

———. *Metropolis: The Chase Suite.* Special Edition. © 2008 by Bad Boy Records. Wondaland 7567-89932-8. Compact disc.

Wondaland Records. "Hell You Talmbout." Streaming audio. August 13, 2015. https://soundcloud.com/wondalandarts/hell-you-talmbout.

Index

300, 128, 129

accumulation: capital, 4, 15, 16, 17, 55, 107, 114, 115, 117, 138, 172, 191, 195, 197, 199; flexible, 63–64, 129; primitive, 198
activism: antiracist, 185, 190–94; fan, 117, 134, 135, 145–47, 149; political, 14, 19, 30, 33, 65, 117, 134, 135, 149, 169, 190, 191, 192, 199
Adama, William (character). *See Battlestar Galactica*
Adorno, Theodor, 11
affect: and fandom, 20, 23–24, 40, 42, 46, 47, 92, 197; and horror, 159
affective labor. *See* labor
affective turn, 130
affirmational fandom. *See* fandom
Afrocentrism, 181, 183
Afrofuturism, 20, 177–85, 193, 195
Agamben, Giorgio, 96, 97
agency, 12, 14–15, 17, 28, 34, 84n66, 151, 152
alienation: and global capitalism, 80, 125, 172, 173, 180, 194; and wage labor, 54, 70, 72, 100, 169–70
Althusser, Louis, 46
AMC, 161

android, 54, 120n54, 151n1. *See also* cyborg
Animal Farm. *See* Orwell, George
anthropocentrism, 194, 200
antiracism. *See* racism/racist
antisubject, 157, 174
appropriation. *See* fandom
Aragorn (character). *See* Tolkien, J. R. R.
The ArchAndroid. *See* Monáe, Janelle
art-horror, 159
Asimov, Isaac, 26, 48
assemblage, 124, 153, 158
attention economy, 131, 148
austerity, 69, 97, 147, 163
authoritative, 175–76, 179
authorship, 8, 68, 80, 104, 105, 176, 184, 190

Bakhtin, Mikhail, 175
Balibar, Étienne, 53, 166
Baltar, Gaius (character). *See Battlestar Galactica*
Barclay, Reginald (character). *See Star Trek*
Batman (character), 2, 25
Batman (film), 42
Battle Royale, 136

Battlestar Galactica (*BSG*), 19, 55, 71,
    92–105, 106, 129, 197; *Battlestar
    1980*, 93, 102; *Caprica* (prequel
    series), 94, 98n109; Cylons, 92, 93,
    95, 98, 102, 103n130; Gaius Baltar
    (character), 95, 96, 101, 103n130;
    Laura Roslin (character), 98n112, 99,
    102; original series, 92, 93, 96, 98;
    religion in, 100–103; William Adama
    (character), 98nn111–12, 100, 102
Baudrillard, Jean, 164
Baum, L. Frank, 5, 7
Bean, Sean. *See Game of Thrones*
Benjamin, Walter, 21, 189
Berardi, Franco, 142
Big Daddy (character). *See Land of
    the Dead*
"big Other." *See* Lacan, Jacques
biopolitics/biopolitical, 12, 13, 14, 17,
    19, 47, 60, 61, 82, 91, 111, 112, 113,
    125, 140, 148, 154, 158, 160, 186, 189,
    199; production, 72, 78
biopower, 14, 16, 20, 57, 72, 90, 100,
    154, 192, 199
Black Lives Matter, 110, 192
blacklist, 119, 120
Blade Runner, 7, 152, 187n159
body genres. *See* genre
Boltanski, Luc, 47
Borg Collective. *See Star Trek*
Bowie, David, 186, 190
Bub (character). *See Land of the Dead*
Burroughs, Edgar Rice, 5, 128
Butler, Octavia E., 115, 178n120

camp, 118, 127
Canavan, Gerry, 166
canon/canonical, 3, 10, 48, 103, 142, 157,
    162, 163, 176
capitalism: cognitive, 10, 12, 14–15, 18,
    20, 47, 55, 58, 60, 72, 78, 87, 89, 107,
    111, 113, 118, 137, 140, 144, 147,
    148–49, 163, 172, 191, 197, 198; com-
    municative, 116–17; crisis, 35, 69; fan-
    tastical, 70–74, 79, 80, 82, 83–84, 91,
    96, 101, 106, 138, 141, 148, 194, 198;
    financial, 12, 68, 82, 83, 128, 129, 156;

global, 1–21, 25, 27, 29, 31, 35, 36, 39,
    49, 51, 53, 55, 57, 58, 60, 64, 66, 68,
    69, 71, 72, 73, 83, 84, 85, 87, 91, 92,
    96, 97, 98, 100, 103, 105, 106, 111,
    112, 113, 116, 124, 125, 126, 129,
    131, 135, 140, 141, 142, 143, 144–45,
    146, 148, 151, 154, 156, 157, 158,
    160, 163, 169, 170, 171, 172, 177,
    183, 184, 193, 194, 197, 198–99;
    industrial, 10, 11n37, 13, 34, 36, 46,
    47, 55, 59–60, 66, 69, 106, 125,
    156, 170. *See also* postcapitalism/
    postcapitalist; precapitalism
capitalist realism, 19, 68–69, 70, 71–74,
    83, 84, 92, 95, 100, 101, 106, 117, 138,
    141, 175, 194, 198
Capitol Couture. See The Hunger Games
Caprica. See Battlestar Galactica
carnivalesque, 114, 173
Carroll, Noël, 159
Catching Fire. See The Hunger Games
centrifugal/centripetal, 175–76, 177–85
Chiapello, Eve, 47
chronopolitics, 178
*Cindi Mayweather: The Cyber-Graphic
    Novel. See* Monáe, Janelle
class conflict, 33, 38, 51, 60, 97–100, 115,
    118–21, 132, 138, 171–72
Clinton, George, 183, 191; Funkadelic,
    178, 179n125; *Funkentelechy vs. the
    Placebo Syndrome*, 180; *Mothership
    Connection*, 180; *Motor Booty Affair*,
    180; Parliament, 178, 179n125; P-Funk
    Collective, 179–81
cognition. *See* science fiction
cognitive capitalism. *See* capitalism
Cold War, 13, 26, 49, 50, 52, 96, 98
"Cold War" (music video). *See* Monáe,
    Janelle
collaboration. *See* fandom
collective/collectivity, 5, 13, 20, 106, 110,
    111, 112, 113, 114–16, 117, 120, 123,
    125, 126, 130, 134, 137, 142, 145, 146,
    148, 169, 174, 179, 180, 185, 191, 193,
    194, 198, 200
collective intelligence, 41, 89, 98n112
Collins, Suzanne. *See The Hunger Games*

colonialism/colonialist, 26, 30, 50, 51, 53, 55, 62, 63, 66, 103, 140, 151, 158, 166, 198

Comic-Con, 40, 87, 114–15

commons, 18, 43, 58, 60, 110, 113, 117, 173, 191

Commonwealth, 113, 154, 155–56, 191, 193

communicative capitalism. *See* capitalism

communist, 1, 38, 39, 58, 110; horizon, 9, 113, 116, 117, 134, 199; imaginary, 19, 118–21, 148

The Communist Manifesto, 30, 37, 70

competition, 34, 54, 55, 58, 62, 64, 80, 84, 91, 96, 106, 112, 114, 141, 148

competitive individualism, 55, 111, 112, 113, 114, 117, 123, 126, 129, 135–42, 148, 185, 194, 198

conglomerate, 6, 15, 58, 69, 87, 91, 92, 115, 199

conservative, 28, 38, 66, 100, 114, 139, 175

consumerism, 1, 6, 14, 28, 35, 41, 42, 68, 89, 104–5, 109, 131, 155, 173

continuity, 49n105, 55, 101, 157, 162

convergence, 2, 4–6, 7, 11, 14, 16, 18, 21, 43, 46, 86, 91, 104, 107, 129, 142, 156, 163, 175, 176n111, 181, 197

Convergence Culture. See Jenkins, Henry

copyright, 15, 25, 104

counterculture, 27, 28, 30, 33, 34n46, 35, 40, 43, 47, 48, 65, 66, 147, 191

cowboy, 165, 166

crisis capitalism. *See* capitalism

Cultural Studies, 9, 12

culture industry, 11, 146

cyborg (android), 20, 151–52, 174–95, 200

Cylons. *See Battlestar Galactica*

cynicism, 19, 20, 68, 70, 74, 80, 95, 101, 141, 145, 172

Dardot, Pierre, 69

The Dark Knight, 177

The Dark Knight Rises, 110–11

Dawn of the Dead (1978), 160, 168n79, 172

Dawn of the Dead (2004), 160

Day of the Dead, 160, 171

Dean, Jason, 138

Dean, Jodi, 9, 112, 116

Debord, Guy, 2, 19, 129, 131, 144

decentered, 12, 13, 15, 69, 71–72, 78, 106, 125, 126, 129, 145, 156, 163, 198

DeKnight, Steven S., 134

Delany, Samuel R., 178n120

Deleuze, Gilles, 14, 61; and Guattari, 12, 124, 132, 156

democracy/democratic, 10, 12, 13, 15, 17, 58, 62, 64, 96, 98n112, 111, 112, 113, 114, 117, 140, 155, 199,200

deterritorialization, 13, 19, 26, 30, 31, 37, 38, 46, 52, 53, 63–64, 65, 70, 73, 77, 96, 160, 197–98, 200

Deuze, Mark, 5n16

dialectics/dialectical, 10, 25, 28–29, 31, 33, 35, 40, 41n73, 47–48, 49, 68, 69, 70, 84, 93, 115, 117, 131, 132, 139, 148, 151, 152, 157, 158, 159–60, 161, 164, 168, 173, 174, 183, 187, 189, 190, 194, 200

dialogic, 97, 190

Dick, Philip K., 177, 190

differentialist racism. *See* racism/racist

digital culture, 5, 6, 11, 14, 16, 24, 58, 104, 111, 116, 117, 126, 128–29, 188

Discographies, 179

diversity, 23, 32, 41, 53, 125, 165, 178, 194

Douglas, Kirk, 118, 120

Doyle, Arthur Conan, 5

dystopia, 2, 38, 57, 70, 112, 136, 137n117, 139, 174, 182

Earth, Wind and Fire, 178

The Electric Lady. See Monáe, Janelle

Elysium, 110, 138

Embry, Karen, 157–58, 169, 174

Empire, 4, 11–15, 16, 18, 19, 20, 21, 25, 26, 30, 34, 39, 43, 46, 47, 49, 50, 51, 52, 53, 55, 56, 57, 60, 61, 62, 63, 65, 66, 68, 69, 70, 71–73, 74, 78, 79, 82, 85, 92, 97, 100, 106, 111, 112, 113, 114, 125, 137, 139, 140, 142, 147, 148, 152, 154, 166, 172, 197–99

Engels, Friedrich, 37, 156
enslavement, 13, 98n109, 99, 118, 158,
    184, 189; machinic, 124–25, 126, 129,
    151, 154, 183
Enterprise (starship). *See Star Trek*
entrepreneur of the self, 125, 141, 172,
    194, 200
Eshun, Kodwo, 178
estrangement, 69–70, 115, 117, 128, 132,
    148, 200
Eurocentrism, 28, 36, 53, 76, 178
Everdeen, Katniss (character). *See The
    Hunger Games*
Ex Machina, 187n159
exploitation: capitalist, 19, 38, 70, 99, 117,
    119–20, 123, 124, 151, 172, 194, 195;
    cinema, 118, 126, 127, 130, 134, 148,
    149; colonialist, 62, 63

Facebook. *See* social media
fandom: and affect, 20, 23–24, 40, 42;
    affirmational, 44; appropriation by, 3,
    5, 14, 49, 105, 148, 175; appropriation
    of, 46, 90, 106; collaboration, 15, 17,
    27, 42–43, 46, 57, 72, 88, 90, 91, 104,
    105, 107, 114; and consumerism, 6,
    14, 41, 42, 44–45, 46, 89, 104, 105,
    107; conventions, 3, 40, 41–42, 87–89,
    114–15, 133–34; culture, 3, 6, 14,
    23–24, 25, 29, 40–47, 66, 87, 92, 93,
    103, 104, 105, 115, 135, 142, 148, 194,
    199; fiction, 29, 39, 48–49, 76, 103,
    105, 112, 176, 194; influencer/ambas-
    sador, 6, 42–43, 46, 88, 92, 107, 147;
    just-in-time, 104; studies, 21, 41, 114;
    transformative, 17, 41n76, 44, 87, 105,
    107, 110, 174, 175
fantastical capitalism. *See* capitalism
fantastic fiction/storyworlds, 1, 3, 4, 5, 6,
    7, 10, 13, 15–16, 17–18, 19, 24, 27, 33,
    34, 39, 48, 53, 65, 69–70, 71, 74, 76,
    77, 87, 106–7, 110, 115, 117, 128, 134,
    136, 143, 148, 151, 157, 162, 166, 174,
    177, 179, 181, 189, 194, 195, 197–99,
    200. *See also specific works*
fantasy: high, 19, 24, 27–40, 67, 70, 75,
    76, 77, 80; pastoral, 41n73; popular,

    25, 29, 32, 74, 86, 152; and science
    fiction, 23, 24, 65, 66, 69–70, 157.
    See also fantastic fiction/storyworlds
Fast, Howard, 118, 119–20, 121, 122, 123
*Fear the Walking Dead. See The Walking
    Dead*
Fido, 171
financial capitalism. *See* capitalism
Fisher, Mark, 19, 68, 112, 138, 140, 142
Fiske, John, 23–24, 176
flexible accumulation. *See* accumulation
folk politics, 174
Fordism, 25
Foucault, Michel, 13, 14, 61, 78, 126,
    157n28
franchising, 2, 3, 4–5, 6–7, 15, 16, 17, 18,
    20
Frankfurt School, 9
Freedman, Carl, 28n21, 69
Freud, Sigmund, 61, 187
Frodo (character). *See* Tolkien, J. R. R.
Funkadelic. *See* Clinton, George
*Funkentelechy vs. the Placebo Syndrome.
    See* Clinton, Geoge

Game of Thrones, 16, 19, 55, 67, 69, 70–
    71, 75–92, 94, 97, 98, 100, 101, 106–7,
    111, 116, 127, 128–29, 141, 144, 197;
    and gentrification, 86–92; George R. R.
    Martin, 71n12, 75, 76, 77, 78, 81, 85,
    91, 98, 103; Ned Stark (character), 75,
    77, 79, 98; religion, 79–86, 100; Sean
    Bean, 75; *A Song of Ice and Fire* (book
    series), 75–86; Tyrion Lannister (char-
    acter), 77–79, 141; Varys (character),
    77–79, 141
geek culture, 17, 24, 44, 47, 87
gender, 12, 34, 50n107, 90, 110, 121, 123,
    141n133, 148, 154, 174, 184, 185, 186,
    190, 195, 200
Genette, Gérard, 44
genre: body, 130, 148; conventions, 106;
    disreputable, 135; fiction, 6, 16, 19, 23,
    25, 86, 139; post-, 25
gentrification, 19, 86–92, 106
Gilbert, Jeremy, 11n37, 12, 112, 113–14,
    115, 116n32, 137, 155, 179

The Gladiators, 118–19
global capitalism. *See* capitalism
globalization, 4, 6, 11, 26, 30, 38, 51, 53, 68, 113, 128, 170, 197–98
Google. *See* social media
Gray, Jonathan, 44, 46, 176–77
Grimes, Rick (character). *See The Walking Dead*
Guattari, Félix, 12, 124, 132, 156

Haraway, Donna, 186
Hardt, Michael, 4, 11–14, 15, 16, 26, 29, 30, 41, 51, 57–58, 63, 64, 65, 66, 69, 71–73, 82, 89, 100, 111, 112, 113, 114, 117, 137, 144–45, 147, 154, 155–56, 157, 177, 190, 191, 193, 197
Harry Potter Alliance (HPA), 134n105, 145–47, 149
Harvey, David, 63–64, 129, 158
HBO, 17, 71, 76, 86–87, 88, 90, 91, 127, 144
Hegel, Georg Wilhelm Friedrich, 158
"Hell You Talmbout" (song). *See* Monáe, Janelle
heteroglossia, 175, 176, 179, 184, 190, 191
hierarchy: class, 33, 39, 58; imperialist, 4, 19, 32, 53, 54, 55, 60, 62, 64, 66, 68, 77, 80, 101, 120, 136, 153, 198; of meaning, 186, 189, 194, 200; media, 16, 26, 130, 179
high fantasy. *See* fantasy
Hills, Matt, 3, 104
hip-hop, 180, 183n141, 184, 185
Hobbes, Thomas, 52n119
The Hobbit. See Tolkien, J. R. R.
horror, 3, 17, 84, 85, 127, 151n1, 156, 158, 159, 161n51, 170, 172
Howard, Robert E., 128
Huizinga, Johan, 96
humanism, 19, 48, 53, 152, 153–54, 157–58, 161, 166, 169, 178, 186, 191, 194, 199, 200
The Hunger Games: book trilogy, 135–36; and capitalism, 115, 116, 137–38, 139, 140, 141, 142, 148–49; *Capitol Couture*, 143–44; *Catching Fire*, 137, 138, 143–44, 145, 147; Donald Sutherland, 139; franchise, 19, 110n2, 112, 115, 129, 135, 143–44, 197; Katniss Everdeen (character), 136–37, 138, 139, 140–42; *Odds in Our Favor*, 145–47; Suzanne Collins, 135
hyperdiegesis, 3, 8
hyperreality, 164

I Am Legend, 155, 158
identity politics, 65, 114, 148, 154, 174, 185, 193
ideology: in *Battlestar Galactica*, 92, 95, 100–103; capitalist, 74, 114; dominant, 72, 114; in *Game of Thrones*, 75, 79, 82–83, 85; in *Hunger Games*, 138, 139, 143, 144, 148, 149; in Janelle Monáe, 192; post-, 18–19, 20, 67–107, 111, 121, 141, 163, 172, 173, 197, 198–99; purest, 33, 74, 82, 198; and religion, 100–103; in *Spartacus* (novel), 120; in *Spartacus* (TV series), 123, 124–25, 134, 148; in *Star Trek*, 49, 52, 54–55, 56–57, 62, 65; in Tolkien, 33, 35, 39; in *The Walking Dead*, 166; zombies and, 151, 172–73
immaterial labor. *See* labor
immersion, 5, 6n21, 8, 9, 15, 16, 17, 24, 27, 28, 59, 61, 94, 128, 143, 144, 145, 147, 197, 200
imperial/imperialism, 10, 13, 18, 19, 25–27, 31, 32, 34, 36, 39, 46, 49–57, 60, 62–65, 66, 68, 69, 70, 71–72, 77, 96, 97, 100, 106, 111, 129, 140, 158, 166, 194, 198; administration, 63, 64, 66, 68, 72; power, 120, 154; Roman, 118, 119, 121
industrial capitalism. *See* capitalism
industrial labor. *See* labor
intellectual property, 15, 43, 105, 157
interpassivity, 103–5, 107
interpellation, 46
In the Flesh, 171
In Time, 110
Invasion of the Body Snatchers, 115–16
Inventing the Future, 155, 174, 185, 193
Iron Man (character), 186

Jackson, Peter, 18, 42–43, 44, 45–46
Jameson, Fredric, 8, 9, 16, 32, 68, 82, 83, 103, 183
Jenkins, Henry, 4, 14, 24, 41, 104, 164n62; *Convergence Culture*, 146; *Textual Poachers*, 11
Johnson, Derek, 15
Jones, Grace, 188, 190
joy, 12, 114, 115, 130, 134, 191, 193
just-in-time fandom. *See* fandom

King, Stephen, 136
Kirk, James T. (character). *See Star Trek*
Kirkman, Robert. *See The Walking Dead*
Klastrup, Lisbeth, 8
Klingons. *See Star Trek*
Koestler, Arthur, 118–19, 138
Kotsko, Adam, 64–65

labor: affective, 11, 43, 61, 91, 92, 125, 131, 140, 141, 199; capital's access to, 13, 68, 140; immaterial, 4, 10, 11, 13, 15, 18, 20, 25, 40–47, 51, 55, 57–62, 63, 66, 68, 72, 79, 85, 87, 89, 91, 92, 105, 106, 107, 129, 131, 132, 140–41, 144, 145, 147, 148, 152, 163, 170n89, 189, 191, 198, 199; industrial, 28, 51, 99–100; reproductive, 142; Sisyphean, 163; union, 13, 99–100, 120n54; virtuosic, 145; wage, 54, 60, 70, 136, 169
Lacan, Jacques, 167; concept of "big Other," 73–74, 79–86, 98; concept of the Real, 84–85, 87, 159
La Forge, Geordi (character). *See Star Trek*
Landa, Ishay, 35, 38
Land of the Dead, 160, 171–73; Big Daddy (character), 172; Bub (character), 171
Lang, Fritz, 38, 186, 187n159
Lannister, Tyrion (character). *See Game of Thrones*
Lauro, Sarah Juliet, 157–58, 169, 174
Laval, Christian, 69
Lazzarato, Maurizio, 124–25
The LEGO Movie, 1–3, 10, 110, 115
leisure, 54, 61–62, 136

liberalism, 48, 53, 116, 120
logocentrism, 179
The Lord of the Rings. *See* Tolkien, J. R. R.
love, 23, 45, 111, 113, 114, 115, 117, 145, 146, 182, 191
Lovecraft, H. P., 5, 84n65

mainstream, 6, 24, 40, 41, 43, 44, 46, 47, 89, 114, 134, 135, 173, 178, 179
managerialism, 60, 63, 175
maps/mapping, 9, 10, 26, 27, 34, 36, 67, 76, 78, 162, 163, 174
Martin, George R. R. *See Game of Thrones*
Marvel Cinematic Universe, 88, 194
Marx, Karl, 11, 37, 60, 63, 113, 126, 132, 156, 158, 169
Marxism, 1, 9, 20–21, 28, 35, 58, 72, 85, 129, 138
mashup, 3, 16, 49, 176
Mason, Paul, 111, 155
mass media, 2, 6, 10–11, 17, 21, 25, 26, 29, 41, 43, 46, 112, 129, 144
Matheson, Richard, 155
The Matrix, 2, 136, 141
Mayweather, Cindi (character). *See* Monáe, Janelle
McNally, David, 170
media conglomerate. *See* conglomerate
meta-individualism, 116
Metropolis (film), 38, 152, 187n159
"Metropolis Saga." *See* Monáe, Janelle
Miéville, China, 37, 115
militarism, 51–57, 62, 66
Monáe, Janelle, 10, 20, 174–94, 195, 197; *The ArchAndroid*, 183, 184, 187, 191; Cindi Mayweather (character), 181–82, 183, 186–87, 189, 190; *Cindi Mayweather: The Cyber-Graphic Novel*, 190; "Cold War" (music video), 187–90, 192; *The Electric Lady*, 184, 192; "Hell You Talmbout" (song), 191–92; *Metropolis: The Chase Suite*, 181–82; "Metropolis Saga," 175, 181–84, 183n140, 197; Wondaland Arts Collective, 20, 181, 191, 192

Monty Python, 170
Moore, Ronald D., 94, 95, 102, 103–4, 105
Mothership Connection. See Clinton, George
Motor Booty Affair. See Clinton, George
Mulholland Dr., 189
multitext, 8, 18, 19, 20, 93, 139, 156, 181
multitude, 12–13, 14, 20, 41, 52, 58, 60, 72, 111, 113, 117, 130, 144–45, 147, 152, 154, 174, 177, 185, 190, 193, 194, 199
mythology: Afrofuturist, 178, 180; in *Battlestar Galactica*, 93, 101; capitalist, 62, 85, 125, 131; in *Game of Thrones*, 77, 80, 84; Spartacus, 19, 110, 112, 119–20, 129; in Tolkien, 27, 28, 31, 35, 36, 39, 47, 65, 77, 84, 198; zombie, 156, 168
MythScience, 178, 180

Negri, Antonio, 4, 11–14, 15, 16, 26, 29, 30, 41, 51, 57–58, 63, 64, 65, 66, 69, 71–73, 82, 89, 100, 111, 112, 113, 114, 117, 137, 144–45, 147, 154, 155–56, 157, 177, 190, 191, 193, 197
neoliberal/neoliberalism, 2, 11, 15, 18–19, 20, 30, 52, 63, 64, 68, 69, 70–71, 73, 91, 96, 100, 113–14, 116, 117, 124, 126, 129, 131, 137, 147, 148, 155, 164, 170, 172, 173, 174–75, 185, 193, 194, 197, 198, 199, 200; racism, 166, 192; subjectivity, 61, 125
niche, 44, 121; appeal, 135; audience, 6, 42, 71, 88, 107
Night of the Living Dead, 155, 158, 160, 168, 171
nostalgia, 16, 18, 27, 30, 31, 32, 36, 39n71, 65, 77, 81, 94, 129, 153, 155

Oblivion, 138
Occupy Wall Street, 110, 116, 139, 147, 169, 173, 174
O'Connor, Sinéad, 187
Odds in Our Favor. See The Hunger Games

Orwell, George, 136; *Animal Farm*, 119, 138
OutKast, 184
Oz (storyworld), 5, 7, 67

Paik, Peter Y., 168
panopticon, 14, 61
paratext, 18, 44–46, 143–44, 162, 176–77, 183
Parliament. *See* Clinton, George
particularism, 73, 180, 185, 192–93
pastiche, 16, 136, 161n51
patriarchy, 10, 34, 38, 75, 78, 98n111, 165–66, 167, 180, 189
Pepperell, Robert, 153
Pfaller, Robert, 105
P-Funk Collective. *See* Clinton, George
phallocentric, 28, 163–69, 180
Picard, Jean-Luc (character). *See Star Trek*
polder, 36–37
political: economy, 15, 91, 118, 175; unconscious, 8, 33, 35
politics of difference, 41, 148, 200
popular fantasy. *See* fantasy
pornography, 127
possible worlds, 8n29
postcapitalism/postcapitalist, 18, 20, 25, 47, 51, 53, 54–55, 57, 60, 62, 64, 65–66, 71n16, 97, 98, 111, 151, 152, 155, 161, 164, 166, 168, 169, 171, 173, 174, 185, 194, 195, 200
postdemocracy/postdemocratic, 17, 109–18, 121, 126, 137, 139–40, 142, 145, 149, 193, 197, 199
post-Fordism, 10, 15, 60n150, 66, 68, 73, 79, 124–25, 129, 132
postgenre. *See* genre
posthistorical, 57, 68, 69, 152, 163
The Posthuman Condition, 153
posthumanism, 19–20, 151–95, 197, 199–200; anticapitalism and, 152–56, 192, 194, 195; cyborg and, 186–90; racism and, 192–93; zombies and, 156–74
postideological. *See* ideology
postimperialism/postimperialist, 13, 18, 197–98

postmodern/postmodernism, 16, 31, 32, 57, 68, 74, 80, 101, 156, 158

precapitalism, 18, 32, 35, 39, 47, 65, 66, 71n16, 82

Primary World, 7, 36n53, 177, 179, 184, 187, 194

Prime Directive. *See Star Trek*

primitive accumulation. *See* accumulation

Prince, 190

progressive, 28, 48, 64, 65, 148, 175, 191

prohibitionist, 104

pseudo-medievalism, 31–32, 47, 75, 78

psychoanalytical, 124, 159, 167

Quality TV, 86–87, 94, 106, 118, 126, 127

queer, 78, 79, 118, 141n133, 153, 185

race, 12, 32, 53, 166, 174, 180, 185, 186, 190, 200

racism/racist, 28, 32, 33, 41, 50, 166, 170, 173, 184, 189, 192, 193; anti-, 20, 185; differentialist, 53, 166

radical potential: of cyborg, 151, 186, 195; of digital culture, 58, 116, 117; of fan culture, 115, 147, 149; of fantastic storyworlds, 4, 10, 13, 15, 17, 18, 19–21, 70, 117, 194, 197–200; of *Game of Thrones*, 85; of *Hunger Games*, 142, 149; of Janelle Monáe, 187, 193; of multitude, 130; of posthumanism, 153, 156, 194–95; of *Spartacus*, 118, 120, 149; of zombie, 174, 194–95

Real. *See* Lacan, Jacques

realism, 7, 19, 67, 69, 71, 81, 92, 94–95, 102, 106, 127, 128–29, 132, 148, 199

religion, 19, 38, 79–81, 93, 100–103, 106, 184

reproductive labor. *See* labor

resistance, 13, 20, 61n156, 68, 96, 120, 142, 148, 154, 161, 169, 175, 183, 185, 193, 198, 200

reterritorialization, 17, 25, 40, 43, 47

Les Revenants, 171

revolution, 13, 19, 33, 38, 110–13, 114, 118–19, 122, 132, 136, 138–39, 142, 151, 155–56, 169, 193, 199

Rifkin, Jeremy, 129

Rise of the Planet of the Apes, 110

ritual, 71, 80, 100, 114, 134, 136, 140, 199

Robinson, Kim Stanley, 115

RoboCop (character), 186

Roddenberry, Gene. *See Star Trek*

Romero, George A., 156, 168n79, 171

Roslin, Laura (character). *See Battlestar Galactica*

The Running Man, 136

Saler, Michael, 34

scale, 7–8, 9, 67, 192, 198

schizoanalysis, 124

schizophrenia, 124

Sci-Fi Channel, 93

science fiction, 26, 47–66, 68, 74, 92–100, 106, 115, 157, 177–84, 190–94; and cognition, 69, 115, 117, 132, 148; and estrangement, 69–70, 115, 117, 128, 132, 148, 200; and politics, 110; in relation to fantasy, 23, 24, 65, 66, 69–70, 157

Scott, Suzanne, 104

Secondary World, 7, 18, 36n53, 74, 80, 184, 194

serialization, 4, 8, 26, 96, 161, 162, 169

Shaun of the Dead, 160

Shaviro, Steven, 156, 170n90, 163, 189

the Shire. *See* Tolkien, J. R. R.

The Silmarillion. See Tolkien, J. R. R.

Sisyphean labor. *See* labor

slavery. *See* enslavement

Snowpiercer, 110

Snyder, Zack, 128

social media, 105, 117, 146, 155, 175, 192; Facebook, 16, 17, 58, 109, 133, 134, 143, 147; Google, 17, 58, 76; Tumblr, 147; Twitter, 147; YouTube, 88, 91

society of control, 14, 61, 66

Society of the Spectacle, 2, 19, 131, 132

solidarity, 41, 101, 110, 114, 115, 120, 138–39, 141–42, 192

A Song of Ice and Fire (book series). *See Game of Thrones*

sonic fiction, 178

Spartacus: Andy Whitfield, 122; as communist imaginary, 19, 110, 116, 118–21, 134, 148; fandom, 132–35; historical figure of, 118–19; *Spartacus* (Fast novel), 118, 119–20, 121, 122, 123; *Spartacus* (film), 109, 118, 120, 121, 122n64; *Spartacus* (Starz franchise), 19, 112, 115, 116, 117–18, 121–35, 140, 141n133, 148, 149, 197; and *Star Trek*, 120

spatial turn, 157

spectacle, 2, 19, 112, 115, 117, 118, 126–32, 134, 136, 137, 140, 141n133, 144, 145, 148, 184, 187, 188, 199

Spinoza, Baruch, 11, 52, 191

spreadable media, 43, 144

Srnicek, Nick, 155, 174, 185, 186, 193

Star Trek: Borg Collective, 55, 116; *Deep Space Nine*, 48, 62n158, 94; and diversity, 23, 53, 97, 178; *Enterprise* (starship), 48, 52, 54, 55, 56–57, 62, 63, 67; *Enterprise* (TV series), 48, 56; fandom, 3, 23, 24, 47, 53, 58, 62, 93; franchise, 23, 24, 47–66, 120, 178; Gene Roddenberry, 50, 52, 70, 178; Geordi La Forge (character), 59, 61; James T. Kirk (character), 51, 52, 54, 56; Jean-Luc Picard (character), 54, 55n126, 56, 59, 61; Klingons, 47n99, 51, 55, 56; and managerialism, 60, 63; and militarism, 50–51, 52, 55, 56–57, 62–63, 66; *The Next Generation*, 18, 48, 49, 50, 54, 55–62, 63, 66, 68, 94, 99, 116, 120, 186; original series, 48, 50–51, 52; and postcapitalism, 18, 25, 47, 51, 53, 54–55, 57, 60, 62, 64, 65–66, 71n16, 97, 98; Prime Directive, 53; Reginald Barclay (character), 58–59, 61–62; *Voyager*, 48, 64

Star Wars, 8, 24n6, 93, 103, 128, 136, 141, 194; Expanded Universe, 176n110

Stark, Ned (character). *See Game of Thrones*

state of exception, 93, 96–100, 164

storyworld. *See* fantastic fiction/storyworlds

structure of feeling, 31, 32, 50, 65, 66, 68, 71, 92, 98, 164, 194

subcreation. *See* Tolkien, J. R. R.

subjection, 124, 125, 126, 151

subjectivity, 11, 12–13, 16, 17, 43, 61, 72, 79, 112, 117, 124–25, 151, 152, 157–58, 169, 171, 186, 189, 194, 200

Sun Ra, 178–79, 180, 183, 191

Superman (character), 25

Sutherland, Donald. *See The Hunger Games*

synthetic freedom, 185, 186

the Terminator (character), 186

Teurlings, Jan, 131

Textual Poachers. *See* Jenkins, Henry

thinning, 30–31, 34, 38, 39, 77, 198

Tolkien, J. R. R.: and anticapitalism, 28, 30–40, 116; Aragorn (character), 37, 38; fandom, 23, 24, 28, 29, 31, 32, 39, 40–47, 57, 65, 147; Frodo (character), 33, 36, 38, 39, 46n94; "Frodo Lives!" campaign, 33, 40, 134, 147; *The Hobbit*, 27, 29, 35, 39, 41n74, 46; *The Lord of the Rings* (*LOTR*), 23, 27, 29, 31–39, 42–46, 49, 52, 55, 65, 68, 70, 71, 76–77, 80n49, 84, 94, 104, 111, 128, 131; the Shire, 33, 34n46, 38–39, 40–41, 46n94; *The Silmarillion*, 39; and subcreation, 7, 74, 79–80, 83, 139

topofocal, 27, 76, 157

transformative fandom. *See* fandom

transhumanism, 186

transmedia storytelling, 4

transmedia world-building. *See* worldbuilding

Trumbo, Dalton, 120

Twilight, 136

Tumblr. *See* social media

Twitter. *See* social media

union labor. *See* labor

universalism, 193

utopia/utopian, 20, 21, 31, 32, 47, 48, 51,
    52, 55, 57, 60, 65, 66, 70, 73, 85, 100,
    102, 103, 112, 113, 154, 174, 178, 180,
    186, 191, 193; imaginary, 68, 98, 117;
    impulse, 71, 106, 169, 200; potential,
    58, 168, 195

Varys (character). *See Game of Thrones*
Vercellone, Carlo, 10
Verne, Jules, 48
V for Vendetta, 2
Virno, Paolo, 112, 144–45
virtuosity, 144–45

wage labor. *See* labor
The Walking Dead: comic book, 161,
    162, 163–68; *Fear the Walking Dead*,
    162; franchise, 17, 20, 105, 156,
    161–69, 181, 195, 197; Rick Grimes
    (character), 161, 163–68; *Rise of the
    Governor*, 162; Robert Kirkman, 161,
    162, 163; TV series, 105, 161–62,
    164n62, 169, 171n96
Warm Bodies, 161n51, 171
Whitfield, Andy. *See* Spartacus
Williams, Alex, 155, 174, 185, 186, 193
Williams, Evan Calder, 165
Williams, Linda, 130
Williams, Raymond, 29n24, 41n73, 48,
    55, 114, 159, 160
Wolf, Mark J. P., 7, 177

Wondaland Arts Collective. *See* Monáe,
    Janelle
Wood, Robin, 159
World War Z, 161n51
world-building: Afrofuturism and, 177–85;
    in *Battlestar Galactica*, 92–93, 103;
    and convergence culture, 23–66; in
    Game of Thrones, 75–77, 87, 88–89;
    and global capitalism, 65, 66, 68–69,
    70–71; in *Hunger Games*, 115, 135,
    137, 142, 143–47, 148–49; in Janelle
    Monáe, 175–76, 184, 187, 190; politics
    of, 6–11; postideological, 67–107; in
    Spartacus, 112, 115, 117–18, 121–22,
    129, 132, 135, 148; in *Star Trek*,
    47–48, 60n148; in Tolkien, 19, 24, 27,
    29; transmedia, 3, 4–6, 8, 9, 10–11, 15,
    16, 17, 18, 20, 24, 25, 26, 48, 65, 66,
    68, 93, 137, 176, 177, 190, 197, 200;
    in *The Walking Dead*, 17, 157, 160–63,
    169, 195
worldness, 8

Young, Iris Marion, 40, 41
YouTube. *See* social media

Žižek, Slavoj, 33, 73–74, 79, 83, 101, 105,
    128, 129, 131n101, 173
zombie, 20, 84, 151–52, 155, 156–74, 183,
    194–95
Zombieland, 161n51